A HISTORY OF THE BALKAN PEOPLES

A History of the
Balkan Peoples

by

RENÉ RISTELHUEBER

Edited and Translated

by

Sherman David Spector

TWAYNE PUBLISHERS, INC.
NEW YORK

René Ristelhueber: *Histoire des peuples balkaniques*
in the series *Les grandes études historiques*.
Paris: Librairie Arthème Fayard, 1950. 504 pp.
Copyright F. Brouty, J. Fayard et Cie., 1950.

Dedicated to Pierre Gaxotte

English language copyright © 1971, by Twayne Publishers, Inc.
Library of Congress Catalog Card Number: 78-147184
7–11–7 7

*To Garry, Nancy, and Susan S. who are now
too young to know the Balkans but who will
surely spend vacation week-ends there before
this turbulent century ends.*

S.D.S.

Preface

AT first glance the word "Balkan" produces the impression of inextricable complications, rivalries, and conflicts. "The Balkans"—the "Powder-Keg of Europe"—contain ambitious, envious, intractable, and dissatisfied peoples; such is the image engraved on many minds. A history of that region should prove that the quarrels and the intercessions provoked by these disputes have all too often created clouds in the European sky and let loose some storms. Thus events must be placed in their proper perspective for an appreciation of their origins, an understanding of their development, and an analysis of their interests. The turbulence and temperaments of the Balkan peoples are by no means the results of their youth and inexperience. Although these peoples regained their independence only during the 19th century, their existence goes far back into history. This is obvious in the case of the Greeks. But less known is the fact that the Serbian nation was not born in 1804, nor was the Bulgarian in 1879. The Serbs and Bulgarians were merely revived in the 19th century. Each nation has a long and glorious history. Under Ottoman (Turkish) domination for four centuries, these peoples retained an awareness of their past, despite oppression, and remained faithful to their origins. If the French proudly evoke the grandeur of Charlemagne and the English the Magna Carta, the Bulgarians cherish Tsar Simeon who threatened the Byzantine emperor in the 10th century, and the Serbs recall their great king Stephen Dushan who ruled from the Adriatic to the Aegean in the 14th century. The vitality of these peoples and their rigorous faith are admirable.

The past assists in understanding the present, and vice versa. This history treats the agitations of which the Balkan peninsula has been a theater for one and one-half centuries, and the considerable impact the Balkans have had upon European politics. But before analyzing this period, a brief retracing of the past of the peoples in the tumultuous peninsula is presented. It is an often misunderstood and even unknown past. Such a review furnishes an idea of the eminent role each people has played at a given historical moment, and also depicted are the heroes whose exploits remain ever-present in the memories of these nations. The Balkan peoples still invoke this legacy to justify their claims. This study will provide a better understanding, if not indulgence, of rival ambitions. Such ambitions are not only the consequences of overheated imaginations which launch the Balkan nations on adventures to the detriment of other people's tranquillity. They most often originate in and are explained by ancient developments which cannot be ignored simply because of ignorance.

A definition of the word "Balkan" is a striking example of the case in which a segment gives its name to the whole. What in reality are The Balkans? A chain of rugged, precipitous mountains less than 850 miles in length which, situated south of the Danube River, stretch from west to east starting at the Timok River in Serbia and ending at the Black Sea in Bulgaria. Restricting the word to its geographical sense, the only true Balkan country would be Bulgaria which the mountains cover in its entirety, although they do extend somewhat into Serbia. This chain of mountains (and *Balkan* means "mountains" in Turkish) gives its name to the vast peninsula which stretches from the Adriatic to the Black Sea, and from the Turkish Straits to the Mediterranean. Massive in the north, the peninsula stretches to the south where it is bisected from the trident of old Chalcedon on the Bosporus to the leaf-shaped Peloponnesus suspended from the continent by the narrow stem of the Isthmus of Corinth. A diffuse collection of islands extend it from Euboea to Crete and to the galaxy of islands which extend to the Asian shore.

The name "Balkan" is applied to almost everything included within the peninsula. One is tempted to call indiscriminately by the word "Balkan" the mountains with which the region bristles, whether it be the Dinaric Alps along the Adriatic, the mountains of Macedonia, or the Rhodope Mountains from whose heights can be seen the gleaming Aegean Sea. "Balkan" also applies to rivers which furrow the peninsula from the majestic Danube, which flows into the Black Sea, to the Drina, its tributary, and then down the Maritsa and Vardar rivers which empty into the Aegean.

Especially "Balkan" are the peoples inhabiting the peninsula— Bulgarians, Serbs, Montenegrins, Albanians, Greeks, and—the former masters of them all—the Turks. Thus is established a human bond between the Greek islands of the archipelago and a chain of mountains from which a vast stretch of water separates them. Custom has added the Rumanians to the Balkan peoples. Nevertherless, their country, located north of the Danube, is not actually a part of the peninsula. It is attached on one side to the Carpatho-Danubian region and to the vast Russian steppes on the other. But the Rumanians have been integrated into the great Balkan family regardless of this geographical distinction.

The expression *Balkan peninsula* is further amplified when it is transposed from geography to politics. Rumania is then added. When reference to the Balkan Wars or the Balkan Entente is made, all should know it is a question of conflicts or agreements to which Rumania has been a component. Some people include the Croats and Hungarians (Magyars) in the Balkan grouping, but there the exaggeration becomes so manifest that such an inclusion is fortunately denied in intellectual circles. This history will consider as "Balkan" all the peoples inhabiting the peninsula including the Rumanians. This is a sufficiently ample, varied, and complex field to treat.

Although justifiable from a geographical viewpoint, this grouping must be based on other valid reasons. Would it be a common ethnic origin? Not at all! The peninsula has Greeks, Turks, descendants of the Romans, and a majority of Slavs. Religion? In addition to Islamic groups and a substantial Roman Catholic population, the Orthodox Christian peoples, the most numerous, are divided into autonomous (autocephalous) churches, jealous of their privileges and quite indifferent toward each other.

A common history? The peninsula has suffered incredibly diverse fortunes over the centuries. At times united under a single rule—the ephemeral empire of Alexander the Great, the Roman Empire for four centuries, the Byzantine Empire whose frontiers were threatened by the Slav wave, and then the Ottoman Turks who seized the great capital of the *Basileus,* Constantinople. After its fall, the Balkan peninsula experienced political unity. It was a sad unity—that of the Ottoman yoke for about five centuries. From Cape Matapan at the southern tip of the Greek Peloponnesus to the banks of the Dniester River and beyond, the Turks dominated as masters without any real opposition, crushing all national consciousness and liberation movements, covering the entire peninsula with a stifling veil.

After this prolonged period of oppressive torpor, the conquered peoples began to awaken at the beginning of the 19th century. They stirred, acquired a new consciousness, and gradually revived, claiming their places in the sun with the aid of the great European powers. By the end of the 19th century the Balkan nations had been reconstituted. But the misfortunes borne by all of them failed to teach them the value or spirit of solidarity. They are still jealous of each other and have harshly demanded extensions of their frontiers.

Such are answers to the question of what may be the bonds uniting the Balkan peoples, so diverse in their origins and aspirations. The Turks forged a common destiny for all of them. What contributed to the integration of their community was the almost identical fashion by which they successively broke the Turkish grip to reclaim their rights to life, and, as a result of their courage and tenacity, they obtained a right to take their places in the European family of nations. (As ephemeral as the empire of Alexander the Great, the Soviet Empire in East Europe has disintegrated after failing to suppress the irresistible nationalism of the Balkan peoples. *Ed.*)—RENÉ RISTELHUEBER

This history has no purpose other than to take each of the Balkan peoples from its origins and trace it to the present by treating exploits, reverses, struggles for independence, and participation in contemporary world affairs. The wish to confine a history as long as this and as replete with events to a few hundred pages indicates that this book is an effort in over-simplification. It appears that if this survey contains nothing new, its novelty might consist of a grouping within one volume, easily consulted, of an assemblage of facts hitherto found only in scattered books.

No one-volume basic introduction to the history of the Balkan peoples has been published in the United States since Wesley Gewehr revised Ferdinand Schevill's classic *History of the Balkan Peninsula* in 1933. Of course many excellent surveys of specific eras of Balkan history have been written, and innumerable scholarly studies have been produced, but the demand for an elementary text treating the entire gamut of Balkan history was apparently first raised in France twenty years ago. Now that text is being made available to Americans who wish a basic introduction to this still relatively unknown peninsula.

Preface

As a college student fascinated by such hitherto unknown and exotic places as the Sanjak of Novi-Bazar, the Banat of Temesvar, Plevna, Kossovo, and other sites mentioned by that indefatigable specialist, Ernst Christian Helmreich, Professor of History at Bowdoin College, I have since pursued a career in teaching about these and other places in the Balkans. The opportunity to translate and update the Ristelhueber book, which makes no pretense to be scholarly or original, has resulted in the publication of a text suitable for adoption in basic academic courses. The original book, published in 1950, is still in print. Any text which remains in print for 20 years must have some merit. Ristelhueber's concise survey appeared in a series of basic introductory texts written by noted French historians such as Bailly, Bainville, Daniel-Rops, Funck-Brentano, Gaxotte (to whom Ristelhueber dedicated his volume), Lot, Maurois, and others. The series, *Les Grandes Etudes Historiques,* is similar to the *History of European Civilization Library* (Harcourt, Brace and World, Inc.). In an age of popularization, as a cynic observed, "if you steal from one author, it is plagiarism. If you steal from two, it is research."

To readers seeking a critical, scholarly, or exhaustive history of the Balkan peoples, this book is not for them. This text is expressly designed to stimulate an interest among students for Balkan history. It is aimed at a college audience where, the editor trusts, more attention will be given to this neglected region. Perhaps no other section of the European continent is so replete with melodrama, complexities, or intrigue. The dynamism of the Balkan peoples has prevented the status quo from lasting more than a decade.

I wish to thank Dr. Frank W. Lindsay, Chairman of the Modern Languages Department at Russell Sage College, without whose assistance this book could not have been completed. And gratitude goes to Beryl, my wife, who urged me to make this book available before the Balkans again upset the status quo.

As this book goes to press, I am temporarily situated in Bucharest, Rumania, investigating materials for a biography of Ionel Bratianu (1864-1927), the creator of Greater Rumania in 1918-19. My preparation of this translation of Ristelhueber has greatly facilitated my understanding and appreciation of the Balkan peoples among whom I am spending a sabbatical leave.

S.D.S.
University of Bucharest
May, 1970

Table of Contents

Maps

*(The original French-language maps were drawn
by Henri Jacquinet)*

General Map of the Balkans

René Ristelhueber, 1881-1960

By Henri Ponsot

René Ristelhueber was born March 5, 1881 in Peking, China, to a family of Alsatian origins. He died February 19, 1960 after a brilliant career in the French diplomatic service and in writing. His last post was at the French embassy in Canada during World War II after which he served for seven years as professor of diplomatic history at the University of Montreal. His career throughout the world admirably prepared him as an expert on the Middle East, the Far East, Europe, and North Africa.

The memory of ten years as a boy in Peking, where his father was French consul, prepared him when he was assigned to Peking in 1905 by the French Foreign Ministry. He spoke Chinese, and the history of that country was familiar to him. His last article, written for a military journal, was a study of the Opium War. The period of history which most interested him was 1860 to 1960. He knew the Middle East and the Balkans as well as China. The second period of his career was spent in the Levant, 1908-12. He wrote in *Revue d'Histoire Diplomatique* in 1960 about his diplomatic service in that region. It was a review of the century of activity which he had previously recounted in his *French Traditions in the Levant* (1918), with a preface by noted historian Gabriel Hanotaux.

Ristelhueber participated in the activities of the conference which treated Balkan financial problems. He was called to active military service during World War I, and served at Salonika, Athens, and Constantinople. He witnessed the beginnings of Kemal's revolution in Turkey. After the war he was named director-general of the interior in Tunisia for three years. Then he served in Lithuania and Norway for nine years. In 1937 he became the French minister to Bulgaria. Friendly relations with Kiosseivanov, the Bulgarian premier, enabled Ristelhueber to furnish Paris with information about growing Nazi influence in that country. While in Sofia he collected materials which were later included in his *History of the Balkan Peoples* (1950), a study which aroused greater interest in that region and which is still in print. In 1940 Ristelhueber was appointed French minister to Canada, a return to a northern climate he had enjoyed previously in Norway and Lithuania. He wrote a book on Nansen (*The Double Adventure of Fridtjof Nansen*) in 1945, an account of the International Refugee Organization and the "White" Russians who had fled from the Bolshevik Revolution.

Ristelhueber spent the war years in Canada as a refugee from Nazi-occupied France. Serving on the faculty of the University of Montreal, he wrote a history of France for a young audience, *Little History of France,* 1946. He returned to Paris in 1948 and was appointed to the International Refugee Organization in Geneva. As a result of this new career, he published *The International Refugee Organization, 1946-52* (1955). The last years of his life were devoted to additional writing.

Part I

The Peoples

CHAPTER I

The Greeks

A HISTORY of ancient Greece cannot be related in these few pages. We are children of the civilization to which Greece gave birth, and we offer to our spiritual ancestor our gratitude while faithfully recalling her long and illustrious past. We perpetuate this gratitude by continuing through the centuries to appreciate the value of the contributions Greece has made to us, and by continuing to respect the human values in whose belief she instructed us. The names of Athens, Sparta, Pericles, Plato, Aristotle, and Phidias, as well as Salamis and Thermopylae, echo so memorably in any cultured mind for it to be unnecessary to recall the memories they evoke. Similarly, everyone knows that, reaching its peak in the 5th century B. C., this admirable Greek civilization, which arose in the eastern Mediterranean basin, spread to Asia and Egypt as a result of the conquests of Alexander the Great. After his death the partition of his empire encouraged the dissemination of Greek culture.

It was next the turn of the Romans to appear in ancient Greece. Some Greek cities opposed the Romans with vigorous resistance; others rallied to the side of the invaders. Corinth was destroyed while Sparta was spared. Greece came under Roman domination 150 years before the birth of Christ. Macedonia was reduced to a province, Thebes and Achaea were oppressed by heavy indemnites, while some city-states followed the example of Delphi and became Rome's allies. This was an era of deprivation, disorder, and decadence, marked by pillage of art works and the exploits of pirates who infested the Aegean Sea. Greece suffered even more disastrously because on her soil were fought civil wars in which the Romans were divided among themselves. It was at Pharsalia in Thessaly where Julius Caesar defeated Pompey in 48 B. C. Three centuries of the *Pax Romana* left the country in ruins and exhausted the inhabitants who played a relatively passive role during that era.

Yet the prestige of Greek culture remained strong. So great was its power of dissemination with Athens as its center that, after having been inspired by it, Rome became its propagator throughout the known world. Greek culture (Hellenism) was complementary to Latin civilization and won adherents as the Roman eagle victoriously spread its wings over new regions.

The inhabitants of the Greek city-states migrated far and wide. Smyrna (Izmir), one of several cities designated as Homer's birthplace, became a flourishing cradle of Greek civilization on the coast of Asia Minor. While many Greeks were migrating to the eastern basin of the Mediterranean, populating Thrace and moving into the Black Sea, others directed their steps toward the west and established themselves in Sicily and southern Italy. The founding of Marseilles is attributed to the arrival of a group of Photians.

A city was founded by Greeks from Megara and Argos on the shores of the Bosporus, a unique location commanding access to the Black Sea. This city, named Byzantium, was destined to become illustrious. But for centuries it was only a port of minor importance because the Greeks had established several ports in that region. The Greeks lived by navigation and fishing, and they came under the sovereignty of different powerful empires in the course of events. During his famous siege of Byzantium, Philip of Macedon was held in check. Luminous signals warned the defenders at night of the approach of the enemy forces. To show their appreciation the Greeks placed their city under the protection of Hecate, a lunar deity, and it was that crescent moon of Byzantine origin which the Ottoman Turks adopted as their emblem when they captured Constantinople (earlier Byzantium) in 1453 A. D. Byzantium could not resist the Romans who, after conquering the city, subjected it to rigorous treatment.

Byzantium's glorious fate was due to Emperor Constantine I. Born near Nish in Macedonia, he was distinguished for having appreciated the city's unique location at the juncture of Europe and Asia and promoting Byzantium to the rank of one of the great capitals of the known world. After authorizing the free exercise of the Christian religion and defeating his rivals, Constantine, a friend of the Greeks and admirer of their culture, resolved to leave Rome which held too many evil memories for him and to dwell nearer to Asia whose immensity and riches tempted him. His choice of residence fell on the place where the ruins of Byzantium were found. Desiring to build a "new Rome" there, Constantine assigned to the city considerable dimensions by mapping out a large enclosure protected by thick walls. History established May 11, 330 A. D. as the birthday of Constantinople, the new capital to which the emperor gave his name. At the end of the 4th century, however, the death of Emperor Theodosius led to the final partition of the Roman Empire into two parts: the Western—destroyed a century later by the barbarians—and the Eastern—which maintained its existence for another millennium.

Thus it was from Constantinople, the new capital, that the heirs of the Roman Empire continued to dominate the eastern Mediterranean. They made it a center of Neo-Hellenic civilization. The Eastern Roman Empire experienced the assaults of barbaric tribes. Visigoths, Huns, and Avars invaded it without destroying it. Next came the Slav tide which flowed over the Balkan peninsula as far south as the Peloponnesus, as witnessed by the Slavic names of such cities as Panitza and Dimitzana in modern Greece. The empire likewise resisted this invasion. While these dangers menaced the empire's European territories, its Asian lands were invaded and diminished by the incursions of the Persians and Arabs; the latter stopped at the very gates of Constantinople in 782. To the Slav peril advancing from the north was soon added the Turkish menace approaching from the south. During this period Constantinople was shaken by palace revolutions; more than half of the emperors were assassinated, poisoned, or mutilated, and riots and insurrections were frequent. But, as if by a miracle, Constantinople, despite all these converging threats, held out for a millennium because of its exceptionally strategic location and the acumen of its rulers.

Once established in the east, the Romans were influenced by their new milieu to the point where pervasive Hellenism assimilated them. Greek replaced Latin and became the official language. When the emperor assumed the title of *Basileus,* this assimilation was marked by a solemn consecration. Henceforth the Romans were known as Romaics (*Romaioi*), and their Hellenized Latin became a popular tongue (Romaica). Beyond ancient Greece, where Greek settlers were remote from the Roman influx, a new Greek nation was constituted but it shared the common characteristics of Hellenism. It was Neo-Hellenism fusing Christian and Eastern elements.

The development of Constantinople as the center of culture was detrimental to ancient Greece and particularly to Athens. Attracted by the new capital, many deserted their homes for Constantinople, especially the intellectuals. Many artistic works were conveyed from Greece to decorate the city of the *Basileus*. An atmosphere of mistrust and misunderstanding persisted between ancient Greece and the inhabitants of Constantinople. Simultaneously, however, Christianity experienced considerable expansion. As the capital of a theocratic state Constantinople became the center from which the religion adopted by the emperor spread out over the most remote regions of his territory. Ancient Greece, wishing to remain faithful to her gods, proved reluctant to adopt the new faith. Indeed, Greece was quite late in accepting Christianity. The closing of the pagan university at Athens, decreed by Emperor Justinian in 529, marked the end of a long and glorious era of true Hellenism.

For centuries the two religious centers of Rome and Constantinople competed for influence. The schism of Patriarch Photius in 863 was merely a confirmation of the state of affairs which ultimately led to a complete separation. The Eastern Orthodox Church, however, was the link between ancient Greek civilization and the culture which appeared under the aegis of the Eastern Empire. Greek thought, not the Greeks, still dominates the region. The dynamism of Christianity was so strong that it figuratively leaped over the frontiers of the empire when it penetrated as far as Russia. The marriage of the grand duke of Kiev to the sister of Emperor Basil II in 990 initiated a process of conversion which made Kiev a holy city destined to play the role of communion with a Constantinople whose luxury and refinement exercised much influence upon the Slavs.

Byzantium and Christianity became almost synonymous in the East. As was once aptly stated, "The Greeks ceased to be philosophers in order to become bishops." As for the *Basileus,* he was considered Christ's representative on earth, responsible for seeing that Christ's laws were obeyed. The magnificence and ceremony with which he surrounded himself made the capital into a divine city. Religious ceremonies were most significant. Frequent and passionate theological controversies were accompanied by violent repression of heresies. There was a remarkable development of Christian literature, which produced the poet Romanos, author of a famous hymn to the Virgin Mary and, above all, St. John Chrysostom whose talents contributed to the diffusion of Christianity and the splendor of the Byzantine court. The church, however, was subjected to imperial authority, lost its independence, and became a political instrument in the hands of the emperors.

The fate of ancient Greece was quite painful. After the assaults of the Visigoths, the Greeks experienced the incursions of the Slavs. A revolt against the emperor in 727 only served to aggravate the situation. Later a terrible plague killed perhaps half the population. The Slavs, especially the Bulgarians, profited from this tragedy to infiltrate Greece in even greater numbers. The Bulgarians twice invaded Thessaly at the end of the 10th century. The Normans of Sicily, precursors of the Crusaders, penetrated the shores of Epirus.

Then, in a completely unforeseen manner, the capture of Constantinople in 1204 by the Fourth Crusade was carried out by warriors who had been turned aside from their goal by the Venetian lust for gold. This capture threw the East into turmoil by ushering in a new element of mostly French nobility who divided among themselves the empire they had overwhelmed. The last defenders of the capital found refuge in Asia. The crusaders established a fragile and ephemeral state which lasted only about sixty years. While Beaudoin de Flandres, Pierre de Courtenay, Jean de Brienne, and their successors ruled in Constantinople, Henri de Blois became Duke of Nicea and ruled in Asia Minor, their comrades carved out domains in ancient Greece. At Salonika Boniface de Montferrat, a native of Lombardy, extended his authority over Macedonia and Thessaly. The Peloponnesus also fell to the French. Its conquest was due to the boldness of Guillaume de Champlitte who, commanding a handful of knights, seized the peninsula which was then divided among a dozen French barons. When Champlitte returned home, Geoffrey de Villehardouin, nephew of the historian, succeeded him. The latter established a dynasty which lasted for more than two centuries as a result of marriage alliances. These newcomers proved very tolerant toward the Orthodox faith. They established a combined Greco-Latin feudalism, and their cordial relations with the populace permitted the development of a half-French, half-Eastern culture similar to that which had transformed Syria.

One vassal of the Prince of Achaea was the Duke of Athens, Guy de la Roche, who rebelled and had to be forced back into obedience. All the nobles had to struggle against the vengeful Greeks. In 1261 the Latin Empire of the East began to crumble

as a consequence of the reconquest of Constantinople by the Byzantines, but French domination in southern Greece persisted for
a long time. It was a strangely troubled domination. At the death
of the last Villehardouin in 1277, Achaea became the fief of his
daughters whose successive marriages led the families of Anjou,
Hainaut, and Piémont to claim their rights to the region. Another
claimant was Jean de Majorque (Majorca) who arrived in Greece
at the head of an army of Calabrians who proved to be strong adversaries. Amid this confusion of competitors appeared a Navarese,
Pierre de Saint-Exupéry, who, after being recognized as the regent
of Achaea, became its ruler.

During this confusion, which was aggravated by acts of indisci-
pline, the French had to confront aggression from numerous enemies—Greeks from Epirus, Venetians who were masters of many
islands from Euboea to Crete and Corfu, and the Knights of
Rhodes. But the Byzantine Empire, once reestablished in Constantinople, ultimately succeeded in terminating the Latin domination
by reconquering the Peloponnesus in 1428.

While ruins of churches and fortresses constructed by the crusaders perpetuate the memory of their occupation of Syria, more
modest traces in Greece recall the passing of the French nobles.
Here and there a tower, partially in ruins, the arms of an old
family sculpted on a wall evoke the spirit of adventure and the
courage of the conquerors who seized this region in the 13th and
14th centuries. St. Omeri, the name of one locality, testifies to
their passage.

At the same time the Latin Empire of the East was seriously
menaced at Constantinople. First came the Bulgarians, indefatigable warriors who inflicted a serious defeat on the crusaders at
Adrianople and captured the emperor. Then in 1259 the Byzantine counter-offensive of Emperor Michael Paleologue began and
succeeded in recapturing Constantinople in 1261. But, despite
this recovery, the Eastern Empire, seriously affected by the blow
of the crusaders, was destined never to recover from it.

The Venetians and Genoans, benefitting from the end of Latin
rule, expanded even more in the eastern Mediterranean basin. They
seized several islands, established a foothold in the Galata quarter
of Constantinople, and even pushed into the Black Sea region.
Their advance created contacts between the Greeks and Western
Europe. Corfu, Zante, and Cephalonia became outposts of Venice

who succeeded for about twenty years in dominating the Peloponnesus.

For many years the Seljuk Turks had been menacing Asia Minor. As a sequel to their victory over the Byzantines at Manzikert in 1071, the Seljuk Turks began to infiltrate to the detriment of the Greek populace, imposing their language and religion on the peasants of Anatolia. After establishing their capital at Brusa they began to put pressure on Europe. The Ottoman Turks, successors to the Seljuks, soon crossed the Straits and were thus on European soil for the first time in 1356. It required yet another century for them to seize Constantinople, but they had already begun their conquest of the Balkan peninsula by fighting against the Slavs. Their capital was moved to Adrianople which was near Constantinople. The latter was protected on the land side by its strong walls and on the water by the chain which protected the Golden Horn in which the Byzantine fleet was anchored. Nevertheless, the furious assaults of Sultan Mohammed II overcame the resistance of the bastion of Eastern Orthodoxy, the heir of the Roman Empire. In 1453 the last *Basileus,* Constantine Paleologue, fell with weapons in his hands while defending his capital which was taken by the Moslem invaders. Sultan Mohammed celebrated his victory by transforming the Basilica of Sancta Sophia into a mosque. According to a Greek legend, when a Turkish soldier raised his sword over the priest who was celebrating mass in the church, the latter suddenly vanished like a phantom, and this priest, the legend adds, will reappear when Constantinople is Christian once again.

All hope for vengeance by Orthodox Christendom did not end. About twenty years later the marriage of Sophia, niece of the last emperor, and Ivan III, Grand Duke of Moscow, had considerable consequences for the course of history. By adopting the two-headed eagle of Byzantium as their emblem, Russia's rulers would turn their attention toward the Bosporus. Their dream of expelling the Turks and reestablishing the Eastern Empire, of which they considered themselves the legal heirs, would last for centuries.

Once Constantinople was firmly in their hands, the Turks advanced south into the Balkan peninsula. They seized the Greek islands held by the Venetians. By 1500 the mainland and the Peloponnesus, where Latin domination and then Venetian rule had left traces, fell into Turkish hands. Venice, however, retained Crete until 1669 when the heroic defenders of Candia surrendered to the

Turks after a siege of 22 years. From that time the entire Greek world from Constantinople to Epirus was under Turkish rule.

The passive and paralyzed Greeks, like the other Balkan peoples subjugated before them, had to bow before the conquerors. To sustain their wealth, some of the more affluent Greeks renounced their faith to embrace the religion of the conquerors. The presence of a large Moslem population in Crete (about 20% of the total) did not justify proselytization on the island.

As miserable as they were under Turkish domination, the Greeks benefitted from a relatively less drastic situation than that of their Slav neighbors. Contrary to general opinion, the Turks, at the time of their conquests, did not prove to be fanatical to the point of imposing forced conversions, or intolerant to the point of systematically persecuting the Christians. With undeniable magnanimity of spirit the Turks permitted the free exercise of the Orthodox faith. In Constantinople the Patriarchate of the Greek Orthodox Church was installed in the Phanar quarter on the Golden Horn. The Patriarchate was an ancient, powerful, and well organized institution. Through the activities of many clergy, it ruled all the dioceses and monasteries of the vast Greek world. The Turks respected and maintained it. They used it as an intermediary in dealings with the Christians. While Islam intervened in numerous acts of private life and constituted a civil as well as a religious code of laws, the Christians were excluded from a status which benefitted only the Turks. The Christians became second-class citizens. The sentiment of the Moslem Turks with regard to the Christians was strongly colored by disdain. But, more significantly, they considered Christians as aliens in their empire because the Oriental concept of nationality was strongly bound to the religious idea.

The Christians, nevertheless, had to be ruled by laws, even though such laws were other than of Moslem origin. This was precisely what the Orthodox Church controlled by assuming the initiative in questions of civil status, marriage, and inheritance, which were all matters entrusted to the care of the clergy. The Turks did not modify or disturb these arrangements. On the contrary, the Turks confirmed them by recognizing the Greek nation and its chief, the Patriarch. To the Greek clergy under control of their Patriarch, the Turks left the direction and responsibility for affairs concerning the Christians who thus preserved their personal status.

The Turks recognized the Patriarch, assisted by the Holy Synod, as the representative of the entire Christian nation from a political as well as a religious point of view. Thus the *reis effendi* (the Turkish minister in charge of affairs of non-Moslems) negotiated with the Patriarch.

Distinctions were required between the great majority who were Orthodox and the small minority who were Roman Catholic, and even between the Greek church and those of other peoples who, in a national spirit, aspired to autonomy in ritual practices which were different from the Greek. Such considerations were significant to the Turks, but these subtleties merely complicated a question which was alien to their preoccupations. To the Turks there existed only Moslems and *rayahs* or *roumis* (the latter a distortion of the word "Romans"); and they ignored the national aspirations of those Christians who disagreed with the Greek majority. For that reason the Turks recognized the Patriarch of the Greek Orthodox Church as the spiritual leader of *all* Christians.

The Patriarch exercised his authority over the Greek Christians in Thrace and ancient Greece, and over the Slavs and Rumanians who lived elsewhere in the Balkan peninsula. But by a curious paradox this Christian authority was exercised under Moslem control. The Orthodox Church had been required to submit to imperial authority under the Byzantine Empire; it now became the prisoner of the Turkish regime and had to submit to its caprices.

The Patriarch's monopoly gave him spiritual primacy and exclusive authority over civil affairs of non-Greek Christians as well. Organized on the model of the efficient Byzantine bureaucracy, the Patriarchate controlled a hierarchy of bishops, metropolitans, monks, priests, and friars whose influence was widespread. Naturally the important posts were reserved for clergy of Greek origin. The Patriarchs reduced to a minimum the number and importance of other ecclesiastics. Furthermore, the teaching of religion was done in Greek, not only in Constantinople and Athens but also in Sofia. The Greek language was imposed on everyone and a perfect knowledge of the tongue became indispensable to the élite since the clergy remained in the Balkans as elsewhere the guardians of spiritual values among the cultured populace especially. This was a powerful method of Hellenization placed in the hands of a clergy who benefitted from the diffusion of their own culture.

Conincidental with the political and economic domination of the

Turks, the Bulgarians, Serbs, and Rumanians had to experience the influence of a foreign clergy with privileges granted them by the Turks to carry on propaganda which undermined what remained of the national consciousness of these peoples. Hence the active and constant hostility manifested by most of these peoples, particularly the Bulgarians, toward the Greeks whom they accused of wishing to exercise over them a hegemony as prejudicial and painful as that of their mutual conquerors.

Ecclesiastical offices, like the civil service, became the object of a regular traffic. It was generally the most untrustworthy who secured appointments, and such posts were awarded those who paid for them. They then sought to recoup their money. This explained the accusations of ignorance, simony, and traffic in sacraments which were charged against the Greek clergy. This regime of venality and corruption served the designs of the Turkish authorities in facilitating their control over the Orthodox Church, permitting them simultaneously to realize some profit. Greek priests regularly had recourse to Turkish officials in securing satisfaction. Nevertheless, contrasted with other peoples under the Turkish yoke, the Greeks found themselves in a privileged position from a religious viewpoint. Their bishops and priests were Greek like themselves. They bowed to the spiritual direction of their own compatriots and not of foreigners, and they obeyed an authority whose jurisdiction they freely accepted.

One must hesitate in repeating reproaches of ignorance sometimes directed at certain Greek ecclesiastics. Many monasteries were simultaneously religious centers and active intellectual establishments. Along with theological writings the monks devoted themselves to research and studies which greatly contributed to preservation of classical antiquity. This became evident when the fall of Constantinople hastened the departure to Italy of many Byzantine scholars, many of whom were from religious orders. Many scholars have asserted that these Greeks revealed to the West the treasures of Hellenic culture, and it has been said that it was as a result of this exodus that the Renaissance really began.

The wealth of the Greek Patriarchate constituted another element of its power. The Orthodox clergy controlled valuable riches. Numerous buildings, vast property holdings, and precious objects, often the products of pious donations, were accumulated by the monasteries. Several of these, such as the celebrated monasteries on Mount Athos and at Meteores, were renowned for the magnificence of their holdings.

The qualities of their ancestry gave the Greeks still other advantages. The Turks, a people of warriors and shepherds, were not prepared at the time for the task of organizing the conquered lands, administering them, or watching over their prosperity. But there existed in the conquered lands an entire Byzantine bureaucracy which was highly organized and whose complex machinery had for a long time activated the immense administrative network of the Eastern Empire. The Turks never had the least wish to adopt it or to be inspired by it. But among the numerous Greek officials were some whose subtlety of mind, suppleness, and experience were used advantageously by the new masters. Without forcing them to renounce their religion, the Turks sought the services of those who seemed to offer assurances of loyalty. Thus a significant number of Greeks were furnished with posts in the Turkish administration where their business acumen and ingenuity became useful to the Moslems who were occasionally befuddled by unfamiliar problems. The confidence these Greeks could inspire was such that some reached very high posts, notably in the Sublime Porte (the palace of the grand vizier) and in the administration of the Turkish navy. Their knowledge of foreign languages, whose use then was considered contrary to Koranic prescriptions, made them valuable intermediaries. Many Greeks became *dragomans* whose functions were more significant than that of simple interpreters. Most quite naturally sought to place the largest possible number of their compatriots in secondary posts. From the island of Chios, which had known much prosperity under the Genoan regime, came the first *dragomans* of the Sublime Porte, personages whose role in foreign affairs was quite considerable; the first *dragomans* of the fleet, who were almost adjutants to the *capitan pasha,* were frequently able to mitigate the fate of their compatriots scattered among the Aegean islands. But the most influential were the Greeks of the Phanar quarter of Constantinople, such as the Ypsilanti and Mavrocordato families, who became *hospodars* (governors) of Moldavia and Wallachia (the Danubian Principalities), posts of exceptional importance which required full confidence of the sultans in those who held them.

High official posts were monopolized by certain families whose loyalty to the Turks became traditional. These families were generally grouped about the Patriarchate, lived in the same district of Constantinople, and placed themselves under its patronage. Thus was established between the clergy and the Phanariot aristocracy an alliance which tended to protect the interests of the Greeks by protecting the latter from the oppression and arbitrary treatment which Christians frequently had to experience. Because of this activity, which had to be tactful to be tolerated, certain Greek groups succeeded in enjoying autonomy and even constituting themselves into separate little municipalities. Furthermore, the commercial and maritime skill of the Greeks contributed to the improvement of their fate. Constantinople again became a vital commercial metropolis and a very busy seaport. At first the pillage and negligence which followed the conquest dealt the city a harsh blow, but soon the sense of business, exchange, and distribution inherent among the Greeks asserted itself. This was all the more easily achieved because the Turks, indifferent to such matters, and prohibited from participating by Koranic law which forbade usury, left to the Christians and Jews the traffic in merchandise and especially banking activities. Thus the Phanariot Greeks became the beneficiaries of a true financial prosperity. Some Phanariots accumulated vast fortunes. Possession of this wealth was not entirely assured; at times the cost to holders of great fortunes took the form of exposure to insults. Some of them became victims of extortion by Turkish officials who seized large sums from them. Sometimes the perils were even worse as Michael Cantacuzene learned. The enormous wealth of this Greek businessman having attracted the attention of the Turks, he was actually hanged in 1578 on the pretext of having interfered in politics. The Phanariot merchants had to be sufficiently clever to anticipate the wishes of the pashas and beys by offering bribes to prevent the worst.

The maritime skill of the Greeks similarly made them the carriers of trade in the Mediterranean and Black seas. Not only did the voyages of their vessels serve to connect the islands which dot the Aegean and Ionian seas, but their larger ships went to Italy, Trieste, Alexandria, and even as far as Hamburg. By 1783, after the Treaty of Kuchuk Kainarji, the Greeks enjoyed recognition of their right to navigate under the Russian flag. Greek maritime activities were also a source of wealth. By the beginning of the 19th century the Greek fleet reached such development that it counted more than 500 ships and about 20,000 sailors aboard the innumerable vessels in the eastern Mediterranean. Because of its access to the sea, the Greek world did not suffer from the asphyxiation of which the Serbs, Rumanians, and especially the Bulgarians were victims. This explained the establishment of overseas Greek colonies, especially the valuable one at Trieste, and the wealth these colonies contributed during the Greek war for independence.

To present an optimistic impression of the situation in the Greek world under Turkish rule would not correspond to reality. That certain Greeks in Constantinople occasionally secured important posts or that others enriched themselves was merely the exception to the general rule whereby the majority of Greeks, particularly those in Greece proper, shared the far from enviable fate of other Christians, except that they did not have to suffer under the domination of an alien clergy. This advantage, however, was quite considerable for it permitted them an opportunity to keep national flames from being extinguished. Except for this privilege, they had to submit to the same harsh regime of vexations and arbitrariness which, in Greece as elsewhere, because harsher as the once unassailable power of the Turkish Empire declined. This decline favored the abuse of local powers in the same way as the loss of territory had as its consequence the arousing of the authorities to avenge themselves on the Christians for the reverses they were experiencing. The aggravation of the misfortunes of the Greeks greatly contributed to arousing in them national sentiment and leading them to demand independence.

CHAPTER II

The Bulgarians

THE Bulgarians consider themselves to be Slavs, and they are considered by many to be Slavs. But are they? The reply is negative from the viewpoint of ethnic origin. Nevertheless, they have been Slavicized.

As in many cases, the first era of their history remains shrouded in some uncertainty. The Bulgarians appear to have sprung from a Tatar people who came from Asia in successive waves after the Huns and Avars (the latter having arrived in Europe in the 2nd century A. D.) and whose appearance is definitely confirmed in the 5th century. Their place of origin was probably the steppe region along the banks of the Don and Volga rivers north of the Black Sea. Experts consider the Bulgarians to be early relatives of the Hungarians and Finns and thus members of the Turanian ethnic group, but this view is still controversial.

The nomadic Bulgarians, whose wanderings were prolonged, advanced westward and occupied Bessarabia. Asparuk (or Isparik), one of their chieftains, crossed the Danube in 679 at the head of his horde to settle in the region destined to become the habitat of the Bulgarians. Bulgarian historians claim that their ancestors arrived with the Slavs, the latter having infiltrated among them. It appears evident that the Bulgarians, on the contrary, found Slav populations already settled there and the former were quite rapidly assimilated by the latter. Although the Bulgarians retained their original qualities of courage and endurance as well as certain customs imported from Asia, they lost no time in adopting the customs and especially the language of neighbors who were more civilized. Despite the large numbers of Bulgarians, they soon acquired the Slav imprint to the point of completely forgetting their original language and proclaiming themselves to be Slavs.

Under Asparuk's successors the newcomers spread to the south and came into contact with the Byzantine Empire. This marked the beginning of endless and merciless struggles between the Bulgarians and Greeks whose echo still resounds. The Greeks immediately became the hereditary enemy and Constantinople the goal of national ambitions. Subtle and clever at intrigue, Byzantium was able to defend herself not only with arms, but also by the divisions perpetuated among her enemies thanks to subsidies deliberately distributed to prolong feudal anarchy.

The Bulgarians nevertheless became a powerful people. At the beginning of the 9th century Krum, one of their chiefs, attempted to establish a hereditary monarchy after having crushed the Avars and reducing the nobles to a state of obedience. He was the first to assure order by laws and to develop commerce. Firmly governing a people who respected force, Krum decided to attack the *Basileus*. After seizing the Roman city of Sardic (Sofia), a strategic center located at the junction of vital highways, Krum inflicted a severe defeat upon Emperor Nicephorus in 811. The Byzantine 'army avenged itself by setting fire to the region, but, ambushed in the passes of the Balkan Mountains, they were cut to pieces and their emperor killed. Krum celebrated his victory by drinking from the skull of the slain Nicephorus. Krum then besieged Constantinople in 813 and even prepared to attack the city when he suddenly died. The Byzantines were then able to save their capital by bribing the Bulgarians to lift the siege.

At about this time Christianity began to make considerable progress in the Balkan peninsula. Two brothers, the apostles Cyril and Methodius, played a vital role in the conversion of the Slavs. Their memory has remained so alive and their prestige is such that all these peoples still venerate them. Natives of Salonika, they translated the Bible into the Slavic language by means of a new alphabet, which was called Cyrillic, and which is somewhat analogous to the Greek. The success of their mission among the peoples of the region of the Don River led them to pursue their missionary activities as far north as Moravia where there were other Slavs likewise requiring linguistic adaptation to penetrate the meanings of sacred religious books. It was on this mission that Cyril and Methodius crossed Bulgaria which was governed by Boris, the first of the national heroes. Influenced by the mission and encouraged by his sister who had become a Christian during her captivity in Constantinople, Boris, feeling isolated in a world which was gradually becoming Christian, resolved to embrace the new faith more than a century before the conversion of Russia's rulers. His ex-

ample was soon followed by his reluctant subjects who were baptized with blood.

But, desiring to attach political consequences to his gesture,
Boris vacillated between Rome and Byzantium. Although not yet
separated by the schism, these two religious centers were already
diverging and competing to extend their influence. The aim of Bulgaria's chief was to establish an independent, national church.
Boris negotiated with Rome, posing numerous questions to the
pope who dispatched two bishops to conduct an inquiry. The
claims demanded by Boris resulted in their being recalled to Rome.
So in 864 Boris, already impressed by the pomp of the Byzantine
court, resolved to choose the Orthodox Church and the emperor
himself as his godfather. The Greek Patriarchate immediately sent
clergy to convert the Bulgarians. This was the origin of a spiritual
influence whose exclusive and exacting predominance would soon
reveal itself to be particularly prejudicial to the national development of Bulgaria. Could Boris be reproached for this decision?
Rome was too distant and proved to be too meticulous on matters
of doctrine. Constantinople was closer, more powerful, and amen-
able.

After achieving the peak of his power, Boris anticipated by
seven centuries the example of Emperor Charles V by abdicating
his throne and retiring to a monastery in 888. A few years later,
infuriated by his son's attempt to restore paganism, Boris emerged
from retirement to chase his son from the throne and install his
younger son Simeon in his place. Boris then resumed his place
among the monks.

To this second son, Simeon the Great (893-927), was reserved
the glory of leading Bulgaria to her height. Reared in Constantinople, Simeon was then a young man of 25 years, cultivated, a con-
noisseur of Greek literature, distinguished by his noble character,
rectitude of spirit, and the austerity of his life. Memories of his
youth produced a dream of succeeding to the throne of the *Basileus*. He seized the question of tariffs as a pretext (which indicated
the high development of Bulgarian trade at the time) to wage war
against the emperor. Alarmed by his advance after a brilliant victory, Byzantium asked the Hungarians for assistance, and their appearance at the rear of the Bulgarian forces led Simeon to retreat.

Simeon took advantage of a twenty-year truce to give his country
a vigorous thrust and to make it civilized. Agricultural and com-

mercial development produced a hitherto unknown prosperity while, at the same time, the Greek clergy encouraged considerable intellectual progress. Simeon established his capital at Preslav in the heart of Macedonia. According to tradition one could admire in that city churches and palaces constructed of marble and decorated with frescoes whose richness would have vied with the luxury and splendor of Constantinople.

But war again broke out. Despite the intervention of the Serbs, who forced part of the Bulgarian army to retreat, this war brought such success to Simeon that in 921 he proclaimed himself Tsar (Caesar) of the Bulgarians and Autocrat of the Greeks, a title contested by his neighbors but which his successors also wished to give themselves. After conquering Salonika and Adrianople, Simeon renewed the exploits of Krum by besieging Constantinople. The capital was protected by strong walls, defended by invincible catapults, and perhaps better governed by able statesmen. Once again a Bulgarian leader, anxious for the security of his frontiers, preferred to negotiate rather than fight, and the imperial city was thus saved from assault. These sudden and apparently incoherent capitulations perhaps indicated a lack of perseverance on the part of troops weary of combat and longing to return to their farms.

At any rate the warlike efforts of Simeon were carried to the north against tribes in the Danubian region, then westward against the Serbs whose country Simeon conquered so effectively that he soon ruled an empire extending from Adrianople to the banks of the Drina and Morava rivers. Never had Bulgaria been so vast or so powerful. During Simeon's reign of more than thirty years Bulgaria became the mistress of the greater part of the Balkan peninsula.

Simeon, the savage warrior and authoritarian chieftain, was succeeded by his son Peter whose reign (927-969) was as long as it was unfortunate. A young, weak, docile, pious prince, Peter was dominated by his Greek wife. Deprived of a strong leader, the Bulgarian Empire soon exhibited signs of decadence. The energetic Nicephorus Phocas, who then presided over the destiny of Byzantium, judged the moment favorable to resume hostilities. The Hungarians attacked on their front, and the Serbs profited from circumstances by rebelling and recovering their independence. At the same time, enraged by the decline into which the glorious empire of Simeon was falling, patriots of Tirnovo rebelled against

Peter and assembled under the leadership of a noble of that city, Shishman. After proclaiming himself Tsar of the Bulgarians in 963, Shishman dominated part of the country near Macedonia and Albania. Bulgaria was thus divided between two rival dynasties.

This decline was hastened by the curious heresy of the Bogomils, named for its creator, which increased the confusion in Bulgaria. Despite its mysticism, this doctrine, which separated soul from matter, the temporal from the eternal, and imposed a rigid discipline on its adherents, developed in the Balkans, and particularly in Bulgaria, because it was a nationalistic reaction against the influence of the Greek Church. Its revolutionary and quite nihilistic tendencies led its disciples to disobey the state and the church. According to the heresy, all authority was considered the creation of the devil. Bogomilism was consequently the object of lengthy persecution. Its success may be marked by its influence in the West, notably in France where it inspired that sect known as the Albigensians.

Emperor Nicephorus Phocas resolved to destroy the basis of Peter's strength in eastern Bulgaria. When Bulgarian agents came to demand the tribute imposed since the reign of Boris, the emperor had them whipped and sent home. He called on the Russians to assist him in a campaign against the Bulgarians. From that time on the Russians would have considerable influence in the Balkan peninsula.

Arriving by sea in 967, the Russians appeared for the first time at the delta of the Danube River under the leadership of Sviatoslav, the rude and bloodthirsty ruler of Kiev. The Russians smashed the resistance of Peter. They then advanced so rapidly that the emperor, fearing the aggressiveness of his allies would threaten his own security, hastened to conclude peace with the Bulgarians. Fortunately for the Byzantine Empire, an opportune attack by the Pechenegs forced the Russians to turn about and repel an invasion of their homeland. The successor of Nicephorus Phocas, John Tzimisces, pursued the Russians and lay waste the countryside. While the new emperor was returning in triumph to Constantinople, accompanied by the two sons of Peter who had become his vassals, the last Russians retreated across the frontier. But the Russians retained an unforgettable remembrance of the Balkans and the gentleness of the climate, similar to that perpetuated by the Germans regarding Italy after their incursions south of the Alps.

This memory, stimulated by envy, would be transmitted through the generations across the snows of the Russian steppes.

Eastern Bulgaria became a dependency of the Byzantine Empire after the victories of John Tzimisces. Deprived of his crown, Boris II, successor to Tsar Peter, lived as a simple dignitary in Constantinople. The western part of Bulgaria remained in the hands of Shishman and his successors who, after considerable wandering, finally established their capital at Okhrida on the frontier of Albania where fierce resistance against Byzantine domination was being waged.

From this state stretching from the Adriatic to the Danube would emerge a monarch whose glorious reign again threatened the Byzantine Empire. This role was reserved for Samuel (977-1014), the second son of Shishman, a tenacious, energetic, and cruel ruler, who is considered among Bulgaria's great sovereigns. After murdering several kinsmen and nobles, Samuel was assured of incontestable power and pushed his conquests as far north as Belgrade and south along the Adriatic shore. He then attacked Emperor Basil II because a war against the Greeks was a vital necessity for the Bulgarian ruler. Basil's counter-offensive was soon terminated by treason among the Byzantine officers and by an incipient revolt in Constantinople. The Byzantine army, in complete rout, was threatened by encirclement by the Bulgarians from heights dominating the passes. After defeating the Greeks, Samuel conquered Bosnia, Serbia, and part of Macedonia, and then ruled an empire whose extent compared favorably with Simeon's at the time of its height.

But fortune was fickle. Thirsting for vengeance, Basil II undertook several expeditions against his formidable adversary. During the last of these, Samuel was completely defeated. The emperor then forced his enemies to pay dearly for the harsh treatment inflicted on his troops. Tradition claims that he ordered the eyes of 15,000 prisoners to be extracted. The blinded soldiers were returned to Samuel chained in rows of 100 each; they were led by one who, as their guide, had only one eye put out. This sinister deed, whose horror hastened Samuel's death, produced a new title for Basil—*Bulgaroktonos* ("slayer of the Bulgarians"). Proceeding to more victories despite stubborn Bulgarian resistance in the mountains, Basil arrived at Okhrida. He seized the treasury, captured members of the royal family, and led them in captivity to Constantinople.

The year 1018 marked the triumph of Byzantium over western Bulgaria just as eastern Bulgaria had been conquered previously. Bulgaria was forced to submit to a protectorate which, at first quite respectful of local customs, soon assumed a more oppressive character. The polite fiction of an autonomous church was abolished in favor of control by Greek bishops. Many Bulgarian aristocrats were attracted to Constantinople where they received honors which led them to forget the misfortunes of their country. Lacking cohesion and a dynasty of energetic rulers, the First Bulgarian Empire, twice brilliant under Simeon and Samuel whose glory threatened to tarnish the grandeur of the emperors, sank into an anarchy aggravated by the corrosive influence of the Greek clergy and the divisions perpetuated by the active Bogomil heresy. The Bulgarians were not the only people to suffer this fate. The Serbs and Croats had also been defeated, and the entire Balkan peninsula fell under Byzantine domination.

During the 11th century the Balkans suffered many invasions— the Pechenegs, Cumans, Normans, and even the crossing of the peninsula by the armies of the First Crusade. Each incursion offered the Bulgarians an opportunity to attempt rebellion, but since they were too weak and lacking in unity they could only submit to the Byzantine yoke while some of the invaders settled among them in isolated groups. For 170 years this was the fate of the Bulgarians who were divided in provinces unscrupulously exploited by Greek governors. Byzantium's oppression was intensified by the Orthodox Church, now more than ever controlled by Phanariot clergy. One wondered whether Bulgaria would ever reawaken after so long a slumber.

But in 1186, because of the weakening of the Byzantine Empire and the threats the Hungarians and Normans posed to its frontiers, a miracle occurred. A revolt broke out in the city of Tirnovo, a site well endowed by nature to be turned into a fortress protected by a winding river gorge. Two brothers, John and Peter Asen, who were possibly descendants of Shishman but more likely shepherds of Vlach (presumably Latinized Thracians and Greeks) origin, took advantage of the general discontent to lead a revolt. They attracted nobles and peasants eager to shake off the Greek yoke. The tide of insurgence swelled into a national reawakening. A chieftain was essential for this patriotic movement, and John Asen was crowned Tsar of the Bulgarians and Greeks. His first act was to substitute his own appointee as archbishop in defiance of the Patriarchate. He then enlisted the Cumans and Serbs and even proposed to assist the crusaders in fighting against the Byzantine Empire.

Deceived by the easy suppression of earlier uprisings, Byzantium neglected to take steps to end this threat because a very weak emperor ruled in Constantinople. Byzantium had become weakened by corruption and the intrigues of rival generals. The Greek forces were amazed to learn they had to fight a resolute adversary who, after scaling the heights from which they rolled down rocks, harassed them in an ambush where Emperor Isaac Comnenus was almost captured. This revolt made such headway that John Asen hoped to lead the Bulgarians for a third time against the walls of Constantinople. But at the moment of almost achieving this goal, he was murdered by an assassin paid by the emperor. Nevertheless, a region stretching from the Danube to Thrace had been liberated from Byzantine domination.

John Asen's premature death did not prevent his work from being carried on, not so much by his gentle brother Peter (who would soon be assassinated, too), but by another brother whom Greek chroniclers called Kaloyan ("the handsome John"). Swiftly pursuing the Greeks whom he knew well since he had been raised among them, Kaloyan directed his energy and ability to the reconstitution of Simeon's empire. He allied with anyone who supported his design, including the Cumans, Bogomils, and the crusaders.

An unanticipated event then occurred to disturb the East. In 1204 the crusaders suddenly overran the Byzantine Empire by seizing Constantinople which they would rule for more than fifty years. Kaloyan prudently decided to orient the Bulgarians toward Rome by asking the pope to consecrate him tsar, a title which Byzantium had refused him. This gesture led the pope to dispatch a cardinal to Tirnovo who crowned Kaloyan as "King of the Bulgarians and Vlachs." The Bulgarian Orthodox Church aligned with the Roman Catholic Church but without modifying its liturgy or organization.

To strengthen his conversion to Catholicism, Kaloyan attempted a rapprochement with the Latin Empire of Constantinople. But the crusaders, scornful of this "barbarian," imprudently spurned his advances. This backfired on them. Aided by his former Greek enemies, Kaloyan inflicted a severe defeat on the Latins near Adrianople. Emperor Beaudoin (Baldwin) fell into his hands. Was he treated respectfully or thrown into a river? The circumstances of his death remain a mystery. Even today a tower on the ramparts of Tirnovo is named "Baldwin's Tower."

The attempted rapproachement with Latin Christianity proposed by Kaloyan resulted only in his being treated as an apostate by the Orthodox. Moreover, he would soon fall victim to one of those murders which marked the course of this bloody epoch. The memory of this powerful chieftain remained very strong among the Bulgarians.

After a period of quarrels over succession and renewed persecution of the Bogomils, Bulgaria again experienced glorious days under John Asen II. A courageous warrior, wise administrator, he was a great sovereign noted for his enlightenment, tolerance, and justice. His long reign (1218-1241) marked a revival of Bulgarian power and prosperity. This Second Bulgarian Empire, which John Asen II established, comprised the region between the Danube and the Black, Aegean, and Adriatic seas, and included Albania, Serbia, Macedonia, Thessaly, and Thrace.

John Asen II encouraged commerce which became so flourishing that the Venetians and Genoans began to trade with his subjects in the port of Ragusa on the Adriatic. He also restored the old splendors of Tirnovo, his capital. On that site which nature had endowed with a rare picturesqueness palaces and churches (one of which still has an inscription celebrating his exploits and listing "the peoples submissive to his right hand") were constructed. His prestige was so great that neighboring rulers sought alliances with his family. John Asen himself married the daughter of the king of Hungary, and one of his daughters married a king of Serbia; another wed a Byzantine prince. Only the Latin emperor in Constantinople persisted in his haughty reserve. John Asen II avenged himself by besieging Constantinople whose attraction was still irresistible. The imperial city once again witnessed an army beneath its walls, but the Bulgarians had the Greeks as their allies this time. Excommunicated by the pope because of his alliance with the Orthodox Greeks, John Asen hestitated to proceed with the siege. He decided to make peace with the Latins. This experience led him to break with Rome so that he could create an independent, national church. His generous solicitude resulted in the establishment of many monasteries which became centers of intellectual activities. He contributed to the enrichment of the monasteries at Mount Athos and Rila, where the relics of St. John Rilski, patron saint of Bulgaria, are preserved.

Just as the death of Samuel in 1014 had marked the end of the First Bulgarian Empire, John Asen's death in 1241 marked the beginning of the decline of the Second Empire which had had a lively but shortlived brilliance. The increasing influence of Byzantine customs introduced into the court by the Bulgarians tsars had contributed to this decline. Although the Bulgarian Empire had been revived and enlarged by the talented Asens, it gradually disintegrated as a result of anarchy, quarrels, and murders. The results of their efforts were wasted. For more than a century a very confused period ensued until the Ottoman Turks appeared. There were few interesting developments in this period except for uninterrupted decadence and decline. How common in these countries, which lacked institutions and traditions, for the fortunes of the peoples to be so bound up with the courage of their leaders. For lack of men of the stature of Simeon, Samuel, and the Asens, the Bulgarians were tossed between hands as inept as they were selfish. After a succession of family tragedies and defeats, the last members of the dynasty renounced their rights and, by a curious irony of fate, sought refuge in Constantinople whose very existence the bravery of their ancestors had once threatened. Through contact with Byzantine mores and their degeneracy, the intrepid Bulgarians, who emerged from barbarism to refinement before experiencing civilization, thus passed from virility to decadence.

The Bulgarians next chose as their chief Constantine, grandson of King Stephen Nemanya of adjacent Serbia. To create the impression of perpetuating the former dynasty Constantine married a descendant of the Asens when he acceded to the throne in 1258. As the Bulgarians had once dominated Serbia, it was now their turn to experience the latter's ascendancy. Moreover, they had to support bitter struggles in the north against the Hungarians who infiltrated the frontiers and the Greeks in the south whose hostility was not reduced by a marriage alliance. The pretenders who claimed the throne in a conspiratorial atmosphere imprudently asked the Ottoman Turks for assistance. Finally a descendant of Shishman, Michael, a noble from Vidin, had the honor of closing the history of an independent Bulgaria by attacking the formidable Serbian Empire.

The strength Bulgaria lacked permitted the Serbs to increase theirs dramatically. The time had arrived when one of these nations, the Serbs in progressive development and the Bulgarians in decline, had to bow before the other. In July 1330 King Stephen Urosh III met the Bulgarian army at Kustendil and put it to rout. Tsar Michael was killed, and his fortresses capitulated. Thereafter, while maintaining the fragile image of a national dynasty, Bulgaria was subjected to the unchallengeable domination of the Serbs until the great Serbian hero, Stephen Dushan, proclaimed himself Tsar of the Serbs, Greeks, and Bulgarians. This domination would endure for about thirty years, after which arose the menace of the Turkish conqueror. Not only the Byzantine Empire but all the Balkan peoples were confronted by this dire peril. Incapable of uniting against the common threat, they continued their petty disputes. In Bulgaria religious controversy was added by the persistence of Bogomilism. Serbia's power did not survive King Stephen Dushan. His empire was dismembered while the Turks were marching on Sofia in 1382. The imminence of the Turkish threat did produce one effort by the Slavs, but they paid dearly for their first successes. Sultan Murad I assembled a strong army, defeated the Bulgarians, and then met the Serbs on the plain of Kossovo. His memorable victory of 1389 placed the entire peninsula at the mercy of the Turks. Tirnovo, once the rival of Constantinople, was seized in 1402, its wealth destroyed, and its leading citizens massacred or deported. The collapse of the last political vestige of Bulgaria also marked the abolition of the Bulgarian patriarchate and its relegation to a simple bishopric controlled by the Greek Patriarchate again. Bulgaria thus ceased to exist.

For the next five centuries the glorious past of Bulgaria was barely a memory. When the inhabitants began to stir in the 19th century, the name of their country had been forgotten. Of all the Balkan peoples, the Bulgarians would be those who felt the Turkish yoke most oppressively. The Rumanians were protected by the Danube barrier, and the Serbs found in their mountains a refuge difficult to penetrate. Their skill and resources enabled the Greeks to mitigate their fate. But the Bulgarians, who lived closest to Constantinople, were isolated within the Turkish Empire, cut off from the rest of the world. The long domination of their demanding and combative nobles had bequeathed unpleasant memories to the peasants. Now that most nobles had been killed or exiled, the peasants were left to their own devices, leaderless and forced to submit. Some peasants converted to Islam. These were the Pomaks who inhabited the region near the Rhodope Mountains. Young Bulgarian boys were conscripted into the celebrated Janissary Corps. The masses submitted to the Turkish yoke with a degree of fatalism common to the East.

The Turks installed in Sofia a *beylerbey* (governor) of Rumelia, the new name for the former Bulgaria now divided into twenty *sanjaks* (districts). As long as the Turkish Empire remained strong, its power was not oppressive. The Turks were even interested in fostering the prosperity of the Bulgarians. They had roads constructed and encouraged the growth of commerce. And they appeared remarkably tolerant toward the church. But in Bulgaria, as elsewhere, the situation changed in proportion as the sultan's power declined and his armies began their retreat from the Balkans. Only at the end of the 17th century did forced labor, increased taxes, and exactions become heavier and assume an arbitrary character in the hands of functionaries who grew more corrupt and despotic. The fate of the *rayahs* (Christians) grew intolerable.

To the political and economic oppression of the Turkish administration was added the spiritual domination of the Greek clergy. After the abolition of the Patriarchate at Tirnovo, the entire Bulgarian clergy had to submit to the authority of the Phanariot ecclesiastics. The Greek Patriarch appointed the clergy who taught doctrine in Greek. More educated and sophisticated than the masses, the Greek clergy exercised their influence not only on religious life but also on secular intellectual activities. The administration of the schools was assigned to them. They assumed an obligation to Hellenize the schools. Greek became the obligatory language of everyone regardless of his educational level. The Bulgarian language was scorned as a patois only for uneducated peasants. The miserable peasants were forced to mumble prayers whose meanings escaped them. Since being called Bulgarian was to admit to inferiority, many were ready to claim they were Greek. Even the Cyrillic alphabet was proscribed and replaced by Greek writing.

Not content with imposing its culture, the Phanariot clergy tried to eliminate all traces of Bulgarian culture. Old manuscripts and icons bearing inscriptions in Old Church Slavonic were consigned to the flames. Vandalism went so far as to destroy the precious volumes of the library at Mount Athos and to promise rewards to those who revealed hidden caches of forbidden books. The foreign clergy would so effectively kill the soul of a people that as late as 1834 an English traveler in Bulgaria, having interrogated natives regarding their nationality, heard them reply they were Greek.

Ecclesiastical as well as civil offices were bought and sold. The beneficiaries sought to recoup their investments by making their parishioners pay taxes and rents with the complicity of the Turkish pasha. Already plundered by the Turks, the Bulgarians were again plundered by the Greeks. The latter completed the work of the former. Such explained the morale of the Bulgarians which was more hostile toward the Greeks than the Turks.

However inactive national consciousness may have been during the centuries of submission, sporadic movements of rebellion occasionally arose, notably when Turkish power appeared threatened by the Hungarians, Venetians, Austrians, and finally by the Russians. But, after failing in their efforts, the rebels sought refuge in neighboring provinces, especially in Wallachia. These uprisings arose mostly under the leadership of patriotic bandits variously called Heyduks, Haiduks, Haidots, whom popular Bulgarian legend surrounded with prestigious aura. From a refuge in the forests and mountains, they fell without warning on Turkish troops, murdered a few functionaries, spread disorder, and disappeared again into their inaccessible retreats. There they awaited a signal by accomplices which indicated an opportunity for another raid. When winter came they reappeared in their villages under the guise of peaceful peasants after hiding their weapons and munitions in the forests. Legends and songs celebrated the exploits of these heroes who were really underground fighters who, confronted by incessant peril, scorn, and torture, symbolized a will to resist the occupation forces. One such hero was Ducho Vatach who, "protected by the spirits who deflected bullets from striking him," terrorized the Turks. At one time a woman called "The Amazon" became the leader of a band at the end of the 18th century. Occasionally the Heyduks formed a very strong organization, such as one led by Pasvanoglu, the gallant adventurer. After carving out for himself a veritable fief near Vidin in the very center of the sultan's empire, Pasvanoglu spoke of marching on Constantinople. It required no less than a Turkish army of 100,000 and three expeditions to overcome this rebel.

The flame of patriotism was not carried by the Heyduks alone. Others assured this flame would not be extinguished, but in a quite different manner. These were the Bulgarian monks. At the end of the 18th century monks began resuscitating the glorious past in their writings and making it live again in the minds of the masses. The monasteries became citadels of Bulgarian nationalism. At the beginning of the 19th century a few still rather vague wishes for independence at last became evident. Those few nationalists who nurtured this hope realized the need for support. Where could they seek such support? From Austria or Russia? Nevertheless, fate decreed that of all the Balkan nations the Bulgarians were the first to be crushed and the last to be freed.

CHAPTER III

The Serbs

ABOUT the middle of the 6th century A. D., the Slavs, who were probably natives of the region between the Don River and the Black Sea, established themselves in the vast region bounded by the Danube in the north, the Adriatic Sea in the west, and Macedonia in the south. In 548 their penetration was noted as far north as Illyria (modern Slovenia in Yugoslavia). Although all were of the same ethnic origin, the Slavs were divided into three branches according to the regions they inhabited. The Serbs in Serbia, Montenegro, Bosnia, Herzegovina, the Backa and Banat, and southern Dalmatia; the Croats further to the west in the region to which they have given their name; and the Slovenes forming a compact mass spread over Carinthia, Carniola, Istria, and Styria. All constitute a group known as the Yugoslavs (South Slavs).

For political and religious rather than geographical reasons this group was divided into two parts. The Croats and Slovenes had migrated into regions of the Western Roman Empire while the Serbs found themselves in those regions attached to the Eastern (Byzantine) Empire. Consequently, the division was accentuated at the time of the schism in the 11th century when the Croats and Slovenes remained faithful to the Papacy in Rome, and the Serbs gave their allegiance to the Patriarchate in Constantinople. The South Slavs thus constituted two groups divided between two empires and two churches. This duality persists to the present day; although united in one nation, the two Slav peoples perpetuate their church differences.

The Croats and Slovenes are not considered Balkan peoples, at least prior to the 20th century. Hence only the Serbs will be treated here.

The Serbs inhabit one of the most mountainous regions of the peninsula. Not that the summits are high (the Dinaric Alps reach about 8,500 feet), but the folds in the terrain form an inextricable network dividing the country into a series of deep, narrow valleys which impede communication and in which are located beds of former lakes. This arrangement facilitated defense against invaders. But it also impeded unity by favoring the division of the inhabitants into rival groups separated by the mountains.

As in most of known Europe, Rome extended her domination over these regions—Dalmatia, Pannonia (present Hungary), and part of Macedonia. The Latin influence which still predominates in the Albanian language, the remains of the Via Egnatia which crossed the peninsula from the Adriatic to the Aegean, and the ruins of Diocletian's palace at Split (Spalato) still evoke memories of the *Pax Romana*. Then came the barbaric tribes—Goths, Huns, Avars—to wreck Rome's achievements which the Byzantine Empire later tried to reconstruct.

At the time of the Slav penetration the Byzantine Empire faced so many threats that it could not meet this challenge. Perhaps the empire considered using the Slavs as a dike against more dangerous invaders such as the Avars. Nevertheless, the Slavs who entered the Balkans in the 6th century soon overcame the empire's defenses. In the 7th century the entire peninsula became prey to their pillaging. Alleged to be tall, blond, brave, and resistant to authority, the Slavs were grouped into tribes quite foreign to each other when they were not mutually hostile. Each tribe obeyed its chief, the *zhupan*. Notables of several tribes joined to name a great chief, the *veliki zhupan*.

The first recognizable Serbian state was born on the Adriatic coast between Novi-Bazar and Scutari. This was Old Serbia or Rachka (Rascia). Like their Bulgarian neighbors to the east, the Serbs embraced the Orthodox Christian faith implanted among the Slavs by apostles Cyril and Methodius. In 879 the conversion of a great chief produced a general acceptance of the new faith which had as one result the mitigation of certain barbaric customs.

Of an independent spirit and ignoring the need to unite, the Serbs initiated a struggle against the Bulgarians destined to last through the centuries to the satisfaction of the Byzantine emperors. A unification of these two peoples would have posed a serious threat to the empire. Their rivalry thus constituted a guarantee of stability. From these struggles the Bulgarians ultimately emerged victorious, although their hostility toward their neighbors led the Serbs to seek support of the Byzantines. Tsar Simeon of Bulgaria punished the Serbs for this alliance. In 926, after arranging the murder of their *zhupan,* Simeon imposed on the Serbs a chief of his own who perpetuated an anarchy favorable to Bulgaria's designs. This oppression was so severe that many Serbs abandoned their ruined country to find refuge in Croatia.

Simeon's death changed the situation. A Serbian chief named Chaslav appealed to the Byzantines to rout the Bulgarians. This campaign was successful, but Serbia fell so completely under Byzantine control that for almost one century the question of being Serbian did not exist.

Serbian power reappeared in 1040 when Stephen Voislav, who had escaped from a Byzantine prison, renewed the Serbian struggle against the Greeks. Retreating to the mountains of Montenegro, the insurgents lured the enemy to the south and ultimately secured their independence in a campaign celebrated with justifiable pride by the chroniclers. The decline of the rulers of adjacent Croatia coincided with the rise of those of Serbia. Michael, the son of Stephen Voislav, ruled for about thirty years. His subjects extended their frontier northward toward Italy, and Michael capitalized on this advance by agreeing to a rapprochement with Rome.

Stephen Nemanya (1168-1196) was the able and energetic creator of the Serbian state and founder of a dynasty which ruled for two centuries. Although he had recruited several *zhupans* and had conquered Bosnia, he was still subject to Byzantine sovereignty. The emperor obliged him to fight against the Venetians with whom the Serbs had maintained friendly relations. Venetian maritime power did not threaten Serbia's territorial ambitions, and Ragusa (present Dubrovnik) had become a vital center of trade and contact between the cultures of East and West. Stephen Nemanya, although basically a great warrior, was also animated by a very active religious faith which led him to contribute to his country's spiritual development. He established many churches and monasteries.

After conquering part of Macedonia, he decided to proclaim his independence in 1185. Serbia had by then emerged from Bulgarian as it had from Byzantine domination. Freedom was no longer a vain dream. Unable to force his former vassal to return to obedience, the Byzantine emperor was required to regard him as an equal and to consent to a marriage alliance between their two families. Henceforth marriages between Serbian kings and Greek princesses became common. This was an honor of doubtful value because the ambitions and intrigues of Byzantine women were frequently prejudicial to the tranquillity of the empire. At the time of the Third Crusade (1190) Stephen Nemanya wished to extend his influence and offered an alliance to Emperor Frederick Barbarossa of the Holy Roman Empire. The Holy Roman Emperor may well have been surprised to learn of the existence of the Serbian state.

After realizing most of his ambitions, Stephen Nemanya, apparently conscience-stricken and imbued with mystical tendencies, decided to relinquish his throne. Imitating the gesture of Boris of Bulgaria, he abdicated to end his days in prayer among the monks of Mount Athos. His youngest son had already become a monk and resided at Mount Athos. It was this son, ultimately known as St. Sava, who was destined to become the patron saint of Serbia. Stephen Nemanya named his second son as his successor. When the oldest son disputed the throne with the heir, St. Sava had to intervene to assure the accession of Stephen II (1196-1223). All the Serbian kings of this era bore the same first name. After assuring the independence of Serbia, Stephen was crowned by a papal legate in 1217. This date marked the elevation of the Grand Zhupanate of Serbia to the rank of a kingdom. At the same time Stephen initiated a rapprochement with Byzantium whose Patriarch recognized the autonomy of the Serbian Orthodox Church with St. Sava as its head. After becoming the first archbishop of Serbia, St. Sava organized a national church. Despite efforts of the Papacy, the Serbian clergy favored the Orthodox Church and soon broke the loose bonds which tied them to Rome. Like the conversion of Kaloyan in Bulgaria at about the same time, the plans of the Serbs to adopt Roman Catholicism, more political than religious in their inspiration, were abandoned. St. Sava's pilgrimage to the Holy Land brought new luster to his fame. After devoting considerable energy to educational development, this great man of the church died only to leave to popular piety a memory of his deeds which has never diminished.

Real progress was achieved in the field of culture during the reign of Stephen Nemanya II. Religious establishments were developed; agriculture, commerce, and mines were exploited. Like his father before him, Stephen retired to a monastery at the end of his reign (1223). The following era produced a succession of rulers whose reigns were beset with conspiracies at a time when

Bulgarian power posed a threat to a Serbia still in her birth pangs. Not until King Stephen Urosh I (1243-1276) did Serbia acquire an able king who could under favorable circumstances switch alliances to resist his many adversaries and to consolidate his authority until, dethroned by his son, he too took the monk's habit. Contrite over his usurpation, this son relinquished the throne to his brother, Stephen Urosh II who, during a reign of about forty years (1281-1321), enlarged his domain at Macedonia's expense. This seizure of Byzantine land did not prevent the emperor from offering the hand of his daughter to the Serbian king. At his death Serbia extended as far as the Adriatic and had achieved much prosperity. But, according to a growing tradition, Stephen Urosh II had to suppress a revolt led by his son, whom he had ordered to be blinded.

The successor was a illegitimate son whom the king had thought he had blinded. Due to the connivance of the executioner who merely went through the motions without actually inflicting the torture, the son was able to see and this convinced everyone of a miracle. The new king took the title of Stephen Urosh III. Among his finest military expoits was his brilliant victory over the Bulgarians at Kustendil in 1330. He reduced Bulgaria to the rank of a secondary power without ending her independence. But, as a consequence of fate destined for Serbia, the king was faced by a revolt of his eldest son who had been removed from succession because of the king's second marriage. This rebellious son, who had distinguished himself at Kustendil, gathered troops to his side. Proclaiming himself king, he marched against his father and routed him. Stephen Urosh III was captured and about to be exiled when he was strangled by zealous partisans of his son. Troubled by family dramas which opposed sons to fathers, and inspired royal retreats into monasteries and marriages with foreign princesses, Serbia's power nevertheless persisted during these calamitous times. Her warriors covered themselves with glory. The defeat of the Bulgarians reversed the situation which had so long made vassals of the Serbs. The 14th century, however, would produce a belated but spectacular revenge for the latter.

Already settled in Asia Minor, the Ottoman Turks were beginning to approach the Straits in an alarming manner. This threat had not yet appeared imminent when the next Serbian king, Stephen Urosh IV, acceded to the throne. This monarch is more familiarly known as Stephen Dushan the Great (1331-1355), destined to be known also as the Charlemagne of Serbia. Enthroned at age 22 after a new murder, this king led the power of Serbia to its greatest heights. A great figure, he was simultaneously a rough warrior, a wise administrator, a sovereign sensitive to intellectual activities, and a true statesman. Dushan remains to the Serbs the national hero whose glories they still recall with pride just as they are proud to place their nation under the spiritual patronage of St. Sava.

Marshaling the strength of his people, who followed him enthusiastically and confidently, Dushan undertook a campaign against the Byzantine Empire which, disastrously affected by the victories of the Fourth Crusade, was attempting to avert a deteriorating situation. Dushan swiftly seized Thessaly, Albania, Epirus, and most of Macedonia. After besieging the emperor at Salonika in 1340, he imposed a treaty which assured Serbia sovereignty over regions extending from the Danube to the Gulf of Corinth, from the Adriatic to the Maritsa River, and all Bulgaria up to the environs of Adrianople. Bulgaria's tsar, whose sister Dushan had married, became his vassal. Dushan thus ruled over the entire Balkan peninsula. Only southern Greece, Salonika, and Thrace escaped his authority. The young sovereign did not fear giving sanctuary to the former regent of the Byzantine Empire, John Cantacuzene, in revolt against the government, and agreed to an alliance. After establishing his authority over the vast territory Dushan convened a synod of the clergy. The primate of Serbia was elevated to the dignity of patriarch so that the Serbian Orthodox Church would be freed from its subjection to the Greek Patriarchate. In his capital of Skoplje (Uskub) in Macedonia on Easter 1346, Dushan proclaimed himself emperor of the Serbs, Greeks, Bulgarians, and Albanians. He placed a tiara on his head and clothed himself in imperial emblems. If some Greeks still escaped his authority, at least he dominated all the other peoples.

Dushan was not only talented as a conqueror, but he was also gifted as a legislator. With as much firmness as ability, he supervised the efficient administration of his vast empire. His great merit was to recognize the need of endowing it with a body of laws in written form, an effort his predecessors had only begun. As assembly of bishops, nobles, and provincial governors was charged with creating a code of laws, bringing together the customs of the Slav countries. What was thus created resembled the feudal system then prevalent in Western Europe. This legislation bore witness to the degree of civilization which yielded no place to most other countries of the same era. Having an aristocratic basis, it established a wide distinction between nobility and peasantry, the latter being required to furnish their lords with a considerable number of workdays. Commerce was also the object of Dushan's concern. He gave strict orders to combat piracy to assure the safety of travelers and foreign merchants. A resumption of traditional relations with the Venetians, masters of the Dalmatian coast, contributed to the development of commerce, a part of which was transacted at Ragusa (Dubrovnik). Exploitation of mines produced appreciable resources.

Education, to which St. Sava had given first impulse, progressed remarkably during Dushan's reign. Schools and monasteries secured royal favor. True seats of culture, they took a firm place in the heroic history of the Serbs who have remained grateful to the role of these institutions in perpetuating national traditions. The fine arts, influenced by Italians, were not neglected. Fragments of frescoes and mosaics testify to the artistic level achieved during this period.

Influenced by the clergy, Dushan showed extreme severity toward Roman Catholicism. Those who adopted the Latin rite were condemned to work in mines, and people who propagated it were threatened with death. The Papacy grew concerned about this and the increasing power of Dushan. It had no difficulty arousing the old rivalry of the Hungarians against the Serbs. Once again, however, Dushan overcame his enemies from whom he seized Bosnia and Herzegovina. This annexation marked the height of the Serbian Empire in the Middle Ages.

The most serious menace now confronted the entire Balkan peninsula. Dushan, displaying clear vision, soon realized it. Entrenched on the shores of the Dardanelles, the Turks were the common enemies of Christendom. It was against the Moslems that the question of uniting and directing all forces in the Balkans arose to save Eastern Europe from invasion. The Serbian Empire already included most of the region. To transform the peninsula into a cohesive whole under the rule of a single master required a seizure of Constantinople to add to Serbia what remained of the Byzantine Empire. Dushan dreamed of making himself emperor and defender of Christianity against the Islamic wave.

In 1355 Dushan began military preparations which aroused enthusiasm among people conscious of the noble task to which they were being called. When he had assembled an army of 80,000, an enormous number for that time, Dushan marched toward Constantinople, confident of success. Capturing Adrianople after a fierce battle, the army was about to achieve its goal, Constantinople, located no more than forty miles to the east, when Dushan suddenly died of an unknown illness at age 46. It may be recalled that the Bulgarian chiefs Krum and John Asen had succumbed at the very moment when they were preparing to assault the imperial city. Did a strange curse, wielded by a mysterious force, affect those who menaced the city? Or was Byzantium, inhabited by experts in ruse and perfidy, able at the last moment to wield the dagger or poison to get rid of her enemies?

At any rate, Dushan's expedition ended with him. If it had been successful, history would perhaps have taken another course. A young, strong people occupying the place of the Byzantine Empire, which was deteriorating with age, might have been the renovators of the Eastern Empire and a check on the Turks before the gates of Europe. But Dushan's army retreated, sadly carrying the dead body of the man who had elevated Serbia to the rank of a great power. Byzantium considered herself saved.

Byzantium may have been spared the Serbian menace, but now the Turkish peril came into sharp focus as an agonizing reality. Turkish troops were crossing the Dardanelles for the first time, and the sultan had established himself on Gallipoli in 1354. Islam had secured a foothold in the Balkans. According to the law of contrasts, so frequently observed in successions to thrones, Stephen Urosh V acceded to Dushan's crown. He was a weak, young man of 19 whom nothing but fate qualified to assume the burden bequeathed by his father. Still lacking a strong foundation, the Serbian Empire soon declined as if its fate had been bound to the fortunes of a single man.

The Serbian nobles supported the authority of a ruler so different from the one who had led them to victory. But several declared themselves independent and some were content to be recalcitrant. A semi-anarchy, which favored the designs of the enemy, arose in Serbia. The Hungarians took advantage of the crisis by seizing Bosnia and Belgrade. The Turks pushed north across the Balkans. At a time when the Hungarians had shown no spirit of Christian solidarity in attacking the Serbs, the latter, on the contrary, allied with the Greeks to stop the Moslems. The battle took place near Adrianople. King Stephen Urosh V did not survive it. His death marked the end of the Nemanyid dynasty. Only ten years after Dushan's death did the great empire which he founded break up as a consequence of military disasters and disunity.

The Serbs elected a new ruler, Lazar of the Hrebelyanovich family, who attempted to redress the deteriorating situation. The Turks had already invaded Serbia and seized Nish. Lazar led an army of Serbs, Bosnians, and Bulgarians—the common front of Christendom—against an immense army commanded by Sultan Murad I. The date was June 15, 1389— a decisive one in all Balkan history. It was a disaster for the Christians. The defeat at Kossovo—"the Field of Blackbirds"—still evokes a memory as dolorous as that of Waterloo in French minds. Despite the bravery of the Serbian cavalry, which was decimated, the Christian army was beginning to waver when Murad was killed in his tent by a Serbian noble, Milosh Obilich. After a moment of hesitation, the Turks, led by Bayezid, regained the initiative and finished the rout of the Slavs. As for King Lazar, whose somber premonitions had foretold the results of the battle, he was captured and beheaded before the body of Murad.

The disaster at Kossovo had immense repercussions which have endured for centuries. The anniversary of the battle is a day of national mourning. Legends, poetry, popular songs have immortalized the wild melée which is marked like the expoits of Roland and Charlemagne are noted in France. Far from seeing in this anniversary a subject for dejection, the patriotism of the Serbs derived an ardent desire for revenge. The defeat near Skoplje stimulated their courage and fortified their will to efface it someday, a distant day perhaps, but one whose arrival every Serb, animated by the spirit of Kossovo, awaited with certainty.

For seventy years Serbia remained a Turkish vassal state without being completely dismembered as Bulgaria had been. Serbia's chiefs, successors to Lazar whose sister married Sultan Bayezid, still enjoyed autonomy in the mountains and in Shumadia, a veritable wooded fortress south of Belgrade. There they tenaciously opposed Turkish domination. But, in addition to paying tribute, the country had to furnish mercenaries to the sultan's army and adolescents to the Janissary Corps. Many Serbs fled to Hungary

where they aroused anti-Turkish hostility, especially after Bayezid's reverses in Asia Minor appeared to undermine Turkish prestige as a result of the advance of Tamerlane and his Tatars.

The sultans soon regained the upper hand as a result of the indifference of Christendom. Invoking his status as the grandson of
a Serbian princess, Murad II claimed the throne of Lazar and invaded Serbia in 1439. Serbia was saved by the intervention of the
Hungarians led by John Hunyadi, who crossed the Danube, seized
Belgrade, and forced the Turks to retreat. But this was only a
temporary respite. By violating a truce with the Turks, the Hungarians incurred the wrath of the Moslems who inflicted on them
at Varna in 1444 a terrible defeat whose repercussions would
affect the Serbs.

Soon the reverberating fall of Constantinople imparted a new
impulse to the advance of the Turkish conquerors. The crumbling
but historically rich traces of the Byzantine Empire having finally
fallen under their blows, nothing could then resist the forward
surge of the Turks. Sultan Mohammed II besieged Belgrade in
1456 which was heroically defended by Hunyadi who died just before the capture of that city. By 1459 the Turks took Smederovo,
the last Serbian fortress, and the entire country came into their
hands. Independent Serbia ceased to exist. The nation, strategically
located in the West's vanguard against the Islamic world, succumbed after having fulfilled its sentinel's post with honor. Serbia,
which provided access to Hungary, became strategically important
for the Turks as a base of operations from which they surged forward to conquer Bosnia, Herzegovina, Albania, and inflicted upon
the Hungarians the disastrous defeat of Mohacs in 1526.

Montenegro, however, alone of the Balkan states, sheltered in
her mountains, continued a resistance symbolizing the determination of the Slavs not to bow to the Turkish yoke. As for Serbia,
she had to undergo Turkish domination after two centuries of
grandeur. The lack of unity among her people, their disputes, the
excesses of the feudal regime, the corrosive influence of Byzantine
corruption, religious controversies, a prolonged hostility toward
the Catholic Hungarians, and finally a shortage of courageous
leaders caused the downfall of a country which once dominated
the Balkans and nurtured a dream of replacing Byzantium.

A matchless warrior nation, the Serbs had to be disarmed. The
domination of the pasha who governed from Belgrade was rigor-

ously imposed. The division of feudal estates, crushing taxes, arbitrary authority, and the abduction of children to serve in the Turkish army typified the oppressive and exacting regime which mistreated the unfortunate *rayahs*. In Bosnia many nobles converted to Islam to save their property, but the majority remained faithful to Christianity, the only bond which tied them to the past and served as a point of national aspiration. The church survived with a Patriarchate at Pech (Ipek), but the influence of the Greek clergy grew until these ecclesiastics became masters after the patriarchate was abolished. Then for Serbia, as for Bulgaria, the church became a foreign organism whose domination was added to the Turkish one.

Attempted revolts were carried out in the more mountainous and wooded Serbia. However meritorious, such uprisings were mere wishes because weapons were lacking and reprisals merciless. But the clandestine resistance of a few patriots gave proof of the will to survive which still animated the Serbs. Popular legends surrounded the heroes with a grateful aura. Heroes like Marko Kralyevich appeared as avenging judges to sow terror among the pashas. "Marko, may your name be glorified everywhere as long as there is a sun and a moon," went an old song. Such fidelity to the memory of rebels showed how intensely they embodied the spirit of revolt among the Serbs. But to fight the Turks really required flight into neighboring countries. Numerous Serbs escaped to struggle alongside the Venetians and Croats and even the Hungarians as, for example, at the fateful battle of Mohacs in 1526. In Hungary the Serbian group grew to such proportions that certain privileges were accorded them.

The defeat of the Turks at Vienna in 1683 and their subsequent evacuation of Budapest inspired new hopes. Would the Serbs succeed in liberating their country? Severe reprisals, including abolition of their Patriarchate at Pech, demoralized the Serbs. At the head of about 100,000 believers, the Patriarch of Pech fled to Austria where this mass exodus was favorably received by Emperor Leopold I. But his promise of spiritual and administrative autonomy was not fulfilled.

When the Venetians advanced into Dalmatia and the Austrians into the Balkans, new hopes were generated. The Treaty of Karlowitz in 1699 accorded to the Austrian emperor a vague right to intervene in favor of the Christians in Turkey. The Treaty of

Passarowitz in 1718, signed after the victories of Prince Eugene of Savoy, finally dislodged the Turks from Hungary and ceded to Austria a portion of northern Serbia and western Wallachia. Would Vienna assume the role of protector of the Christians languishing under the Turkish yoke? The Serbs awaited their liberation by Austria, but their confidence was shortlived. Dividing their attention between the east and west, the Hapsburgs were not in a position to pursue efforts in two opposite directions. The Treaty of Belgrade in 1739 wrecked the achievements of Prince Eugene when that fortress city and the Serbian and Wallachian territories were restored to the Turks.

At this point Empress Maria Theresa turned away from the east to struggle against the ambitions of Frederick the Great of Prussia. The dejected Serbian émigrés decided to leave Austria where they had once been welcomed only to learn they would be used to form military colonies along the frontiers with the Turkish Empire. Why did Austria fail to justify the confidence inspired among the Serbs? Was it the difference in religion which hindered the Orthodox Serbs and Catholic Austria? Perhaps Austria was already fearful of the creation of a Slav state so close to her frontier. Whatever the reasons, about 200,000 Serbs, disgusted by Austria's attitude, abandoned the Hapsburg Empire to emigrate to the banks of the Dniester River where they were ultimately assimilated into the Russian mass.

At the same time the rise of a new star in the east attracted attention. The urge to expand to the south manifested by Peter the Great and the role of protector of the Orthodox claimed by Catherine the Great turned Serbian hopes toward Russia. A new power of the same Slav group, Russia shared Serbia's Orthodox faith as well. At first the Serbs expected common action by their two great Christian neighbors. Had not Catherine and Emperor Joseph II combined efforts against the Turks, thus foreshadowing the partition of the Turkish Empire? But this experience proved it was necessary to renounce confidence in the Austrians and the wisest course was to trust to one's own forces.

Although never as severe as that experienced by the Bulgarians who lived closer to the Turkish capital, the Moslem occupation of Serbia was nevertheless oppressive. But Serbian national consciousness was never entirely obliterated. Intellectual centers set up outside the Turkish Empire, whose influence only feebly reached Serbia, perpetuated among some Serbs the permanence of Slavic thought and ideas. The Republic of Ragusa (Dubrovnik) on the eastern Adriatic coast maintained its independence from Venice and carried out the dual mission of a commercial metropolis and a melting pot for east and west in the 18th century. Scholars added to its fame. Dosithee Obradovich, the creator of Serbia's literary language, resided in Ragusa.

An intellectual movement was the forerunner of a national revival in Bulgaria. In Serbia, where the spiritual role was strong, recourse to arms predominated in the beginning. The time was approaching when the descendants of Dushan's warriors would soon raise their heads.

CHAPTER IV

The Rumanians

THE Rumanians (also spelled "Romanians" or "Roumanians")
derive from a branch of Indo-European peoples of Thracian
origin who originally settled in a region extending from the Carpathian Mountains to the Adriatic, and southward to the Greek
archipelago. To the west were the Illyrians and to the east their
rivals, the Dacians, often called Getae in antiquity, hence Dacian-
Getae designating one people, the ancestors of the present Rumanians. The original Rumanians were nomadic tribesmen who
wandered between the frontiers of Germany and the Crimea where
they encountered the Scythians in the 7th century B. C. The
Scythians, superb horsemen and archers, but barbaric and cruel,
were attacked by King Darius of Persia in 513 B. C. Objects of
Scythian manufacture have been unearthed along the Black Sea
coast to attest that the Scythians once inhabited the region. The
Sarmatians, who had migrated from central Asia, inflicted a severe
defeat on the Scythians and thus contributed to their disappearance
at the beginning of the 2nd century B. C.

As for the Dacians (or Getae), they were successively conquered by Darius when he was campaigning against the Scythians
and later by Philip and Alexander of Macedonia. At that time the
Dacians inhabited the vast plain north of the Danube around
which the Transylvanian Alps and the Carpathians formed a
rough circle. Their level of civilization was quite advanced. They
believed in the immortality of the soul. Agriculture and herding
were their major occupations. A legend relates that when Philip
of Macedonia attacked them, they sent against him priests dressed
in white robes who were playing lyres. Perhaps this is an indication of the poetic influence exercised over them by their contact
with numerous Greek colonies on the Black Sea coast, such as
rich Tomis (Constantsa), Dionysopolis (Balchik) and Olbia on
the Borysthene (Dniester River). Herodotus cited the Getae and
described their characteristics. Citing his theory of an actual

[43]

Thraco-Scytho-Hellenic civilization, Professor Nicolae Iorga (1871–1940), the distinguished Rumanian historian, wrote that "the Mediterranean world had conquered that of the interior." Nevertheless, he added, the great synthesizing of East and West was reserved for the Romans. Research did reveal traces of Greek civilization in the region. Some Greeks may have been invited to the court of Getae rulers to teach their language. During his exile in Tomis, the Latin poet Ovid alluded to the son of a king who wrote Greek verse while he himself was still trying to learn the Getae language. The legend of Orpheus probably originated in this region. Philip of Macedonia married a Getae. Priests undoubtedly played a considerable role in Getae society. They were assigned the drafting of written laws in verse form so that the imagination could be aroused. To these cultural qualities these people added warlike virtues which made them tough enemies of Alexander the Great and Lysimachus, one of the former's generals. After reaching Bessarabia Lysimachus was forced to capitulate before the Getae and pay a ransom to escape captivity.

Dacia really enters history's pages in the 2nd century B. C. At that time the Romans had established control over Moesia (present Bulgaria) south of the Danube. The Romans made contact with the Dacians by concluding an alliance to defend Moesia from the advancing Sarmatians. Architects were sent to Dacia to construct fortresses and to furnish the inhabitants with materials and subsidies. The Romans soon realized the Dacians were actually preparing defenses against their protectors. What the Romans had believed to be an act of political wisdom was interpreted as a sign of weakness by a people who were ambitious to affirm their power. The Dacians then attacked the Romans south of the Danube. Their king, Boerebista (or Bourbista), whose authority extended from the Danube to the Black Sea and from the Bug River to the Carpathians, led an army of about 200,000 and began to pillage Macedonia and Illyria. Strabo wrote that "he was the terror of the Romans."

When these reverses forced the Romans to evacuate their legions from Moesia, the Dacians took advantage of the retreat by invading the province in 85 A. D. They were led by their most famous king, Decebalus, a great warrior. Confronted by this peril, Emperor Domitian personally took command in Dacia and won a few battles. Nevertheless, Decebalus signed a very honorable treaty with Rome which preserved for him title to his domain and recognition as its sovereign. This capitulation did not deter Domitian from celebrating his questionable victory in Rome.

When Trajan became emperor in 98 A. D., he determined to end the threat the Dacians posed on a vulnerable frontier. He prepared a vast expedition for the purpose, not of conquering the Dacians, but of preventing them from menacing Rome's security. In 101 a road was constructed along the Danube to a new bridge near present-day Turnu-Severin. The Roman legions then progressed slowly against stubborn resistance. Decebalus and the Dacians were forced to submit. Their fortresses were razed and troops disarmed. Trajan's goal seemed to have been achieved. His success over a reputedly invincible people produced a profound impression in Rome.

But Decebalus did not accept defeat. He broke the treaty by again attacking the Roman legions. Now Trajan brought everything to bear in suppressing his irreconcilable enemy. The Danube was again crossed and this second Dacian campaign, more than the first, revealed the superiority of Roman equipment. The war assumed a savage character. The adversaries gave no quarter. Before surrendering the Dacian capital located in central Transylvania, Decebalus and his officers drank poison hemlock. Dacia became a Roman province in 106 A. D. As a result of the savage campaign of which it had been the theater, Dacia was almost devastated and depopulated.

Rome joyously received news of the victory. Trajan returned in triumph dragging captive chiefs chained to his chariot who were followed by an immense crowd of war prisoners. Enthusiastic celebrations on this occasion illustrated the importance attached to the conquest of a warlike people. Trajan's column in Rome has immortalized his exploits. The 2,500 figures on the column commemorate changes of fortune during the campaigns and the ceremonies of the triumph. The column is a precious document showing the costumes and arms of the Dacians. Even today Trajan's memory remains very popular and respected in Rumania, probably because he brought a superior culture to the ancient inhabitants.

Ruins of many edifices and still more numerous inscriptions point with eloquent precision to the great work completed by the Romans in Dacia. A governor was appointed and Rome's legions had established camps. According to Roman tradition, several great military highways were constructed, and fortresses were erected at strategic points to repel invasions. But the Romans attempted more than this. They strived to revive the prosperity of the fertile region and to repopulate it. Land was distributed to legionnaires who wished to establish homes in Dacia. Many colonists were attracted from other regions of the empire because of a skillful propaganda campaign boasting of the advantages of Dacia. Settlers came from Italy, Dalmatia, Gaul, Spain, and even Syria. Archaeological discoveries have identified very diverse national origins and professions of the colonists—veterans, farmers, merchants, artisans seeking less miserable conditions, adventurers searching for wealth. The newcomers mingled with the original inhabitants, and thus was created the Daco-Roman ethnic group.

As is the usual rule, the language of the more civilized country prevailed over the Dacian tongue which became extinct. Classical Latin, already in its popular form in the 2nd century, was even more corrupted. Furthermore, after becoming an island surrounded by Slav or Slavicized territories such as that inhabited by the Bulgarians, Dacia experienced linguistic infiltrations as well as new customs. Such influences are older than the Russian because Russia was separated from Dacia by non-Slav peoples and did not make contacts until the 18th century. Thus Slav influence was the consequence of close proximity to the Bulgarians, especially during the hegemony of the Asens, the Serbs, and the Poles.

Today it is estimated that about one-half of Rumanian words are of Slavic origin. In fact, not until the middle of the 19th century did the Rumanians scrap the Cyrillic and adopt the Latin alphabet. But words representing significant ideas and particularly verbs clearly show a Latin origin. If numerically the Latin vocabulary is less than the Slavic, it does surpass it in value. Furthermore, the grammar reveals a Latin construction—indisputable evidence that Rumanian culture is inherited from the Romans. Slight differences do exist among the regional dialects, in Transylvania for example, which experienced the same influences as the language spoken in Moldavia. All philologists, even the Hungarians, agree in classifying Rumanian within the family of Neo-Latin languages. Such linguistic findings definitively affirm that the Rumanians are the product of a fusion of Daco-Roman elements with certain Slav elements.

Slav influences can also be noted in the judicial organization of the country which came about at a late date to enjoy real autonomy about 1330. An even more significant consequence of Slav influence was the adoption of Orthodox Christianity by the Rumanians, the only people of Latin origin who rallied to the Orthodox Church. For a long time the Rumanian Orthodox Church used Old Church Slavonic and for a while was dependent upon the Bulgarian archbishopric of Tirnovo. Despite these Slav influences, the inhabitants of ancient Dacia remained so Latin that when national consciousness arose in the 19th century it would be toward their cousins in Rome and Paris that they turned for inspiration and assistance.

The Roman province established on the ruins of the kingdom of Decebalus included mountainous Transylvania. This explains and possibly justifies Rumanian claims to a region also contested by the Hungarians. Cities were founded during the Latin domination, agriculture and commerce were developed, and exploitation of Transylvanian gold mines reached such heights that the damages caused by the war soon disappeared. Protected by the *Pax Romana,* the Daco-Romans, content with the prosperity encouraged by their conquerors, resigned themselves to their fate and forgot their warlike qualities.

But the era of the great barbarian invasions was approaching. The barbarians whose menace was felt all over Europe did not spare the provinces prematurely designated as "Happy Dacia." The Goths invaded Dacia in the middle of the 3rd century, despite their defeat near a tower constructed on the Danube by Emperor Severus Alexander, at a site now called Turnu-Severin. Emperor Aurelian was forced to evacuate Dacia in 271, the retreating legions thus recrossing the Danube which they had victoriously traversed almost two centuries before. Rome was resigned to yield the province, but not until after her domination had transformed a primitive people into a group henceforth marked by the Latin genius. This was an example, even more than that of Gaul, of the power of assimilation Rome could impose on her subjects. How could the evacuation be explained? Dacia was a vulnerable salient in an empire which, weakened and exposed even in Italy to the attacks of the Vandals, decided to reduce its frontiers, the first sacrifice and the beginning of the inevitable dismemberment.

The evacuation was a disaster for the Daco-Romans. Some specialists, especially certain Hungarian historians, claimed that the entire population followed the Roman legions south of the Danube. Hence the origin of the name "Aurelian Dacia" which is infrequently substituted for "Moesia," and which is distinct from "Trajan Dacia" located north of the Danube. The theory of a mass exodus appears inadmissible. If many urban inhabitants quit Dacia, one cannot conceive of the same action by peasants strongly attached to the soil. The urban residents probably remained and became reconciled to the invaders. Moreover, the Roman retreat was not accomplished in a day; it was done in successive stages. The emperors for some time entertained hopes of regaining a foothold in Dacia. Fortifications subsequently maintained by Justinian in the 6th century on the left bank of the Danube near Turnu-Severin testify to this intention.

Certainly a few nobles and some people did accompany the Romans in their retreat. Still others sought refuge in the mountains of Transylvania from which their descendants would return ten centuries later. As a consequence of the barbarian incursions, other Daco-Romans spread over the Balkans, into Macedonia, Epirus, and even into the Peloponnesus where they today form small enclaves. But on the Danubian plain remained the peasants who were unconsciously obstinate in perpetuating their ethnic entity. Descending from a young and vigorous people, these simple men, full of vitality, succeeded in maintaining amid anarchy and chaos and under several foreign yokes the tradition of Latinity dating from the colonies established by Trajan. The survival of this people for more than a millennium through all kinds of vicissitudes has been a mystery. This may be the explanation of what has been termed, with sufficient justification, "the Rumanian miracle."

From the evacuation of Dacia by the legions beginning in 271 to the retreat of the Mongols in 1241, the Daco-Romans were caught up in a confusion which disturbed their country, a corridor for invaders some of whom remained and others who merely crossed it. But these crossings did not change the country. The flood receded, and the stones remained—a Rumanian proverb depicting the continuity of a people who suffered in exemplary fashion.

During the reign of Emperor Constantine (306-337), who tried to expel the Goths, Dacia was the first of the Balkan countries to embrace Christianity. The fierce Huns, defeated in Gaul, succeeded the Goths in Dacia and were then forced to yield to the Avars. These successive waves were the repercussions of population displacements in central Asia which drove tribes westward in search of new homes. Then the Bulgarians arrived. They integrated a large section of ancient Dacia into their territory in 676. This contributed a durable influence on Dacia. From that time dated the introduction into the language of numerous Slavic words as well as the usage of Old Church Slavonic as the language of the church which contributed to separating the Daco-Romans from the Latin world.

There next appeared another savage tribe which spread terror. This was the Hungarians (Magyars) advancing from the steppes of central Asia. They penetrated Transylvania where they claim to have been the first arrivals on a territory that long domination made their own. The Rumanians nevertheless contend that their ancestors settled Transylvania long before the arrival of the Hungarians. This is the origin of an interminable dispute in which ethnic arguments conceal political claims.

After the Hungarian invasion Dacia suffered the incursion of the Cumans. And it was then the turn of the Mongols (Tatars) who all but ended the long and troubled succession of invaders. Thus Dacia was thrown into a torment of continual melée among the inecessant ebb and flow of populations between the Carpathians and Macedonia. After an era as prolonged as it was confused, the Daco-Romans made their reappearance in the 13th century as Wallachians (Vlachs) and Moldavians.

According to legend, Radu Negru, a *voevod* in Transylvania, founded Wallachia in 1290. He settled near Fagarash and, according to Rumanian historians, began to play a role analogous to that of Piedmont in creating Italian unity. Many nobles followed Radu Negru, and the result was a weakening of the Rumanian base in Transylvania. Deprived of their leaders, the Rumanians would become subject to Hungarian domination in Transylvania. Thus Radu Negru and his group settled in the region inhabited by their ancestors a thousand years before. Since the Mongols had already devastated the region, the newcomers were welcomed by the local populace because many derived from the same ancestry had remained faithful to the homeland. Thus, after a long absence, the course of Rumanian history was reestablished and the spirit of Latinity revived.

The Basarab family succeeded Radu Negru and boldly assumed leadership of a growing principality. The development of the new state was favored as much by the decline of the Asens in Bulgaria as by the Mongol invasions menacing Hungary. Furthermore, the difference in religion of the Wallachians who had rallied to Orthodoxy and the Hungarians who remained Catholic accentuated the separation of the two peoples.

The year 1330 marked the real beginning of Wallachian history. In that year Basarab I consolidated the basis of his state by intervening on Bulgaria's side in the war against the Serbs and by combating the Angevin dynasty of Hungary. Nevertheless, Basarab had to recognize Hungary's sovereignty over Wallachia. In exchange, however, Hungary agreed to an enlargement of his domain. The Wallachians then secured authorization for the establishment of an Orthodox metropolitan in Wallachia. Such recognition by the Greek Patriarch affirmed the creation of the Principality of Wallachia to which it granted an ecclesiastical seat. Navigation down the Danube by Italian merchants encouraged contact between Wallachia and the west. Nevertheless, conditions favoring the development of Wallachia deteriorated as a result of Turkish incursions which deprived the Danube of its free outlet to the Black Sea.

Moldavia, the other Rumanian principality, had a less difficult birth. Legend relates that a *voevod* named Dragosh, a native of Maramuresh in the Carpathians adjacent to the Polish frontier, was the first to settle on the slopes overlooking the Moldavian plan. He must have found an almost deserted region covered with forests and inhabited more by beasts than men. One of his descendants, Bogdan, did settle in the region, but at the loss of domains on the other side of the Carpathians to the Hungarians. When Mongol attacks on Hungary caused the migration of Rumanians from Transylvania into sparsely populated Moldavia, Bogdan, at first a Hungarian vassal, declared his independence in 1359. Rumanians date the creation of Moldavia from that year. By the end of the 14th century this territory extended from the mountains to the sea. Moldavia served as a corridor and a stop on the commercial highway between the Baltic and Black seas. Thus two groups of the same ethnic origin, the Wallachians and Moldavians, coexisted on the Danubian plain.

The preponderant role fell for some time to Wallachia because of the energy of the Basarabs whose relations with Hungary alternated between war and peace. The Wallachians finally freed themselves of Hungarian domination in 1380. One of the Basarabs, Mircea the Great (1386-1418), was the real organizer of Wallachia although his reign was marked by much trouble caused by Turkish victories in the Balkans. Wallachian soldiers fought alongside the Serbs at Kossovo in 1389. Bent on revenge, Sultan Bayezid crossed the Danube to crush Mircea, but the latter escaped into Transylvania.

Mircea's prime objective was to fight the Turks, and he did not hesitate in allying with Hungary for this purpose. Both, however, were defeated at Nicopolis in 1396. Mircea continued to resist, but the consequences of Nicopolis obliged him to pay tribute to the Turks who in turn granted him a degree of autonomy. His people were grateful to Mircea for his exploits and aggrandizement of the country by annexing the Dobrudja (also Dobruja, Dobrogea), a region south of the Danube which furnished Wallachia with an outlet to the Black Sea.

The geographical location of the two principalities and their economic advantages explained their rapid development. "As the door opening on the steppes," both had attracted invaders from the east who constantly crossed the provinces. When the era of migrations ended and the populations became somewhat sedentary, the two regions became routes over which trade passed from the German Hanseatic League south through Poland to Danubian ports where Genoese and Venetian merchants had already established markets. As Greek and Roman traders had earlier done, the Italians came to the Black Sea coast, sailed up the Danube to sell textiles, and purchased cargoes of grain. This very active commerce was a major source of prosperity. The Wallachian rulers were led to extend their authority on the Black Sea coast by seizing Kilia on the northern arm of the Danube delta. The taking of that port explains the name of Bessarabia given to the region of the Danube delta dominated at that time by the Basarab family.

Mircea's death in 1418 ushered in a decline which ironically contributed to the elevation of his prestige among the Wallachians. The Moldavians and the latter soon struggled over the question of succession. Elections of rulers encouraged intrigues among candidates who sought support from Hungary and Poland. There was a succession of 11 princes in 25 years, three of whom claimed to rule simultaneously. This anarchy and resulting corruption facilitated the advance of the Turks whose threat hung over the principalities. The misery of the peasants, who were mercilessly exploited by their landlords, added to the instability.

The hostility between the two groups of Rumanians did not prevent some princes from occasionally playing significant roles. Such was the case of a Wallachian prince, Vlad the Impaler, whose nickname sadly indicated his barbarism. He warred on brigandage, intimidated the nobles into obeying his authority, and considered himself sufficiently strong to refuse tribute to the Turkish sultan. Mohammed II sent a strong army against Wallachia. Concealed in the disguise of a Turk, Vlad engaged in such successful espionage that the information he secured permitted him to defeat the Turks. He then justified his nickname by having the Turkish prisoners impaled. While pursuing the Turks, an attack by Stephen the Great, prince of Moldavia, obliged Vlad to seek refuge in Hungary.

Stephen the Great of Moldavia ruled for almost 50 years. He warred so courageously and successfully against the Turks, upon whom he inflicted the defeat at Racova in 1475, that the Papacy applauded him and Venice sent him ambassadors. Stephen also fought the Hungarians. He was victorious over Matthias Corvinus and took a region of Transylvania from Hungary. Then he fought the Poles. But he could not defend the vital ports of Kilia on the Danube and Akkerman (Cetatea Alba) at the mouth of the Dniester River. The fall of these ports to the Turks in 1484 seriously compromised the economic development of the two principalities which were now removed from access to the Black Sea. Then in 1511 the Turks forced Stephen's son to recognize their authority which had been imposed a century earlier on Wallachia. Despite assurances of autonomy, Turkish domination became effective. Sultan Suleiman the Magnificent subsequently occupied Moldavia in 1538 and established a Turkish garrison there.

Despite this turmoil, the 16th century marked a period of intellectual development and prosperity for the two principalities. Both contained few towns, but soon urban areas grew rapidly. The princes ceased changing residences and decided to establish permanent capitals. The nobles abandoned their rural estates, where they oppressed the peasantry, and took up residence at court. Arts and literature developed, and tastes became more refined. Chronicles cite the care taken by the nobles to array themselves in sumptuous clothing and their penchant for the fine velvet of Genoa. The Orthodox clergy attempted to mitigate harsh customs. Churches were erected, and the monasteries multiplied in number to carry on cultural activities.

At the end of the 16th century a spirit of resistance was revived. Prince John ("The Terrible") won several victories against the Turks until he was betrayed by nobles who judged him too favorable toward the peasants. He was tortured to death. Michael the Brave, prince of Wallachia, despite the brevity of his reign (1593-1601), elevated his country to a position of power never before equalled. In a gesture of rebellion against the Turks, Michael burned the records of tribute paid to the sultan. He then repulsed a Turkish force sent against Wallachia by the irate sultan. The Wallachians then crossed the frozen Danube, ravaged Bulgaria, and even threatened Constantinople. Confronted by an advancing Turkish army, Michael allied with Sigismund Bathory, prince of Transylvania. He routed the Turks and then turned against the Hungarians whom he also vanquished. After a triumphal entry into Transylvania, Michael was proclaimed its ruler at Alba Iulia in 1599. He then conquered Moldavia. Thus at the beginning of the 17th century Michael the Brave, probably Rumania's greatest national hero, realized the national dream. Wallachia, Moldavia, and Transylvania were united under his rule. This was a brilliant but ephemeral success.

Michael was greatly envied and thus surrounded by enemies at home and abroad. Having failed to conciliate the peasants, he also offended certain nobles who were always quick to rebel or betray their leaders. To the tenacious hostility of the Hungarians and Turks was added that of the Holy Roman Emperor, Rudolf II, who was disturbed by the appearance of this new power in the east. So a vigorous attack was launched by Austria, and Michael could not repel it. He fled into the Carpathian Mountains and was subsequently assassinated. After losing his acquisitions as quickly as he had secured them, Michael became for the Rumanians a symbol of hope. He had sown the seed of the patriotic ideal of which the resurrection of his empire was to remain their supreme goal. His statue in Bucharest today recalls a great epoch of Rumanian power just as that of Louis XIV in the Place de Victoire in Paris recalls one of France's greatest centuries.

Turkish preponderance was restored after Michael's death. At no time, however, were the two principalities incorporated into the

Turkish Empire (as Bulgaria and Serbia experienced) or treated as provinces. Turkish administration was carried out by the occupation of several fortresses and the recruiting of Rumanian troops to fight within the ranks of the sultan's army. The Turks did exact an important tribute, partly in money and partly in the form of deliveries of livestock and grain. The sultan permitted the investiture of Christian governors chosen by the nobles and higher clergy from among the great families of the principalities. These governors administered the country through the intermediary of Greek representatives who readily acted as businessmen for the Turks. Such was the seductive ability of the Greeks that they were often favored to the detriment of the autonomous Rumanian nobility.

This Greek-controlled regime perpetuated various abuses. The post of governor was frequently sold at auctions in Constantinople where the occupants were frequently changed so that the maximum in bribes could be secured. Governors were frequently transferred from one capital to the other to facilitate additional bribery. Payment was the normal practice for obtaining a post. It was then necessary to pay for the privilege of retaining it. To retrieve his investment the beneficiary merely turned to his subjects who were forced to pay the cost of the entire affair. This was organized spoliation. Everything was a pretext for taxation, whether it be a thimble or a herd of cattle. Such a system in which intrigue excelled might well have befitted the skill of a few nobles or functionaries from Constantinople, but it profoundly wronged the Rumanian peasantry while implanting in them an urge to rebel against such injustice.

During this turbulent period two remarkable princes ruled Wallachia and Moldavia in the first half of the 17th century. Matthew Basarab (1633-54) and Basil the Wolf (Vasile Lupul) (1634-54) ruled each principality, respectively. With nationalist support, both reacted against Greek influences but had to proceed carefully since the Greeks were very influential in Constantinople. But unfortunately the similarity of ancestry, which should have encouraged common interests, did not deter the two princes from perpetuating the nefarious tradition of warring on each other and further aggravating this error by frequently summoning foreign powers to their assistance.

Both princes nevertheless are memorable for beneficial innovations on the domestic scene. A revision of the laws led to a degree of equality before the law. They promoted education and attempted to reestablish the original character of the national language. With this intention in mind, they substituted Rumanian for Old Church Slavonic, the latter having been imposed during the earlier Bulgarian domination. The first printing presses were set up in Bucharest (Wallachia's capital) and Jassy (Iasi), the capital of Moldavia.

Efforts to improve agrarian conditions and extend education were pursued by Sherban Cantacuzene, prince of Wallachia (1679-88). As the sultan's vassal he was obliged to assist the Turks in their last siege of Vienna in 1683. Cantacuzene furnished only nominal aid for which Emperor Leopold I was grateful.

The Wallachians and Moldavians realized the assistance of a great power was essential if they wished to liberate themselves from the Turks. The episode of the siege of Vienna might have inclined them toward Austria if there had not arisen at that time Russia's star as a result of the rapid and prodigious development given his country by Tsar Peter the Great. During the reign of Tsar Alexis (1645-76) the Rumanians sought Russian aid by invoking Christian solidarity against the Turks. Only vague promises were secured. When Peter the Great (1682-1725) took Azov in 1696 and founded Taganrog on the Black Sea in the same year, Russian power secured a foothold on the shores of the Black Sea and approached Rumanian territory.

Princes Demetrius Cantemir of Moldavia and Constantin Brancovan of Wallachia initiated diplomatic relations with the Russians. In 1711 the former signed an alliance by which Tsar Peter agreed to furnish assistance against the Turks. This was the creation of a union of the Cross against the Crescent. After suspecting Peter might become the defender of Christianity, Sultan Ahmed III (1703-30) feared his subjects would revolt on the Tsar's instigation. The role of leading a crusade served Peter's ambition to make the Black Sea a Russian lake.

Russian soldiers entered Moldavia for the first time; it would not be the last. Peter was given a triumphal welcome in Jassy. The theft of gold decorations and valuable religious vestments during the visit was a surprise, but it did not dampen popular enthusiasm. Later the Russians were surrounded by the Turks and forced to recross the Dniester River. A major consequence of this first Rus-

sian campaign in the Balkans was to arouse the anger and vengeance of the Turks. The prince of Wallachia, Brancovan, was taken
to Constantinople in 1714 and beheaded, together with his four
sons. A scion of the rival Cantacuzene family was elected on the
sultan's orders, and he, after exhausting the principality for the
benefit of the Turks, was in turn deposed and executed in 1716.

The Turkish government terminated the privilege of the native
nobility to govern the two principalities and entrusted the jobs to
Phanariot Greeks. Thus began the era of the Phanariots which
would last until 1822. The first, Nicholas Mavrocordato, a former
dragoman (interpreter) at the Sublime Porte, was a typical en-
lightened despot of the period, but he left the peasants huddled
in their misery. Succeeding governors, as many as 35 in 90 years,
accentuated every defect of the preceding regime. These *hospodars*
thought only of recovering the prices which their jobs cost them.
Their first concern consisted of discharging functionaries so that
favorites could have jobs. From them arose a fever of intrigue
and corruption which led every official to be concerned for his
position and oblivious to the common welfare.

The Greek governors imported the customs of Byzantium.
Clothed in sumptuous vestments and adorned with jewels, they
were surrounded with Oriental luxury and lived in soft, sybaritic
ease as they governed a scandal-ridden society. The native nobility, inspired by their example, fell into step and the entire populace
was affected by the prevalent corruption from which even the
clergy were unable to escape. The nobles borrowed only the worst
from Byzantine customs. It should be realized that Greek influence
did contribute to intellectual development, but this progress was
felt only in those circles whose level had remained quite low until
then. The salons were Hellenized, the language sprinkled with
Greek words whose meanings were misunderstood, and Greek was
used in teaching. An influx of Greek clergy favored the introduction of their language into the church to the detriment of Old
Church Slavonic. Rumania's orientation toward the French language and literature stems from this period. But while in the cities
the nobles competed in prodigality and wit, the distress of the
peasants, ignorant victims of greed and violence, inspired considerable pity.

While the two principalities were cursed by the double domestic
evil of a nominal Turkish domination and an inefficient Greek

administration, the Russian colossus hovered over the region. Would Russia assist or menace the principalities? Whatever the answer, the destiny of the region would be closely bound to the designs of Russian policy.

Empress Anne of Russia, who inherited the projects of her uncle Peter the Great, declared war on Turkey in 1736 on the pretext that the Turks had violated Russian soil. After occupying the Crimea, the Russians entered Moldavia for their second occupation. Russian general Münnich conducted himself as a conqueror, not as a liberator. His brusque methods inspired the formation of an anti-Russian party among the Rumanians. Finally, Austria, allied with Russia, was defeated by the Turks and forced to sign the Treaty of Belgrade (1739). The Russians then evacuated Moldavia over which they had planned to establish a protectorate.

It was reserved for Empress Catherine the Great (1762-96) to resume these ambitious projects with vigor and to assure the fulfillment of some. This time the Turks declared war (1768), but their troops were quickly defeated and, for the third time, Russian forces occupied Moldavia and Wallachia in 1770. The *hospodar* of Moldavia was received in St. Petersburg with much honor. Was this a prelude to annexation? Since the army of General Suvorov was marching toward Constantinople, events suggested this was a Russian plan. But Austria, disturbed by Russia's expansionism, revealed her opposition to a disruption of the balance of power in the Balkans. Austria's reaction may have prevented a Russian annexation of the principalities.

As for the Russo-Turkish war (1768-74), it was settled by the Treaty of Kuchuk Kainarji in 1774. The treaty restored the two principalities to the sultan but obliged him to respect religious freedom there and recognize Russia as the protector of all Christians in the Ottoman Empire, and of those in the Danubian Principalities particularly. Tsarist diplomacy thus acquired the privilege of protecting the Balkans which was the main object of Russia's ambitions. Furthermore, Russia's annexation of Azov, the mouth of the Dnieper River, and the right to navigate on the Black Sea enhanced her power in the Danubian regions.

Russia's treaty with Turkey was considered too favorable by Austria whose government now believed it had been cheated in the first partition of the Kingdom of Poland. So Austria forced Turkey in 1775 to cede the Bukovina (also Bukowina), the northwest part of Moldavia including its capital of Czernowitz (Cernauti, Chernovtsy), to the Hapsburg Empire. Austria was thus the first European power to threaten the territorial integrity of the principalities whose inviolability she had just forced Russia to respect. Having been a pawn in the competition between these two powers, whose rivalry was brewing in the Balkans, the Danubian Principalities now became its victim. In fact, Empress Catherine resolutely pursued her expansionist policy by establishing consulates in Bucharest and Jassy which soon became active centers of Russian influence. In the Ukrainian regions taken from Turkey in 1774, situated close to Moldavia, Prince Potemkin, one of Catherine's favorites, was colonizing the area and establishing new cities. In one, Kherson, Catherine met Emperor Joseph II of Austria in 1780, and he suggested a partition of the Turkish Empire. The fate of the principalities was discussed at this meeting. Although they agreed to permit the Rumanians a degree of independence, each insisted upon installing a sovereign and, consequently, the project was abandoned. Alarmed by these discussions, Turkey again declared war on Russia (1787). For the fourth time a Russian army occupied the principalities. The Turks commanded the *hospodars* to resist, but the nobles refused.

Distractions produced by the French Revolution led to peace. The Treaty of Jassy was signed in 1792. Once more Russia restored the principalities to Turkey, but she retained her former advantages there. Russia gained the Black Sea coast as far south as the mouth of the Dniester River. The Dniester formed the frontier between Russia and Bessarabia, thus increasing Russia's influence in the affairs of the adjacent principalities.

Tsar Alexander I of Russia (1801-25), angered by the frequent changes of *hospodars,* extracted from Turkey the privilege of nominating *hospodars* for seven years. He imposed two puppets on the principalities. Their policies so ignored Turkish interests that the sultan threatened to remove them. Alexander, however, insisted on improving Russia's security against increasing French hostility. He thus ordered Russian troops into the principalities for the fifth occupation.

Relations between Napoleon and Alexander deteriorated after 1808. A threat of war led Alexander to conclude the Treaty of Bucharest with Turkey in 1812. Once again the Russians evacuated the principalities, but only after annexing that region of

Moldavia known as Bessarabia. The Russian frontier, formerly fixed along the Dniester River, was extended south to the Pruth River. The vast region between the two rivers became a Russian possession, and Russia now controlled the northern arm of the Danube delta. Having been deprived of the Bukovina two decades before by her Austrian protectors, Moldavia was now deprived of Bessarabia by her Russian protectors.

After suffering the loss of land in the north and east, pillaged, requisitioned, ransomed, battled over, Moldavia and Wallachia would soon demand independence when the spirit of freedom swept over the Balkans. The ideas spread by Napoleon's victorious armies were awakening the consciousness of peoples in East Europe.

CHAPTER V

The Turks

THE role of the Turks has often been cited in the preceding chapters, but only in an indirect manner to indicate their attitudes toward the other Balkan peoples and the reactions they provoked. Now a survey of Turkish history is presented to provide a coherent picture of their evolution.

The term "Turk" is generally considered inappropriate. The Turk or Turcoman is, strictly speaking, a native of Turkestan. Doubtless those who are now designated Turks emigrated from Central Asia across the Altai plateaus and settled in Turkestan, but that region was merely a temporary abode for them. Shepherds and warriors, with an essentially nomadic character, they were constantly on the move looking for pasturage and warlike adventures. Once converted to Islam, they were considered among the most fervent adherents of that religion, sober, courageous, and disciplined. Such qualities were stressed by Koranic doctrines.

From Turkestan they crossed into Persia, where many settled, and at the end of the 7th century A. D. they appeared in Mesopotamia and Syria. A significant group of Turks, the Seljuks, settled in Asia Minor after the 11th century. Their incomparable warriors seized cities by storm, sent Byzantine armies reeling, and imposed their beliefs and language upon conquered peoples. At the end of the 13th century their capital was established near the shores of the Sea of Marmara, part of the Straits separating Asia from Europe. About the year 1300 a Turkish border chief, Osman (or Othman), assumed the title of sultan. He is considered not as the creator of a nation, which had proved its power before his reign, but as the sovereign who gave the Turks great ambition and assured them a great destiny. Proud to bear his name, his subjects considered themselves the peoples of the Osmanlis (or Ottomans). But the name "Turk" nevertheless became more popular.

The Ottoman Turks established their capital at Brusa (or Bursa) in 1326. As masters of Nicea and Nicomedia in Anatolia, these

Turks could henceforth look across to Europe, a feeble, weak, and divided continent at the edge of which was the Byzantine Empire, seriously weakened by the blows of the crusaders and now struggling against the Slavs. The Serbia of Stephen Dushan threatened Constantinople to such a degree that within the emperor's circle were statesmen who considered appealing to the Turks to protect the capital.

The day soon arrived when the Moslem Turks crossed the Straits to seize the peninsula of Gallipoli in 1357 after its fortresses had been destroyed by an earthquake. Following the route of Darius, descendants of tribes which had migrated from the depths of Asia were now marching on European soil.

Serious problems afflicted the Turks as a result of their westward march. They became embroiled in struggles which involved the various Balkan peoples—the Greeks, Serbs, Bulgarians, Rumanians, Albanians, and even the Hungarians to the north of the region. While the Turks were engaged in almost interminable conflicts, Byzantium appeared protected from the storm. But the Turks were invincible warriors who could not rest. In 1361 their capital was moved from Brusa to Adrianople, a city close to Constantinople. The imperial capital was now isolated and directly threatened. But not until a century later would the Turks succeed in taking Constantinople.

In the interim the Turks crushed the Serbs and their allies at Kossovo in 1389. Next it was the turn of the Hungarians who experienced at Nicopolis a bloody defeat in which many of the élite of the French nobility, who had come to the aid of Christendom, perished. Henceforth Serbia, Bosnia, Macedonia, Thrace, and almost the entire Balkan peninsula were in the hands of the Turks whose dominions extended to the Danube, Morava, and Drina rivers.

The sudden defeat of Sultan Bayezid by Tamerlane in Asia Minor (1402) merely restrained Turkish pressure for a brief period. Following Tamerlane's retreat, the Turks resumed their march despite the resistance of Skanderbeg, courageous leader of the Albanians, and John Hunyadi and Vladislav Jagiello of Hungary and Poland, respectively, who were defeated at Varna in 1444.

All that remained of the Byzantine Empire was the tip of the Balkan peninsula. In 1453 this last rampart was overthrown by

Sultan Mohammed II. When the conquerors rode their horses into the holy basilica of Sancta Sophia, the corpses, according to legend, formed such a heap that the top body imprinted upon a column a red spot which can still be seen halfway up the vault. The Crescent replaced the Cross on the dome, and for Byzantine rule was substituted that of the Ottoman Turks whose strength was derived from an efficient feudal system.

The Turks arrived in Europe as conquerors, not as fanatics. Contrary to their practices in Asia Minor, they did not impose mass conversions or persecutions on the Christians. Allowing the Christians to practice their religion, the Turks even granted privileges to the Greek Patriarch who became the official representative of the entire body of Christian communities in the view of Ottoman authorities. This recognition entailed serious inconveniences for the non-Greek peoples, but the Turks were not responsible for this.

Although settled in Europe, the Turks nevertheless remained profoundly Asiatic. Their language, beliefs, institutions, customs, and all else bore the imprint of their origin, an imprint so profound that it would persist and never be fully erased. Hence that picturesque exterior, that mixture of fatalism and violent reaction, of chivalrous spirit with ruse, of magnificence and misery which, by their piquant contrast, count among the characteristics of Oriental life.

The Turks, required to govern a numerous non-Asiatic population, were obliged to forget that they were, above all, a nation of shepherds and warriors so that they could administer vast territories which had fallen into their hands. Nevertheless, they never mixed with their subjects. Rumanian scholar Nicolae Iorga pointed to only one rare foreign influence on the Turks—Byzantine pomp. Impressed by the lavish ceremonials of the Greek Orthodox Church and by memories of the splendor of Oriental rulers, the sultans, who had until then been crude warriors, occasionally dismounting from their horses to seek shelter in tents, gradually adopted the sumptuous manners of the Byzantine rulers. Henceforth they lived secluded in closely guarded palaces surrounded by dignitaries subject to a complex and meticulous etiquette. The sultans became semi-divine personages who rarely appeared in public. The Asiatic origin of the Turks and the differences in mentality which it implied was a reason for the lack of contact between the victor and the vanquished.

More profound was the difference in religion. Confusing religious with civil law, Islam was integrated to such a point that in all human affairs it dug an abyss between believers and infidels. Excluded from the circle of the initiated and from privileges reserved to Moslems, the Christians formed a class of inferior subjects which prohibited assimilation. This system explained why the two refractory layers of the population were superimposed for six centuries, except in rather rare cases of conversions to Islam in Bosnia, without assimilation contrary to occurrences in other countries, such as in Romanized Gaul.

As soldiers and peasants, with little ability for administration or taste for jobs as functionaries, the Turks found among certain subjects collaborators who supported them in these tasks. Former Byzantine bureaucrats offered their services, and some succeeded in attaining high positions in the Danubian Principalities. Some Albanians followed this example. The Albanians were considered trustworthy because many had converted to Islam, and they provided many zealous soldiers and administrators for the empire. The most celebrated of them, the Kiuprili family, held the post of grand vizier (prime minister) in the second half of the 17th century.

One may deplore the sad fate of peoples subjected to the domination of conquerors of a different race and religion, but it must be realized that, during a period generally devoid of gentleness, the conditions of the Balkan Christians in the early years of Turkish rule were not much more burdensome than under their former rulers. The Turks remained conquerors. Of almost legendary bravery, their well-trained army, animated by a fervent faith, continued to be incomparable. One of the best fighting units on earth, the army realized the importance of provisioning and medical services to which it attached a concern often neglected by other armies. Its ranks were swelled by adventurers attracted from all classes. Some were captivated by the promise of heroic exploits and others were more realistically attracted by the prospect of plunder. Not all were volunteers. The Ottoman government, and this was one of the most painful features of its domination, exacted annually from the Christians a certain number of adolescents to be trained in the army. Converted to Islam, turned into fanatics, and subjected to iron discipline, they constituted an élite body—the famous Janissary Corps. This recruiting of children, a veritable human tribute, had an especially odious character because it obliged Christians to hand over the flower of their youth in order to make of them the instruments of their own oppression. An obligation of celibacy was imposed upon the Janissaries for many years. When they were freed of this requirement, the character of the corps assumed the defects of a hereditary caste which became undisciplined. But at least the Christians were finally relieved of this blood tax. The intrepid Janissaries, conscious of their esteem and intoxicated by battle successes, made exorbitant demands and acquired political ambitions which produced crises of which they themselves became the victims.

Although beyond the scope of this survey, Ottoman expansion beyond Europe cannot be ignored. Armenia, Kurdistan, Mesopotamia, and Arabia with the holy cities of Mecca and Medina passed into Turkish hands. In a third continent, Africa, Turkish power was installed in Egypt. In 1517 Sultan Selim I exiled the last of the Abbasids from Cairo so that he could acquire the title of caliph. Until then the Abbasids, who had been expelled from Baghdad, were recognized as the chiefs of Islam because they were considered Mohammed's successors. Henceforth this honor was conferred on Turkish sultans who were simultaneously sovereigns of one of the most powerful empires in history and religious chiefs of the entire Moslem world, the commanders of the faithful. The sultanate and caliphate conferred on the person who assumed this dual office a power and prestige of which there are few examples. State and religion were combined.

Continuing their successes, the Turks engaged in a long struggle in the Mediterranean with the powerful Republic of Venice, the Knights of Rhodes, and the Genoese who had already penetrated into the Black Sea. Gradually all had to yield, and from the originally nomadic Turks emerged bold pirates who sailed the seas of the Levant extending Ottoman domination as far as Algeria, the future nest of pirates.

It was nevertheless on the European continent that the Turks played their most important roles. The submission of the Balkan peoples reduced Serbia to a Turkish province. Then it was Bosnia's turn. Elsewhere the khan of the Crimean Tatars was recognized as the sultan's vassal. Although alerted, Europe could not unite to stem the flow incessantly pressing further into the continent. In 1520 the sultan who would carry Turkish power to its height assumed his throne. Suleiman I ("The Magnificient")

(1520-66) seized Belgrade, annihilated the Hungarians at Mohacs in 1526, took Budapest by storm and made it the advance fortress of Islam in Europe for 150 years, and finally made vassals of the Hungarians. Ovewhelming everything in his path, he arrived at the gates of Vienna to which the Turks laid siege for the first time in 1529. But after two months of vain effort they had to retreat.

Thus in Europe's center the proud Hapsburgs, hereditary adversaries of France, were being menaced. King Francis I of France conceived of an alliance with the Turks. An alliance of His Most Christian Majesty and the great Turk, commander of the faithful, appeared impious. However, the French gained considerable advantages for themselves and even for Christendom. The famous capitulations of 1535 accorded to the French the exclusive right to navigate and trade in the eastern Mediterranean. Although a half-century later similar concessions were granted to England and other powers, France nevertheless maintained a considerable advance which assured the primacy of her prestige increased by the privilege of protecting all Catholic missionaries whatever their nationality.

The Turks were masters of a vast empire extending in the north from the plains of Hungary to Yemen and the Persian Gulf in the southeast, and from Algeria in the west to the Caucasus in the east. The peoples of Asia and Africa were apparently resigned to this fate. But those in Europe who were menaced by the prospect of this domination were prepared to resist an enemy who was doubly terrifying because he was both Asiatic and Moslem.

Suleiman the Magnificent was a glorious conqueror and a wise administrator concerned with reforming his empire in order to consolidate it. Although his immediate successors were inferior in ability, the skill of their energetic grand viziers retarded the decline of Ottoman power. Nevertheless, that power was already placed in the balance. Successes and reverses cancelled each other. Cyprus and Crete were captured after a fierce struggle with the Venetians, but the Turkish navy experienced a decisive defeat at Lepanto in 1571 at the hands of a Christian fleet of Spanish, Venetian, and Genoese vessels. In Asia the Persians recovered Georgia, part of Armenia, and Baghdad, while in Europe the Austrians continued to advance.

Despite efforts at recovery undertaken by the Kiuprilis, decadence became apparent. The failure of the second siege of Vienna in 1683, partly due to Polish aid led by King John Sobieski, clearly marked its beginning. From then on the wheel of fortune turned. After having attained its greatest extent, Moslem domination began to recede and would never cease its retreat. A new period was begun.

The sultans could not escape the fate of all great conquerors. To assure the security of territories already conquered, the sultans had to secure new buffer zones by extending the empire's frontiers. Its excessive proportions caused the empire to lose its cohesion and stability. By 1700 it had become infinitely more vulnerable. If the courage of the troops had never flagged, the soldiers were not demonstrating the same enthusiasm. Their discipline had relaxed. The most courageous of them, the Janissaries, even set the example for insubordination. Sultans had once commanded their troops in person, but they lost their taste for battle and entrusted commands to generals whose authority could not compare with that of the ruler.

Extension of the empire further from Constantinople weakened controls by a central authority. The weakening of this power encouraged desires for independence on the part of local governors. They assumed the mien of feudal lords whose link with Constantinople became more tenuous and who administered according to their own ideas, using arbitrary methods, and attending more to personal rather than state interests. Moreover, the empire was failing to recruit functionaries able to govern the immense domain.

While the incessant pursuit of costly wars was draining the treasury, receipts were arriving with an irregularity accentuated by an inefficient administration. Finances rapidly deteriorated. Lacking normal resources, the government procured needed sums by expedience. The pashas hastened to imitate this example for their own greater profit. Finally, awareness of the common danger having led Europe to unite against Islam, the Turks realized they had become objects of a general hostility which repeated reverses made more visible and even more painful.

About this time a change in Turkish attitude toward the Christians became apparent. For disdainful tolerance was substituted a hostility which subsequent events explained. The Christians—were they not the co-religionists of those who fought the Turks so savagely? Were not Christians praying for the victory of Turkey's enemies? Thus the Turkish government found within its own empire a mass of traitors. What was called Moslem fanaticism, for which the Turks had been quite infamous, was not a spontaneous phenomenon; it was unleashed as a reaction to the hostility of Christian Europe. The Turk was not an inherent fanatic. He was capable of becoming a fanatic, and the Ottoman authorities did not fail to arouse Islamic sentiment to serve its designs.

The Balkan peoples became the sad victims of this vicious circle. The hateful distrust shown toward them could only increase as the empire disintegrated under the blows from the outside and as setback was added to setback. The formerly unconcerned regime gave way to a reign of systematic and severe oppression. A most urgent need was for money, and Ottoman functionaries strived to find it among the *rayahs*. Imposts, taxes, arbitrary levies, and insults were rained upon the Christians, denying them the pleasures of wealth however modest it might be.

After the retreat of the Turks before Vienna in 1683, the Austrians remained formidable adversaries for some time. Under excellent generals, of whom one was the celebrated Prince Eugene of Savoy, Austria's forces took Budapest and expelled the Turks from Hungary, Transylvania, and the Banat of Temesvar. At the same time Venice took Dalmatia and secured a foothold in the Peloponnesus. The Turks yielded to the combined forces of Austria, Venice, Poland, and their latest enemy, the Russians, who took Azov. Was the Ottoman Empire about to collapse? The Treaty of Karlowitz of 1699, which ceded Hungary to Austria and granted Vienna the right to protect the Christians, led the *rayahs* to anticipate liberation by Austria. The Treaty of Passarowitz of 1718, which ceded Belgrade, part of Serbia and a section of Wallachia to Vienna, appeared to herald a vigorous Austrian push into the Balkans.

But fate turned the Hapsburgs from their eastern ambitions toward preoccupations in western Europe. Moreover, Prince Eugene's successors proved unequal to the task. By the Treaty of Belgrade in 1739, Suleiman III managed to regain that city and other territory located south of the Danube River. The aggression of Frederick the Great of Prussia forced Empress Maria Theresa to devote her energies to the defense of the Austrian provinces of Bohemia and Silesia. Thus relieved of the Austrian threat, the Turks regained part of Persia, chased the Venetians from the

Peloponnesus, and the Russians from Azov. But these were Pyrrhic victories.

The Ottoman Empire was menaced by two formidable foes. In the west was the Austrian, a precursor of later Pan-Germanism; and in the east was the Russian, champion of Orthodoxy and later of Pan-Slavism. Austria and Russian occasionally despoiled Turkey separately while at other times they both plotted her demise until the time when her lands would become the stake of their rival ambitions.

Arising suddenly in the east, the Russian menace would soon reveal itself in disquieting proportions. After liberation from the Mongol yoke in the 15th century, Moscow began to assume the form of a national state when Ivan III married the niece of the last Byzantine emperor. The two-headed eagle of Byzantium was added to the Russian emblem, and the Russians, always impressed by the glory of Constantinople, dreamed of making Moscow the third Rome. But Russia had to await the deeds of Tsar Ivan IV ("The Terrible") (1533-84), the gatherer of Russian lands, and of the Romanov dynasty, the restorers of unity after a period of anarchy, to permit Peter the Great (1682-1725) to initiate the realization of these projects. Among his ingenious initiatives was the birth of the slow but formidable advance which would send Russian forces almost incessantly to the south like an irresistible lava flow. An eternal goal of Russia's policy was to secure openings to the sea for the immense empire locked in the depth of the steppes. Once an opening to the Baltic Sea was secured, Russia had to secure a window on the Black Sea to open the road to the east.

Azov had the same importance to the Russians as Belgrade had for Austria. Peter was determined to secure a seaport which would provide an outlet to the Black Sea. After seizing Azov in 1696, Peter was forced to retrocede it in 1711. During the reign of Empress Anne, Peter's niece, the conquest of Azov was achieved at last. The defeat of Austria, Russia's ally, and Turkish resistance encouraged by the French ambassador led to Turkish recovery of Belgrade, however.

At length ambitious Empress Catherine II succeeded in realizing the dreams of Peter the Great. The victories of her armies in the Crimea and the Danubian Principalities led to the Treaty of Kuchuk Kainarji (1774) which marked Russia's solemn entry into the Balkan scene. Catherine secured the privilege of navigation on the Black Sea which thus furnished Russia with a southern route to the Mediterranean. Furthermore, Russia's privilege of protecting the Orthodox Christians in the Ottoman Empire was recognized. Thus Russia was assured the opportunity of interferring in Turkish affairs and especially in the principalities, Montenegro, Serbia, Bulgaria, and even in Greece.

The First Partition of Poland in 1772 excited the beneficiaries to pursue their policy of dismemberment by applying it to the Ottoman Empire. Before the Crimean peninsula was annexed, Catherine met Emperor Joseph II of Austria in the regions developed by Potemkin to discuss plans to partition the Turkish Empire (1780). Although the two monarchs did not fulfill their plans, Turkey was alarmed by the meeting to the point of declaring war on both in 1787. The general crisis produced by the French Revolution hastened the signing of peace at Jassy in 1792 which confirmed Russian sovereignty over much of the Black Sea coast. Catherine pushed her southern frontier to the banks of the Dniester River and thus to the very boundary of the Danubian Principalities. This proximity would enable Russia to promote her interests in the Balkans with greater energy.

The 19th century marked a new era in Turkey's decline. European Turkey was threatened with internal collapse. A weakening of central power was manifested by general insubordination which even affected the army. A revolt of Janissaries stationed in Belgrade (1804) indirectly aroused the movement for Serbian independence. Directing an indolent, corrupt administration amid disorderly financial embarrassments, the governors had tendencies of becoming autonomous chieftains.

By 1815 such was the case of several governors. Ali Pasha was acting like a rebel at Janina (Jannina, Yanina, Jannena) in Epirus; Pasvanoglu (Passwan Oglu), a Moslem Bosnian, was a brigand at Vidin; and Mehemet (Mohammed) Ali, the pasha of Egypt, was a rival to the sultan, Mahmud II (1808-39). Mahmud realized the need for reforms, and his first concern was to eliminate the unruly Janissaries which was accomplished by his massacring most of them in 1826. Nevertheless, it was in Asia, the real reservoir of Turkish power, that the change was most felt. In the entirely Moslem Ottoman realm in Asia, the strong social and national bond represented by loyalty to the sultan-caliph was most effective. But in Europe the different Christian peoples began to seethe and revolt in rapid succession. Thus sapped and undermined by several coincidental misfortunes, Ottoman authority was clearly declining. Officially declared a "sick man," the sultan was surrounded by avid, jealous powers watching each other as they slyly observed Turkey. But Turkey was one of those decrepit old men who keeps his heirs waiting. The powers contributed to perpetuating Turkey's life as a consequence of bitter rivalries.

Austria and Russia, formerly accomplices, now became adversaries. The former, favored by proximity, considered the Slav regions of Bosnia, Herzegovina, and Serbia as natural extensions of her provinces of Carniola and Croatia; Austria even aspired to obtain Macedonia and an outlet to the Aegean Sea at Salonika. The latter, claiming kinship of ethnic origin and identity of religion, considered the vast plains in the east where rivers originated to be stepping-stones, not barriers, for her plan to seize the road to the Straits and Constantinople. By neutralizing each other, the thrust of their conflicting ambitions produced a certain equilibrium.

This equilibrium was sustained by the attitude of France and England. The former nourished no ambitions regarding Turkey. On the contrary, France favored Turkey's integrity in order to preserve the traditional influence she had acquired since the 16th century in the Turkish provinces of Egypt and Syria. It appeared as if the temporary Napoleonic domination over Illyria and the Ionian Islands had made France conceive a project of securing a series of stepping-stones to the east. Even more than France, England desired respect for the territorial integrity of the Ottoman Empire. It was not a question of prestige for England but rather security for her vast empire. Mistress of India, England had to assure freedom of the routes leading to the Far East. No great power could be permitted to supplant weak Turkey in the Levant. What England most resisted, and the other powers joined her, was the laying of Russian hands on the Straits and Constantinople which Napoleon once called "the key to the world." What would be the value of the hegemony which England had created in the Mediterranean basin? With as much skill as patience England had assured for herself a strong position in the Mediterranean by stringing out strong naval stations at Gibraltar and Malta, and by dominating the Ionian Islands after Napoleon's final defeat.

Inspired by ideas of freedom spread by the French Revolution, the awakening of the nationalities was to be disastrous for the Ottoman Empire. One after another the Balkan peoples rose in revolt at the beginning of the 19th century. The Serbian insurrection, encouraged by Russia, was observed suspiciously by neighboring Austria. The claims of Moldavia and Wallachia earned support from Russia who took advantage of her proximity to seize Bessarabia in 1812. Despite such agitation in the Balkan theater, no mention of the peninsula arose at the Congress of Vienna in 1814-15. But immediately afterward, when the Greeks demanded independence in 1821, the French and English attitudes were modified. Because the location of Greece affected their commercial interests, both did not wish to permit Russia the benefit of exclusively intervening in the crisis. Russia profited from the occasion to undertake against Turkey a war which resulted in the Treaty of Adrianople (1829) giving her additional advantages—free passage through the Straits and territorial acquisitions in the Caucasus region.

Contrary to all predictions, the gravest threat to the Ottoman Empire arose in Africa, not in Europe. Proud of his reorganization of Egypt and the strength of his army, Mehemet Ali, the Albanian-born ambitious pasha in Cairo, raised the banner of revolt against the sultan from whom he planned to wrest Syria. Ibrahim, his son, advanced on Constantinople in 1832. Would Turkey collapse under these blows, or, on the contrary, be regenerated under Egyptian influence? This was an alarming, double eventuality for Russia. Suddenly reversing his policy, Tsar Nicholas I became the protector of an empire whose defense he insisted on reassuming for the exclusive purpose of Russia's remaining the determinant of Turkey's fate. Russia's military intervention in 1833 did indeed save Sultan Mahmud II. Prior to withdrawing his troops Nicholas imposed at Unkiar Skelessi (Hunkiar Iskelesi) a treaty of alliance which placed Turkey at Russia's mercy. The only stipulation Nicholas required prior to future aid to Turkey was the latter's closing of the Straits to all foreign warships. Thus the sultan became the doorkeeper of the Straits for the benefit of Russia who was now invulnerable in the Black Sea.

In 1839, when Sultan Mahmud attempted to punish Mehemet Ali, fate was just as merciless. At England's instigation Europe almost unanimously opposed the ambitions of Mehemet Ali, who was supported by France only. After a grave crisis Turkey's terri-

torial integrity was again assured and, according to the terms of
the London Convention in 1841, Russia was forced to see the
Straits closed to all warships, including her own, in time of peace.

Acceding to the throne during this crisis, Abdul Mejid (1839-
61), the new sultan, continued his predecessor's reforms. At his
inspiration the era called *Tanzimat* sought to reform the foundations and institutions of the empire. Too radical and precipitous
to be effective, *Tanzimat* aimed to transform an old empire of
essentially Asiatic character into a modern European state. Equality before the law and equitable taxation were promised to the
Christians. Although Koranic law denied them all political rights,
the Christians now found themselves suddenly granted them. Such
reforms angered conservative Turks and filled the *rayahs* with
suspicion.

The Crimean War (1853-55) interrupted the reforming era. A
dispute among monks at the holy shrines in Jerusalem provided the
pretext for the Franco-Russian crisis, but it was really only one
phase of the classic conflict between the ambitions of Russia and
the resolve of England to bar her, with French aid, from a sphere
of influence whose control England did not intend to relinquish.

The peace signed at the Congress of Paris (1856) was harsh for
Russia. According to the principle of Ottoman territorial integrity
established in London in 1840-41, the treaty reversed Russian influence in the Near East. The powers declared their recognition of
the sultan's promises to institute ethnic equality and free worship
among the Christians. Thus the privilege of protection claimed by
Russia over Orthodox Christians was deprived of its basis. The
same regression of Russian influence was noted regarding the
Danubian Principalities and Serbia. Henceforth a collective guarantee of the powers was substituted for the *de facto* Russian protectorate. Furthermore, Russia was required to cede southern
Bessarabia to Turkey, thus denying the former of control of the
northern arm of the Danube delta. The powers reaffirmed the
London Convention (1841) to which was added neutralization of
the Black Sea. Henceforth littoral powers, including Russia and
Turkey, could not maintain navies or arsenals there. This was the
final ruin of the progress achieved by the tenacious efforts of
Russia's rulers since Peter the Great. Turkey, however, emerged
from the Crimean War with considerable advantages. Until that
war Turkey had been denied membership in the family of nations.

The Turks were now admitted into the general European community. The great powers began to treat the Moslems as equals, and this was really new. The authority of the sultan was strengthened and confidence in his word was affirmed. These attempts to resuscitate a dying empire were the other aspect of a settlement in which the Russian colossus was relegated to the remote interior of the Black Sea.

The decade following the Crimean War witnessed increased agitation arising from application of the reforms promised by the Ottoman government. The Balkan Christians had accurately judged Ottoman promises to be worthless. They preferred the old system of taxation to that of military service and guarantees to their clergy to promises of equality made to gleam before their by no means dazzled eyes.

During the sultanate of Abdul Aziz (1861-76) the question of reforms continued to exist, particularly a reorganization of finances imposed by depreciation of the currency and a budgetary deficit. These domestic difficulties aroused Russia, who had been humiliated in 1856, to seize an opportunity to recover her former privileged status. Russia began by taking advantage of the crisis produced by the Franco-Prussian War in 1870 to denounce unilaterally that article in the Treaty of Paris (1856) regarding neutralization of the Black Sea. At a conference in London (1871) the powers recognized Russia's action by restoring her freedom of movement in those waters. Agitation among the Balkan Christians would soon furnish Russia with a long-awaited pretext to launch a new offensive against the Ottoman Empire, tottering but still standing erect.

Part II

Independence

CHAPTER I

Greek Independence

O F all the Balkan peoples, the Greeks possessed the most favorable conditions for securing their independence. Greek national spirit had never been eliminated because of the activities of their strong and patriotic clergy. Around the Patriarchate in Constantinople were grouped a number of Phanariots whose positions made them influential personages. Activities of a strong Greek merchant marine had preserved trade relations with Europe. In many large cities abroad were large and prosperous Greek settlements. Although the Greeks were the first Balkan people to secure their independence, they were not the first to rebel. That honor went to the Serbs who raised their standard in 1804.

During the 18th century one could not discern aspirations for liberty in Greece any more than one could perceive evidence of sympathy for them in the outside world. Doubtless Ivan III (1462-1505), by his marriage to the niece of the last Byzantine emperor, considered himself the heir of Byzantium. But this sentiment was inspired by an ambition to become master of Constantinople and not by an urge to assist the Greek people. The same was true of Peter the Great (1682-1725) when he attacked the Turks in order to seize Azov (1696), and when, as a result of Suvorov's victories on the Danube, Catherine the Great (1762-1796) conceived the dream of a "Greek Project" it was a question of little more than a restoration of the Byzantine Empire for Russia's advantage.

Attracted by common religious ties, clergy from Mount Athos went to Russia in the 17th century. In 1657 the Greek Patriarch paid with his head for maintaining ties with the Tsar and other Russians. But it was only during the war against the Turks in 1769 that Catherine first decided to utilize Greek aid against the Turks. An insurrection fomented in the Peloponnesus received Russian support and even the aid of warships which Catherine dispatched to the Greek coast. This was the Maina insurrection during which the patriotism of Mavromichalis (Mavro the Black) began to distinguish this family which was destined to give many illustrious sons to the struggle for independence. When this diversion lost her interest, Catherine did not hesitate to abandon her Greek allies and to make peace with the sultan. The Treaty of Kuchuk Kainarji (1774) did provide for the establishment of Russian protection over the Balkan Christians. But the inhabitants of Greece, situated far from Russia, could hardly benefit from an interest whose effects the Balkan Slavs would feel more. Because of their proximity to Russia, the Rumanians were privileged in this regard, if one considers as a privilege the fact of having their homeland the scene of many Russian occupations.

At the beginning of the 19th century all of ancient Greece, oppressed by almost six centuries of misrule, appeared resigned to continued Turkish oppression. Travelers in Greece at that time expressed little confidence in a reawakening of national consciousness. Such was the impression of the French envoy to Constantinople, Comte de Choiseul-Gouffier, as contained in his journal of the 1780's. A similar account was by Baron de Beaujour, a French consul, who alluded to a people enslaved by long servitude. The most illustrious of French travelers, François René Chateaubriand (1766-1848), the famous writer and statesman, was more pessimistic. Visiting Greece in 1807, he wrote in *Itinerary from Paris to Jerusalem*, "I indeed fear that the Greeks will not very soon be disposed to break their chains. When they have gotten rid of the tyranny which is oppressing them, it will be a long time before they lose the mark of their chains." He saw them "pulverized under the weight of despotism."

After the fall of Constantinople in 1453 Greek intellectual activities found refuge in monasteries in Thessaly, the Peloponnesus, and on Mount Athos, where pious monks achieved in silence and solitude the conservation of traditions and the preservation of a precious spiritual heritage. At the end of the 18th century the idea of the survival of Greek civilization began to leave the cloisters and to reach the people. An example of this was the secondary school of Dhiminitzana in the Peloponnesus which became a center of aspirations. Its students were taught to repudiate the name of "Romaics" and to adopt that of "Hellenes," and thus to demonstrate a will to revive a tie too long broken with the past.

Other Greeks contributed differently to the resurrection of national spirit by resisting Turkish authority, whether on the high seas, in the mountains, or on the islands. Such were the Klephts and the Palikars, wild brigands whose exploits approximated those of the Slav Haiduks. In an atmosphere receptive to ideas of freedom, such thoughts germinated especially after Napoleon's troops penetrated to the shores of the Adriatic Sea. Moreover, these ideas developed further when the Ottoman Empire began to decline as marked by successive agitations by Moslem theologians in Constantinople, the sultan's guard, and finally the turbulent Janissaries.

In the provinces a relaxation of the central power permitted the pashas to give free rein to arbitrariness. The excesses of their rule provoked rebellious sentiment against the more burdensome yoke. The governors acted independently of the central government whose authority they flouted in order to carve out semi-independent domains for themselves. They extorted and pressured the Christian peoples. By 1815 the sultan's sovereignty appeared to be restricted not only by popular uprisings in Serbia, stubborn resistance in Montenegro, demands of the Rumanians, but even by the ambitions of Mehemet Ali and the insubordination of Ali Pasha in Epirus.

Ali Pasha, an Albanian Moslem, had made Janina, located in a Pindus Mountain valley, the veritable capital of a small state almost totally removed from Constantinople's influence, which he administered with the aid of Greek functionaries. He had succeeded in securing from the sultan the privilege for his sons to govern Thessaly and the Peloponnesus so that a major portion of territory inhabited by Greeks was under his control. Ali Pasha, in open defiance of the sultan, thus offered the Greeks an opportunity they sought to rebel in their own turn. Contrary to the testimony of superficial observers, the Greeks were experiencing a spiritual rebirth. The school of Dhiminitzana inspired imitators who undertook a linguistic reform to restore in its literary form a language that had been neglected and corrupted, and they published classical writings to make them better known among the people. Adamantios Korais (Coreas, Coray, or Koraes) (1748-1833), the great scholar, was devoted to this task. Konstantinos Rhigas (Rhegas, Regas, or Rigas) (1754-98) composed patriotic verse. As in all countries seeking to escape foreign clutches, the national idea began by taking the form of a literary renaissance and a return to past traditions. In this setting Western ideas were most attractive because numerous émigrés contributed to transforming former ways of thinking. Greek children had adopted ideas in places where they had lived abroad. The seeds of a new life were about to bloom, and the Greeks, passive until this time, were ripe for rebellion.

In the spring of 1820 the Turkish Empire, threatened by anarchy and at loggerheads with Persia, resolved to undertake an expedition to force Ali Pasha into submission. The arrival in Epirus of an Ottoman army was the signal for the Greek insurrection. Connected to the continent by the narrow isthmus of Corinth and bristling with rugged mountains, the Peloponnesus, the last Greek territory occupied by the Turks and the region where the symptoms of intellectual rebirth had recently been manifested, was called upon to become the center of the revolt. Changing his frock for a uniform, Bishop Germanos of Patras became head of the rebels in February 1821. Another group was led by the Mavromichalis family. In July the insurgents merged at Tripolitza in the central Peloponnesus.

Everywhere patriots responded to the call. The Klephts led by Theodoros Kolokotronis fell upon Turkish troops from mountain ambushes. The Armatolis, another outlaw band, completed the work. Greek sailors, who were really semi-pirates, pillaged Turkish vessels. In all these activities a savage patriotism was complemented by an ardent religious faith. Competing in feats of boldness and courage, each group achieved exploits whose popularity aroused a hope which previously had not seemed possible. Tripolitza fell after a harsh struggle, and 8,000 Turks were massacred. The entire Peloponnesus fell into the hands of the rebels. Greek sailors, after forcing the Turkish fleet to seek shelter in the Dardanelles, became the masters of the Aegean and liberated its islands. These swift victories emboldened a national assembly at Epidauros to proclaim Greek independence on January 13, 1822 and to draw up a constitution providing for a liberal parliamentary system and an executive directory of five. Alexander Mavrocordato, scion of a rich Phanariot family who had been reared in Wallachia where his uncle had been a *hospodar,* was elected president of a provisional government.

Greeks throughout the world were aroused by the revolution. There were Greeks scattered across Europe from Odessa to Hamburg, in Trieste and Marseilles, Alexandria and North Africa, on the shores of Asia Minor and especially in Smyrna. The Phanariots of Constantinople hesitated compromising themselves in the eyes of the Turks. But this was not true of members of a powerful society founded in Odessa in 1814, the *Philiké Hetairia* (League of Friends). The Russian government supported the growth of this vigorous seedbed of nationalism. With Alexander Ypsilanti (Hypselantes, Hypsilantis, or Hypsiltanti) (1792-1828), a Phanariot and former aide to Tsar Alexander I, at its head, the league spread its influence afar, even in the principalities, but above all in Constantinople where it recruited numerous members. Another center of this movement developed in the Ionian Islands, close to the shore of Epirus. The islands had become an English protectorate in 1814.

In March 1821 Ypsilanti tried to provoke an uprising in the Danubian Principalities which was intended to support the Greek insurrection. Leading a group of partisans from Odessa, he crossed into Moldavia and appealed for a revolt. But, mistrusted by the Rumanians and inspiring hardly more confidence among the Serbs, he experienced total failure and had to flee to Austria, leaving his brother Demetrius to assume the leadership of a few remaining dissidents.

From the start a division within the Greek movement appeared between the rough combatants who had risen from their country's soil and who relied upon themselves exclusively, and the intellectuals who had come from the outside with cosmopolitan tendencies and sought foreign assistance for the cause. Although animated by the same nationalism, conflicts between these two groups of divergent composition and orientation were destined to sow useless obstacles in the already difficult path to independence.

Since Russia lent a helping hand to the agitation in the Danubian Principalities and Serbia, she also encouraged Greek aspirations. As the sanctuary for numerous refugees, Russia favored active agents of the insurrection, such as Ypsilanti and Count Giovanni Capo d'Istria (Capodistrias) (1776-1831). The latter enjoyed the confidence of Tsar Alexander, a contradictory, imprecise, and hesitant sovereign. The Russian emperor for some time remained quite reserved about a revolt contrary to his conception of international morality.

Turkish reprisals led Alexander to modify his attitude. To the manifestations of Christian faith which accompanied Greek patriotism, Moslem fanaticism lost no time in furnishing an echo. The struggle assumed the savage character of a religious war. To avenge their reverses, the Turks engaged in acts of wanton cruelty and regular bloodbaths. After executing several Phanariots, they even hanged the Greek Patriarch on Easter Sunday in 1821. Holy Orthodox Russia, bristling with indignation, then took up the cause of her persecuted coreligionists.

Confronted with demands for vengeance, Alexander I could not remain indifferent, especially since he saw in these events an occasion to realize the old Russian dream of dominating the Balkans. In June 1821, therefore, he had his ambassador present in Constantinople an ultimatum in which he demanded the protection of the Balkan Christians, restoration of ruined churches, and the reestablishment of the privileged regime in the principalities.

The Greek question also confronted Europe. In the beginning the powers did not welcome the revolt. Were not the Greeks rebels and the sultan a representative of legitimate authority? Since the Congress of Vienna in 1815 Europe under Metternich's leadership had strived to suppress popular agitation in the German and Italian states. By what right should they accord to the Greek rebels a favorable treatment, demanded the Austrian government. England anxiously observed the growing threat of Russian intervention and feared the course of events. Prussia remained indifferent. France would have been disposed to supporting Russia's views on condition of receiving some compensation. Thus Europe did not evince any great urge to assist the Greeks. Europe was more concerned with the intentions of Russia who was now massing troops along the Dniester River.

Such international reactions subdued in Alexander a zeal already weakened by pretensions of the Greeks who were proclaiming complete independence and proceeding to establish a constitutional regime. Such a procedure in no way corresponded to his wishes. He wished the creation of a monarchy or, at the very least, autonomous provinces over which Russian influence could be exercised. On their side the rebels distrusted Ypsilanti and Capo d'Istria who, they claimed, were more zealous in serving the Tsar's ambitions than the cause of Greek independence.

This situation did not escape the Ottoman government which capitalized on it by rejecting Russia's demands. Austria and

England strived to appease the crisis. When the great powers met at the Congress of Verona (1822) to treat a crisis in Spain, the Greek delegate was not permitted to speak, and Tsar Alexander did not intervene in favor of the Greek position. The Greeks were abandoned just when events were about to take a very unfavorable turn.

The Turks sent reinforcement to Epirus, overcame the resistance of Ali Pasha who was killed, and captured his capital of Janina by assault. The victorious Ottoman forces then turned on the Greek rebels. The struggle doubled in intensity, with various changes of fortune and increased ferocity. The most horrible episode occurred on Chios, a densely populated and flourishing Aegean island. When the Turks had pacified the island, they then slaughtered the entire male population of about 25,000; the women and children were sold into slavery and scattered abroad. The savagery of this terrible episode filled Europe with indignation.

Meanwhile the Peloponnesus (also called Morea) remained in the hands of the rebels who now began to penetrate into the continent. To the exploits of Kolokotronis were added those of another Klepht, Markos Bozzaris, and on the high seas those of Konstantinos Kanaris. But Ottoman resistance became more savage, notably at Athens and even more so at almost impregnable Missolonghi.

To complete their misfortune discord seized the Greek movement. To the so-called "Militares" such as Mavromichalis and Kolokotronis were pitted the "Politiques," Mavrocordato, Ypsilanti, and Kolettes. The latter, scions of great Phanariot families, had donated their fortunes to the national cause and actively participated in the revolution. Instead of appreciating their support, the Militares considered them to be rivals. President Mavrocordato encountered opposition from the senate and navy, the latter refusing to obey his orders. Unfortunate as this split was, it did not inhibit the rebels from proving their courage which attracted almost universal sympathy.

Initially lukewarm and hesistant, public opinion, aroused by the resolute and brave spirit shown by an unanticipated resistance and by the unsuspected vitality of the Greek people, turned in their favor. Now considered heroes worthy of ancient Greece, the rebels inspired general enthusiasm. Greek communities abroad, like that at Marseilles, expressed sympathy while the more prosperous settlements became bankers of the revolt. Committees of friends, the Philhellenes, were formed in different countries, London, Paris, Geneva, and in the German states where they found active support from King Ludwig I of Bavaria who was so avidly interested in Greek antiquity that he sought to give his capital the architectural aura of ancient Athens. Almost everywhere much enthusiasm arose in favor of the rebirth of Greece.

In France, royalists, liberals, and Bonapartists shared the same favorable sentiment toward Greek independence. The revolt was considered a humanitarian cause, a new crusade against Islam, while it became a curious pretext for a reawakening of militarism and a desire for revenge on the Congress of Vienna (1815). The royal court and press echoed this. The movement attracted literary and artistic circles. In the romantic verse of his *Orientales,* young Victor Hugo exalted the patriotic fervor of the Greek child, the blue-eyed child who preferred "powder and shot" to other gifts. Greek heroism found in Casimir Delavigne a bard to celebrate it in classical verses. Ignoring the disdain he had expressed earlier, Chateaubriand joined the movement, placing his prestige and talent at the services of the cause, "France is the eldest daughter of Greece," he proclaimed. In ardent words he declared, "The extermination of the Hellenes would be a grave thing for the entire civilized world. Greece rises heroically from the ashes." Finally, Delacroix, in his famous canvas, forever condemned the massacre on Chios. As had been done for the Americans during their war of independence, shipments of arms and an influx of volunteers came to the Greek rebels. General Fabvier, a veteran of the Napoleonic wars, was a fine example, Commanding a handful of men, he put up a splendid resistance to the Turks in the ruins of the Acropolis.

England experienced a similar movement. The name of Lord Byron symbolizes English Philhellenism for all eternity. The great poet was in Italy leading a life in which pleasure vied with work when he was suddenly seized with enthusiasm for Greek independence. In a burst of energy he embarked in 1823 to fight for liberty. Six months later, attacked by a fever caused by the infestations in the lagoons surrounding the city, he succumbed at besieged Missolonghi. This great poet was followed by other compatriots such as Admiral Cochrane, a champion of freedom who was proud to fight for it, and General Church, a friend of the Greeks even before the revolt, who would become their generalissimo and die in Athens, the object of universal respect, at age 90.

To struggle for modern Greece was for these idealists a way of rendering homage to ancient Greece. Arriving in Greece and observing the divisive conflicts among the Greek leaders, they found reality different from what they had imagined. The liberation of Greece was, in fact, achieved in the midst of a civil war. Mavrocordato was forced to flee because of the hostility of Kolokotronis. The latter then saw a rival arise in the person of an adventurer with the classical name of Odysseus. An English loan served to intensify these quarrels, each side claiming a share of it.

In 1822 English foreign affairs came under the direction of George Canning, a great statesman with broad, liberal views. Adhering to traditional English foreign policy, Canning's efforts were directed to the achievement of peace in the Balkans and the containment of Russian expansion. He also wished to check increasing French interference especially when the candidacy of the Duc de Nemours, a member of the Orléans family, for a Greek throne was being considered in Paris. Canning also realized the need to furnish aid to the Greeks even if it would merely signify English interests.

Canning then suggested a project to bring about peace. He proposed that Greece, a new state enclosed within still very narrow frontiers, enjoy a degree of independence while still recognizing the sultan's sovereignty. Tsar Alexander spurned this proposal, and he insisted upon intervening in the crisis to secure from the sultan autonomy for three Greek provinces which would be protected by Russia. Discussions were held in St. Petersburg in 1825, but to his great disappointment his project met with general opposition.

A new development then occurred whose consequences were destined to change the course of events. Sultan Mahmud II, hoping to crush the Greek revolt completely, appealed to his vassal in Egypt, Mehemet Ali. The latter had not always been disciplined, but at least he had a strong army and a well equipped fleet. So Mehemet Ali sent his son Ibrahim Pasha, reputed to be an excellent general, to assist Turkey in return for a promise that the Peloponnesus would be ceded as a price for the services.

The Egyptian fleet joined the Turkish ships at Rhodes. After subjugating Crete in the spring of 1826, Ibrahim led 18,000 troops in invading the Peloponnesus and regaining inch by inch the territory conquered by the rebels at such cost. Ibrahim captured Missolonghi by storm despite a glorious resistance of 11 months. Even Athens was taken after General Fabvier had conducted a strong defense. Cochrane and Church also suffered reverses on sea and land. Thus the Greek situation appeared very critical.

As the Egyptians were apparently on the verge of complete victory, Tsar Alexander died suddenly in December 1825. The continued disappointments had apparently exhausted the nerves of a sovereign whose bitterness and misanthropy bedevilled his final years when merely ten years before success had smiled on him. This dreamer was succeeded by his brother Nicholas I, realistic, brutally energetic, and very determined to assure the success of Russian ambitions in the Balkans. In March 1826 he addressed an ultimatum to the sultan indicating Russian interests in the Danubian Principalities and Serbia. This was not merely a question of the Greeks; the new emperor was seeking a settlement of old quarrels with the Turks while apparently leaving to England the responsibility of caring for the Greeks. By the Convention of Akkerman (1826) the sultan agreed to reestablish Russian privileges in the Principalities and to grant similar ones in Serbia. Russian merchant ships were to have freedom of navigation in the Black Sea. In the same year Canning furthered the Greek cause by having the Duke of Wellington, who was attending the coronation of Nicholas, sign a protocol stating the support of England and Russia for the establishment of an autonomous Greek state under Turkish sovereignty.

France pursued a similar policy, but was unwilling to associate herself with a *post facto* protocol when invited to do so by Canning. The French requested the drafting of a new protocol. The crisis was becoming desperate. A series of successes in 1826, such as the capture of Missolonghi and Athens, had made the Turks intransigent and placed the Greeks in jeopardy. A treaty was finally signed in London on July 26, 1827 by which England, France, and Russia expressed sympathy for the Greek cause in accordance with the terms of the Anglo-Russian protocol and the powers proposed an armistice. A secret article envisaged coercive measures such as verbal threats which none wished transformed into military action. The powers thus sided openly with the Greek rebels. The Holy Alliance was now dead. It had hardly survived

Tsar Alexander, its creator. Moreover, the Treaty of London deprived Russia of the exclusive power to defend the Greeks who were now considered wards of the three powers. The Turks, however, refused the hand extended to them.

Translating words into deeds, the three powers, without any aggressive intentions, dispatched a combined fleet to the Ionian Islands to prevent Turkish reinforcements from being landed on the Greek coast and to bring pressure to bear on the Ottoman government. The command of this joint task force went, by reason of seniority, to Admiral Codrington of the English navy. But Admiral de Rigny, his French colleague, would play the decisive role. Codrington wished to have Turkey yield without fighting, but de Rigny was secretly encouraged by King Charles X of France to use force for purposes of securing prestige. As for Admiral Heyden, the Russian officer, he was instructed to "treat the enemy in the Russian manner."

During negotiations with Ibrahim Pasha, whose fleet was anchored in the Bay of Navarino in the southwest Peloponnesus, Codrington was patient while de Rigny was provocative. The opinion of the French admiral ultimately prevailed and an order was dispatched to the Turco-Egyptian fleet to leave Greek waters. Legend states that on October 20, 1827 a shot fired from a Turkish ship signalled a battle which none had wanted or foreseen. At most it was a symbolic gesture which furnished de Rigny with the pretext he was seeking. A fierce battled ensued which cost the Turco-Egyptian fleet about half their force of 100 ships.

Echoes of Navarino were loud in France. Dreaming of military glory, public opinion chose to see in this an exploit of arms which unleashed a passionate enthusiasm. Press articles saluted the event as the "beginning of a new era" and "a right to glory." Liberals as well as Bonapartists celebrated it as a victory for *la Patrie,* a new July 14, which aroused desires to expand the frontiers and occupy the left bank of the Rhine River. French writers competed in their zeal to glorify the event. In England, however, regrets were cited over a "sinister accident," a battle resulting from a surprise if not from a lack of restraint. Canning had died in August 1827 at a time when he could not witness this blow which wrecked his efforts at conciliation.

The battle at Navarino Bay was impressive proof of the active support by the powers for the Greeks whose cause was vastly improved. Again led by Fabvier and Church, the Greeks resumed the offensive to push the future frontiers of their country as far as possible. News of the naval battle stupified and then infuriated the Ottoman government. Christians in Constantinople, notably the Armenians, were expelled from the capital. This was an opportunity for Russia to resume her action against Turkey. Since Turkish troops had not yet evacuated the Danubian Principalities as promised in the Convention of Akkerman, Tsar Nicholas took advantage of this to declare war in April 1828. Turkey retaliated by proclaiming a holy war. The Russians fought in the Caucasus, Armenia, and the Balkans. The Turks concentrated against them all available forces at the risk of weakening their positions in Greece. England and France deliberated over the fate of the Greek rebels during the Turco-Russian war.

Engrossed in her struggle with the Turks, Russian displayed little interest in the Greek cause. But the Tsar had in Capo d'Istria an agent devoted to Russia who had become chief of the provisional Greek government in April 1827. Then, after the insistence of a Grecophile premier, France decided to send troops to assist the Greeks. In August 1828 14,000 troops embarked from Toulon under the command of General Maison. This force assisted in liberating the Peloponnesus in October. When he learned of the arrival of this French expedition, Admiral Codrington secured from Mehemet Ali a promise to evacuate Egyptian troops from Greece. As a consequence, the French force encountered little opposition. Resistance by a few, scattered garrisons obliged the French to use force. If the expedition was thus transformed into a military promenade, it nevertheless served French prestige in the Balkans. Moreover, the French could be pleased in averting encounters with the Egyptians with whom the former had had a long friendship.

The English, who were furnishing naval support to the Greeks, jealously observed the exploits of General Maison. After the Moslems evacuated the Peloponnesus, French troops prepared to cross the isthmus of Corinth to penetrate into Attica. But General Maison was suddenly recalled to Paris. His troops continued to remain in Greece until 1829 where they trained the Greek forces.

While Capo d'Istria served Russian interests by controlling the Greek senate, England and France strived to remove Greece from Russia's sphere. A conference in London attempted to convince

the sultan to recognize the autonomy of Greece. By a protocol of
March 22, 1829, Greek frontiers would extend from the Peloponnesus to the Cyclades Islands and from the Gulf of Arta in the
west to Volo in the east. But Capo d'Istria refused to evacuate
territory located north of this frontier.

After encountering severe resistance, Russian troops advanced
toward Constantinople while these negotiations were in progress.
Tsar Nicholas imposed the Treaty of Adrianople on the sultan on
September 14, 1829. The Russians, decimated by disease, were
hardly in a position to take Constantinople, and decided not to try
lest the powers intervene. The terms of the treaty were quite
lenient. Russia abandoned her conquests in the Balkans, but the
frontier on the Pruth River was extended from the northern to the
southern mouth of the Danube. Russia would occupy the Principalities pending the payment of an indemnity. The *hospodars*
would be appointed for life and the Turks would withdraw all
Moslems and raze all fortresses in the Principalities. The sultan
agreed to accept the London Protocol of 1829.

These conditions were the subject of a new London protocol
signed February 3, 1830. This new understanding was an improvement over the old because it provided for the complete independence of Greece. But the territorial extent of Greece was now
less generous. At the insistence of England, who wished to prevent
the coast of the new country from being too close to the Ionian
Islands, where she had a protectorate, the southern frontier was
pushed back from the Arta-Volo line to the mouth of the Aspro-
potamo in the west and to the Gulf of Lamia in the east, i.e.
almost to the Gulf of Corinth. This was a considerable loss of
territory. The three powers decided to recommend for the Greek
throne a candidate from the Saxe-Coburg family. He refused the
offer, and Capo d'Istria, whom the English and French hoped to
remove, remained dictator.

Born in Corfu, educated in Vienna, former Russian foreign
minister, with a subtle and complex mind, Capo d'Istria was not
prepared to govern a nation of mountaineers and sailors upon
which he wished to impose a European-style administration. He
ruled the country as a veritable autocrat. Although exhausted by
the long revolution, Greece continued to experience the disputes
which had aggravated her difficult struggle for freedom. Clan
hatreds remained active and were now aggravated by conflicting

views on domestic policies. President Capo d'Istria, a partisan of strong government, was opposed by the liberals. Dissident liberals established a government on the island of Hydra. Strong opposition also came from Petros Mavromichalis, a Russophobe, whom Capo d'Istria imprisoned. In October 1831 Capo d'Istria was murdered by the brother and son of his rival, Mavromichalis.

Would Greece, whose rebirth had been hailed with so much enthusiasm, now sink into anarchy so soon after leaving her cradle? The powers were disturbed by the appearance of rival authorities who condemned each other and fought bitterly among themselves. The installation of a monarchy of foreign origin appeared indispensable for the reestablishment of stability and the assuaging of passions. The choice fell on young prince Otto (Othon in Greek), the second son of the king of Bavaria, in March 1832, in recognition of the Philhellenism of Ludwig I. The frontier of the kingdom was moved to the Arta-Volo line to celebrate this occasion, and the Turks resigned themselves to the new state of affairs in consideration of a sizeable indemnity.

Thus the Greek phoenix was reborn, not without an intense struggle, from its ashes. The Acropolis in Athens, although in ruins, was no longer a Turkish arsenal. Standing proudly against the enamel of the Attic sky, it would become a shrine to which so many come to render homage to that freedom of which the ancient Greeks taught us the price, but of which a cruelly ironic destiny had so long deprived their descendants. The road to freedom had been arduous. If the Greeks of the early 19th century proved themselves worthy of their ancestors of Marathon and Thermopylae, their disputes unfortunately testified to that propensity for quarrels which remained very alive and which recalled in various forms the ancient rivalry between Athens and Sparta.

Foreign assistance had been indispensable for Greek success. The first aid from Russia had ulterior motives. Then England supported the cause until French enthusiasm unleashed a naval battle in their favor. And finally it was again Russia who, due to her victories over the Turks, made the cause of independence triumph. This was independence for some Greeks only, for beyond the frontiers assigned in a rather niggardly fashion many Greeks were excluded and impatiently awaited the moment to join their brothers and bring about a reunification of all Greeks. These were the Greeks of Thessaly, Epirus, Macedonia, Thrace, Crete, the Ionian

Islands (which England still retained), the Dodecanese Islands including Rhodes, and those inhabiting the coast of Asia Minor. Greek independence had only been traced in the form of a nucleus around which Greeks scattered over the eastern Mediterranean would try to bind themselves together to form the homogeneous bloc which their patriotism required.

CHAPTER II

Serbian Independence

A SURVEY of the steps leading to Serbia's independence should begin with homage to the courage of those rugged people, the Montenegrins. The wildness of their country and their bellicose disposition led the Montenegrins to play a significant role in this era. They were the first to emancipate themselves from Ottoman oppression. The forests of tall pines which covered the slopes of the mountains fully justify the name Montenegro or Black Mountain (Chorna Gora in Serbian). Bounded by Herzegovina in the north, Novi-Bazar to the east, and Albania in the south, Montenegro extends along the Adriatic from the mouth of the Cattaro (Kotor) River south to Dulcigno (Ulcinj). In the interior the Dinaric Alps form a steep, jagged range which renders Montenegro difficult to traverse.

After the disaster of Kossovo, the region became the natural refuge of numerous Serbian chieftains. Nominally vassals of the Turks, the Montenegrins did not cease to rebel against Ottoman rule from which they freed themselves in the 18th century. Despite their small population, the Montenegrins occasionally inflicted resounding defeats on Turkish troops sent to subjugate them.

At the beginning of the 16th century a group of tribes in Montenegro elected a chief who was granted a princely title. In 1696 this choice fell on a young monk, Danilo Petrovich-Njegosh, who was soon promoted to bishop. One of his nephews, also a monk, was his successor and founder of the dynasty of prince-bishops whose power was transmitted from uncle to nephew until the middle of the 19th century. Montenegro enjoyed a patriarchal existence under this theocratic regime.

Seclusion and difficult traveling did not prevent the inhabitants from being the first south Slavs to establish close contact with Russia. In the 18th century they appealed to Peter the Great in the name of the dual solidarity of the Christianity and Slavism of their powerful neighbors to the north. Tsar Peter replied by proclaiming his interest in the little Slav nation and his resolve to liberate Orthodox Christians from the infidels' yoke. Montenegrin officers serving in Russia's army were intermediaries between the two countries. One ruler of Montenegro once resided at the court of St. Petersburg. Another conveyed gifts from Russia, and a third died enroute to Russia. His successor won from Emperor Paul an annual subsidy to aid Montenegro in her struggle against the Turks. Everyone apparently expected moral and financial support from Russia.

At the end of the 18th century the Montenegrins succeeded in expelling the Moslems and pushing them as far south as Scutari in northern Albania. Montenegro's independence was not recognized, but it was acquired *de facto* and had to be maintained by constant vigilance and recourse to arms at the first alarm. This privileged situation led the Montenegrins to take initiatives in resisting the Turks. Serbian nationalists merely awaited an opportunity to imitate their Montenegrin cousins.

In 1787, when Turkey was fighting Austria and Russia, many Serbs joined the latter against the Moslems. They participated in Austria's capture of Belgrade. That city was restored to the Turks at the end of the war, but the decline of Ottoman power had become quite apparent. The moment had arrived to take advantage of the disintegration menacing the Ottoman Empire.

The process of liberation would be relatively slow. The Serbs were surrounded by the Turks; their only Christian neighbors were the Austrians whose assistance experience had taught them to be as ineffective as it was motivated by self-interest. After many Serbian leaders had fled to Austria and Montenegro to escape Turkish revenge, the Serbian people, deprived of their chiefs, remained illiterate peasants who raised sheep and pigs and who subsisted on the products of their fields. The lack of an aristocracy and descendants of the medieval national dynasties favored competition among families who claimed leadership of the national movement.

Such was the situation at the beginning of the 19th century when the Turkish pasha, who was governing justly and moderately in Belgrade, was confronted in 1804 with a revolt of the Janissaries. Courageous but insubordinate troops, the Janissaries indulged in outrages from which the Turks themselves were not even exempt. After joining forces with the adventurer Pasvanoglu who was terrorizing Vidin, they ended up by murdering the pasha.

Prior to this crisis many Serbs had sought refuge south of Belgrade in the region of Shumadia, bristling with steep mountains and punctuated by abrupt valleys, which was the cradle of their liberation movement. There they assembled around chiefs who were simple men almost spontaneously animated by a profound patriotism and indomitable energy. The mayor of one village, Alexa Nenadovich, took the initiative of dispatching a request to the sultan. Swiftly punished by the Turkish authorities for this insubordinate gesture, Nenadovich refused to flee so that "others might not have to suffer in his place." He paid with his life for this brave deed, leaving to his brother the responsibility of carrying on the struggle.

More fortunate was George Petrovich (1766-1817) who was the creator of a great destiny for his family. The Turks called him "George the Black"—Kara George—because of the fear he allegedly inspired. He was 34 years old and illiterate like the vast majority of his compatriots when the crisis began. A former swineherd and livestock merchant, Kara George enlisted in the Austrian army where he acquired basic military knowledge which, combined with his energy and a small fortune amassed in his business, brought him much prestige in Serbia. A veritable Cincinnatus, albeit a violent and brutal one, he was very simple in his habits, refusing to leave his crude wooden house or abandon simple peasant clothing. Taciturn in character, he displayed a violent temper when insisting upon imposing his will. "Obey or I shall kill you," he told his entourage and, in fact, one of his brothers fell under his blows. He was the founder of the Karageorgevich dynasty to whom modern Serbia owes its resurrection.

In 1804 partisans led by Yakov Nenadovich, who had resolved to avenge his brother, were keeping the Turks in check. But the leader with incontestable authority was really Kara George. After assembling many outlaws and exasperated peasants, he finally created a veritable army of about 10,000 men. Encountering Turkish troops at Michar in August 1806, he inflicted upon them a rout which marked the first step in the long and difficult road to Serbia's independence. The rebels then captured Belgrade where they smashed the resistance of the Janissaries and unleashed a massacre of the Turks. These victories encouraged his ambitions by leading Kara George to transform a purely local insurrection into a general liberation movement. He appealed to the confraternity of the Montenegrins and Bosnians, inviting them to follow his example and restore the unity of the Serbian nation.

The Serbs realized they could hardly hope to achieve unity without foreign assistance. Aid could not be expected from Austria. Napoleon's forces were advancing toward the Adriatic in 1806. Would they show any interest in the Slavs? The French were a new element, replete with unknown qualities. So the Serbs turned to Russia more readily because Montenegro had already found a protector there. Serbian envoys received promises, not aid, in St. Petersburg. The general European crisis was diverting Tsar Alexander's attention. Despite this disappointment Serbia's hopes were not dimmed, especially since the country had advantageous natural defenses and was still celebrating triumphs over the Turks.

Sultan Selim III feared Russian intervention in Serbia. So he conceded a degree of autonomy to the Serbs and agreed to withdraw most of his garrisons except the one at Belgrade, which was an advance outpost facing Austria. But after Russia was defeated by Napoleon at the battles of Eylau and Friedland (1807), the sultan did not hesitate in reneging on his agreement. Hostilities were resumed, and the Serbs again occupied Belgrade where similar excesses were committed.

Master of a region south of the Danube whose extent was quite considerable, Kara George decided to organize a rudimentary administration by creating a senate and organizing his partisans into a regular army. A popular assembly, the Skuptschina, conferred on him the functions of a supreme chief. Then Kara George planned to attack Turkey while the latter was involved in a war with Russia. Perhaps Serbia would have achieved complete independence if Tsar Alexander had furnished serious support. A few Russian troops did arrive in 1810 to swell the ranks of the insurgent army and to assist in holding Belgrade, but the prospect of a struggle against Napoleon led Alexander to conclude a hasty peace with Turkey so that he would have a free hand against the French. Alexander thus sacrificed the Orthodox Serbs who had trusted him. Turkey and Russia signed the Treaty of Bucharest (1812) by which the former accorded Serbia vague promises of autonomy. The Turks nevertheless retained a certain number of garrisons in Serbia.

The Ottoman government, profiting by Napoleon's invasion of Russia in June 1812, dispatched a large force to subdue the unruly Serbs. Serbia was quickly defeated. Kara George, suffering from illness and the criticism of those who had felt his temper, displayed the quite unexpected spectacle of completely losing his composure. After hiding his wealth and then accompanied by many partisans, he abandoned Serbia and sought refuge in Austria where he was interned. This retreat marked the collapse of hopes which brilliant successes had produced only six years before.

Among those who, after having fought bravely, preferred to remain in Serbia was Milosh Obrenovich (1780-1860). He too was a former swineherd who had become rich and had acquired a stature which let him serve as an intermediary with the Turks. Aware that Ottoman strength rendered defiance imprudent, Milosh decided to make peace with the sultan. He succeeded in inspiring confidence to the point of having his authority recognized as that of a semi-independent chieftain. His actions then and now remain quite debatable. Was he merely an ambitious man driven by egotistical views onto the road of treason? Or was he a beguiling patriot who awaited the hour to unmask? Entitling him a "village Louis XI," whose services did not compensate for the moral decadence inspired by his lack of scruples, Ernest Denis, in his *La Grande Serbie,* recognized that in such circumstances the patient and flexible intrigues of Milosh were the only available weapons. Whatever the truth, his collaboration went quite far, even as far as collaborating in the arrest of some compatriots. By playing the always difficult and dangerous game of negotiating, not to mention playing the fox with a cruel and demanding occupant, Milosh succeeded in preserving the foundations of the Serbian state. Contrasted with the military feats of Kara George, the cautious politics of Milosh offered nothing heroic. But he nevertheless assured the future of the country.

Tsar Alexander made broad declarations in favor of the south Slavs at the Congress of Vienna, but the powers had other concerns and, although they appreciated humanitarian gestures, they took no effective measures to mitigate the lot of the Orthodox Christians. Confronted by indifference, the Serbs decided to claim their own rights. An uprising inspired by Milosh in 1815 earned for him confirmation of his recognition as chief of the Serbs and to his subjects freedom of religion and a degree of antonomy. Milosh unhappily abused his powers as much to enrich himself as to persecute his opponents. Kara George, deciding to profit from rising discontent, returned to Serbia in 1817. A mortal rivalry was thus inevitable between the old and new leaders of the liberation movement. Kara George was soon assassinated (1817) by his Obrenovich opposition. Since that murder a relentless duel was carried on by the Karageorgevich and Obrenovich families which tragically darkened the already troubled history of re-emerging Serbia of which the duel bloodied more than one page. Temporarily relieved of a rival, Milosh was proclaimed prince with a hereditary title in 1817.

The attempted revolt led by Ypsilanti in the Danubian Principalities would perhaps have found an echo among the Serbs, but their new prince, skeptical of the consequences, contented himself with fine words. Meanwhile, the Greek insurrection began. Faithful to his strategy of nibbling away at Turkish authority, Milosh did not seek to profit from the sultan's difficulties to provoke open rebellion. He preferred to await an opportunity to validate the right to independence.

Events proved Milosh correct. The accession to the throne of Tsar Nicholas in 1825 was followed by the Convention of Akkerman and the Treaty of Adrianople, both of which notably advanced the Serbian cause. The Tsar, however, refused to recognize the hereditary title of Milosh lest the latter display too much independence. By a policy which, though logical at first glance, seemed paradoxical, Sultan Mahmud II hastened to accord to Milosh what Nicholas had refused. In 1830 the sultan's decree conceded heredity of power to the Obrenovich family merely to attract Milosh from Russia's exclusive influence. Furthermore, the sultan granted Milosh freedom to administer a territory whose frontiers, encompassing about 700,000 inhabitants, would remain the same for about 50 years.

Serbia nevertheless remained a small principality, subject to Turkey's sovereignty, a prisoner in her mountains, deprived of access to the sea, lacking Bosnia and Macedonia and even the region of Nish, and still occupied by several Turkish garrisons. Confirmed as prince, Milosh then became as demanding as a pasha. He was a feudal tyrant who treated his people as serfs. But his brutal methods and terrible temper should not obscure his achievements: a campaign against thievery, road improvements, extension of education, and commercial development. He brought to trade a very personal interest which accrued to him profits which he did not scorn. Milosh secured the emancipation of the Serbian Orthodox Church from the Greek Patriarch and the appointment of a metropolitan at Belgrade. A view of this illiterate prince to whom newspapers were read so that he could know the news, a clever manipulator, alternately energetic and flexible, with a keen sense of the opportune, indicated again that political skill is not so much a matter of study and knowledge as of common sense. But this virtue did not diminish his arbitrariness and violence from arousing opposition and the formation of conspiracies.

Milosh believed he could avert hostility by summoning the Skuptshchina which he had earlier suspended. In 1835 he attempted to transform Serbia into a constitutional state. Since the Serbs lacked political experience or even the required sophistication, the project was unrealizable and Milosh reverted to the despotic formula which responded to his temperament. He practiced it with such excess that Tsar Nicholas sent an agent to Serbia to counsel moderation. Despite concessions, the prince of Serbia suspected his advisers, felt abandoned by his supporters, considered his good name undermined by envious rivals, and apparently suffered from paranoia. He decided to abdicate in favor of his son Milan in 1839. The new prince died in the same year. The Skuptshchina appointed the 16-year-old brother Michael on whom the sultan imposed two regents. After a reign of two years, Michael, having become quite unpopular, was forced to abdicate.

These successive setbacks marked the failure of the Obrenovich dynasty. Twenty-five years of misrule failed to fulfill the needs of Serbia. The Serbs then turned to the family of the old national hero whose memory had not died. Alexander (1806-85), son of Kara George, was summoned from exile and, against Russia's will, appointed prince. These events occurred in such swift succession that the young prince was elected and installed before he had time to understand the sequence of events. The Turkish government took advantage of this situation to grant Alexander a restricted investiture of temporary character. This was an appreciable reversal for Serbia, and for Alexander an award of very fragile authority. The new ruler acquiesced because he was as desirous of not offending Turkey as he was of pleasing Austria. In a country accustomed to considering Russia as her natural protector, such a reversal of traditional policy was unpopular.

Alexander did introduce some practical reforms. He dared in

1844 to move against the ancient institution of the *zadruga,* a regime of the family commune, to encourage individualism and authorize the acquisition of private property. This was a beneficial change whose consequences were not realized for some time. At the outset the reform did provoke a certain unease by breaking the old ties of family solidarity.

In 1848 revolution broke out in neighboring Hungary. In turn, Serbs living in Hungary rebelled against their Hungarian oppressors. Alexander supported the efforts of his kinsmen on the northern side of the Danube and permitted numerous volunteers to join their ranks. Favoring the cause of the Serbs of Hungary earned the approval of his subjects, but participation in the struggle against the Hungarians was simultaneously contributing to the preservation of the Austrian Empire, an act which was appreciated in Vienna.

Alexander's cautious policy estranged him from Russia. St. Petersburg forcefully reminded him of his obligations. During the tension preceding the Crimean War Tsar Nicholas called upon Alexander to discharge his foreign minister whose policy shocked the Russians with its demands for independence. The prince had no alternative but to yield. The Serbs keenly felt this insult which, much to the chagrin of Nicholas, resulted in Serbia's decision to maintain neutrality during the Crimean War. The Treaty of Paris (1856) confirmed the liberation of Serbia regarding the protectorate Russia had hoped to impose. For the guarantee of Russia was substituted that of the powers. A native administration, religious freedom, and unrestricted commercial activities were guaranteed to Serbia, but Turkish sovereignty remained in effect. The Ottoman government continued to levy tribute and maintain garrisons.

Although these achievements were of value, Alexander was losing the little popularity he enjoyed. His excessive submission to the sultan was reproached. His servility toward Austria and certain procedures of his government which excluded the masses (the Skuptshchina had not been convened since 1842) alienated the populace. By the natural swing of the pendulum, Serbian favor oscillated toward the Obrenovich family whom many Serbs began to miss. As happened often in the Balkans, discontent was manifested in the form of conspiracies. A plot against Alexander was arranged by several politicians who were apprehended and sentenced to death. Intervention of the powers resulted in having the penalty commuted to exile. Nevertheless, Alexander's days as prince were numbered. When it convened in November 1858, the Skuptshchina displayed such hostility toward Alexander that a committee of public safety was hastily formed to demand his abdication. Upon learning of this, the prince ignominiously sought refuge in the Turkish garrison. Aged Milosh Obrenovich, in disgrace for 20 years, was recalled to power.

After a long exile Milosh returned to Belgrade in January 1859, still as vigorous and crude despite his advanced age. If, in his style of governing, he showed that he had learned nothing and forgotten nothing, at least he gave the Serbs the pride of appreciating his independent attitude toward foreign influences. Servility toward Austria, of which the Karageorgevich family had been accused, now disappeared. Milosh also jeered at Turkey when he proclaimed and the Skuptshchina approved the heredity of his power. The Ottoman government protested, but, when Milosh died only eight months after returning home and his son Michael (1825-68) succeeded him, the sultan recognized the *fait accompli*.

The death of Milosh marked a turning point in Serbia's history. His passing marked the end of the generation of the first heroes of independence, fervent patriots, crude peasant soldiers, but only half-civilized, whose survivors then offered an image of an outmoded type. Prince Michael was a new type. Since his first brief reign during his adolescence (1839-42), he had spent 18 years in exile traveling throughout Europe and adopting the manners of a Westerner. The outlook of his compatriots had likewise evolved. The Serbs were no longer simple men whose elementary instinct to rebel impelled them to seek liberation from an oppressor of different ethnic origin and religion. Education and reflection had given the Serbs a clearer consciousness of the national sentiment animating them. Everywhere in Europe peoples in the process of achieving independence utilized history and philology as weapons. The Serbs found in historical sources an urge to join with other Slav groups inhabiting the Balkans and the Austrian Empire. Within the latter country Ljubljana (Laibach) in Carniola had remained the center of Illyrianism since the arrival of Napoleon's troops. At Zagreb (Agram), capital of Croatia, a Slav and Roman Catholic city, the scholar Ludovit (Ljudevit) Gaj (1809-72) purified the popular language which would become

Serbo-Croatian and created the concordance between the Latin and Cyrillic alphabets.

Special recognition must be given to Vuk Karadzhich (Karadzic) (1787-1864), the Serbian scholar who led a movement to break the tenuous bonds with Vienna. This erudite, nationalistic scholar strengthened Young Serb nationalism by simplifying the Cyrillic alphabet as used in Serbia, determining the spelling and rules of the language by publishing a dictionary and grammar, and producing a Serbian-German-Latin lexicon. Then producing an anthology of celebrated popular songs, the *pesmes*, and historic legends, Karadzhich furnished sustenance to a people in love with idealism and their past. His efforts were appreciated abroad and attracted Europe's attention to the still relatively unknown claims of the Serbian nation. It was due to Karadzhich's efforts that Serbian in its Western form (Croatian) owed its becoming one national language of the south Slavs (the contemporary Yugoslavs) whose common ethnic origin it emphasizes. "There are no longer even rivers or mountains between us," wrote a Croat at the time. A movement toward unity was supported by propaganda of which Russia was the natural center because she claimed her right to the historic mission of "protector of the Slavs."

Thus Prince Michael oriented Serbia towards Russia. He came to power with a precise program—to introduce progressive reforms and liberate Serbia from Turkish sovereignty. The Skuptshchina met regularly to voice its wishes. The army was the object of special attention. Doubtless the Serbs had always been excellent soldiers, but primarily in guerilla warfare. Assisted by French officers, Michael created a disciplined, trained, European-style army.

The occurrence of a commonplace incident enabled Michael to free Serbia from control by the Turkish garrisons. The presence of Ottoman troops had always produced squabbles with the populace, especially in Belgrade. In June 1862 a Serbian child was killed during a quarrel, and a riot ensued. The unrest appeared to have been quelled and peace restored when the Turkish garrison began to shell the city from the citadel. This senselessly cruel act provoked much distress in Europe. A conference was held in Constantinople at French insistence to discuss the evacuation of the Turkish garrisons. Austria and England opposed the French move, and the latter had to be content with a demolition of two fortresses. However, by 1867 the powers were no longer opposed to evacuation and in that year the last Turkish soldiers left Serbia. For all Serbia it was a great satisfaction to be deprived of the daily spectacle of foreign domination, and for Michael it was a personal success to have presided over Serbia when Ottoman occupation finally vanished.

Despite wise administration and actual progress, Michael had many relentless enemies. In June 1868 conspirators ambushed Michael and his companions in a Belgrade park. He was assassinated and his companions were wounded. Was this nefarious murder, which was disastrous for Serbia, plotted by partisans of the Karageorgevich family? Such were the rampant suspicions, but the motives have remained mysterious. The Skuptshchina was immediately summoned and chose Milan, the 14-year-old son of Michael, to succeed to the throne. Milan (1854-1901) left his Paris school to return home. The Ottoman government recognized Milan II. Guided by a distinguished statesman, Jovan Ristich (Ristic) (1831-99), the regency council promulgated a new constitution, more liberal than the preceding one, which called for an assembly of 90 elected members and 30 appointed ones which met annually. But most power was entrusted to the ruler.

Severe judgements have been passed on Milan II. Quite intelligent and attractive, the young prince reared far from his family had assumed the manners of a cynic, a bon vivant, and a roué. Bored by Belgrade, a primitive city of 30,000 inhabitants undistinguished in backgrounds and capacities, Milan frequently abandoned his capital to find amusement in Vienna and Paris where he led a life of debauchery and gambling. The gap between this precocious and corrupt young man and a nation still quite backward but healthy, virile and full of virtue, was complete. Furthermore, Milan despised his subjects and lacked no opportunity to advise them of his attitude. A regime of intrigue, favoritism, and venality which arose during his reign created a most disastrous influence. Not as much on the people who remained simple and attached to their old customs as on the official milieu who were anxious to get into step with the strange ruler who was so anti-Serb despite his ancestry and who was always seeking money for his pleasures. Corruption went its free and unfettered way. Austria's influence was shamelessly applied. A nation of peasants still under the influence of oriental customs was given over to the caprices of a young, ineffectual sovereign who believed himself a disciple of the West because he had adopted its vices.

Although attached by a theoretical bond of vassalage to Turkey, Serbia had really become independent. But new and grave problems confronted the Serbs. If those inhabiting the principality were confined in very modest limits, such was not the fate of numerous brethren who inhabited Bosnia, Herzegovina, Macedonia, the Sanjak of Novi-Bazar, and Montenegro, the latter owing their relative independence only to a stubborn armed resistance to the Turks. The Croats and Slovenes, on their side, were likewise groaning under the Hungarian yoke. All aspired to independence, looking toward Belgrade for support and toward St. Petersburg for encouragement. Would Serbia assume leadership of a Slav revolution? Would Serbia become a center of attraction for all the south Slavs?

The rebirth of national sentiment aroused difficulties in Bosnia as early as 1850. Omer (or Omar) Pasha (1806-71), a native of Croatia whose real name was Michael Lattas, a convert to Islam, became the specialist of Ottoman repression in the Balkans. He quickly subdued the Bosnian revolt in that year. It was next the turn of the Montenegrins to demonstrate Slav nationalism. In 1852, when prince-bishop Peter II died, his nephew and successor, Danilo, decided to secularize his authority with the approval of Tsar Nicholas I of Russia. This modification aroused Turkish anger and resulted in military intervention which was vigorously repulsed. The Congress of Paris in 1856 discussed the question of Montenegro. Turkey claimed annexation of the little principality, and the latter demanded independence. Despite the support of Emperor Napoleon III, who was sympathetic to the Montenegrin cause, the bond of sovereignty with Turkey was reaffirmed. The Turks then sent an army of 20,000 to subjugate the country. The Ottoman forces suffered a humiliating defeat at Grahovo in 1858. Danilo's victory provoked an uprising in neighboring Herzegovina. Would Montenegro become the rallying-point and standard-bearer of the Slavs because of the indomitable valor of Danilo? Would the liberator role move from Belgrade to Cetinje, the capital of Montenegro? But in 1860 Danilo was assassinated by a disgruntled Montenegrin. He was succeeded by his nephew Nicholas (1860-1918).

Although officially neutral, Montenegro furnished arms and volunteers to the rebels of Herzegovina, and Turkey assigned Omer Pasha the task of invading the country at the head of an army of 60,000 in 1862. The Montenegrins resisted for four months in their "citadel of the rocks" only to end up crushed by Turkish artillery. But the Ottoman army could not take Cetinje, the capital. Intercessions by the powers compelled Turkey to mitigate her conditions. The Convention of Scutari (1862) was quite severe, nevertheless. No Montenegrin fortresses were to be erected on the Turkish frontiers, no one was to enter Montenegro without a Turkish visa, and war materials were not to be imported. Although required by the agreement, Turkish troops were not stationed within Montenegro.

After a decade of smoldering, the fire was rekindled in 1875. This time it was the peasants of Bosnia and Herzegovina who revolted against the Ottoman government. These two mountainous provinces were located on the natural prolongation of the very rough terrain of Serbia and Montenegro. Both provinces were transition zones between the Serbs and Croats and the Orthodox and Roman Catholic religions. Many Bosnian Bogomils became Moslems after the Turkish conquest. They had been persecuted by the Orthodox and Catholic hierarchies and not unnaturally they embraced Islam. Also, there were practical considerations to conversion. The noble who became a Moslem could retain at least some of his former lands and privileges; the serf who converted became a free peasant. Thus the Moslem conquerors attracted more converts in Bosnia than in any other Balkan region. The population remains today almost one-third Moslem. Nevertheless, the Orthodox and Slav majority had grown exasperated by the arbitrary and extortionate regime of the Turkish authorities and took up arms in revolt.

Serbia could not remain indifferent to the heroic resistance of her brethren. At Belgrade Jovan Ristich, the premier, urged his prince to intercede. Milan hesitated lest Austria react against Serbian intervention. Finally, he decided to intervene and he was imitated by Nicholas of Montenegro. Would a Slav federation be created to form a league against Turkey?

Frequently prompted to assist her co-religionists in the Balkans, Russia assigned one of her best officers, General Michael Chernyaiev (1828-98), to command the Serbian army. Nevertheless, the Serbs provided a disappointing resistance. While the Montenegrins again resisted the Turks, the Serbs, defeated by them, were forced to seek an armistice in March 1877. Despite defeat, the Serbs managed to emerge without loss of territory or payment of an indemnity. Still fearful of Austria and cowed by his recent defeat, Milan was prudent to abstain from hostilities when war broke out between Russia and Turkey in 1877. He stood by when the Rumanians alone came to the aid of the Russians at the siege of Plevna, but when Russia's triumph appeared assured he abandoned neutrality to seize the towns of Nish and Pirot in Macedonia.

When Austria and Russia met at Reichstadt in July 1876, Gorchakov, the Russian foreign minister, and Andrassy, the Austrian foreign minister, informally agreed to a division of spheres of influence in the Balkans. Both agreed that the *status quo ante bellum* should be restored if Serbia and Montenegro were defeated by Turkey. But if the two Balkan states won, Austria and Russia would cooperate in regulating territorial changes. Both agreed that no large Slav state should be created, but a misunderstanding arose from the start about details of new frontiers. Russia maintained that Serbia and Montenegro, if victorious, would acquire the larger part of Bosnia and Herzogovina and that Austria would receive only a small portion of Bosnia. Andrassy, however, believed the larger part of Bosnia and Herzegovina would accrue to Austria-Hungary. This misunderstanding would produce acrimony between the two great powers before the crisis was partially resolved. Both agreed, nevertheless, that if the Ottoman Empire in Europe collapsed completely, Constantinople might become a free city, Epirus and Thessaly annexed by Greece, and Bulgaria and Rumelia become autonomous or even independent states. Russia would regain southern Bessarabia.

Faithful to her understanding of the Reichstadt agreement, Russia imposed on Turkey the Treaty of San Stefano (March 3, 1878). Russia was primarily interested in creating a greater Bulgaria. Stipulations about Serbia were reached at the Congress of Berlin in July 1878 to which her delegates were barred despite the preeminence of Premier Ristich. The Congress did recognize the complete independence of Serbia, symbolized by termination of the tribute to the sultan and by enlargement of her territory to include the region of Nish. Courageous Montenegro had her independence confirmed and her territory enlarged by addition of the port of Antivari in which she was prohibited from maintaining warships.

Having acquired her independence in 1878, Serbia thus arrived at the end of long trials and tribulations which since 1804 had hindered attainment of freedom. Four years later Milan Obrenovich crossed the last hurdle when he was proclaimed king. The Kingdom of Serbia was thus established. It was of quadrilateral shape quite limited in its northern region by waterways—the Danube and the Save; in its western region by the Drina River which separated Serbia from Bosnia; and in the east by the Timok region which formed the frontier with Bulgaria. Serbia had no natural frontiers in the south and bordered directly on Macedonia and the Sanjak of Novi-Bazar. The Morava River, a Danube tributary, divided Serbia into two equal parts. Her geographical position made Serbia a corridor as much for the Turks and their advance toward Hungary and the west as for the German nations in their drive to the east in the direction of the Vardar valley and the Aegean Sea, with Salonika as their objective.

It was in Serbia that national sentiment, even before that of Greece, had first arisen among the Balkan peoples. Serbia achieved her independence by her own efforts without that foreign aid of which her neighbors, Greeks, Rumanians, and Bulgarians, would be beneficiaries. But these meritorious achievements were troubled by internecine struggles between rival dynasties, murders, and family dramas of which the series, which stemmed from the origins of her history, had not yet ended.

The advantages secured by Serbia by the Treaty of Berlin (1878) entailed a disturbing reversal. Austria was granted administration of Bosnia and Herzegovina as well as a right to maintain a garrison in the Sanjak of Novi-Bazar. Fears expressed by Ristich at the beginning of Bosnia's insurrection in 1875 had materialized. Austria now encircled little Serbia and cut off all access to the Adriatic Sea. Serbia's frontiers were so reduced that the location of Belgrade, separated from Hungary only by the Danube River, placed the capital under the fire of foreign cannon.

Serbia's destiny was thus inscribed on a map. Destined to become the nucleus of a great Slav state, Serbia was threatened with strangulation by a stronger neighbor who was the vanguard of Germanism in the Balkans. Would Serbia be subjugated by Austria who, after having added new Slav peoples to the Croats and Slovenes already subjects of her empire, would incorporate the last remaining intact island in the midst of the regions she dominated to realize under her wing the unification of all south Slavs? Or would Serbia, assisted by Russia, succeed in overturning this obstacle and fulfilling this mission herself? Nature assigned

Serbia the perilous role of a battlefield in the test of strength which would inevitably pit German and Slav against each other over the principle of domination in the Balkans where the two cultures confronted each other.

"Arise, falcons! Bear the name of 'Slavs' nobly. Go! Unite with the eagles of the north," so went a popular song.

CHAPTER III

Rumanian Independence

THE movement from which Greek independence emerged had its birth in the Danubian Principalities. Were not these Rumanian provinces administered by Greeks to whom the Ottoman government had permitted a considerable latitude? When an insurrection broke out in the Peloponnesus (the Morea), Alexander Ypsilanti, nephew of a former *hospodar* of Wallachia and an officer in the Russian army, aroused the Rumanians to rebel. The Phanariot *hospodar* of Moldavia, Michael Sutsu (1819-21), was attracted into joining the rebellion. Neither secured an appreciable following, however. The populace accurately estimated that failure would produce Turkish reprisals and success would have been advantageous only to the Greek Phanariots. The Rumanians had to suffer much from the Greek administration, and were not tempted to compromise themselves in the latter's favor. Opinion was divided. A peasant leader, Tudor Vladimirescu, who had considerable wealth and had gained experience fighting the Turks in 1806 on Russia's side, attempted to arouse a popular uprising in Wallachia independent of Ypsilanti who was criticized for acting at foreign instigation. Vladimirescu's bold attacks against Phanariot rule inevitably produced a collision with Ypsilanti. The former was captured and murdered by Ypsilanti's henchmen. This internecine struggle played into Turkish hands and subsequently resulted in Ypsilanti's defeat and flight into Austria.

These incidents made the sultan realize the danger of awarding the posts of *hospodar* to Greeks who were inclined to sympathize with the revolt their own homeland had raised against his authority. This resulted in the end of the Phanariot regime. Appreciating the loyalty of most Rumanians, Sultan Mahmud II appointed native nobles (boyars) as *hospodars*—Ioan Sturdza in Moldavia and Gregor Ghica in Wallachia (1822). If this restoration of the Rumanian princes gave legitimate satisfaction to the principalities, the masses remained discontent as they realized the nobility still clung obstinately to outmoded privileges while the former were still excluded from all political rights.

Russia's southward expansion, substituted for that of Austria, continued to be of increasing anxiety for Rumanian liberty. The crisis in Greece furnished the ambitious Nicholas I with the occasion to resume Russia's push into the Balkans. Prior to engaging the Turks in battle, Nicholas secured by the Convention of Akkerman (1826) recognition of the privileged position Russia had in the Danubian Principalities. Henceforth the native princes, elected by assemblies of nobles (boyars) for seven-year terms, would secure the sultan's approval only after consultation with the Russian emperor. Moreover, the princes were instructed to accept the opinions and advice of Russian agents. The sultan's self-esteem was flattered while the tsar secured substantial advantages.

Less than two years later Nicholas declared war on Turkey (1828) because of alleged non-implementation of the Convention. As had happened on previous occasions, Russian troops immediately crossed the Pruth River to occupy Moldavia and Wallachia, which were now subjected to a Russian occupation for the sixth time in about 125 years. Tsar Nicholas won a victory, but it was seriously disputed. His success permitted Russia to impose on Turkey the Treaty of Adrianople in 1829 which marked a considerable advance of Russian influence. Following a custom which had assumed the character of a tradition, Moldavia and Wallachia were to be evacuated by Russian troops and restored to the sultan, but only after full payment of an indemnity. Finally, while continuing to pay tribute to the sultan, the two Principalities were to enjoy additional autonomy because their *hospodars* would henceforth be elected to life terms.

Russia's occupation lasted almost six years during which Count Paul Kiselev (or Kisselev), the Tsar's viceroy, strived to implant his master's influence in the principalities. Kiselev, apparently an honest, able, and liberal official, supervised the drafting of an internal constitution known as the *Règlement Organique*. This constitution, though perpetuating the feudal privileges of the boyars, who formed the majority of its framers, was valuable in introducing western administrative ideas. The document granted to Russia effective power and left Turkey with only a shadow of sovereignty. Under the provisions of the *Règlement* each principality was to have an autonomous government headed by a native *hospodar,* who was to be elected for life by a small group of higher clergy, nobles, and landed proprietors. Despite the limitless admiration of Tsar Nicholas for autocracy, the *Règlement* embodied some principles of constitutional government (separation of powers, representative elected assemblies, although on the basis of a limited suffrage), as well as provisions for the development of a school system and the regulation of relations between landowners and their peasant farmers. The *Règlement* was approved by a specially appointed committee in St. Petersburg and by assemblies of Moldavian and Wallachian boyars. The Ottoman government had merely the doubtful privilege of formally approving the *Règlement* and putting it into effect. The Kiselev regime deepened the abyss already dug between the nobility and peasantry. The latter had no other rights except paying taxes. By flattering the nobility, Russia hoped to erase national sentiment and simultaneously maintain the peasantry in its servitude. The Principalities had actually escaped from Phanariot domination only to fall under that of the Russians. Kiselev favored their outright annexation by Russia, but his government doubted the economic gains to be derived from this move and dreaded its international repercussions. Tsar Nicholas decided against incorporation and after the Ottoman government legalized the *Règlement* in 1834 Russian troops were withdrawn.

Russia's steps in the Principalities nevertheless produced an effect opposite to what was envisaged. At the same time an awakening of national sentiment could be perceived. Influenced by the ideas of the French Revolution, many Europeans who had not yet emancipated themselves began to dream of independence and freedom. They aspired to free themselves from alien domination and to assume direction of their own destinies. The inspiration of German romantic idealism led them to return to the sources of their history and language to find therein a patriotic motive for their nationalism. Such were the tendencies evinced by Italians, Czechs, Hungarians, and Rumanians in the middle of the 19th century.

A strong attachment to their religion and the development of education had contributed to a preservation of national sentiment among the Rumanians. Russia became alarmed and sought to raise obstacles by declaring that expansion of education was a useless activity since the offices of functionary would be reserved for the cultivated class of boyars.

Despite Russia's efforts, educated Rumanians gained consciousness of their nationality. Those in Transylvania under Hungarian domination, many of whom had rallied to Roman Catholicism as members of the Uniate (Roman Catholic Church of the Byzantine Rite) Church, traveled to Rome where they encountered reminders of the Dacians and of the epoch of Emperor Trajan. Study of the past apprised them of their ancient traditions, and they were proud to resume contact with their Latin origins. It was reported that a Wallachian peasant made a pilgrimage to Rome where he, having fallen asleep at the base of Trajan's column, was identified as one of the figures sculpted on the monument. To the taste for history was joined that of philology popularized by scholars such as Samuel Clain (or Klein) (1745-1806) who tried to restore the language closer to its Latin origins. A remarkable development of historical, archaeological, and linguistic studies served as a basis for the awakening of Rumanian national consciousness.

France, in addition to Rome, served as another attraction. The former was the source of ideas of liberty toward which there had been formed a clandestine national party which placed hopes in Napoleon's victories. This tendency oriented the Rumanians toward France for whom a common ideology and intellectual affinity, through a taste for the French language, had been strong. Highly educated Phanariots had flatteringly spoken French with ease and elegance like all gentlemen of their time. They frequently appointed Frenchmen to teach their children. The frequent occupations of the Principalities by Russian troops only accentuated the state of affairs. Empress Catherine the Great, a zealous admirer of French manners, undoubtedly influenced the Rumanian aristocracy in Francophilism. Furthermore, Russian officers, rarely inclined to learn a language which was not spoken elsewhere, quite naturally used French in their contacts with Rumanian officials.

After 1840 many Rumanians, and particularly students, began to travel and study in France. They found there an atmosphere corresponding to their tastes and one which widened their appreciation of freedom. Liberal university circles welcomed them. Michelet and Quinet, the famous French historians, became advocates of Rumanian independence. In no other country but France did the Rumanian cause acquire so much support. Paris became the headquarters of young Rumanian patriots who appreciated and assimilated French culture to the point of adopting it when they returned home. The first official teaching of the French language in the principalities began in Bucharest under the auspices of a French teacher. Since the 1840's were dated cultural ties destined to develop to the point of producing several excellent Rumanian writers who have contributed to French literature.

Such were the diverse elements which combined to arouse a rebirth of national consciousness. This rebirth, having an essentially intellectual basis, was manifested especially among the educated élite. The latter labored to spread it among the masses. From the archives and literature ideas exalting Rumania's past appeared in the press and theaters. Animators of Rumanian nationalism resuscitated old legends and songs to recall the glorious past in forms designed to strike the imagination. Gheorghe Lazar, a Rumanian from Transylvania who studied at Vienna, gave up his ecclesiastical career to settle in Bucharest as the great innovator who gave a new impulse to Rumanian consciousness. From 1816 to 1821 Lazar taught homage to Rumania's Latin ancestors in Bucharest and aroused a love for the glories of imperial Rome. Schools proliferated after the impetus furnished by Lazar. Rumanian folklore soon began to celebrate the era of ancient Dacia, the empire of Michael the Brave (1593-1601), prince of Wallachia, who united the two principalities with Transylvania, Bukovina, and Bessarabia, and the epoch of Stephen the Great (1433-1504).

As revealed in folk songs, hostility was less directed against the Turks, the distant sovereigns, than against the Russians, a self-interested and more demanding protector, and even more against the Hungarians, the hereditary enemies upon whom an ancient hatred was concentrated. For the Turks the Danubian Principalities were less conquered territories than advance outposts destined to protect them from Russian pressure. Under Russia's advance this bastion had crumbled and the dangerous rival had finally entered the stronghold.

This propaganda led to the idea of a reconstitution of a greater Rumanian state which gradually penetrated into minds ready to transform it into a reality. The efforts of Ioan Heliade Radulescu (1802-72), reputed founder of Rumanian literature, Michael Kogalniceanu (1817-91), the great nationalistic historian and statesman, and Gheorghe Shincai (1753-1816) who edited a collection of archival sources in Latin and Rumanian, stimulated

The Balkan States in 1881

||||||| Limits of the Great Bulgaria of the Treaty of San Stefano
(1878)
——— Frontiers of Turkey
- - - Other frontiers in 1881

repercussions soon felt even in the huts of the most humble peasants. The national idea took on such strength in Rumania that it spread beyond the principalities where it became the source of propaganda favoring the freedom of adjacent peoples. Bucharest became an active center of patriots seeking asylum. Bulgarian nationalists secured refuge and encouragement there.

Such was the atmosphere in the Principalities when the revolution of 1848 broke out in Paris. Stirred by the proclamations favoring nationalism, Rumanian students in Paris, carrying flags, acclaimed the principle of nationality. This storm swifty reverberated throughout Europe, even to the depths of the Carpathians and the shores of the Black Sea. All nationalities soon demanded independence. While the Hungarians rebelled against Austrian rule, the Rumanians of Transylvania rebelled against their Hungarian masters. This movement penetrated the Principalities, which were impatient to repudiate Ottoman rule and even more impatient to free themselves from Russian influence and its autocratic methods. Among the intellectuals attracted to the cause were Ioan Bratianu (1822-91) and Dimitrie Bratianu (1818-92), two brothers noted for their nationalism; Nicolae Balcescu (1819-52), a foremost liberal historian; and Constantin Rosetti (1816-85), mayor of Bucharest in 1848. They attempted to win over the governor of Wallachia who was intimidated by Russian agents. Failing to overcome his hesitations, the intellectuals created a revolutionary committee which unleashed agitation in Bucharest. The native *hospodar* was forced to abdicate. The revolution spread to Moldavia where a more sympathetic *hospodar* introduced certain reforms. Appeals were addressed to Rumanians in Transylvania where the idea of a greater Rumania uniting members of a common ethnic and linguistic ancestry was beginning to appear.

Reaction was not long in coming. Unwilling to tolerate on her frontiers such a hotbed of nationalist agitation, Russia sent on July 10, 1848—for the seventh time—an army of 20,000 to occupy the Principalities under the pretext of protecting the region against revolutionary excesses. These troops were soon followed by 40,000 more. Rumanian nationalists who lacked the prudence or chance to flee were arrested, imprisoned, or exiled. The Ottoman government, on its side, sent a force to occupy Bucharest. The Tsar and the Sultan—and this is a fact too unique not to be stressed—apparently agreed to stifle Rumanian nationalism.

A Russo-Turkish convention signed at Balta-Liman on May 1, 1849 sealed the fate of the Principalities. Adjudged too nationalistic, the assemblies of the boyars were suppressed. Moldavia and Wallachia, which demanded union, were to be kept separated, each one continuing to be governed by its *hospodar*. The *hospodars* would no longer be appointed for life but for terms of seven years subsequent to Russo-Turkish approval. Barbu Shtirbey was installed in Wallachia and Gregor Alexander Ghica in Moldavia. Russia's occupation would be continued until the restoration of stability. This provision prevented the stipulation of a deadline for its duration. Thus the revolution of 1848 was followed by a cruel disappointment for Rumanian nationalists. The Principalities were restored to their former status under the watch of two protectors.

These developments, however, failed to extinguish the flames of nationalism which had been ignited, especially since the West began to exhibit interest in the fate of Moldavia and Wallachia. The principle of nationality was encountering increasing favor on the part of liberal public opinion. It found an ardent champion in Emperor Napoleon III for whom the questions of Italian and Rumanian unity were somehow related. Rumanian nationalists who had sought refuge in France pleaded the cause of their nation and succeeded in securing audiences in France and England. The Rumanian question was not yet formally raised, but people were beginning to learn of Rumanian claims.

When the dispute over shrines in the Holy Land broke out in 1853, it was for Tsar Nicholas merely a pretext to impose on Sultan Abdul Mejid the acceptance of a protectorate over the Orthodox Christians. Met with Turkish opposition encouraged by English foreign secretary Palmerston and Emperor Napoleon III, Nicholas resorted to preventive measures which had become classic. In the summer of 1853 the Russians occupied the Principalities for the eighth time. After crossing the Pruth River the Russians, profiting from numerous prior experiences, strived to appear as liberators and secure support of the Rumanian aristocracy. But, after encircling Russian troops at Silistria, the Turkish forces under Omer Pasha crossed the Danube and began to repulse the Russians. At length, Austria's hostile attitude and the priority of operations in the Crimea obliged Nicholas to evacuate the Principalities. Squeezed between two strong neighbors, the unfortunate Principalities escaped the ambitions of one only to become the prey of the other. Austrian troops soon arrived to assume the places vacated by the departure of Russia's forces.

The Congress of Paris in 1856 was for Russia a considerable step in her faltering Balkan policy. As far as the Principalities were concerned, the protectorate established by Russia was abolished and replaced by a collective guarantee of the powers. Turkey's sovereignty was reaffirmed, but the sultan was obliged to grant Moldavia and Wallachia the privilege of an independent, native administration. Moreover, Russia was required to retrocede the districts of Ismail, Cahul, and Bolgrad in southern Bessarabia which had been acquired by the Treaty of Bucharest of 1812 and whose possession had given Russia control of the Danube mouths. Freedom of navigation on the Danube was established and an international commission was created to guarantee respect for that principle which was of incalculable significance for the Rumanians whose fate was inexorably bound up with that of the great water artery. The Rumanian determination to secure Bessarabia was explained by a need to control the Danube delta located in southern Bessarabia. Occupation of southern Bessarabia was of vital interest for the peoples of central and eastern Europe because it offered much more security for freedom of navigation on the Danube than that of a great power.

Although frequently asserted that Rumania owed her independence to Russian intervention, this affirmation is only partially accurate. If Russian policy had always been very active in this regard, it was by no means disinterested. Rumania's progress toward independence was sometimes aided by Russia and sometimes hampered by Russia. The most striking example of this dualism was furnished by the Congress of Paris when the diminution of Russian strength permitted a discernible improvement in the fate of the Principalities. The Crimean War had restored Turkish authority over the Principalities. For the protectorate which Russia had previously acquired over the Orthodox Christians in the Balkans was substituted the solemn promise of the sultan to improve their lot—a promise noted by the powers who declared their recognition of its value.

But difficulties soon arose. Removed from Russia's protection, the Principalities became uncertain of their fate. An active campaign for union of the two Principalities had arisen. Promoters of a national, literary movement were active in inspiring this campaign. Among them was Vasile Alecsandri (1821-90), the Rumanian lyric poet and a noted nationalist. The Moldavians and Wallachians, of the same ethnic origin and having similar histories, interests, and enemies, were about to share the same destiny. Nothing really justified a prolongation of the separation of the two Principalities. But the powers did not agree on this topic. As an ardent partisan of a solution which would gratify his nationalism, Emperor Napoleon III supported the union which appeared to him to offer the advantage of establishing a barrier to Russian expansionism. But the Turks naturally opposed this French scheme. The sultan had the unconditional support of England who was fascinated by the dogma of the territorial integrity of the Ottoman Empire. Austria, who rarely failed to oppose national aspirations on the part of her subjects, also supported the Turks.

Confronted by these policies, Napoleon III, according to a procedure dear to his heart, suggested consultations by the interested parties. Special assemblies called *divans* were convened in the Principalities for the purpose of discussing unification. Turkish intrigues and Austria's occupation vitiated a plebiscite because the electoral lists were arranged to exclude a sizable number of voters. Threats and corruption did the rest. The result was such as might have been anticipated. Only a minority of electors participated in the plebiscite, and this minority voted against unification.

It was more than a scandal; it was really derision. Napoleon III was not a person to be duped. He demanded of the Ottoman government the nullification of the elections and supported his demand by recalling his ambassador from Constantinople. Russia imitated his example. At the same time, Napoleon, meeting with Queen Victoria at Osborne, convinced England of the need for a new consultation. It took place in September 1857 under unrestricted circumstances. The consequence was a complete reversal of the preceding results. Only three candidates opposed to union were elected this time and 84 in favor of union were the victors. The newly elected candidates immediately demanded complete autonomy, a constitutional government, and the appointment of a foreigner as prince of the united Principalities.

A conference met in Paris in May 1858 to decide on a regime for the Principalities. England opposed union, and Napoleon III could not satisfy the wishes of the Rumanian nationalists. Not only was Turkish sovereignty reaffirmed, symbolized by continued tribute, but also the separation of the two Principalities was affirmed despite the plebiscite. Although two distinct governments were to be maintained, the powers created a common organism to unify laws, coinage, justice, defense, etc. A concession to the impatience of the patriots was the coining of the title "United Principalities" to denote their country. This indirect manner of arriving at administrative union was nevertheless a deep disappointment for the Rumanians who did not anticipate the powers would create a situation which failed to conform to their wishes.

Filled with rancor, the Rumanian nationalists resolved to mistrust the benevolence of their protectors and to proceed toward unification themselves. They arrived at this triumph with skill and elegance. In January 1859 the assembly at Jassy in Moldavia first and then the one at Bucharest in Wallachia elected as governor the same person, Alexander Cuza (or Couza) (1820-73), a native boyar from Moldavia, who had participated in the 1848 revolution and had been a prefect of the port of Galatz. Unlike most of his fellow nobles, Cuza recognized a sense of political and social responsibility. He was assisted by Michael Kogalniceanu, the historian and social reformer. Thus by an artful ruse the two Principalities were united at a time when the attention of the powers was directed at another question of union. Austria, the principal opponent of union, was embroiled in an effort to prevent the Kingdom of Piedmont-Sardinia from unifying the Italian states. France supported Italian nationalism, and war was imminent.

Under such conditions the powers could only acquiesce in the clearly expressed will of the Rumanians. Turkey even accepted the *fait accompli*. Emboldened by these developments, Cuza moved ahead. Although required to submit to an investiture ceremony by the sultan, he nevertheless bestowed the title of prince of Rumania on himself. In December 1861 the name "United Principalities" was abandoned in favor of "Rumania." Cuza attempted to abolish all traces of differentiation between the two Principalities and to merge into a single unit their legislatures and administrations. After succeeding in this task, Cuza then boldly introduced reforms, uprooting institutions and habits which he expected to modernize with a wrench of his wrist. No area escaped his notice.

Of the numerous reforms Cuza undertook, all were not equally welcomed. So, confronted by a growing opposition, he engineered a *coup d'état* on March 28, 1864 in order to carry out his plans to reorganize the country. Although all could rejoice to see education become compulsory, two universities founded, and communications improved, the nobility could not cheer Cuza's great agrarian reform by which serfdom was abolished. Emancipated from obligations to the nobility, who were compensated for their losses, the peasants could become small landed proprietors. Secularization of ecclesiastical property was injurious to the Greek Orthodox clergy who had been the major holders of this wealth.

Cuza, however, was gradually losing popular support. If his private life and personality had acquired respect, perhaps his reforms would not have provoked animated reaction. Having been hailed as a liberator, he was now alienating the country by his dictatorial manners which were imitations of those of Napoleon III, his protector and model, and also by his haughtiness and lax morals. The nobility and clergy, whose interests he had injured, united so well against Cuza that a conspiracy was plotted which, during the night of February 23, 1866, forced open the doors of his palace and obliged him to abdicate.

Rumania then faced a problem experienced by Greece almost a half-century earlier. The designation of a ruler from a foreign dynasty was imposed to calm local passions and to reestablish order among a young people who were still groping along. The crown was offered to the son of Leopold II, King of Belgium, who declined. Napoleon III intervened in favor of his candidate, Prince Charles of the Catholic Hohenzollern-Sigmaringen family of southern Germany. Memories of his childhood in Germany and distant family ties between the Bonapartes and Hohenzollerns were hardly an adequate excuse to justify the French emperor's choice.

The choice, moreover, encountered scant favor among the powers. King William I of Prussia, fearing complications on the eve of his war with Austria, hesitated granting approval. Russia did not conceal opposition to having a German prince directing the destiny of a country on her frontier. But Napoleon upheld the candidacy with tenacity equal to that he would use in 1870 in fighting the candidacy of Charles' brother Leopold for the Spanish throne. He persuaded the Rumanians to elect the German prince, and, encouraged by his support, they chose Charles in a plebiscite.

Would the powers again accept a *fait accompli*? Bismarck, the

Prussian chancellor, persuaded the young prince to accept the summons. When the latter expressed misgivings, Bismarck said to him, "Why not try the experience? If you succeed, so much the better for you. If you fail, you will return to us with interesting memories." Apparently convinced by this subtle advice, Charles departed, crossed Austria in disguise, and, after arriving in Bucharest, was enthroned amid general acclamation. The Austro-Prussian War had just broken out and was distracting Europe's attention. Only Turkey pretended to resist the accession of Charles by mobilizing some troops, but the sultan yielded because of general European indifference. Thus was installed on Rumania's throne a Prussian prince who was crowned by the grace of a French emperor who, more effectively than anyone, had done a service for the King of Prussia. This was a strange aberration whose consequences would become significant in 1914.

Charles, a 27-year-old officer in the Prussian army, became "Carol" according to the Rumanian appellation. A very serious but liberal prince, he had a high conception of his duties. After learning the needs of his new subjects, Carol methodically applied himself to improving conditions and introducing obedience to discipline in a country where it had not been very prominent until his reign. Disturbed by years of agitation, hasty reforms, and corrupt regimes, Rumania finally came to appreciate order and respect for obedience. In July 1866 a constitution, based on the Belgian charter of 1831, established a bicameral legislature and assured freedom of conscience, press, and assembly, and promised equality before the law. The Orthodox faith was declared the state religion under the leadership of a church which was independent of the Greek Patriarch. From this dated a really new epoch.

The new ruler wisely administered a country which would be indebted to him for facilitating its true beginnings and rapidly consolidating its international status. The dignity of his personal life, contrasted with the atmosphere of callous frivolity preceding his reign, was shared by his wife, Princess Elizabeth of Wied, who was completely devoted to her new homeland. Under the pseudonym of "Carmen Sylva" she publicized Rumania by her poems, novels, and collections of folklore.

Two political parties vied for power in the country. The Conservatives supported by the nobility and clergy, had Germanophile tendencies. The Liberals, led by the Bratianus, had a growing middle class basis and leaned toward France. Prince Carol governed by adroitly arbitrating their differences and by his personal prestige which assured Rumania's fame abroad. Because of the energetic and perceptive impulse of her ruler, who presided over the destiny of his new homeland from 1866 to 1914, Rumania soon took a very honored place in the European family of nations while Serbia was still being disturbed by violence and Greece was still hesitatingly seeking her way. But Rumania was still not a fully independent country. Still under Turkish sovereignty, Rumania's vassalage was quite nominal until 1876 when, as a result of Turkey's plan to impose Ottoman citizenship on all subjects in the empire, the last tie had to be broken. The occasion was soon available. It was the outbreak of the Russo-Turkish War which allowed Carol to show the magnitude of his spirit by joining Russia on Bismarck's advice. According to a secret agreement of April 1877, Carol gave free passage to Russian troops and then joined the Russians against the Turks at the siege of Plevna. The Turks demanded Carol's removal to which the Rumanian ruler replied by proclaiming the independence of his country on May 11, 1877.

At the outset Russia ignored Rumania's military assistance which appeared initially negligible. But when Russian troops were pinned down at Plevna, they were glad to see Rumanian detachments arrive and conduct themselves quite brilliantly. It was due to Rumanian valor that Plevna would ultimately surrender. The fall of that fortress permitted the Russians to advance to the suburbs of Constantinople and to impose on Turkey the Treaty of San Stefano (March 3, 1878). The Rumanians were not invited to participate in the negotiations which was for them a bitter disappointment. Despite the appreciable effort the Rumanians had contributed to Russia's victory, the latter showed no gratitude. On the contrary, Russia required the cession of southern Bessarabia taken away by the Congress of Paris in 1856. The Russians explained this away as a mere retrocession. As compensation Russia gave Rumania the northern Dobrudja, a rather infertile region inhabited by more Bulgarians and Turks than Rumanians located south of the Danube delta and north of Silistria. This exchange did not deny Rumania the status of a riparian state on the Danube River, whose southern banks the

Rumanians continued to own. This advantage plus an extension of her coastline along the Black Sea did not mitigate the discontent and indignation aroused in Rumania as a consequence of Russia's high-handed treatment of her southern neighbor.

The Congress of Berlin in July 1878, to which Rumanian delegates were denied admittance, ratified this situation, including the retrocession of southern Bessarabia to Russia. This award was considered adequate compensation for Russia's abandonment of her project to create a greater Bulgaria in the Treaty of San Stefano. Although Rumania had to suffer the consequences, at least the Rumanians could find some consolation in having their independence affirmed and freedom of navigation on the Danube assured.

In 1880, at the insistence of Russia, a commission to delimit the boundaries of the Dobrudja refused to award the fortress of Silistria to Rumania. This was an additional disappointment which accentuated hostility toward Russia and provoked protests in Rumania. Russia's attitude had been dictated by a design to favor the Bulgarian state of which the former hoped to make a satellite. By securing for Bulgaria the stronghold of Silistria, Russia hoped to ring Rumania with reminders of her power. "It is preferable to have Russia as an enemy than as a protector," Carol would have said.

With recognition of Rumania's independence, the last tie with Turkey was broken after a vassalage of five centuries. But the new state was still only a principality. In March 1881 Carol crossed the last hurdle by proclaiming himself king and having his crown fashioned from metal melted down from Turkish cannon seized at Plevna. With 5 million inhabitants forming a homogeneous group except for a large Jewish minority of about 200,000, whose persecution would soon cause international anxieties, Moldavia and Wallachia, transformed into an independent kingdom, became the most powerful country in the Balkans. But the unification of all Rumanians was by no means achieved. Beyond the frontiers, their brethren in Transylvania, already demanding liberation from Hungarian rule, as well as their brothers in Bessarabia and Bukovina, were calling for a reunion of the common fatherland. A great task remained to be achieved.

CHAPTER IV

Bulgarian Independence

THE long Turkish domination succeeded in making the Bulgarian national consciousness more torpid than that of other oppressed Balkan peoples. Reasons for this have already been cited. Constantinople's proximity to Bulgaria caused the Turkish yoke to weigh more heavily on the Bulgarians than other peoples. Furthermore, the Greek Orthodox clergy also repressed their Bulgarian co-religionists. The abolition of the Bulgarian patriarchate at Tirnovo, proscription of the Bulgarian liturgy, the incineration of Bulgarian manuscripts—such were the means used to Hellenize the Bulgarians.

While inevitably suffering a foreign administration, it did not appear in the beginning as if the peasantry was noticeably more persecuted than before the Turkish domination. The peasants had long before grown accustomed to the harshness of the Bulgarian nobility. But now it was quite different for the nobility who, deprived of their privileges and denied all influence, were eliminated to the point of complete disappearance. Attempts by Bulgarians to rebel were very infrequent prior to the end of the 18th century. Even at the beginning of the 19th century the insurrections of the Serbs and Greeks and the agitation of the Rumanians produced only feeble reactions among the Bulgarians. Some outlaws attempted to arouse the peasants and a few volunteers joined Russian forces, but no actual movement arose. Was this due to indifference, resignation, or the impossibility of action? Whatever the reason, the Bulgarians remained aloof from a great movement which was convulsing the Balkans. Even their name was more or less unknown.

If the existence of most Balkan peoples went unnoticed, it was not so in the policy of Russia. Frequent incursions of Russian troops into the Danubian Principalities had furnished St. Petersburg with an awareness of a people on the southern banks of the Danube River who spoke a language akin to Old Church Slavonic, practiced the Orthodox religion, and claimed ties to the Slav community. After Russia's annexation of Bessarabia in 1812, the number of Bulgarian refugees seeking asylum in that province increased. During the Russo-Turkish War of 1828 some enlisted in the Russian army to combat the common enemy. Nevertheless, the Bulgarians were still hesistant about turning to Russia for protection as the Montenegrins and Serbs were doing.

Awakening of Bulgarian national consciousness stemmed from an intellectual rebirth of which the monasteries were cradles. Not only the distant one on Mount Athos, but also the one at Rila perched on the cliffs of the Rhodopes and hidden in a thick forest. In both studies were pursued which revived the past and recalled to the Bulgarians their ancient glories and rekindled in them a spirit which had lain dormant for centuries. This revival was all the more meritorious because the Greek clergy made strong efforts to suppress it. It was a monk at Mount Athos, Father Paisy (or Paisi), who wrote in 1762 his *History of the Bulgarian People, Tsars, and Saints* in the Bulgarian language. "The Greeks and Serbs often insult us," he wrote in his naive preface, "because we have no history. That is why I have undertaken to bring these materials together." His work was an act of patriotic faith which appealed to the Bulgarians to return to traditions of a forgotten past and to break the ties which bound them to an alien culture. Abandoning the use of Greek in his writings, which until then was required, Paisy was the first Bulgarian intellectual to demand liberation from Hellenic culture. His name has since been surrounded with infinite respect as the animator of the national revival. As Louis Léger, the French historian of the Slavs, wrote— every cultivated Bulgarian had believed himself to be Greek just as formerly Czechs of high station thought in German. Until then a peasant dialect, the Bulgarian language was suddenly promoted, thanks to Father Paisy, to the rank of a cultural tongue worthy of figuring in literary publications. Paisy's book was a revelation.

Bulgaria's steps toward emancipation henceforth developed slowly but with deliberate continuity. An impulse having been provided, Paisy's example being the first, imitators were thus inspired. The most famous was Bishop Sofroni of Vrasta who attracted attention by preaching in Bulgarian and writing in his language a set of memoirs which, more than the splendors of the past, evoked the misfortunes of the present. Published in Bucharest in 1803, Sofroni's book was the first printed in the Bulgarian language. Efforts to spread and promote the national language and culture contributed to a gradual revival of national consciousness and pride in a common origin. Did not Bulgarian have as much right as Greek to exist in the literary realm? Proof of this was furnished by the works of Bulgarian scholars.

Bulgarians living abroad, mostly businessmen in Rumania or Russia (about 40,000 lived in Bessarabia), encouraged this movement. Their contacts with already developed nations had awakened their spirit more rapidly than if they had remained in their own country, stifled under the Turkish yoke. In the same way their fortunes, generally greater than those of their compatriots, permitted them to uphold the national cause with financial support. This was a phenomenon analogous to that which had impelled the Greek Phanariots in the Danubian Principalities to play a vital role in the first struggles for Greek independence.

In Bucharest was a relatively large Bulgarian colony with considerable financial resources. Another flourished in Odessa. Both envisaged emancipation of their homeland. These exiled patriots found zealous support from a Ukrainian known as Yurii Venelin who was in favor of their cause. With Russian money, Venelin undertook to make the Bulgarians known in Europe by one of his books, *The Ancient and the New Bulgarians,* published in 1829. Venelin also began to study the Bulgarian tongue, but he died a young man at Odessa not without the satisfaction of having "recalled to the world a forgotten nation."

Efforts to purify the language and restore its original characteristics soon gave Bulgarian the rank of a literary language. Works in modern Bulgarian began to be printed about the year 1825. Schools soon opened to assure the propagation of the language and culture. In 1835, a significant date in the history of modern Bulgaria, a disciple of Venelin, Vasili Aprilov, who was a wealthy Bulgarian merchant in Odessa, opened the first secondary school offering education in the national language to pupils at Gabrovo, not far from Sofia. This example was so swiftly imitated that within a decade about 50 similar institutions were opened. The first printing press to utilize the Bulgarian language was set up in Salonika in 1839. Another was established in Constantinople. Soon presses were introduced into Bulgaria where the first newspaper was founded in 1844.

Quite unanticipated was the fact that this nation of tenacious peasants, hard workers little attracted by intellectual activities, soon revealed itself to be curious about knowledge, avid to learn, and very well endowed. The industriousness with which Bulgarians tilled their soil also showed in their learning and assimilating knowledge.

By the middle of the 19th century Bulgaria was slower than other Balkan nations in the march to independence. But the Bulgarians would succeed by obstinate labor in hastening their progress to reach the pace of their neighbors by the turn of the century. About the middle of the 19th century a leader appeared. He was George Rakovski (1818–68), poet, historian, journalist, and agitator. After studying in Paris, Constantinople, and Moscow, he wandered in the countries bordering Bulgaria to awaken national consciousness. Inspired by rebellion in Serbia, he provoked an uprising at Gabrovo which the Turks suppressed. This did not deter him from establishing a revolutionary committee in Bucharest. At his side were Luben Karavelov (1840–1903), his nephew, and Dragan Tsankov (1827–1911) who would be later distinguished as leaders of the intellectual awakening. Karavelov, who had also studied abroad, agitated among émigré Bulgarians and was one of the first to write in his native language short stories which made him the precursor of his nation's novelists.

A few young men from the small minority of wealthy families attended Robert College (founded in Constantinople in 1871), the great American educational establishment in the Balkans. After being educated along western lines, they returned home with ideas of freedom. Gradually such notions spread beyond the restricted circle of the élite to reach an increasing number of people. The movement's leaders realized it would be senseless to expect immediate liberation. They had a more modest goal, namely to awaken national consciousness and then to gradually shake off centuries-old bondage to a foreign yoke.

Russia observed this evolution with considerable interest. The prospect of extending Russian influence over a new Balkan people whose Slavic sympathies and aspirations were being aroused was brought to the attention of the government by the Pan-Slavs. Russia had already encouraged rebels at Nish in 1841 and Vidin in 1851. Although lacking weapons, the insurgents fought with daggers, sickles, and pickaxes, and were fiercely crushed by the Turks. Murder, rape, and arson were the means by which the rebels sought revenge. As for hopes aroused by the approach of Russian forces during the Crimean War, only disillusionment resulted. The situation worsened when the Turks sent Kurds and Circassians into Bulgaria where they conducted themselves as robbers, pillaging and holding luckless peasants for ransom. The just administration of Midhat Pasha, the Turkish governor 1864–68, who attempted implementation of the reforms contained in the *Tanzimat,* improved the situation to a limited extent. Of Pomak (Moslem Bulgarian) ancestry, Midhat Pasha established schools, agrarian banks to lend to the peasants at minimum interest rates, and a degree of stability in the country. But the era of administrative reforms had vanished; that of national demands was beginning.

After the Congress of Paris required Russia to withdraw from the Balkans, the tsar's government, seeking venegeance, pursued a still more active policy by giving it a Pan-Slav basis. In 1856 a Slavic rescue committee was created in St. Petersburg which did not ignore Bulgaria's awakening. By subsidies, book distribution, and other activities, the committee encouraged the development of schools and religious centers to fortify national sentiment and to relate it to a Slav idealism. A Bulgarian committee founded in Odessa received active encouragement as did all agents involved in propaganda work. The national concept had always been closely bound to religious idealism among the Balkan peoples. The symbol of belief, the church, was also a type of flag. Hence the determination of the leaders of Bulgaria's awakening to concentrate upon ridding their church of Greek influences.

The struggle would be arduous, but the Bulgarians were patient and tenacious. Their pretensions collided with the opposition of the Greek Patriarchate, which was very influential in Constantinople and resolved to perpetuate its religious authority upon which was superimposed Turkish political power. After the Crimean War Turkish promises to respect freedom of worship encouraged the Bulgarians to double their efforts to secure the appointment of native bishops. But the Greek clergy still hindered them. Disappointed, angered, and determined to be free from Greek domination, a few patriots hinted at turning to the Papacy and Roman Catholicism. An alarm quickly resounded in Holy Orthodox Russia which refused to countenance any such moves. Anxiety also arose in England where it appeared as if France

were attempting to extend influence over the Balkans. Assured of
Russian support, a Bulgarian priest in Constantinople one day
ignored the name of the Greek Patriarch in his public prayers.
This was tantamount to rejecting the latter's authority and constituting an act of defiance. Protests arose on one side and
obstinacy on the other until Russia demanded a solution to the
crisis. The dispute dragged on amid violence. Greek clergy in
Bulgaria had nationalists thrown into prison. At length, despite
its hesitation to intercede in religious controversies among Christians, the Turkish government, angered by prolongation of the
dispute and fearful of its becoming the pretext of new intercession
by the powers, agreed to creation of a Bulgarian Exarchate
separate from the Greek Patriarchate. The Exarchate was first
established in Constantinople but later moved to Bulgaria in
1870. Fifteen ecclesiastical districts were established between
Nish and Veles over which the Bulgarian Exarch was given
authority. This circumscription was interpreted as recognition of
the essentially Bulgarian character of large parts of Macedonia
and Thrace as well as Bulgaria proper.

This was considered a victory for the cause of Bulgarian nationalism. The Bulgarians finally had a national church. Ignoring
the excommunication by the Greek Patriarch, the nationalists rejoiced in adhering to an institution which was representative of
their unity and which was theirs exclusively. One consequence was
the phenomenal growth in school development. If the religious
emancipation denoted significant progress, it served all the more
to inspire political liberation. After 1870 agitation among the
peasants, who had been more difficult to arouse than other classes,
assumed considerable proportions under the stimulus of émigré
committees.

Although students and journalists were less patient than businessmen and landowners, a single patriotic ideal animated all.
Rakovski had been succeeded by Vasil Levski, of violent revolutionary temperament, who, after eluding the Turkish police for
years, was finally betrayed and hanged in 1873. Another agitator
destined for a greater role was Stefan Stambulov (Stambolov or
Stambuloff) (1855–95), a crude but very energetic statesman
known for his eloquence, who pursued his career while eluding
all attempts to capture him. Hopes were aroused when the
northern Balkans were about to erupt into war in 1875.

The uprising of the Bosnians in 1875 activated numerous revolutionary activities. Serbia soon supported the claims of her kinsmen by declaring war on Turkey. More than 2,000 Bulgarian volunteers joined the Serbian army. In April 1876 the Bulgarians revolted against Turkish rule under Stambulov's leadership. The Turks repressed them with utmost vigor. Assisted by Bulgarian Moslems (Pomaks) and Circassians, the latter having been settled in Bulgaria to colonize the region, Turkish troops raided insurgent villages and drowned the rebellion in blood. Among a defenseless people this was a veritable carnage which did not spare women and children. Estimates of the number of victims varied between ten and fifteen thousand. About sixty communities were destroyed, and many churches were pillaged and burned. At Panagyurishte in central Bulgaria the resistance of about a thousand rebels infuriated the Turks who massacred all of them indiscriminately. In the small town of Batak at the foot of the Rhodopes, the bloody folly exceeded all imagination. The entire population of about 5,000 was massacred after two days of defense. This deed coincided with the accession to the throne of Sultan Abdul Hamid II (1876–1909) who could have claimed the title of "Red Sultan" which the later massacre of the Armenians gained for him in 1894–95.

News of these "Bulgarian Horrors," followed by the burning of villages and monasteries and the theft of cattle, aroused intense emotions abroad. A general revulsion was manifested. It appeared with greatest impact in England where William Gladstone, the former prime minister, wrote a celebrated pamphlet inveighing against the atrocities. James Bourchier, the noted journalist of the London *Times,* hastened to Bulgaria where he reported scenes of cruelty with a reportorial realism which aroused Europe's indignation and for which the Bulgarians held for him much gratitude. The atrocities excited the Bulgarians into demanding an immediate end to the Turkish regime which had just given irrefutable proof of its incapacity as well as of its cruelty.

The powers named commissioners to investigate the situation. They merely confirmed the sad reality. Suddenly the fate of the Bulgarians, almost totally ignored until then, became a general preoccupation of the powers. In December 1876 a conference was called at Constantinople to discuss the situation. Still hesitant about compromising the territorial integrity of the Ottoman Empire, the powers suggested the appointment of Christian governors who would administer a Bulgaria divided into two provinces. Abdul Hamid rejected all concessions and reverted to an old device. He issued a new constitution, drawn up by Midhat Pasha, which conferred on all his subjects the rights of liberty and equality. This document, issued on December 23, 1876, declared the indivisibility of the empire and promised parliamentary government based on general representation.

Russia was not deceived by this maneuver. St. Petersburg had taken the Bulgarian cause to heart and was not about to abandon plans to regain influence in the Balkans. In April 1877 Russia declared war on Turkey. After signing a secret agreement with Prince Carol, Russian troops crossed Rumania and arrived at the banks of the Danube. These forces met with a warm welcome but received little military assistance from the Bulgarians. The latter had been oppressed for so long that they were poorly prepared to take any appreciable part in the war against Turkey. But despite the terrible reprisals just experienced, the people used their ingenuity to feed the liberating forces, serve as guides, and to furnish them with information. Doubtless many volunteers, reviving the exploits of the medieval heyduks, joined the Tsar's regiments. Their limited cooperation was appreciated when the Russians had to traverse the Shipka pass which, from a height of about 2,000 feet, overlooks the plain leading to Adrianople and the Straits. Despite tenacious resistance, the Turks were obliged to yield before the Russian advance which was guided by Bulgarian scouts. Today a church and seminary stand near a cemetery in which are interred Russians and Bulgarians who died in combat to clear the pass. Their brotherhood-in-arms is thus commemorated.

Although the Bulgarian volunteers lacked training and experience, they did fight bravely. The Russian forces, after assigning the Bulgarians the duty of cleaning up Turkish garrisons to the rear, advanced rapidly and captured Adrianople. By mid-January 1878 the walls of Constantinople, the coveted city, appeared before the eyes of the astonished Russian soldiers. To assault the capital would have aroused all Europe against the Tsar's ambitions. Alexander II had to be content with imposing on Turkey a severe treaty signed at San Stefano, a suburb of Constantinople, on March 3, 1878.

Almost unknown before the war, Bulgaria now found herself promoted to the rank of an autonomous principality of immense size. The Russians had literally resurrected the empire of Simeon and the Asens. After having slumbered for six centuries, Bulgaria was reborn with frontiers extending from the Danube to the Aegean, from the Black Sea to the banks of the Timok River including the city of Nish in the west, and it even dipped into Macedonia to include Skoplje, Okhrida, and Presba, then down the Vardar River to end at Lule Burgas and Midia in the east. As a result of the treaty, Bulgaria became the largest country in the Balkans. With 4½ million inhabitants it occupied about three-fifths of the entire peninsula. Severed into two parts by the new delimitation, the Ottoman Empire in Europe possessed only Constantinople, Adrianople, Salonika, a small part of Macedonia, and Albania.

Having renounced plans to seize the Straits, Russia sought to be assured of fruitful compensation by the creation in the center of the Balkans of an enormous state which, entirely indebted for its creation to Russian intervention, could only gravitate in St. Petersburg's orbit. At a single stroke Russian influence leaped from the banks of the Danube to the warm waters of the Aegean Sea. This new situation aroused an alarm in Europe which was as critical as if Russia had laid hands on Constantinople. The creation of a great Bulgaria by the Treaty of San Stefano was an inadmissible deed. It was deemed so in the European chancelleries and contrary to the articles of the Treaty of Paris (1856) guaranteeing the territorial integrity of the Ottoman Empire. The San Stefano peace had to be revised. England was the most vocal power to protest, and exhibited her opposition by dispatching a flotilla to the Straits and mobilizing troops on Malta. Faced with firm protests, England's determination, and general disapproval of the treaty, Russia, after three months of hesitation, was resigned to having her achievements challenged again. This was the objective of the Congress of Berlin.

Great Bulgaria emerged from the Congress mutilated and divided into three parts. The territory between the Danube and the chain of the Balkan Mountains in the north was set up as an autonomous principality, with its capital at Sofia, under Turkish sovereignty. The region between the mountains and Adrianople, entitled Eastern Rumelia, remained within the Ottoman Empire and governed by a Christian pasha appointed by common accord of the powers. As for Thrace and Macedonia, both provinces were restored to Turkey. Since no one was really satisfied, these decisions bore the seeds of conflict. For a brief moment conveyed to glorious heights, the Bulgarians saw their dream give way to an infinitely more modest reality, a little principality of less than 2 million inhabitants, at a time when they had expected to be more than double that. This disappointment would be engraved on their minds. In the years to come Bulgaria would feel cheated of her rights. The territorial awards of the Treaty of San Stefano would remain those Bulgaria claimed as legitimate, and her policy would always aim to recover the land the Congress of Berlin had denied her.

The 800,000 inhabitants of Eastern Rumelia, disappointed at their separation from brethren in Bulgaria, did not conceal a resolve to rejoin them as soon as possible. The people of Macedonia, restored to Turkish domination from which they expected to be released, would pursue their agitations even more. To cap the entire demoralization, young Bulgaria was deprived of the districts of Nish and Pirot, which were awarded to Serbia and whose attribution would embitter relations between the two Slav states.

While awaiting the appointment of a prince, Bulgaria, freed but worn out and ravaged, was governed by a Russo-Bulgarian commission with the weak assistance of the sultan's representative and the consuls of the other powers. Forced to accept the wreck of her designs, Russia strove to bend the new Bulgaria to her will. The importance of the sacrifices for Bulgaria which Russia had made caused St. Petersburg to hope for a docile vassalage by grateful Bulgarians. Prince Dondukov, the Russian commissioner, supported by a strong military occupation, governed as a great lord the region he regarded as a virtual Russian province. All command posts were in his officers' hands. His primary concern was to organize a Bulgarian army as support for Russian forces.

If Bulgaria appreciated the services rendered by Russia, she was nevertheless quite jealous of a long-awaited independence, won at great cost, and whose privileges she wished to exercise immediately. Inexperienced as the Bulgarians were, there existed certain young groups full of zeal and patriotism, who were impatient to give everything to assume control of their homeland's destiny. Russia's protectorate, lacking subtlety and discretion, offended the proud, xenophobic Bulgarians whose peasant temperament was based on jealousy and mistrust. The Russians so quickly lost their popularity that certain Bulgarians became oriented toward Austria. Vienna very skillfully dangled before their eyes certain commercial advantages which were attractive to a people whose existence depended almost exclusively upon the sale of agricultural produce.

Bulgaria's first task was to create a constitution. This was an effort which complete lack of political experience, ignorance of the workings of parliamentary government, and even the existence of an illiterate population rendered particularly hazardous. As Bismarck once remarked about Bulgaria, which had passed from oppression to freedom without real transition, "Bulgaria was being placed in the saddle before having learned to ride horseback."

At Tirnovo (also Trnovo), a city rich in memories, a motley constituent assembly was convened under Dondukov's chairmanship in February 1879. Representatives from the clergy, the professions, and especially peasants in heavy boots and sheepskin hats vainly attempted to raise the question of Eastern Rumelia. The assembly of 233 members finally framed a very democratic constitution which provided for a bicameral legislature elected by universal manhood suffrage. But such a radical creation could not be implemented because of a provision incorporated into the constitution. Suffrage was granted exclusively to the very few literate voters. Freedom of the press and elections were among other rights included in the constitution.

The selection of a prince still remained. Since Bulgaria lacked a nobility, the prince had to be an alien. The choice of the Sobranie, the new assembly, fell by acclamation on Prince Alexander of Battenberg (1857–93), nephew of Tsar Alexander II, whose candidacy was more agreeable to Russia than that of Prince Waldemar of Denmark who was also considered. Twenty-two years old, Alexander was a model Prussian officer without political inclinations. He had served in the Russian army against Turkey in 1877–78.

The Bulgarians required a capital. The Sobranie chose Sofia, still a rather small village, rather than Tirnovo because it offered better prospects for growth as well as easier contacts with the West.

Many obstacles led the Bulgarians to stumble in their first steps.

There were exaggerated hopes for the new regime, competition among aspirants for government appointments, bitterness toward the powers, and impatience with Russia's protectorate. "Have we escaped the Turkish yoke only to bow under the Russian knout?" they asked. For their apprenticeship in politics the Bulgarians, "who were simultaneously inert and recalcitrant," had accepted as their guide a very young man as ignorant as they of viable government.

Prince Alexander betrayed the impression of being instructed by the Russian emperor. When he arrived in Sofia Russian commissioner Dondukov departed, but he left Russian officers to command an army of 100,000 Bulgarians whom they had carefully trained. The prince was surrounded by a team of Russian advisers who considered Bulgarian nationalists to be dangerous revolutionaries. This was a grave miscalculation of a people whose tendencies were quite democratic. The Russian view soon aroused hostility toward the young prince whose welcome had been acclaimed at first. Tall, elegant in his uniform, seriously involved in his post and eager to secure good will, Alexander was sincerely full of ambition. But unfortunately torn between the struggle among conservatives and liberals, the prince developed, under Russian pressures, a following of conservatives only when the majority in the Sobranie was liberal. Confronted by vigorous opposition, Alexander's cabinet was forced to resign and it was not replaced. This provoked a dissolution of the Sobranie.

When elections returned a considerable liberal majority, Alexander had to select a cabinet from among them. The liberals had no specific political views, preferring satisfaction for their petty vengeances over organization of a country where everything remained to be created. The conservatives were still in a strong position to compensate for their loss, so much so that Alexander decided upon a *coup d'état*. In April 1881, encouraged by Tsar Alexander III, his cousin, who was less cautious than his predecessor, the prince took advantage of the anarchy to suspend the constitution and install again a regime dominated by the Russians. The latter rigged the subsequent elections so that only four liberals were elected to the Sobranie. However, they refused to take their seats. The Sobranie was then dissolved after the prince delivered an address in which he arrogated to himself exclusive powers. His dictatorship by no means restored stability. Prince Alexander summoned two Russian officers to terminate resistance. They were expected to exert pressure, but their attitude soon made Alexander regret having summoned them. By a curious paradox the officers flattered the liberals by alienating the conservatives in such a way that the prince was becoming suspect, even by the Russians. Alexander, impatient to remove the Russian officers, decided to restore the constitution in September 1883. Most of the Russians were immediately recalled home, and the unfortunate prince, who had originally accepted Russia's patronage, incurred an enmity which would soon be fatal.

While Bulgaria experienced obstacles to her development, an agitation of another type was exciting the Bulgarians in Eastern Rumelia. Deeply disillusioned by having been restored to Turkish rule, the latter Bulgarians vehemently clamored for union with Bulgaria. A very complex political regime had assured them certain privileges, such as the convening of an assembly and the appointment of a Christian governor. The latter, Aleko Pasha, an experienced diplomat of Greek ancestry, had a breadth of spirit which gave Eastern Rumelia the advantage of an administration quite superior to that prevailing in adjacent Bulgaria. But this did not suffice to appease popular demands. The powers appeared disinterested in the fate of Eastern Rumelia. But by a strange shift, Russia, now a trustee of the Treaty of Berlin signed at her expense, became hostile to a union which would have enlarged Bulgaria, whose ingratitude had seriously wounded her pride.

The Bulgarians of Eastern Rumelia, frustrated in their hopes, decided upon a show of force. In September 1885 a plot was conceived during which Aleko Pasha was seized and union with Bulgaria was proclaimed. Prince Alexander's unionist sympathies were well known. He had perhaps been too favorable at the risk of alienating his Russian protectors. Although he could not resist rejoicing to see union demanded, he was quite anxious about anticipated reactions. The sultan would certainly oppose a further amputation of his shrinking empire. Serbia, jealous of her neighbor's expansion, would also oppose union. And what about the attitude of the powers and especially Russia?

The powers again decided upon convening a conference in Constantinople to treat the crisis. Prince Alexander, anticipating hesitations by the powers and realizing any action might threaten his crown, decided to confirm the union by proclaiming himself at Tirnovo "Prince of Northern and Southern Bulgaria." The powers including Turkey bowed before this *fait accompli,* but Russia displayed ill-temper in recalling her officers from Bulgaria. Their departure produced no regrets in Bulgaria.

The most serious opposition came from Serbia. As expected, Belgrade demanded compensation. The crisis was exacerbated because several disputes regarding their mutual frontier had previously embittered relations. Was this not, Belgrade pondered, the occasion to delay the development of a young nation which was hardly constituted? How strong could Bulgaria's army be now that its Russian officers had departed? The Serbs dreamed of recreating the empire of Dushan at their neighbor's expense. Austria interceded in this crisis to offset Russian influence. Anticipating a swift and facile victory, Serbia's army crossed the Bulgarian frontier on November 1, 1885 before a declaration of war was issued.

Reality prepared an excruciating disappointment for the Serbs. The Bulgarian army, taken by surprise, retreated to Slivnitza. Sofia was threatened. After securing reinforcements the Bulgarians assumed the offensive and penetrated the Serbian lines. Threatened by encirclement, the Serbs retreated and were pursued toward Nish. This was a bloody defeat for the Serbs. Austria demanded an immediate cessation of hostilities. The war had lasted two weeks at a cost of 6,000 men on each side. The peace treaty, signed in Bucharest in February 1886, was a disappointment for Bulgaria. Serbia was not required to yield any territory or pay an indemnity. Nevertheless, the union of the two Bulgarias remained a *fait accompli,* recognized not only by the sultan but even by King Milan of Serbia. Young Prince Alexander returned to his capital a conquering hero whose bravery at Slivnitza had been quite spectacular.

Alexander's renewed popularity angered Russia whose government now strove to arouse opinion against him. The powers had consented only to a personal union of Bulgaria and Eastern Rumelia, a half-measure which could not restrain the course of events. The prince did not hesitate to convene a single national assembly which solemnly proclaimed union. This act not only enlarged Bulgaria, but it also added to her administrative personnel several Bulgarians of Eastern Rumelia who were considered more refined and less violent than their counterparts in Sofia.

Meanwhile, Tsar Alexander III (1881–94), harboring a personal grudge against Alexander of Battenberg, struck his name from the lists of the Russian army. The Tsar's rancor, which nothing could assuage, was even more prejudicial because a section of Bulgaria's public opinion realized how it could compromise the young nation's future. Moreover, a few high-handed acts of the prince alienated numerous officers. Encouraged by Russia, a group of army officers conspired with Tsankov, Karavelov, and others to remove the prince. Threatened with pistols, Alexander was taken from his bed, forced to abdicate, and exiled from Bulgaria (August 21, 1886).

Immediate repercussions arose. Bulgarians loyal to their sovereign reacted all the more promptly because pro-Russian expressions uttered by the conspirators alarmed their national susceptibilities. A counter-revolution was hatched in which Stephen Stambulov played a leading role, and Alexander was recalled. He returned to Sofia on August 29 quite disillusioned. He was greeted by a crowd who enthusiastically acclaimed the prince as the only one who could assure order in the turbulent country. Although Alexander sent a humble and deferential note to Tsar Alexander, he could not succeed in softening the latter's opposition. The Russian emperor replied with a very pointed reference to abdication. Prince Alexander was thus forced to admit defeat.

Abdication on September 4 was a cruel and ironic fate for the young man who had vainly devoted seven years to an effort to preside over the birth of a violent and susceptible nation. As a Russian protégé, Alexander had found himself incessantly torn between a protector who reproached him as an ingrate for wishing to secure independence and a people still in political limbo, torn by petty disputes, who accused him of being too submissive to Russia. The first years of free Bulgaria had seen nothing but a series of willful acts which made of her the bad child of Europe whom she seemed to be always flouting.

A group of his subjects remained thankful to Alexander for having organized an army which was victorious over the Serbs. For them he was the hero of Slivnitza, who had fought like a lion against a greedy and perfidious neighbor. As for Alexander, he left discouraged. More disgusted by demands of Russian imperialism than by the conspiracy of his own officials, Alexander did not long survive his Bulgarian adventure. He died in Austria in 1893.

A council of regency next directed affairs in which the energetic

Stambulov became the leader. Of modest origins, son of an inn-keeper, he was called upon to be dictator for about a decade. A small man with broad shoulders whose mongol-like face revealed a violence and opinionated rigidity inherited from his Asiatic heritage, cloaked in the prestige which his active role in the struggle for independence had won for him. Stambulov displayed an intransigent patriotism and anti-Russian sentiment as well as strong ambitions. He exercised power with harshness bordering on brutality which aroused considerable protest. Despite his almost total lack of culture and even more of formal education, it was impossible to deny his real political sense and incontestable domination. Perhaps it was especially necessary to use harsh methods to govern a people respectful only of force.

Stambulov relentlessly pursued his adversaries under the guise of reestablishing order. He demanded the absolute independence of Bulgaria. This was an intolerable pretension to Tsar Alexander who sent General Kaulbars to Sofia on a mission to restore Russian influence. The inevitable impasse arose through an exchange of angry notes. Bulgaria was about to announce her demands. Elections arranged according to a manner dear to Stambulov gave the Sobranie a heavy majority of anti-Russian nationalists. This constituted popular approval which encouraged Stambulov to double the severity of his hounding of suspects. Embittered by his failure, Kaulbars and his mission decided to leave Bulgaria. Russia denounced Bulgaria's choice of Prince Waldemar of Denmark to succeed Alexander. Plots continued to agitate the country. It was all the more urgent to name a ruler since the powers would never approve the confirmation of Stambulov's dictatorship.

A delegation combed Europe in quest of a prince only to learn that Bulgaria's throne could not attract candidates because of Russia's ostracism. Finally, after approaching Prince Ferdinand of Saxe-Coburg, an officer in the Austrian army, the Sobranie offered him the throne on July 7, 1887. Without awaiting Europe's reaction, Ferdinand arrived three days later in Sofia and took the constitutional oath.

Of royal German ancestry on his father's side and French on his mother's (Princess Clémentine, daughter of King Louis Philippe), the twenty-six-year-old prince began his reign under difficult circumstances. After securing for Bulgaria final admission to the family of nations, Ferdinand would end his reign in defeat and treason. He was a physically handsome man with a high forehead, light blue eyes, and a rather Bourbon type of nose. His relations with numerous royal courts gave him an assurance and authority which would profit Bulgaria. Very learned, he was interested not only in politics and literature, but also in the natural sciences, particularly botany about which he wrote a book of impressions gained on a journey to Brazil in 1879. A tireless worker, he soon began to learn the Bulgarian language and contributed to his adopted homeland the resources of a fertile, adroit, and supple mind. Ferdinand made a strong impression at the beginning of his reign, leaving to its end the revelation of his true character. He needed a strong resolve to face the prospect of governing a nation whose quarrelsome disposition was only too well known and for whom Russia's wrath remained unabated. Russia, in fact, refused to recognize the new sovereign. The other powers, influenced by Russia's rigidity, delayed granting recognition to Ferdinand. Bulgaria remained under the ban of Europe for several years. Deprived of a choice of policy and unable to anticipate a détente from Russia, Prince Ferdinand, ignorant of internal affairs, had to depend upon the formidable Stambulov. The presence of Ferdinand's mother in Sofia, whose famed goodness touched Bulgarian hearts, contributed to his popularity.

Stambulov had not changed his arbitrary or violent procedures. His opponents continued to concoct plots which provoked more repression and, consequently, hatred. United only in their desire to remove the dictator, these opponents split into several parties which were not associated with any programs but rather to chiefs under whose names members were grouped. Of these plots the most serious were organized by a Russian officer who led a force which landed at Burgas and by a Bulgarian major who in 1890 turned against Ferdinand, a former friend. Stambulov suppressed these plots and others which attempted to murder him. Acts of violence were also perpetrated elsewhere such as the case of Bulgaria's representative in Constantinople being murdered.

Nevertheless, conditions within Bulgaria, so long neglected by the Turks, had become considerably better under Stambulov's iron fist, especially from the points of view of economic development and the difficulties of maintaining effective communications in the mountainous terrain. In foreign affairs, except for Russia's hostility which remained a preponderant factor, Bulgaria gradually emerged from her status of being a chastised, young nation. A rapproachement with Turkey, which was a bold stroke of initiative, produced a real détente in the Balkans. As a guarantee of its sincerity, the Ottoman government authorized the installation of Bulgarian bishops at Uskub (Skoplje) and Okhrida in the heart of Macedonia, which Belgrade considered Serbian. Prince Ferdinand actively worked toward dissipating mistrust and raising the barriers which isolated Bulgaria. Commercial agreements with foreign governments accorded *de facto* recognition, and a tour undertaken by Ferdinand to several capitals revealed a less reserved orientation towards his principality.

As Ferdinand learned more about his profession, his relations with Stambulov, called the "Bismarck of the Balkans," became tense. Between two men of such different origins and temperament, relations could not be cordial or confident. The sovereign frequently suffered from Stambulov's tactlessness and intransigence. Furthermore, retention in office of a dictator, still considered a provocation by Russia, was regarded with considerable distrust by a growing section of public opinion. Stambulov regularly threatened to resign while simultaneously organizing demonstrations in his favor. Finally Ferdinand's patience ended. The prince, convinced he was now master of the situation and avid to remove all obstacles to a rapprochement with Russia, decided to break with Stambulov in May 1894.

Forgetful of the services rendered by a crude and brutal statesman, whose concern for the common welfare had really contributed to progress, the Bulgarians, whose political passions were usually revealed in paroxysms, exhibited the most shameful ingratitude toward Stambulov. "Down with the tyrant," cried a mob outside his protected residence. Full of rancor, the dismissed dictator published abroad an article critical of Ferdinand who, consumed by a desire for vengeance, had Stambulov prosecuted for defamation. Deprived of his property and hounded like a wild animal, the man who had for so long controlled the destiny of Bulgaria ended up, as was feared in this country renowned for its murders, by being savagely attacked in the street. Stambulov succumbed to frightful wounds (July 15, 1895). His assassins, who were called Macedonian revolutionaries, were never apprehended. In a strange manner, Prince Ferdinand, a man of cosmopolitan tastes and refinement, now appeared to relish an atmosphere of conspiracy and violence. His complex personality found pleasure in this contrast.

Prince Ferdinand married Princess Marie Louise of Bourbon-Parma in 1893. The prince broke a promise to his mother to have his first child baptized in the Roman Catholic Church and, consequently, the crown prince was christened according to the Bulgarian Orthodox rite. He thus won the good graces of his subjects and furnished evidence of his desire for rapprochement with Russia, a détente more realizable since the death of Tsar Alexander III in 1894. The late tsar's passionate hatred for Bulgaria would not be imitated by his successor, Nicholas II (1894-1917). The birth of crown prince Boris, soon followed by his brother Cyril, was joyously hailed by the Bulgarians. The future of the Saxe-Coburg dynasty was assured.

From this time on relations with Russia steadily improved. The unveiling of a statue of Tsar Alexander II on the square opposite the Sobranie and the erection of a monument commemorating the battle at Shipka pass were signs of this reconciliation. After a passionate but ephemeral dispute provoked by growing pains, the Bulgarians returned to the traditional path of friendship with Russia. Re-entry into a state of Russian grace, exhibited by a welcome given to a Bulgarian delegation by Tsar Nicholas in 1895, transformed Bulgaria's international status. Since much international antipathy toward Bulgaria had disappeared, she could assume normal relations with the powers and occupy a respected position among them. From this moment a new era for Bulgaria began.

Similarly from the viewpoint of internal affairs, Ferdinand placed himself above politics, as sovereigns should, and smoothly presided over the formation of different cabinets which followed each other in office. This tranquil period following years of turmoil allowed Bulgaria rapid development and an opportunity to observe events in adjacent Macedonia which became the object of her foreign policy.

Bulgaria still remained a vassal of the Ottoman Empire. The Young Turk revolution and Austria's annexation of Bosnia and Herzegovina in 1908 furnished Ferdinand the occasion of severing this last tie with Constantinople. He declared Bulgaria's complete independence on October 6, 1908, and in the old city of

Tirnovo was proclaimed Tsar of the Bulgarians by reviving that title used by the great rulers of medieval Bulgaria. Tsar of the Bulgarians, not of Bulgaria—he intended this to mean that he would someday become the ruler of Bulgarians still scattered beyond the frontiers of his country.

Clouds were already gathering which presaged the outbreak of the First World War. That conflict would reveal the calculating mind and duplicity of a sovereign who earned the name of "Ferdinand the Felon," a Machiavellian ruler similar to the despots of the Renaissance.

Part III

Establishment of
the Balkan States

CHAPTER I

Greece, 1830-1881

ALTHOUGH the Balkan peoples secured their independence in gradual steps only to acquire it finally in 1878—and even later for Bulgaria—the Greeks, forerunners of other Balkan peoples on the road to freedom, had already established an independent state in 1830. For this reason a treatment of the Greeks between their proclamation of independence and the Congress of Berlin has been ignored. But it is now essential to examine Greece's evolution during this half-century so that all Balkan states can be given equal consideration. All Balkan states entered the game of European politics as liberated nations about the year 1880.

Young Prince Otto of Bavaria, the first king of modern Greece, disembarked at Nauplia (also Nauplie and Nauplion) in the Peloponnesus in 1833. Since he was only 18 and ignorant of conditions, he was assisted by a regency council of three Bavarians. He was also accompanied by a Bavarian general staff and army of 3,500. Although the new monarch bore a loan of considerable proportions from the powers, a gift greatly appreciated by a people whose finances had been depleted, the deployment of Bavarian troops wounded Greek pride. Even if order had been established and security assured by this foreign army, the Greeks might not have resigned themselves to the change. But brigandage continued to ravage the country.

The young king lacked authority, the regents lacked courage, and both failed to cooperate. Torn between absolutism and liberalism, the support of Tsar Nicholas I made the absolutists prevail. The regents exercised their authority, but they could not secure adequate revenue or appease the pretensions of the many heroes of the liberation movement who clamored for rewards as compensation for yielding to the foreign rulers.

In June 1835, when King Otto, known in Greece as Othon, reached his majority, he moved his capital from Nauplia to Athens, which had begun to rise from its ruins. The regents were still unpopular. Their difficulties were aggravated by England's hostility. The first Greek insurgents saw how Canning had maneuvered to deprive Russia of an opportunity to intervene in the crisis. A competition for influence continued. After France entered the contest, Greece became an arena for the rivalry of three powers who considered themselves protectors and insisted upon protecting the Greeks in their own fashion and to the best of their interests. This competition intensified when the Bavarian regency council, obliged to depart because of its growing unpopularity, yielded to a government of Greek ministers. Each Greek was under the patronage of a foreign power, and so party disputes were aggravated by international rivalries. Internal squabbles merely became frequent reflections of foreign influences. Conditions became very favorable for the creation of a new regime.

Other obstacles hindered development of the young nation. Far from incorporating a majority of her people, Greece's frontiers, too narrowly delimited in 1829, contained only 752,000 people in an area of 18,378 square miles. Greece was merely an enclave in the Ottoman Empire, an island whose communications with the West depended almost exclusively upon the good will of the sultan who was in a position, except via the sea, to paralyze the Greeks. Reacting to this strangulation, the very nationalistic Greeks dreamed of acquiring all their ethnic territories. By concentrating on this irredentist dream, the Greeks failed to organize and improve what they had gained in their struggle for independence. Thus the Greeks indulged more in imagination than in industriousness.

To these difficulties was added a financial crisis. In 1843 England and Russia demanded interest on a loan granted when Otto ascended the throne in 1833. The Liberal Party took advantage of this to demand the granting of a constitution. Italian nationalists encouraged this demand, and Giuseppe Garibaldi considered landing in Epirus to assist the Liberals. But Russia resisted these tendencies.

An uprising by military officers forced King Otto to convene a national assembly. A new constitution was proclaimed which provided for a senate chosen by the monarch and a chamber of deputies elected by universal manhood suffrage. The evils from which Greece was suffering were not cured by the introduction of parliamentary government. On the contrary, party squabbles were intensified and extended to the mass of the electorate. Corruption became widespread. The powers soon found clients ready to accept foreign controls. Greek politicians overthrew and replaced each other with the connivance of foreign governments. Kolettes, the Francophile, removed Mavrocordato, the Anglophile, in 1844. The former was supported by the French government of King Louis Philippe; the latter had no English support. But Russia supported a third politician, Metaxas, whom Kolettes also removed.

As for King Otto (Othon or Otho), he failed to acquire prestige or an heir. The question of royal succession inevitably arose. Russian pretensions were envisaged, and England was beginning to be concerned. London therefore began to weaken the influence of her rivals by inciting in Achaea and Euboea uprisings which led in 1847 to the downfall of Kolettes' regime. Greek territorial ambitions still flourished despite the internal crises and English efforts to dissipate them according to London's insistence upon the territorial integrity of the Ottoman Empire. Not only did Greek claims threaten English rule over the Ionian Islands, but the dream of a greater Greece including Constantinople threatened London's policy.

England decided to restrain the turbulent spirit of young Greece. Palmerston, the foreign secretary, was determined to teach the Greeks a lesson. He took as a pretext an affair whose modest origin did not seem destined to be transformed into an international incident. The Don Pacifico affair would create considerable anxiety in 1850. Pacifico was a Jew who had profited from the enviable status of being an English subject. His home and shop were looted during a riot in Piraeus, the port of Athens. Was English honor at stake? Palmerston, whose national pride was always intransigent, thought so, and he avenged this insult in a spectacular fashion. He dispatched an English flotilla to the shores of Greece to blockade Piraeus. Admiral Parker, commander of the squadron, accomplished his mission by seizing about 200 Greek vessels.

France and Russia considered this to be a very exaggerated reprisal. Both attempted to intercede, but nothing could soothe Palmerston whose maneuver even encountered opposition in England. Summoned before Parliament, he delivered one of his most celebrated speeches lasting five hours. It was on this oc-

casion that he uttered that declaration which remained famous:
every subject of Her Britannic Majesty must be as proud to bear
this distinction as a Roman citizen who once proudly proclaimed,
"Civis Romanus sum." Like a Roman citizen, an English subject
had to be assured of finding complete protection on the part of
his government regardless of where on earth he might be.

This argument failed to convince the French government which
considered English pressure to be disproportionate to the initial
cause. Relations between the two governments became so tense
that the French envoy in London was recalled home. But this
was a temporary squabble whose memory Napoleon III ultimately
decided to forget. Nevertheless, Greek authorities gave complete
satisfaction to English demands in the form of apologies and a
generous indemnity to Don Pacifico.

Russia then initiated difficulties about religious questions when
she supported the claims of monks whose activities were disturbing
the Peloponnesus. The first symptoms which were to lead to the
Crimean War were arising in the Balkans. Aroused by Russian
agents, some Greek nationalists believed the time had come to
realize their territorial ambitions at the expense of Turkey who
was now threatened with armed conflict. But England and
France, allied against Russia, were determined to concentrate their
activities in the Crimea in 1854 and not to be diverted by actions
in the Mediterranean Sea. Any untimely disturbance to Greece
would have constituted a serious distraction to Russia's opponents
in the Crimean War. So England and France decided to repress
Greek disturbances. In May 1854 an English flotilla guarded
the approaches to Piraeus while French troops landed there. The
French occupation lasted for more than three years.

Many Greeks refused to pardon their king for failing to take
advantage of Turkey's embarrassment to realize the dream of a
greater Greece, even though Otto had been prevented from taking
action. The refusal of the Congress of Paris in 1856 to discuss
the Greek question was considered an injustice and humiliation.
Whereas other Balkan peoples derived certain satisfaction from
the Congress, the Greeks failed to secure anything. If Greece
had been led by a Cavour who advised her to align with Turkey's
allies, she would have been indubitably unable to suppress her
rancor to listen to the voice of reason. The king had deferred
to England during the Don Pacifico affair, and France was more

hostile since the death of Kolettes. King Otto was confronted by hostile public opinion and soon lost all remaining respect. Plots were organized. A hero of the war of independence, Admiral Kanaris, led an uprising at Nauplia and established a provisional government in Athens. The national assembly then voted for the overthrow of the king who, discouraged and aware of his short-comings, abdicated and returned to his native Bavaria in 1862.

During his long reign of 30 years, without actual authority or prestige, King Otto had presided over considerable progress—the development of agriculture as a result of judicious agrarian re-forms, increase in an already flourishing merchant marine, begin-nings of an organized army, and extension of public education which inevitably aroused national awareness. But in other fields matters remained static. Disorders continued and communications remained precarious. There were few roads, incomplete road-building projects, and travel rendered almost impracticable by the lack of bridges. In this mostly maritime country, Piraeus was still the only effective port while the others remained mere road-steads. Nevertheless, the total population did increase, the standard of living was raised, and improved working habits had been encouraged. But Greek nationalists considered all of this progress to be negligible compared to their national disappoint-ment.

The throne of Greece was vacant. Succession to the throne was a delicate problem. England and Russia had considered suc-cessors to Otto even before he abdicated. London considered offering it in 1854 to the brother of the King of Piedmont-Sardinia, but the clever Cavour rightly judged the Greek throne to be a "bramble bush." The Russians had their candidate, the Duke of Leuchtenberg, a grandson of Tsar Nicholas. But the Greeks soon forgot their rancor toward England and offered the crown to Alfred, Queen Victoria's second son. By flattering England the Greeks hoped to secure cession of the Ionian Islands, which would have been the first realization of their grandiose ambitions. A plebiscite in January 1863 produced an overwhelmingly plurality for the English prince. But the powers, who had agreed in 1830 to deny the Greek throne to members of their ruling dynasties, deemed the choice to be unrealizable. England then hinted her readiness to cede the Ionian Islands if the Greeks elected a favor-able candidate before Russia forced them to accept her favorite.

The interregnum produced a rather troubled period. A triumvirate was overthrown by the national assembly which then arranged the election of Prince George, a nephew of the Danish king, who became King George I of Greece in 1863. He was welcomed with greater acclamation because England agreed to cede the Ionian Islands, a vital maritime station and an ancient center of Hellenism, which were annexed to the motherland. Nevertheless, the island of Corfu was to be demilitarized and its fortresses razed.

The new monarch, like his predecessor, was only 18 years old. His arrival did not terminate the troubles which had become endemic since the end of the preceding reign. Greece continued to be a theater of agitation. Riots were followed by executions of politicians. Ministerial crises were innumerable. A semi-anarchical situation prevailed which led deputies to the national assembly to convene wth pistols and daggers in their belts.

In 1864 a new constitution was framed in an attempt to remedy the evils. It provided for a bicameral legislature elected by universal manhood suffrage. This was assuredly a radical step for a people who were inexperienced in politics. Nevertheless, parties and coteries developed even more. In a cascade of ministers, Delyannis succeeded Zaimis, who succeeded Rouphos, and the cycle then reversed itself. Sixteen premiers were counted in eighteen months. The first task of each new government was to depose the functionaries of the previous regime. Thus a virtual administrative paralysis ensued. Such was the unenviable situation in Greece when the inhabitants of the island of Crete rose in a general rebellion. After the Turks suppressed it, the people of Greece, although still politically divided, united in a single purpose of aiding their brethren who were being oppressed. If the Greeks had regularly revealed themselves as contentious and fickle, one could not deny their nationalism. The common aspirations of the Greeks and their ambition to unite all Greeks scattered over the eastern Mediterranean constituted a bond of inalienable solidarity.

Crete had a population of about 350,000 of whom most were Orthodox Christians. The Cretans rebelled against the Turks in 1821 when their Greek brethren on the continent initiated their war of independence. Egyptian forces rigorously suppressed the Cretan revolt. After Mehemet Ali, the pasha of Egypt, achieved victory, Crete was awarded to him in 1832. But Crete was restored to the sultan in 1840 when Mehemet Ali was restrained by the powers. The Turkish regime then governed with shocking harshness because the Moslem population constituted only a small minority. This produced a second revolt in 1856 which ended with promises of reforms, such as freedom of religion and equality for the two religious groups, which were infrequently honored.

Again in 1866, after ten years of unfulfilled Turkish promises, the Cretan Christians rebelled. A revolutionary committee presented a series of demands which the sultan rejected. The uprising intensified and led to a proclamation of union with Greece. The rebels then attacked and forced the Turks to retreat. Strong reinforcements arrived from Constantinople to subdue the rebels. The latter, overwhelmed by numbers, put up an honorable defense in the mountains, notably in the Spakia range which was an almost inaccessible stronghold.

The Cretan revolt, of course, attracted Europe's attention. France, Italy, Russia, and even Prussia expressed interest in aiding the rebels. But Austria and England refused to take sides in the crisis. The sultan was in the enviable position to refuse concessions to the rebels while the powers failed to agree on concerted action.

The Cretan revolt produced very natural repercussions in Greece, especially after 60,000 Cretan refugees were granted sanctuary in Piraeus and other places. The Cretan cause became very popular in Athens. Heretofore the Greeks had sent good wishes and proclamations to the rebels, but in 1866 they sent food, arms, munitions, and volunteers who, led by the chief of the national guard, sailed to join the rebels in the struggle against the Turks. Greek premier Delyannis declared that free Greece incorporated only a fraction of greater Greece and thus the liberation of oppressed brothers was a duty.

This policy obviously evoked a protest from Constantinople. An ultimatum was sent to King George to stop supplying the rebels with arms and volunteers. Relations became so embittered that some Greeks were expelled from Constantinople and the Athens government contemplated declaring war on Turkey. This was a possibility which the powers had to avert lest a general conflict erupt in the Balkans. If the Cretan rebels were deprived of Greek assistance, the sultan could swiftly subdue them. Consular agents of the powers, who urged their governments to intercede for humanitarian reasons, convinced the sultan to grant a new organic statute. Among other guarantees in this charter were provisions granting 49 of the 80 seats in the assembly to the Christians, mixed tribunals, and recognition of Greek as an official language. Calm was temporarily restored.

As a consequence of a relative peace on Crete, Greek nationalism, which had supported the Cretans, again fragmented into internecine squabbles. King George's popularity, which had increased after his marriage in 1867 to Grand Duchess Olga, niece of Tsar Alexander II, and the birth of an heir, Constantine, failed to produce a truce. The quarrels were aggravated by an evil of long standing. This was the poor state of public finances caused by a considerable debt arising from loans floated at exorbitant interest rates. General waste and exaggerated expenses for grandiose projects had depleted the national treasury. To achieve solvency the government did not recoil from such despicable procedures as seizing silver mines at Laurium, which had been granted to a Franco-Italian company and were finally restored after the owners protested. Brigandage, an old vice, reappeared worse than ever. In fact, the secretaries of the English and Italian legations in Athens were captured and held for ransom by bandits. Parliamentary disorder, a major source of these evils, persisted. Political parties still formed around leaders and not around ideas; they were clienteles. Ministerial crises and parliamentary dissolutions followed in rapid succession. Greece was merely marking time, failing to realize any important reforms and achieving no real progress.

When the Russo-Turkish war of 1877 broke out, Greece mobilized her army which only worsened her financial situation to the point of requiring debasement of the currency. A loan could not be guaranteed. Thus the Athens regime was unable to play an effective role in the significant events occurring beyond the frontiers. Nevertheless, Greek representatives at the Congress of Berlin of 1878 demanded an extension of their frontiers. They obtained assurances of sympathy if Greco-Turkish negotiations could ensue. A mixed commission could not agree on frontier rectifications. Turkey's opposition and a lack of agreement among the powers threatened to ignite another war. Finally, in July 1881, a conference of the powers in Constantinople agreed to enlarge Greece. The frontier with Thessaly was moved north to give Greece the districts of Volo, Larissa, and Trikala with a population of about 36,000. Turkey retained Janina in western Epirus. Greece nevertheless remained embittered and disappointed at securing frontiers which would not be modified again for thirty years.

CHAPTER II

The Balkan States, 1878-1908

THE Kingdom of Rumania, the largest and most powerful of the Balkan states, experienced a rather long period of stability and prosperity after its creation. Rumania enjoyed a period without serious incidents, unlike that of her Serbian neighbor, which might substantiate the saying that happy peoples have no history.

Nevertheless, two unhappy features marred Rumania's bright horizon: the Jewish and agrarian questions. Jews formed a large minority of the population in Moldavia and were found chiefly in the cities. Many had fled from Russian Poland after the 1830 revolution in that country and then settled in the Danubian Principalities where they lived as a distinct caste engaged principally in money lending and innkeeping. Their presence produced an economic, not a religious, problem. The Rumanians, exploited by the Phanariot Greeks and Turks, committed abuses against the Jews who, as a weak minority, performed their ancient role of scapegoats. Frequently violent reactions against the Jews involved pillaging of shops and burning of synagogues. A tragic pogrom occurred in 1872. The Rumanian government did stop riots, and to diminish public anger it decided to prohibit Jews from selling alcoholic beverages. Agitation nevertheless continued, and the Jews of Rumania found vocal support from their co-religionists in Western Europe, and especially in France, who accused the Rumanian government of anti-Semitic discrimination.

The 1866 constitution denied citizenship to the Jews. The Liberal Party led by Ioan Bratianu had invited Carol to the throne in that year. This party leaned for support on the commercial and industrial middle classes, and these, constituting the majority in the legislature, were determined to destroy Jewish competition. Old discriminatory legislation was revived, and large numbers of Jews were expelled from rural places in the districts of Jassy, Bacau and other parts of Moldavia. Those who fled to the cities were sent across the frontier as vagabonds. Expulsions of Jews continued during the Conservative government of Catargiu (1869-77). President Grant of the United States appointed Benjamin F. Peixotto, grand master of the Order of B'nai B'rith, American consul in Bucharest for the purpose of protecting Rumanian Jews. The Alliance Israélite Universelle in Paris convinced the powers to make representations in Bucharest. But Russia, an avowed persecutor of Jews, and Austria were mild in their protestations. Rumania remained committed to her policy of denying civil and political rights to the 250,000 Jews in the country. The Jews were considered as aliens, although they were not citizens of any other country, and were held subject to all obligations in the state, including army service and taxation.

The Congress of Berlin, in recognizing the complete independence of Rumania, required the Bucharest regime to admit non-Christians to citizenship. The principle that differences of religious beliefs could not hinder enjoyment of rights was embodied in the Treaty of Berlin and applied to the Balkan states. But the phrasing of the article left a technical loophole for Rumania to revive an old law declaring Jews to be aliens whose naturalization must be granted by the legislature. Thus individual Jews had to be naturalized by special acts of parliament. And even if a Jew did secure citizenship, he was denied the right to own property. The vast majority of Jews remained aliens until after World War I and had to endure a special body of legislative restrictions about residence and occupations. Rumania acquired considerable hostility on the part of those countries where Jews constituted a powerful group, and her reputation abroad was sullied.

In another sphere the development of agriculture was of special concern in a country whose inhabitants were principally peasants. Not until 1864 were the peasants able to secure possession of land by the first agrarian reform of Alexander Cuza. Consequently, about 33% of the arable land, but not the most valuable, came into peasant hands. The establishment of a land bank in 1873 stimulated productivity. But the domains of great landlords were still numerous. About 2,000 landowners owned more than one-half of the total land. From this unbalanced situation arose a smoldering discontent among the land-hungry peasants. Two agrarian laws tried to remedy the inequity, but the effect was partly vitiated by the maneuverings of speculators whose actions precipitated a peasant uprising in 1888. This led to a new reform which gave only partial satisfaction to the claims of the disgruntled peasants. Indisputable evidence of this unrest was provided in 1907 when the great peasant revolt occurred. The army was mobilized to terminate the plundering of the property of the landed aristocrats. Actual battles took place between the army and rebels who had vaguely anarchistic ideas and were attempting a march on Bucharest. As a result of this jacquerie, about 10 million acres were divided into holdings of 2½ to 150 acres each, while 7½ million remained in the hands of owners of more than 1,500 acres each.

King Carol, who was only casually interested in the agrarian problem until 1907, now realized the problem was extremely serious and required careful scrutiny. He applied himself to this task with appreciated firmness and conscientiousness. Eager to erase all vestiges of his foreign birth, Charles of Hohenzollern-Sigmaringen sought to act like an authentic Rumanian sovereign who had only the interests of his country in view. Perched above and beyond party considerations, Carol governed according to the constitution and mediated political disputes with an almost infinite authority and tact. Two great political parties divided public opinion. The Liberals were supported by commercial interests and the bourgeoisie, and the Conservatives by the great landowners. For many years the Liberals, led by Ioan Bratianu (1822–91), enjoyed Carol's complete confidence. Holding office again from 1881 to 1888, Bratianu achieved much by reforming the suffrage and reinforcing administrative centralization. The Conservatives under Lascar Catargiu (1823–99) and Petru Carp (1837–1919) were again in office until the peasant revolt of 1907 when the Liberals returned to power under the leadership of the second Ioan (Ionel) Bratianu (1864–1927), one of the three sons of the founder of the party, whose family constituted a type of rival dynasty.

Years of peace were wisely used to advantage so that by 1900 Rumania could note considerable progress. The population reached about 6 million of which 90% were Rumanians and the rest mostly Jews. Since the achievement of independence about 9,000 miles of roads and 2,000 miles of railways had been constructed. Most locomotives were powered by petroleum fuel whose use was simultaneously cleaner and more economical because of the abundance of oil deposits in Wallachia. The construction of a bridge over the Danube at Cernavoda, improvements in the port of Constantsa, and creation of a steamship line connecting Rumania with Egypt indicate some aspects of economic progress. Commerce valued at 200 million francs in 1870 jumped to 675 million by 1898. This is another indication of undeniable prosperity. But from the financial view, the situation was less brilliant because of heavy borrowing. Despite heavy debts, general conditions remained healthy. At the initiative of Take Ionescu (or Jonescu) (1858–1922), a brilliant statesman, member of the Conservative Party, a strong stimulus was given to the development of rural schools by his education act of 1893. True to his training as a Prussian officer, King Carol organized a well-equipped army which became an influential factor in the Balkans.

King Carol succeeded in establishing enviable rapport between his subjects and himself. This admirable situation was not duplicated in foreign affairs, however; but a divergence between the ruler and his people in this regard did not become apparent until years later. When, for example, the Rumanians sympathized with Paris during the Franco-Prussian War in 1870, Carol favored a Prussian victory. This crisis led the king to consider abdicating, but he was dissuaded. He never abandoned a strong faith in Rumania's need to orient her policies toward the German-speaking states.

This royal inclination did not stem exclusively from Carol's ancestral background. It was fortified by Russia's attitude. The seizure of southern Bessarabia in 1878, although compensated by the acquisition of the northern Dobrudja, profoundly wounded Rumanian pride and especially Carol. Russia's refusal to award the fortress of Silistria in the southern Dobrudja carried disappointment to a climax. From that time fear of a Russian descent upon the Danube became a Rumanian obsession. Fearful of being isolated and with England and France located at a great distance, Rumania inevitably sought a rapport with the German-speaking powers. Carol could not resist the advice of Bismarck who, setting aside his usual disdain for troublesome little states, suggested an entente between Austria and Rumania. So in 1883 a treaty of alliance was concluded. Germany adhered to this completely secret treaty, and Carol attached special significance to this. Italy subsequently joined the arrangement. The Rumanian people, ignorant of this alliance, were thus drawn into the Triple Alliance very few statesmen knew of its existence. Even the parliament and system. Only the king, the foreign minister who signed it, and a the bureaucracy did not know about it. The outbreak of World War I in 1914 would reveal Rumania's commitments. Rumania's alliance with Austria-Hungary failed to improve relations between the two countries. History would show the treaty to have been an unwise move by King Carol.

Public opinion and the government evinced considerable concern for the many Rumanians of Transylvania who were subjected to Hungarian rule. A policy of systematic Magyarization provoked protests in Rumania which made Carol hesitate renewing his alliance with Vienna. After emotions subsided, he decided to renew it in 1893. But this did not prevent the Transylvanian question from remaining a serious cause of friction between Bucharest and Vienna. The arrival in Rumania of refugees from Hungarian-ruled Transylvania contributed to arousing opinion against enforced Magyarization of the schools and the Uniate (Roman Catholic Church of the Byzantine Rite) clergy. A national Rumanian party was established in Transylvania, led by Iuliu (Julius) Maniu (1873-1953), which demanded equal rights for the Rumanian inhabitants.

The question of succession to the Rumanian throne arose when it was realized that Carol and his queen would remain childless. The king selected his nephew Ferdinand (1865-1927), son of Leopold of Hohenzollern-Sigmaringen who was the unsuccessful candidate for the Spanish throne in 1870, who settled in Rumania to learn as an apprentice the tasks which would someday be his. As heir apparent he married in 1893 a granddaughter of Queen Victoria, Princess Marie (1875-1938), the daughter of Alfred, Duke of Edinburgh, and Grand Duchess Marie, daughter of Tsar Alexander II. This was a brilliant marriage arrangement which added to Ferdinand's prestige.

By 1900 Rumania had proof of her vitality, homogeneity, and wealth. The Rumanians began to look beyond their frontiers to their brethren living under foreign rule. They considered the 4 million in Transylvania subjected to Hungarian domination which was growing harsher, the 1 million incorporated by the Russians when Bessarabia was annexed, and the 300,000 in the Bukovina who were Austrian subjects. Rumania's dream of uniting all of these in a single homeland was assuming increasing momentum. Nationalist propaganda was encouraged in the universities. King Carol and a few of his associates were convinced that the dream was premature and could not materialize in their lifetime.

The Kingdom of Serbia experienced a pro-Austrian orientation after 1878. Bismarck once said, "I am Russian at Sofia and Austrian at Belgrade." In effect, when Milan Obrenovich succeeded Michael on the Serbian throne he adopted a clearly Austrophile position. Milan considered absorption by Russia infinitely more to be feared than threats from Austria. If this view was sincere, it proved Milan to be astonishingly lacking in perception. Nevertheless, he accorded Austria commercial agreements, railway concessions, and continued to contract heavy debts in Vienna. But the Serbian Radical Party, intellectuals, and students returning from Paris remained faithful to the traditional Serbian sympathy for Russia. Ristich, the premier and a man of broad vision, vainly warned Milan of perpetuating this policy. He predicted the terrible price such a friendship would cost and warned of a war to guarantee Serbia's freedom from Austria's expansionism.

Austria had powerful means to influence Serbia's actions. Vienna exercised economic pressure on Serbia whose agricultural economy could look only to Austria as her customer since the other Balkan states had the same economies. Austria cleverly took advantage of and abused this situation. Vienna absorbed almost 80% of the total Serbian production of pigs, fowl, beef, wheat, and fruit. If Belgrade refused to remain passive, Vienna closed the tariff barriers and thus deprived Serbia of export outlets. Thus asphyxiated, Serbia always hastened to yield. This recurrent crisis has been picturesquely but justifiably called "The Pig War." An Austrian concern secured the right to construct the Orient Railways linking Vienna with Salonika and Constantinople. Thus Austrian capital took a lively interest in Serbian enterprises. King Milan was always sure of obtaining credit in Vienna where he "hawked his crown in usurers' shops."

These developments facilitated Austria's stranglehold on a feeble neighbor which reduced Serbia to the status of a satellite. Milan's submission led Serbia to react obediently to Vienna's demands. There was even a rumor of a secret treaty by which Milan had pledged to forbid all Serbian propaganda in Austria in exchange for a vague promise of recognition of his rights to the Vardar River valley in Macedonia. When Bulgaria annexed Eastern Rumelia in

1885, Milan disgraced himself in an attempt to gain prestige. His envy, aroused by Austria, launched Serbia into war with her neighbor. The disastrous results have already been related. Weakened by demoralization of army officers and lack of confidence of her troops, Serbia, who had anticipated a swift victory, retreated in haste. Austria's diplomatic interference ended the hostilities after the defeat at Slivnitza, and forced the belligerents into a peace which restored the prewar situation. Thus Vienna, by shrewd use of money and agents, dominated Serbia economically and politically.

The pleasure-seeking regime instituted by Milan was hardly designed to secure the esteem of other states or respect for order and tranquillity. The ineffectual constitution had given way to arbitrary rule. Financial waste increased the public debt to alarming proportions. The Serbs apparently realized all this, and their discontent was manifested as much as severe police measures allowed. The partisans of the Karageorgevich dynasty clandestinely raised their heads.

To a deplorable public administration was added the private life of Milan who was increasingly alienating his subjects. He was married to a Rumanian from Bessarabia, Natalia Kechko, a dignified and respected queen. But the royal couple were incompatible because of political differences. Their quarrels became public knowledge. Milan decided upon a divorce, but the clergy was reluctant to respond to his demands. So he himself announced the divorce. This cavalier step discredited him so much that the Radical Party, in the ensuing elections, emerged greatly reinforced as a result of its opposition to the divorce. Milan understood the message. He decided in 1889 to abdicate in favor of his son Alexander, then only age 12, an unhappy child who had been reared amid the acrimonious quarrels of his parents. A regency council under the aged Ristich, who had always offered wise advice, assumed power during the minority of the new ruler. Former king Milan did not neglect his own interests. He assured himself a munificent financial grant as the price of abdication even before he departed from a nation which did not regret his parting.

The first years of the new reign passed in relative calm until 1893 when Alexander, age 16, carried out a *coup d'état*. Abruptly leaving a dinner to which prominent personages had been invited, and assisted by carefully concealed accomplices, he arrested the regents and cabinet ministers and proclaimed himself an adult. He then abolished the constitution. All this came as a double surprise because the *coup* was never anticipated from this mediocre, dull-witted adolescent.

Suspicions arose that Milan, the evil genius, was behind this plot. In fact, despite his solemn promise, Milan returned to Belgrade in 1897 and was granted special privileges by his son. Popular discontent led Alexander to muzzle the press and to hound the vocal intellectuals. The malevolent influence of Milan over his son was widely noted. When the king broke with Milan in 1900, conditions failed to change.

When Alexander was 24 years old he fell in love with his mother's lady-in-waiting, Draga Mashin, age 32, widow of a Czech engineer, and whose reputation was somewhat dubious. The young king's passion ignored all remonstrance. He married Draga in an act which added more scandal to that which had already marred the reputation of the Serbian royal court.

Already overwhelming, Alexander's unpopularity could only increase. The new queen was as hated as she was scorned. A tragedy appeared inevitable, but few could envisage the cruelty of the drama that occurred. As the result of a military conspiracy, King Alexander and Queen Draga were savagely murdered during the night of June 10, 1903—the anniversary of Prince Michael's assassination thirty-five years before—and other members of the Obrenovich family were killed during a veritable butchery. This plunge into barbarism at the dawn of the 20th century brought Serbia back to the worst era of obscurantism and produced a devastating impression on a civilized world shocked by the horrible tragedy.

The Karageorgevich family was not directly involved in this plot, but they nevertheless profited. With Alexander the Obrenovich line perished. Peter Karageorgevich, grandson of Kara George, was designated the new king by the Skuptshchina and mounted the unenviable throne after an exile of forty-five years. The liberal constitution of 1889 was restored.

In the thirty years since achieving independence, Serbia, shaken by constant agitation, had achieved only minimum progress. Although she had preceded Bulgaria on the path to freedom, the former was considerably behind her neighbor. Serbia had every reason to envy Bulgaria's domestic tranquillity, finances, railway development, army organization, and general European respect. This was the situation faced by King Peter I, age 58, when he came to the throne. A graduate of St. Cyr, the French military academy, Peter had fought in the Franco-Prussian War under the alias of Lieutenant Kara and distinguished himself by winning the Legion of Honor. Wounded and captured by the Prussians, he escaped and continued the struggle in the ranks of the French Army of the Loire. He again saw action with the Bosnian rebels in 1875. His marriage to Princess Zorka, daughter of King Nicholas of Montenegro, created strong ties between the two neighboring and related peoples, although personal relations between the two monarchs were not cordial.

Of medium height, thin, his face divided by a thick mustache, with a nervous temperament, King Peter (1844-1921) was primarily a soldier. He did find time to devote to literature, history, and philosophy. Of very simple habits, detesting all pomp and ceremony, endowed with clear and precise ideas, the new king was devoted to an arduous task. What he was required to accomplish was no less than the restoration of order and tranquillity in a country which had not only been disorganized by a deplorable administration, but where morale had been seriously undermined by cynical neglect. Moreover, Peter had to inspire Europe with confidence in a Serbia which had been ostracized as a result of the recent murders. He soon overcame these difficulties by resolute labors, tact, and moderation. His first concern was to rule as a constitutional monarch whereas the constitution had been for his predecessors merely a disguise to conceal their absolutism. Elections, no longer rigged, brought to the Skuptshchina a majority of Radicals who had solid roots in the country and were grouped about their respected leader, Nikola Pashich (Pasic) (1845-1926), once involved in a plot against Milan, who escaped into Austria and remained in exile, premier in 1891, ambassador to Russia 1893-94, banished from Serbia for conspiracy against the king in 1899, returned in 1903 and supported the Karageorgevich dynasty in its accession to the throne. His program included a reform of finances which had been ruined by extravagance of incredible proportions, improved education, revitalization of army morale, commercial development, and liberation from Austria's influence.

Foreign affairs presented even greater problems. How could King Peter elevate Serbia from the depths into which his predecessors had sunk her, and how could he shake off Vienna's stranglehold? The king first appealed to France, his second homeland. The French government responded by floating loans and selling arms made by Creusot. The Serbs had no need to depend further on weapons from Krupp and Skoda. In 1905 Austria avenged herself by closing her frontier to Serbian imports. France came to Serbia's assistance by purchasing most of her products, notably livestock, fowl, and fruit. Thus rescued by the creation of a new market, the little kingdom could better resist Vienna's demands. A trade agreement signed with Austria in 1908 was not as unfavorable as had been anticipated.

Peter's firm administration reestablished Serbia on a solid basis and restored her prestige. It was during his reign that a movement appeared which, initially rather vague, promoted union of the south Slavs. An idea to unify them took root in the minds of a few nationalists. Encircled in their mountains and realizing the need for an outlet to the Adriatic Sea, the nationalists looked toward the coast where their ancestors had established the prosperous medieval city of Ragusa (Dubrovnik) which was once a brilliant intellectual center. Union with Montenegro appeared even more natural because family ties had brought the two adjacent dynasties closer. Also inhabited by Slavs who had been freed of Turkish rule only to find themselves subjected to that of Austria, Bosnia and Herzegovina were considered similar to Alsace and Lorraine which had been separated from their homeland.

A Greater Serbia movement within Austria-Hungary spurred the Slavs there to demand freedom. While 3 million Serbs were free in their homeland, 5 million other south Slavs—Serbs, Croats, Slovenes—suffered under the Hapsburg yoke in Austria, Hungary, and particularly in Bachka, the Banat of Temesvar, Croatia-Slavonia, Bosnia and Herzegovina. About 400,000 more languished in Macedonia under Turkish rule. Many repeated the patriotic verses of the poet Jovan Jovanovich (1833-1904), who lamented the mutilation of medieval Serbia and cried, "Lord, give back to the martyrs of Kossovo the place among the nations which belongs to them."

By 1900 national aspirations which would have grave consequences for Europe's fate were arousing difficulties in Austria-Hungary. The south Slavs realized they had a common spirit and, even more, a common adversary in Austria-Hungary. The latter would strive to hinder south Slav unity by multiplying intrigues to incite the Catholic Croats against the Orthodox Serbs, and by vigorous economic discrimination and penetration. Austria's construction of highways and railways, especially a line from Mitrovitsa to Uskub (Skoplje) in Macedonia was indirectly intended to interfere in south Slav affairs.

Despite her small size and weakness, Serbia constituted for Austro-Hungarian authorities a constant source of anxiety because of the attraction she exercised over neighboring Slav peoples. Metternich, Austria's chancellor in the first half of the 19th century, had declared, "Serbia must be either Turkish or Austrian." Thus, from the time of her liberation from the Turks, Serbia had to become Austrian or at least subordinated to Vienna's influence. A theory was manufactured in Vienna and Budapest that the Slavs, who were considered inferior peoples, were destined to remain German and Hungarian subjects.

Belgrade still remained the focal point of the south Slavs and became the center of an intellectual if not yet political movement. In Croatia a party seeking union was formed, but some of its members envisaged it incorporating only Catholic Slavs. Would Serbia succeed playing in the Balkans a role analogous to that of the Kingdom of Piedmont-Sardinia in the fulfillment of Italian unity? This was doubted in many quarters. Serbia was still a weak, little country with negligible resources. Despite considerable improvement, her finances remained precarious, and Europe had not yet dismissed her recent disorders and scandals. Furthermore, Russia, her traditional protector, had been exhausted by an unfortunate war with Japan. Russia's humiliating defeat had also coincided with a revolution in St. Petersburg. Under such conditions Russia was quite hesitant about risking new adventures in the Balkans. Thus Austria was in an enviable position to suppress aspirations of which Serbia was becoming the center. Vienna's new chancellor, Count Alois von Aehrenthal (1854-1912), hastened to push toward Macedonia and Salonika the railway which emerged from the Sanjak of Novi-Bazar. Russia's defeat in the Far East encouraged Austria's imperialist tendencies, of which Aehrenthal was a fervent promoter, and her natural and inevitable area for expansion was in the Balkans.

The Kingdom of Greece remained dissatisfied by the frontier rectifications of 1881 which still failed to correspond to her grandiose ambitions. But Athens had to submit in exasperation. A period of calm and stability was maintained by Kharilaos Tricoupis (Trikoupes or Trikoupis) (1832-96), frequently premier between 1875 and 1895. More realistic than his predecessors, this cold, taciturn, industrious statesman, son of a hero of the 1821 revolution, educated in England, was probably the greatest Greek politician next to Eleutherios Venizelos (1864-1936). He realized fulfillment of the dream of greater Greece depended first on achievement of domestic tranquillity, restoration of army morale, and improvement in the economy. Despite opposition by extremely nationalist groups, Tricoupis secured foreign aid. He built better roads linking the mainland with the Peloponnesus, extended the railway system, and drained marshes to combat malaria. His plan to exploit mines near the coastline to facilitate simple export required foreign assistance. But how could foreign investors undertake such an enterprise if they lacked confidence in Greece's financial policies? Tricoupis had to inspire this confidence. The marriage of Crown Prince Constantine to the sister of Emperor William II of Germany contributed to this by elevating Greek prestige and creating an illusion of German support.

Probably too advanced for his time, Tricoupis was unappreciated and even unpopular because of his ultra-western orientation. He had to increase taxes to construct roads and railways. He was reproached for being too docile to foreign influences, and he was forced to retire in 1895, dying abroad the next year in voluntary exile and enforced disillusionment. His successor, Theodoros Delyannis (Deliyiannes, Deligiannes, or Delijannis) (1826-1905), a murky megalomaniac, ultra-nationalist, and premier when Tricoupis was out of office, revived dreams of grandeur despite internal unrest and financial disorders. His government presided over a very somber chapter in the tormented history of modern Greece. The fate of the Greeks in Crete and Macedonia preoccupied the Delyannis regime more than the instability of the country.

The situation on Crete had remained very unstable. The mainland Greeks watched the island, the ancient center of the oldest (Minoan) Greek culture, where the vast Christian majority constantly resisted the Turkish administration. Concessions granted by Constantinople had only been a stop-gap measure. Moreover, the Turks strove to diminish the inadequate privileges so that the original oppressive regime could be restored. Europe heard the continuous and justifiable complaints of the Cretans, but reaction was slow in coming. The powers finally decided to intercede in 1895. Sultan Abdul Hamid II again yielded by designating a Christian, Alexander Karatheodory Pasha (1833-1906), governor of the island. He was a Greek in origin and a long-time Turkish statesman who negotiated the treaties of San Stefano and Berlin in 1878. The Moslem inhabitants, however, resisted this appointment. The sultan declared his original policy had been vindicated and dismissed Karatheodory whom he replaced with Turkhan Pasha, a Moslem. Unrest increased, and instability became so widespread that the foreign consuls in Constantinople asked their governments to dispatch ships to protect the Cretan Christians. Cretan rebels sought refuge in the mountains to struggle against Turkish troops.

This new Cretan crisis naturally aroused excitement in Athens. Nationalists clamored to annex the island. Numerous volunteers sailed to Crete to support the rebels. King George was urged to intervene, but he was restrained by the powers who tried to persuade the sultan to appease the rebels. Every concession offered the Christians, however, offended the Moslems, and vice versa, and the crisis worsened. In January 1897, Canea, the capital of Crete, was the scene of destructive fires and the massacres of Christians. The indignation of the mainland Greeks could no longer be moderated. If the king refused to become involved, his second son, George, did embark with torpedo boats, and the chief of the royal guard arrived with volunteers. The urge to aid all Greeks under Turkish rule and thus achieve final unity threatened the peace of Europe.

But Europe watched in hopes of avoiding menacing complications. Emperor William of Germany, more concerned for his friendship with Turkey than his marriage ties to the Greek dynasty, resolved to stop Greece. England and France wished to have Crete granted autonomy within the Ottoman Empire. The powers agreed on the need to localize the crisis. Thus the Athens government was called upon to evacuate its forces from the island. An international flotilla then blockaded Crete. The island became a trusteeship of the six powers who landed troops to occupy strategic points and to restore order (February 1897).

Bitter disappointment overcame the mainland Greeks. National pride had been wounded. Indignation became so vehement that

King George would have risked his throne if he rejected the almost unanimous opinion of his subjects. Crown Prince Constantine, apparently without authorization, led a volunteer army in an invasion of Thessaly on April 10, 1897. The Greeks soon fled in wild retreat after their first encounter with Turkish troops who had recently been trained by German officers. Hostilities lasted only three weeks during which the Greek forces were crushed by the superiority of the Turks whose officers were advised by German generals. The Turks swiftly captured Larissa and Volos (or Volo) in Thessaly, which had been awarded to Greece in 1881. The Greek defeat was resounding. Athens had no recourse but to seek an armistice and consequently renounce her ambitions on Crete. Furthermore, Greece was forced to recognize modifications of her frontier with Turkey in Thessaly and to pay an indemnity. Turkey, however, accorded Greece valuable moral satisfaction by appointing Prince George, the second son of the Greek king, governor of Crete which was granted autonomy within the Ottoman Empire. Thus was established the first legal bond between the rebellious island and mainland Greece.

The required payment of an indemnity to Turkey aggravated the already deplorable state of Greek finances. An international commission was created to restore order to this precarious situation. Like Egypt in a prior era, Greece was subjected to a trusteeship for her financial affairs. This was the origin of the Commission on Greek Finances. Representatives of six great powers formed a commission which began its operations in 1898. Its first business was to negotiate a loan which was guaranteed by revenues from monopolies and port rights collected in Piraeus.

The Turks believed themselves invincible in the wake of their exhilarating victory over the Greeks. But the Greeks were aroused to the point of securing vengeance. If the Greeks had emerged deeply embittered by the series of ordeals, they had also disappointed many who had supported their cause. But these circumstances should have pardoned the Greeks. Of the two foreign dynasties imported by the Greeks, the Bavarian never comprehended the situation, and the Danish experienced considerable difficulty in being accepted. The great fault of Greece was that of being gnawed by the political virus of discord. An Athenian schoolboy could be heard uttering, "Why, sure, I politick now and will politick all my life just as my father and grandfather did." The error of Greece was to think too excessively of the role as "gatherer of the Greek lands" to the detriment of the development of already liberated territories.

An exaggerated taste for debate and an overflowing imagination hindered Greece's first steps. Greece was too long inclined to neglect the present for the future. These truths should not obscure the fact that Greece would ultimately achieve prestige in European eyes as a result of the valor of her soldiers, her breadth of view, and the perspicacity of Venizelos, her greatest statesman.

Despite these disasters and misdeeds, Greece did manage to progress since the establishment of the kingdom. When the first census was conducted in 1838, the country had about 750,000 inhabitants. By 1909 the country had a population of about 2,632,000 of which about 600,000 inhabited recently acquired Thessaly and the Ionian Islands. In the same period the area of Greece grew from 18,379 square miles to 24,042. The budget, estimated at only 20 million drachmas in 1837, reached 142 million in 1912. Whereas highways were almost impassable in 1840, they formed a relatively modern network of about 145 miles in 1867. The first railway, linking Athens and Piraeus, was completed in 1870. By 1912 almost 1,000 miles of railway furrowed the country. Exploitation of the mines employed about 10,000 workers in 1902. The growth of the merchant marine was perhaps Greece's greatest feat. Tonnage of ships increased from 8,240 in 1875 to 387,000 in 1911. Piraeus, a simple fishing village in 1830, became a great Mediterranean port as a result of increased trade with England and the United States. It was also the embarkation point for innumerable Greek emigrants. About 30,000 departures per year were estimated between 1900 and 1910; a sad commentary on the state of affairs in Greece.

The fate of the Kingdom of Bulgaria contrasted quite remarkably with that of neighboring Greece. Ferdinand, who would soon reveal his perfidy, had shown a methodical and realistic spirit at the beginning of his reign. An indefatigable worker, he imparted to Bulgaria an active stimulus that assassination attempts did not deter. Progress between 1887 and 1908 was as remarkable as it was rapid. Credit went to the ruler, but his task was greatly facilitated by the industrious temperament of the Bulgarians who were apparently ready to accept discipline when they realized the fortunate results obedience could guarantee.

Ferdinand maintained a stability which discouraged brigandage whose continuation the revolutionary era had served to excuse. Virtually everything had to be created in the realm of law. Numerous laws voted in a minimum of time endowed Bulgaria with an indispensable judicial apparatus borrowed from the French and Italian legal codes. The same was true in the military sphere. Compulsory military service for men aged 21 to 35 permitted the mobilization of a relatively large army, equipped with modern weapons, and whose troops had already proved their valor at Slivnitza. The regular army had 2,000 officers and 47,000 men, comprising a force which would ultimately affect the entire nation.

Agriculture played a principal role in Bulgaria's domestic affairs. The production of wheat and maize, the major crops, was quadrupled as a result of improvements in agronomy, experimental farms, agricultural banks, and the introduction of new techniques. After the exceptional quality of Bulgarian grapes was discovered, vine culture was heavily encouraged. Although the forests in the Balkan Mountains had suffered from Turkish spoliation, the reforestation of the Rhodope chain was methodically carried out by French experts and it produced notable results. The improved raising of livestock also had appreciable consequences.

Improvement in communications is always vital to the development of a new country. Bulgaria had only few and mediocre roads and one railway of questionable utility leading from Rushchuk on the Danube to the port of Varna on the Black Sea. Construction of highways and bridges did increase the length of the roads from 4,000 to 9,000 miles in 20 years. Foreign loans enabled the railways to increase their mileage in the same period, chiefly as a result of the construction of a branch of the Orient Express. A similar effort was achieved in port facilities. Great achievements were made almost in all spheres, especially in Sofia which was transformed from a sleepy Turkish village into a small European capital.

Bulgaria's embryonic industry also secured encouragement. The relatively primitive state of the country was more favorable for crafts than for industry. Small artisan workshops increased so much that by 1908 about 8,000 craftsmen could be recognized. This encouraged the establishment of a labor exchange and an unemployment compensation system. These signs of economic progress encouraged foreign commerce. From 1880 to 1908 the volume of foreign trade increased threefold. This gratifying development spurred the creation of chambers of commerce, trade schools, and the conclusion of trade agreements with several foreign governments. The national budget of any country in such a rapid process of transformation could only increase. Thus Bulgaria's budget increased from 39 millions in 1887 to 87 millions in 1908. French experts had reorganized the financial apparatus. Loans were negotiated for railway construction despite the prudence of Bulgarian financiers so that a deficit would not be experienced. Bulgaria sought loans in London, Vienna, and Berlin. But most borrowing was transacted in Paris which assured France an influential role in the economic sphere.

As a result of the rapid improvement in her economy and resources, Bulgaria, after the Russians decided to end their ostracism, was admitted to the family of nations. Relations with other states developed along normal channels after ambassadors were exchanged with Turkey, the other Balkan states, Austria, Russia, and finally with France, England, and Germany. Bulgaria's international orientation was determined by two factors, the one which attracted her toward Russia and the other which alienated her from Greece.

Bulgaria's activities in various fields did not neglect questions of public health and education. In two decades the number of hospitals was quadrupled, while that of schoolchildren rose from 120,000 to 335,000, the latter remarkably including 50% females. The schools assumed a fundamental role in Bulgaria after they had actively participated in the propagation of ideas about national independence. The number of illiterates declined sharply in the rural areas. Secondary and higher education was organized and marked by the establishment in Sofia of the first university in 1888. Since Bulgaria's resources were inadequate to nourish youthful demands for education, many of the new middle class studied in foreign schools. Vienna and St. Petersburg attracted many, but most went to France. Because of their modest means, many decided to study in the provincial universities at Aix, Montpellier, and Grenoble instead of expensive Paris. Many Bulgarian politicians were educated in the more modest French universities. Thus France profited from a wide intellectual influence in establishments operated by the Roman Catholic orders of Assumptionists, Christian Brothers, and Sisters of St. Joseph. But mention must be made of one non-French influence which greatly contributed to illuminating Balkan darkness. This was Robert College, founded by Cyrus Hamlin (1811-1900), an American Protestant missionary in Turkey who established this institution in Constantinople in 1871. Future premiers Geshov and Stoilov, as well as other leading politicians and scholars, would be educated at this college.

During this formative period Bulgarian literature gained a reputation due to Ivan Vazov (1850-1921), poet, novelist, and a great patriot upon whose head a price was placed in 1876. He was first occupied in restoring the Bulgarian language to its primitive state by eliminating the numerous Greek and Turkish words introduced into it. Vazov wrote works which earned for him the title of Bulgaria's Victor Hugo. He dedicated his talents to furnishing a literary form to national folklore, popular songs, and ancient legends.

Bulgaria's vassalage to the Ottoman Empire was more theoretical than effective. Stambulov had the wisdom to renounce the traditional hostility toward Turkey so he could effect a reconciliation. His gestures were appreciated in Constantinople in view of the sultan's authorization to the Bulgarian Exarchate to appoint bishops in several Macedonian cities, a very significant concession since it was interpreted as recognition of the Bulgarian character of the region.

Like the Rumanians, Serbs, and Greeks who aspired to enlarge their countries to incorporate co-nationalists under foreign rule, the Bulgarians had their irredenta in Macedonia. Acquired by the Treaty of San Stefano in 1878, lost at the Congress of Berlin, Macedonia might someday be annexed as Eastern Rumelia had been. To attain this, Sofia carried on active propaganda. Many Macedonians held important posts in Sofia and constantly urged the government to act. After Ferdinand's ambitions were aroused, Bulgaria's claims to Macedonia took a leading role in Sofia's policy.

Bulgaria's progress in all fields was demonstrated by an increase in population from 3,150,000 in 1887 to 4,200,000 in 1908. Thus Bulgaria became the second most populous state in the Balkans next to Rumania. Earnest hopes were raised regarding a brilliant future to be achieved by hard work, prudence, and continued prosperity. To attain this goal, Bulgaria had to "wait for fortune's favors without doing violence to fortune." But this was precisely what King Ferdinand, who was considered loyal and prudent and would soon become rash and untrustworthy, could not resolve to do.

CHAPTER III

The Macedonian Question

MACEDONIA was the region in the southern Balkans which remained in Turkish hands after the liberation of the Balkan states. It has always been a region of indefinite boundaries. In the very heart of the Balkan peninsula, it was the meeting-place of all the ethnic groups, and was claimed by all. From Salonika on the Aegean Sea it followed the valley of the Vardar River northward to Uskub (Skoplje), westward to Lake Okhrida on the Albanian frontier, and eastward to the Strumitza region on the Bulgarian border. The course of the Vardar formed the axis of this mountainous lake-dotted region. It was comprised of the three Turkish vilayets (provinces) of Uskub, Monastir, and Salonika (or Thessaloniki). Macedonia had about 3 million inhabitants in 1900, but it was losing population. Not only were the Macedonians seeking to circumvent Turkish surveillance by migrating into adjacent states, but they were also a prey to brigandage and misery.

Most of the nationalist struggles in the Balkans have centered on Macedonia. The question of who or what a Macedonian is will never be resolved. Until the middle of the 19th century the Greeks were assured preponderance there because of the influence of their powerful clergy. After the establishment of the Bulgarian Exarchate in 1870 and the installation of Bulgarian bishops in several cities, all those who did not consider themselves Greek declared themselves Slavs and acknowledged the spiritual leadership of the newcomers. Encouraged by an active propaganda network, the Bulgarians made progress. They claimed all Macedonia except the Chalcidice peninsula south of Salonika, whose Greek character they admitted. Independent of the clergy and schools, the Bulgarians had a real revolutionary association, the Internal Macedonian Revolutionary Organization (IMRO), which engaged in terrorist acts publicly ignored by Sofia, but probably financed by the Bulgarian government.

The Greeks, however, claimed to be the oldest inhabitants of

Macedonia, the birthplace of Alexander the Great, where Orthodox clergy had strived to Hellenize the population centuries ago. The Greeks, having an indisputable majority on the Aegean coast of Macedonia, claimed the entire southern region, including Salonika, Kavalla, and Seres, and sought to extend their pretensions as far north as possible so that they could appear as heirs to the Ottoman Empire. They also organized bands called *komitadjis* (committee-men) of patriotic brigands. The Bulgarians sponsored similar groups, and savage struggles broke out between these bands which were animated by ancient hatreds. Blood flowed in ambush encounters. Like their rivals, the Greeks used the clergy and schools for their active propaganda.

Serbs were scattered throughout Macedonia, and it was difficult to distinguish them from the Bulgarians. Not until 1902 was their first bishop installed at Skoplje (Uskub in Turkish). Hence the Serbs had little time to compensate for their exclusion. They claimed the northern region including Skoplje, their ancient capital, and they invoked the memory of the great Dushan to extend their claims south into the Vardar valley. Denouncing the abuses of the Greek and Bulgarian clergy, the Serbs proposed to unite all Christian Slavs under their rule.

In religion the Macedonian Slavs, apparently of both Serb and Bulgarian origins, who acknowledged the Bulgarian Exarchate, were more numerous than those who followed the Serbian Orthodox Church. For this undoubtedly there was an historic reason, since the Exarchate, recognized in 1870 by Turkey, worked amid favorable circumstances. The best test of the nationality of a Slav was, as a rule, his own consciousness. But so much political pressure was brought to bear on the Slavs that it was doubtful whether much confidence could have been placed in a plebiscite. The Bulgarians did more to establish schools, and education did much to stimulate a Bulgarian orientation.

A fourth Christian group was recognized by the Ottoman government. This was the Kutzo-Vlachs (Vlachs or Aromunes), a tribe of sheepherders concentrated in the Pindus Mountains, whose language suggested survival of a Rumanian group in the region. They were probably descendants of ancient Thracians, numbering between 4,000 and 22,000, who engaged in pastoral occupations, migrating annually from winter quarters to summer pasturages. Although relatively few in number, official recognition of their existence in a Greek region contributed to complicating the ethnic question whereby tensions arose between Athens and Bucharest. The Rumanian government had developed a peculiar interest in these kinsmen. The sultans, in admitting the existence of the Kutzo-Vlachs, intended to provoke this Greco-Rumanian discord. Thus Macedonia became the most complex of all the many Balkan problems which required solution at the beginning of the 20th century. The region aroused jealousies to such an extent that the Balkan states actually preferred a prolongation of Turkish rule to a triumph of their rivals.

Inhabiting the easternmost region and the Adriatic coast were the Albanians (Skipetars), descendants of the ancient Illyrians, numbering about 1 million. Although mostly Moslem, they did have a significant Orthodox minority. The relatively undeveloped Albanians were favorites of the Turkish government. The sultan had an Albanian guard just as the former king of Naples once had his royal Albanian regiment. A people of sheepherders and brigands, dependent upon Turkey's indulgence toward their violent acts, the Albanians frequently plundered Macedonia. This habit was a right which tradition had rendered respectable. "The Albanians plowed with the spear," went a saying.

The Jewish population of Macedonia was quite considerable, concentrated in the cities where they engaged in commerce. They formed about two-thirds of the population in Salonika to which they had come as refugees expelled from Spain by the inquisition in the 16th century. The survival of this ethnic group, which preserved intact its religion, language, and customs, was remarkable proof of the spirit of religious toleration which the Turks could display if warranted. Salonika was a strange city, inhabited by a Jewish majority, administered by the Turks, and claimed by Greeks and Bulgarians.

A small but quite distinct minority were the Gypsies, who had no political aspirations, national consciousness, or real pretensions. They stood wholly apart from the people in whose midst they dwelled. Their number was very small, and they were insignificant in the ethnic problems of Macedonia. But their presence added complexities.

To round out this view of the groups inhabiting Macedonia, the ruling Turks must not be omitted. They were in evidence as numerous soldiers housed in large, yellow-painted barracks which, placed on the heights, constituted along with the *Konak,* the governor's palace, a symbol of the Ottoman domination. With a rifle slung over his shoulder, the silhouette of a Turkish sentinel guarding a bridge or checkpoint served to remind anyone who might be tempted to forget the instability in Macedonia. Alongside the soldier was the Turkish peasant, a peaceful worker asking only to cultivate his plot, who was always unnerved by the struggles around him. He was all the more exasperated by this because quarrels among Christians did not at all interest him.

Agitation intensified as the result of heated propaganda which did not recoil from recruiting many supporters. Bulgarians, Greeks, and Serbs quarreled not only with rifles, but also with historical, geographical, and philological arguments. All published statistics with glaring differences. As noted in 1906, Bulgarian statistics had 1,184,036 Bulgarians and 57,600 Serbs in Macedonia. The Serbs claimed they numbered 2,048,320 and the Bulgarians only 700! This game gave rise to the saying that "all those in Macedonia who are neither Greek nor Turk are Slavs, but which Slavs? Bulgarian or Serb? They pass from *ich* to the *ov.*"

The Greeks estimated themselves to total 656,305, the Serbs to number about 200,000, and declared there were no Bulgarians in Macedonia at all. As for the Turks, they numbered about 400,000. After invoking various scientific methods to fortify their theses, it became a question of who could assemble the most bishops, churches, schools, teachers, and students. Amid the shouts of everyone who was trying to shout down his neighbor, it was impossible to be heard.

Macedonia was like a skein of wool, an inextricable skein in which nationalities were mixed to such a point that it was impossible to distinguish among them. One village counted a Bulgarian population while its neighboring community was Greek. Within each village the nationalities were juxtaposed without even coming together in death since each group scrupulously maintained its own cemetery where, sheltered by high walls, its dead were preserved from contamination by the other accursed peoples.

The miserable inhabitants of Macedonia, constant prey to propaganda and terrorism, were incessantly solicited to inscribe their names on a list or to attend a certain church. Many moved from one camp to another because of intimidation and threats, alternately calling themselves Bulgarians *("ov")*, Serbs *("ich")*, or Greeks in hopes of finding that most desirable advantage of all, namely peace and quiet. What an illusion! Arguments became only more bitter. In these quarrels the worst fury came from intellectuals who, as passionate patriots, believed they were serving their cause by perpetrating assassinations or inciting conflicts, and who usually ended up in Turkish prisons. These nationalists involved in internecine struggles kept a naturally fertile country in a state of incessant agitation. Macedonia's sun-drenched and well-watered valleys could produce ample harvests of cotton, tobacco, mulberry, and maize which grew on mountainous slopes rich in pastures and forests. But disorder made the country miserable. A mere handful sowed agitation and hatred among the inhabitants, and the latter, torn between the parties, ended up by being oblivious to what was happening. If recognition of a distinctive Macedonian nationality would have sufficed to restore order, how happy the people would have been to be considered Macedonians. But when passions were heated, neutrality was denied them.

The intensity of contradictory propaganda naturally facilitated Turkish domination. The Turks strove to favor one and then the other to divide their adversaries and lead the game whose strings they unscrupulously pulled. The Turks were content to see their enemies struggle; this was eloquent proof of Turkish skill in governing. Sultan Abdul Hamid II was a master of this craft. A thin, timid, little man, with large slanted eyes and hooked nose, reputedly the son of an Armenian mother, he inspired the terror he was experiencing within his own palace overlooking the Bosporus. Like a real Asiatic despot, he reigned by intrigue, espionage, informing, and even massacres. Nevertheless, he was a clever diplomat who profited from rivalries among the great powers.

To the Cretan and Armenian questions was added that of Macedonia which, during the first years of the 20th century, would intensify Europe's atmosphere already charged with tension. The crisis was not entirely new. The Congress of Berlin had examined the Macedonian question when the Turkish yoke was weighing down in a very arbitrary manner. The Turks had agreed in 1878 to undertake reforms. Since then the powers were morally obliged to assure fulfillment of the sultan's promises. But for a quarter-century the powers failed to act.

At this juncture the Balkan policies of the great powers should be noted, at least until the Macedonian question became acute. The crisis discussed by the Congress of Berlin in 1878 had been partly provoked by Russia's aid to the insurgent Bosnians, Serbs, Montenegrins, and Bulgarians, and by her old design to secure the Turkish Straits. Confined to the northern depths of the Black Sea and trapped by the double locks of the Bosporus and the Dardanelles, Russia strove to be liberated from this isolation. To political aspirations were added economic requirements since the bulk of Russian wheat and petroleum was transported across the Black Sea. Two obstacles blocked Russia's expansion—the Turks, on the one hand, and the Austrians and English on the other.

Austria, checkmated in German affairs by her defeat in the Seven Weeks' War in 1866, was obliged to leave Germany to Prussia. By a very natural alternative Austria sought compensation in the Balkans. Bismarck encouraged Vienna in that region. In that way, he believed, Austria would think less of revenge. He followed the same logic when he pushed France toward Tunisia. Moreover, by increasing her influence in the Balkans, Austria, the harbinger of Germanism in the Balkans, could only serve Pan-German interests. This was a new direction for the renowned *Drang nach Osten* whose goal was acquisition of Salonika and the shores of the Aegean Sea. Austria's ambitions were supported by the anti-Slav attitude of Count Gyula Andrassy (1823-90), the Hungarian statesman and delegate to the Congress of Berlin. This policy aroused Russia's hostility, and the two powers had either to yield or fight.

The two began by conceding. When agitation broke out in Bosnia in 1875, Austria, Germany, and Russia, members of the Three Emperors' League created in 1873, agreed to the Berlin Memorandum which called on Turkey to introduce reforms in the Balkans. This request called for a cessation of hostilities, resettlement of the Bosnian insurgents, concentration of Turkish troops in a few localities, retention of weapons by the rebels, and supervision of reforms by the consuls of the powers. The Berlin Memorandum was accepted by France and Italy but rejected by England because London was not involved in drafting it. In May the Bulgarians rebelled against Turkish rule, and on June 30 Serbia declared war on Turkey. After the Turks repulsed the Serbs and invaded their country, Austria and Russia met at Reichstadt on July 8, 1876 to discuss the crisis. The two powers agreed to insist upon a restoration of prewar conditions if Serbia were defeated and to demand implementation of the reforms of the Berlin Memorandum. If Serbia was victorious, she would secure a part of Bosnia and Herzegovina, but the larger part of the provinces would be awarded to Austria. Russia would obtain southern Bessarabia (lost in 1856). In the event of Turkey's collapse, Bulgaria would become independent, Greece would acquire additional territory, and Constantinople would become a free city. Thus Russia secured freedom of movement from Austria in the eastern Balkans in exchange for assurance of support to Austria's ambitions in the western Balkans. This entente enabled Russia to abandon Serbia temporarily so that a protectorate over the Bulgarians and an opening to the Straits could be established. After occupying Bosnia and Herzegovina, according to this Reichstadt agreement, Austria would be in a position to threaten Serbia and to annex the two provinces. Furthermore, Austria could station garrisons in the Sanjak of Novi-Bazar, a province separating Serbia from Montenegro.

Although England was located far from the Balkans, an intransigent English opposition to Russian imperialism was maintained in the 1870's. No compromise was possible with England's policy. Determined to safeguard her communications with India, England insisted upon maintaining freedom of the route to the Far East and Australia and resolved never to tolerate Russia's advance on the Straits and Constantinople since mastery of the Mediterranean was a vital necessity for the English. This policy had become even more vital since Prime Minister Disraeli purchased Egypt's majority shares in the Suez Canal Company in 1875.

When Russia declared war on Turkey in April 1877 and advanced on Constantinople, England reacted at once. English warships appeared at the Prinkipo Islands near Constantinople and troop concentrations were made on Malta. England's policy was supported by most of the powers who opposed creation of a greater Bulgaria and subsequently revised the Treaty of San Stefano at the Congress in Berlin. Thus England succeeded in preserving the territorial integrity of the Ottoman Empire. England, wishing to assure improved protection, convinced the sultan to cede the island of Cyprus from which London would be in a better position to observe Russian activities in the eastern Mediterranean. By the same stroke England was assured of an advanced bastion near Syria and Egypt which could dominate the waters of the Levant.

After spectacular military success Russian troops reached the very walls of Constantinople, but they were denied the fruits of victory. Russia merely acquired the creation of a small Bulgaria, which was rather unappreciative of her liberator's efforts, and retrocession of southern Bessarabia from Rumania. Russia even had to witness her Serbian protégé fall under Austria's influence. Nevertheless, Russia's military victories once more demonstrated to the Balkan peoples the strength of the Tsar's armies as well as the interest which Holy Orthodox Russia had in the peninsula.

France did not play a very active role at the Congress of Berlin because she had not yet fully recovered from the ordeal of 1870. France was faithful, except during the Crimean War, to a policy of preserving the territorial integrity of Turkey, inaugurated by King Francis I in the 16th century. Paris thus supported London in this policy. France enjoyed an enviable intellectual and moral influence in all Turkish territories, and it was to French advantage to preserve the empire under the sultan's authority to safeguard her privileged position. Thus the Treaty of Berlin (1878) accorded France considerable moral satisfaction when that peace granted her a traditional protectorate over the Roman Catholics in the Ottoman Empire. Many religious orders had a vast network of schools in the Holy Land which by 1912 numbered more than 100,000 students who were taught French and a love of France. Thus France had a moral patrimony in the Ottoman Empire. If France exported ideas rather than merchandise, she did indeed invest considerable capital in a series of enterprises (railways, ports, docks, lighthouses, loans) whose total value affected the Ottoman public debt and activities of Ottoman banks.

The Kingdom of Italy, a relatively new state, had not yet acquired a status to interfere in the Eastern Question. But compelled by her proximity, Italy did evince concern for the Adriatic coastline. Because her western Adriatic coast lacked suitable ports, Italy was ambitious to secure ports on the Dalmatian and Albanian coasts in addition to Trieste and Fiume. The marriage of King Victor Emmanuel III (1900-46) to Elena, the daughter of King Nicholas of Montenegro, attested to Rome's interest in the eastern Adriatic. By reviving Venetian traditions, of which Italy was considered the heir, Rome aspired to play a role in the Balkans. A first indication of such interest was Italy's attempts to thwart French influence in the schools and churches. Italy took advantage of the breach between France and the Papacy in 1904-05 to commence active missionary work in the Balkans.

As for Germany, Bismarck had declared that the Balkans did not interest him. He once said, "The Balkans are not worth the bones of a Pomeranian grenadier." At the Congress of Berlin, pretending to act as the honest broker, Bismarck strove to assuage Russia's chagrin since he wished to befriend that power and support Austria whom he was grooming as Germany's ally. But while proclaiming Germany's disinterest in the Balkans, Bismarck was encouraging Austria in the peninsula.

By 1878 the new Balkan states were pieces on an international chessboard and in the hands of the European capitals who were about to begin the game of maneuvering them. The peninsula was a triple hotbed of trouble produced by the revolt of the Christians against their Moslem rulers, quarrels among the Christians themselves, and, not the least of their woes, rivalries of the powers who were their protectors. The Balkans became the powder-keg of Europe; that has been repeated quite often. But was it not Europe who had placed many of the explosives there? Aggravation of the troubles ultimately put the Macedonian Question before public opinion.

Although he could not ignore Macedonia, Ferdinand of Bulgaria hesitated to change the status quo. Bulgaria was tempted to send her strong, well-disciplined army to the Aegean Sea and annex Macedonia in the process. This policy was advocated by the Supreme Committee or External Macedonian Organization, established in Sofia in 1895, in opposition to IMRO (founded in 1893 at Salonika) which wanted autonomy of the province within a great Balkan federation. The Supreme Organization began raids, and its resort to violence forced IMRO, which had originally abjured the use of terror, to engage in similar tactics. The rival groups soon fought each other.

In 1903 disorders became widespread. Bulgarians, Greeks, Serbs, and Albanians were at loggerheads. Macedonia became the scene of wild anarchy. By the end of October the Turks had suppressed the fighting. The sultan selected one of his most experienced administrators, Hilmi Pasha (1859-1923), for the new post of inspector general of the three Macedonian vilayets. Despite his extensive powers and sincere efforts, the disorders intensified. This crisis prompted Austria and Russia, the two closest and most concerned of the powers, to extend their accord of Reichstadt (1876). Emperor Francis Joseph and Tsar Nicholas II met at Mürzsteg near Vienna in September 1903 to propose reforms for Macedonia. Convinced that foreign gendarmes were needed to support the Turkish authorities, the two emperors proposed to offer the services of Austrian and Russian agents. The other powers were not prepared to permit the two emperors to intervene alone.

Thus a project was created in which the six great powers participated in an international police force and designed financial arrangements. But the sultan rejected the offer because he considered it an unwarranted intervention in Turkey's internal affairs. The powers refused to yield. Only Germany, persevering in a policy of extreme circumspection about Sultan Abdul Hamid, abstained from joining in the démarche. Although lacking Germany's insistence, the will of Europe had been so clearly expressed that the sultan had to capitulate. It was agreed that part of the levies would be designated for a reorganization of Macedonia. Several foreign financial advisers would assist in the project. Moreover, a corps of sixty officers from the armies of the powers was charged with training the Turkish gendarmerie and operating a school for training the police. The center of this project was at Salonika which had the advantage of being near Constantinople, to which it was linked by a railway, and at the entrance to the Vardar valley through which travel into Macedonia was made accessible.

An explanation of Germany's abstention was due to the policy of friendship adopted by Emperor William for Sultan Abdul Hamid and the Moslems. In 1889 the emperor had made a sensational journey to Constantinople, and in 1898 he visited Syria and the Holy Land. This friendship was manifested by Germany's hesitant support for Europe's intercession in the Cretan and Armenian crises. William's attitude toward Macedonia merely accentuated his benevolence toward the Turks.

Germany was thus protecting Turkey. Baron von Marschall, the German ambassador at Constantinople, adroitly served German interests. But German friendship was not motivated by good will.

Efforts to make Turkey an economic satellite and eventually a military ally were concealed by this show of friendship. General Kolmar von der Goltz (1843-1916), supported by a staff of capable officers, arrived in Turkey in 1883 and for about a quarter-century trained the Turkish army on the German model. Turkish officers went to Berlin to study. The Ottoman army was equipped with Krupp cannon. Turkey was descended upon by a veritable army of German financiers, engineers, and merchants. The Orient Bank was founded by the Germans in 1904 to accelerate commercial development and to finance German traveling salesmen. Germany created a special line, the Deutsche Levant Linie, to complement the ships of the Hamburg-America Line in the eastern Mediterranean.

German industry achieved especially remarkable success in the Ottoman Empire. The Turks granted to a German company the right to construct a railway across Asia Minor to Baghdad and the Persian Gulf. This was to be the Berlin-to-Baghdad Railway. To furnish this line with an attractive point of departure from Europe into Asia, Sultan Abdul Hamid permitted Berlin engineers to construct a monumental depot in the new port of Haidar Pasha on the Asian shore of the Bosporus. Thus, at the beginning of this century, a new factor had appeared in the Balkans. This German political, economic, and strategic penetration was indisputably active, ambitious, and versatile. Germany was not alone, however. Berlin pushed Vienna since the latter's interests were bound up with the Germans. Antagonisms whose shock would set Europe afire came into focus at this time. Pan-German aims would collide with Russian imperialism.

CHAPTER IV

Social Evolution of the Balkan Peoples

THIS chapter of Ristelhueber's book, written a quarter-century ago, generally reflected almost universally held opinions about the inhabitants of the Balkan peninsula. Labeled myths, canards, or prejudices today, many reputable scholars shared these judgments which were not creations of Nazi German propagandists or other ultra-nationalist polemicists. Readers of this text may consult many studies of the Balkans published over the years in which Ristelhueber's opinions will reappear as those of other scholars. For that reason this chapter is retained in the translated work so readers may become familiar with opinions still cherished by those motivated more by emotions than by reason. *Critical notes by the editor appear in bracketed sentences.* [*ED.*]

After considering the origins, historical evolution, and the processes by which independence was secured, this survey of the past of the Balkan peoples has shown the essential differences among them. Thus their particularisms, rival ambitions, and reasons why they became pawns in great-power struggles have also been treated. Before proceeding to trace their history in the 20th century, certain parallels should be established by comparing them as to ethnic characteristics [This item was always the source of the greatest controversy because scholars generally held that most human characteristics could be adduced from racial origins. Such a method is no longer considered viable in the rational sociological methodology employed in free societies today. *ED.*], historical origins, their fate under Turkish domination, and their progress toward liberation.

To affirm that no nation can justify its creation merely on the basis of the idea of race alone is commonplace. A pure race, the favorite theme of Nazi ideology, does not exist today. All races, herein cited as ethnic groups, have mixtures in which such and such an element may predominate, but without any exclusive priority. More than elsewhere this is a fact of life in the Balkans. Situated on the natural route of invasions from Asia, the peninsula was successively infiltrated by most of the so-called barbarian tribes which arrived in Europe. Conversely, the peninsula was located on the strategic route which led European armies into Asia whether they were those of the Romans, Crusaders, or German tribes.

Greece, located at the southern extremity of the peninsula, might have claimed a relative immunity from invasions. But her people were not isolated from contacts such as the Macedonian conquest in the 4th century B. C., then the Roman occupation, and finally by the infiltration of Slavs even into the Peloponnesus. [Assertions that Slavs penetrated Greek soil were bolstered by Jakob Fallmerayer (1790-1861), author of famous works on the Slav origin of the modern Greek people, *Geschichte der Halbinsel Morea während des Mittelalters* (1830) and *Das Albanische Element in Griechenland* (1857-60), who wrote that "not a drop of genuine and unmixed Greek blood flows in the veins of the Christian population of modern Greece." The debate still rages today. According to a dispassionate scholar, Samuel Hazzard Cross (1891-1946), place names still yielded abundant traces of Slav occupation south of Epirus and Thessaly, but historians have long since disproved the famous Fallmerayer thesis that the race of the ancient Greeks had been annihilated. The native Greek element in Greece was too populous and the Slav colonists too few to make Slavic civilization survive there. *ED.*] Also to be noted were the brief domination of the Crusaders, that of Venice which was more durable, and finally that of the Turks which lasted about five centuries. Thus a mingling of ethnic groups was certainly inevitable. The Greek physical type, if it offered examples corresponding to the classical age, may well have acquired new characteristics common to the peoples of the eastern Mediterranean basin.

The Rumanians, like the Greeks, may have stemmed from an indigenous (autochthonous) population. the ancient Dacians, who were relatives of the Thracians called Getae. Among the Dacians there was a more systematic mingling as a consequence of Roman colonization policies in Dacia after Trajan's conquest in the 2nd century A. D. The modern Rumanian language is of Latin (Romance) origin which attests to Roman influence in Dacia. [Rumanian historians, bourgeois and communist, consider themselves descendants of the Daco-Roman people and defend historical claims to Transylvania, the ancient Dacia, which Hungarian historians, bourgeois and communist, challenge. The Hungarians argue that Trajan massacred all the Dacians in 106 A. D., and Emperor Aurelian evacuated all Roman legions in 271, and modern Rumanians inhabiting Transylvania arrived there in the 13th century in a reverse migration at least 4 centuries after Hungarian tribes arrived. This complex historical dispute still rages. [A clear exposition is given by Robert Lee Wolff in his *The Balkans In Our Time,* pp. 31-36. *ED.*] Inhabiting the route of numerous invaders, principally the Slavs, who came from the north, the Daco-Romans could not remain unaffected, all the more because the invaders apparently stopped for some time before attempting a crossing of the Danube River. The presence in modern Rumanian of numerous words of Slavic origin reveals these infiltrations which have been accentuated by the proximity of a great Slav reservoir—Serbs, Poles, Bulgarians, and Russians.

The case of the Bulgarians and Serbs is quite different. Contrary to the Greeks and Rumanians, they did not spring from the soil which is their habitat today, but they came from far off to occupy it at a relatively recent time fixed at about the 7th century A. D. The Bulgarians, of Turanian or Mongol origin, were Slavicized by mingling with the local conquered peoples and by their enthusiastic adoption of the subordinate culture. The Bulgarians are significantly pleased to call themselves Slavs just as the Rumanians recognize themselves to be Latins. Nevertheless, evidence of Mongol-appearing Bulgarians is still found in the country. Whether this is due to perpetuation of a pre-Slav strain or mingling with the Turks, who are likewise of Turanian origin, is conjectural. Although disputes still flourish regarding what the Bulgarians are, few should be so immature as to blame their faults on any specific ethnic origin.

The Serbs, who are apparently the most authentic Slavs in the Balkans, would be accurate in claiming to be people who have experienced a minimum mingling, at least in certain regions. North of the Carpathians and east of the Vistula River, stretching east to the Dnieper River, is a region where, many scholars assert, the Indo-European-speaking Slavs had their original home. [According to Wolff, the name "Slav" remains something of a mystery, perhaps derived from a root meaning "speech" or "word," but more likely from the name of a place whose location is now unknown. From this original home the Slavs dispersed in all directions, and the southern branch reached the lower Danube about the year 600. The Danube was the frontier between the Western and Eastern Roman Empires, and the Slavs began to appear in Byzantine chronicles. An objective treatment of Slav migrations is in Cross, *Slavic Civilization Through the Ages,* chapter 2. *ED.*] Doubtless the region these Slavs penetrated was already inhabited, but the Slavs appeared to prevail without being appreciably altered. These south Slavs, known ultimately as Serbs, were protected by mountain barriers from future foreign incursions.

Mountainous obstacles also favored the ethnic integrity of the Albanians, the least numerous nationality in the Balkans. The Albanians are supposed to be derived from the Illyrians or from the ancient Thracians, mixed perhaps with an earlier settled group. Some scholars assert they descend from a Pelasgian race established in the Balkans in prehistoric times. The Albanians call themselves Shkypetars (Skipetars), the "Children of the Eagle." Like the Greeks, they claimed to be the most ancient people in the peninsula. Slav incursions from the north, Greek penetration from the south, and a long Turkish domination resisted by the Albanians have modified the religious beliefs and political tendencies, but did not alter the mode of existence of these underdeveloped peoples or their language, whose origins have perplexed philologists.

Generally speaking, the Balkan peoples have not mingled in recent times because of their constant antagonisms. Their ethnic characteristics may have had some influence on their development, but such arguments are fraught with ambiguity, emotions, and such uncertainty as to assign their examination to disreputable racists. Far more scientific would be a quick comparison of the historical evolution of these peoples who can boast, in varying degrees, of ancient and glorious pasts.

As already stated, it would be superfluous here to treat the history of the Greeks who derive, and rightfully so, a double pride as heirs of ancient Hellenic civilization and as participants in the pomp and luxuries of the Byzantine Empire. After the Greeks the Rumanians claim the oldest titles of renown because of the heroic deeds of their Dacian ancestors. The rejoicing in Rome after victory over the Dacians suggested the degree of resistance the latter gave to Trajan's legions. Although an ensuing silence shrouded them for a millennium, their reappearance on the plains north of the Danube, either from slumber or migration, showed a people of vitality who, despite the approach of the Turkish threat, still enjoyed a period of grandeur under prestigious princes. But soon Wallachia and then Moldavia had to bow under the Ottoman yoke.

As for the Bulgarians, from the time of their arrival in the Balkans they displayed remarkable dynamism. About 1½ centuries after the crossing of the Danube, their expansion became so formidable that their invincible chief Krum besieged Constantinople, a feat the Bulgarians would repeat on four occasions. Reaching its height under Boris and Simeon, the first Bulgarian Empire then declined, and its enemy, Byzantium, absorbed it. Nevertheless, a brief and glorious rebirth was witness to the formidable forces animating this people who reemerged as the Second Bulgarian Empire until absorbed by the Serbs, who had been previously conquered by the Bulgarians.

The Serbs were the last to rise. History had to wait until the mid-12th century to see Stephen Nemanya impose his authority on the tribal chiefs and establish an organized state. At that time the First Bulgarian Empire had vanished, and the Second was about to arise. Although somewhat belated, the Serbian Empire shone with a bright light. The bellicose Serbs made vassals of the conquered Bulgarians. Under the rule of the great Stephen Dushan, Serbia attained a territorial extent and power which were unequaled. Never had the frontiers of a Balkan state been so farflung. Never had prosperity so flourished. A quarter-century of victories and prestige inspired Dushan with the dream of making himself the Byzantine emperor when, close to his goal, death overtook him. Only thirty years after his glorious reign the disaster at Kossovo in 1389 determined the fate of the Serbs and, at the same time, that of all Christians south of the Danube. This tragic defeat marked the beginning of the Ottoman yoke for all of them.

The fate of the Balkan peoples differed under the Ottoman yoke. The Turkish repression did not weigh on them in an equally direct and heavy manner.

The Rumanians, the furthest from Constantinople and separated by the Danube barrier, were indisputably privileged. Turkish sovereignty lasted only four centuries for the Wallachians, and only three for the Moldavians. Furthermore, the two principalities were never entirely occupied by the Turks nor reduced to the status of Ottoman provinces administered by Moslem governors. As vassals of the sultan, the Rumanians were required to pay tribute, secure the sultan's investiture of their princes, and suffer the presence of only a few Turkish garrisons on their territory. For many years the princes were selected from among members of a native aristocracy, and national life was not disrupted to the point of experiencing paralysis. Such life, on the contrary, flourished because of the relative autonomy of the Rumanians. Indeed, certain princes were veritable sovereigns under Ottoman rule. Michael the Brave was the outstanding example. He rebelled against the sultan in 1600 and succeeded, after victories over the Turks, Hungarians, and Moldavians, in establishing a greater Rumania whose resurrection would be the ideal of Rumanian nationalists for more than three centuries. The Rumanians may well have learned lessons in artful diplomacy in their dealings with the Turks, and they may have bequeathed this propensity to their descendants. But this inheritance, like so many other legacies, is still subject to considerable dispute.

Rumania's national spirit was never fully obliterated. Moldavia and Wallachia certainly used prudence regarding their relations with the Turks. Nevertheless, did not their princes act boldly in contracting an alliance with Tsar Peter the Great in 1711? Thus there was evidence of a continuity of national and cultural development and a perpetuation of traditional social classes, with a native nobility preserving its influence. Rumanian relations with Russia did produce reprisals. The Ottoman government abandoned confidence in the native princes and transferred the administration to Phanariot Greeks. The era of Phanariot governors, which endured for more than a century, is considered among the darkest in Rumanian history. It was a regime of intrigue, corruption, and spoliation which threatened to injure national spirit. Nevertheless, the Wallachians and Moldavians, even during this sad era, escaped the direct servitude weighing on their neighbors. For the Rumanians a menace henceforth came less from the south than from the north. The numerous occupations by Russian forces bore witness to the fact that protection by the tsars was as demanding as the sovereignty of the sultans. If any doubt remained about this observation, then Russia's amputation of Bessarabia in 1812 should have dissipated it. Caught between the Turks and the Russians, the Rumanians still continued to enjoy their national life. The idea of a national state persisted in the minds of an intellectual élite who strove to spread it in all directions and who maintained fruitful foreign contacts.

Greek destiny was quite different. Less favored, the Greeks saw their country become directly administered by the Turks. Nevertheless, recognition of the Greek Orthodox Patriarchate in Constantinople as the symbol of their nation constituted a privilege of considerable significance. The Greeks enjoyed the benefit of a national church. While the Church strove to maintain religious beliefs, one of the bases of Hellenism, it also worked for the perpetuation of a national sentiment while fostering the flame of the Greek idea with equal piety. The Greek Orthodox clergy even strove to force the Slavs into their orbit. Residence in Constantinople of influential Greek personalities, famed for their wealth, permitted them to become protectors of their less favored compatriots. The appreciable development of a navy, encouraged by the industriousness of distant Greek colonies in the Mediterranean, contributed to the maintenance of relations with the Greek Orthodox world. Despite such advantages, the fate of the inhabitants of ancient Greece remained quite dim. This view led Chateaubriand to believe they "would not very quickly lose the mark of their chains."

The Serbs and Bulgarians experienced a harsher fate than the Greeks. Not only did Turkish domination bend them directly under its yoke, but they did not even benefit from a national church. The Bulgarians, on the contrary, were made subject to an active propagandizing campaign by Greek priests. After the disaster at Kossovo, when many Serbian nobles sought refuge in Montenegro and Austria, the masses were separated from their élite. The fate of the Bulgarians was even worse. At first subjected to Serbian domination after their defeat at Kustendil (1330), they and the Serbs swiftly came under Turkish domination after Kossovo (1389). Their nobility, like that of the Serbs, vanished completely.

Contrary to the Greeks and the Rumanians, the latter having perpetuated their nobility, the Serbs and Bulgarians became a people almost exclusively of peasants whose great majority remained illiterate. These painful circumstances explained the marked and lengthy interruption of the march of their civilization. But they at least preserved intact a precious heritage which would someday be brilliantly revealed. One of their legacies was a propensity for war, indubitably induced by the harsh Turkish rule. The Serbs, compared to the Bulgarians, were more distant from Constantinople, more sheltered in their mountains, and thus able to maintain a semblance of autonomy for some time. Even when the Turkish yoke fell upon them in brutal fashion, the persistence of a resistance movement in Montenegro and Serbian enlistments in the Austrian armies contributed to nourishing a strong spirit of revolt. This survival of a national ideal burst forth into full light at the time of the 1804 insurrection of Kara George.

The Turkish domination, harsh for both Slav peoples, was particularly oppressive for the Bulgarians who lived too close to Constantinople, capital of the enemy empire. Constant pressure, severe and extended, succeeded in so completely obliterating their national consciousness that it was the slowest of all to revive. A sudden resurrection of that spirit had to wait until the end of the 19th century.

The Ottoman domination, by its very nature and duration, presented a gradation whose two extremes were represented by the Rumanians and the Bulgarians, the former at the top and the latter at the bottom of the scale, then moving to the Greeks who enjoyed certain privileges, and then to the Serbs who were subjugated but less harshly oppressed than their neighbors, the Bulgarians.

If the steps by which independence was achieved are examined, remarkable differences may be noted as much from the viewpoint of the nature of individual efforts as from that of the support given by the great powers. The privileged people in this field were the Rumanians. Having preserved their nobility, they were guided in this path by their princes. This aristocracy of birth and wealth encountered the competition of of an intellectual élite who were not always identical to the nobility. After studying abroad, especially in France where young Rumanians like Ioan Bratianu played a role in the 1848 revolution in Paris, these students returned home to spread ideas of freedom which they had learned to appreciate during their sojourn abroad. Thus the Rumanian liberation movement was directed by an intellectual élite which gradually carried the masses with it.

The situation was more complex among the Greeks. Aspirations for independence emanated from two sources. The patriots emerged from the native soil as rough mountaineers or sailors, who were the first to demand freedom. Simultaneously an intellectual élite from abroad, notably from Constantinople, Odessa, and Bucharest, sought to assume leadership of the movement. This duality of tendencies complicated efforts toward securing independence. The military leaders, who relied exclusively upon their own efforts, were opposed to so-called politicians who were inclined to seek foreign aid so that, while the latter were equally dedicated Greek patriots, both parties came to loggerheads in a disastrous civil war.

There was a strong resemblance between the independence movements of the Serbs and Bulgarians. In both nationalities a desire for liberty was born of a strong feeling of revolt arising from popular sentiments. Deprived of an aristocracy, the peasant masses rose against the foreign, Moslem oppressors. Their leaders were recruited from the peasantry. The Serbian heroes, the Karageorgevich and Obrenovich families, were swineherds. Specific Bulgarian names cannot be cited because the anonymous reaction of the entire populace rose against those who were oppressing them.

This historical evolution was quite extended. It was slow in Serbia because Turkish strength remained quite constant at the beginning of the 19th century and, consequently, the Serbs had to proceed in stages to move successively from vassalage to autonomy, to principality, and finally to becoming a kingdom in 1878. Only in Serbia did a national dynasty reign. Furthermore, Serbia had two national dynasties whose rivalry darkened the beginnings of her rebirth. Everywhere else, in Greece, Rumania, and Bulgaria, the reigning dynasties were foreign imports.

The speed by which Bulgaria achieved independence at the end of the 19th century was due to the increasing debilitation of Turkey, the numerous rebellions which broke out in the Balkans, and especially to the vigor of Russian intervention in favor of the Bulgarians. This leads quite logically to the role and significance of the assistance given by the powers to the liberation of the Balkan peoples.

The role of foreign assistance was fundamental for Bulgaria. Almost unknown in 1875, when the Bosnians rebelled, Bulgaria awakened from a long slumber to be promoted suddenly to the rank of an independent state in 1878. The Russians created an independent Bulgaria by the Treaty of San Stefano in that year. However reduced Bulgaria may have been after the Congress of Berlin, the Bulgarians still owed their liberation to Tsar Alexander II of Russia.

As for Rumania, Russia's intervention, although less exclusive, remained preponderant and offered a unique character. After making the Danubian Principalities her immediate neighbors, geography rendered competition impossible. Thus the tsars became the guardians of Rumania's autonomy and occupied the territory eight times in 1½ centuries. Russia as a protector did not hesitate to annex an intervening province, Bessarabia, then restore part of it, and retake it several times.

Serbia's case was quite different. Russia evinced considerable interest and lavished encouragement, especially upon the adjacent Montenegrins who were actually Serbs. Serbia, however, had a common frontier with Austria who strove to exercise influence over her Slav neighbor so that the latter was pulled in two directions by two protectors. The Karageorgevich and Obrenovich dynasties oscillated between the two. This conflict of influences, which was destined to become serious for Europe's fate, originated over little Serbia, whose territory would become the scene of a colossal struggle between Germanism and Slavism.

Finally, the fate of Greece assumed another orientation. In contrast to the peoples of the northern peninsula who lacked outlets to the Mediterranean, the Greeks had a maritime advantage without peer. Greek shores were washed by the Adriatic in the west, the Aegean in the east, and the Mediterranean in the south. Greece commanded the entrance to the Turkish Straits. Thus England could not remain indifferent to the fate of the Greeks. As a consequence of the influence of her agents, Capo d'Istria particularly, Russia could only show concern for the liberation movement. But the English government, led by George Canning, intervened in that movement. France followed, and ultimately the Kingdom of Greece was carried to the baptismal fountain by three protecting powers who kept a jealous eye on each other.

Liberation of the Balkan peoples was due primarily to Russia's intervention. To Russia fell the major role in her dual capacity of protector of the Slavs and of the Orthodox Christians. But in Serbia the Russians encountered the rivalry of Austria and in Greece that of England and France.

All nations of the peninsula were of different ethnic origins. All could claim glorious historical eras at different periods. All of them, except the Rumanians, fought each other before the 20th century—Bulgarians against Greeks, Serbs against Bulgarians and Greeks, and finally all of them against the Turks.

When the Turks subjugated the Balkan peoples, their submission to a common domination failed to inspire any spirit of solidarity. As soon as independence was achieved, however, all the peoples revived their ancient hatreds. All called upon the powers to assist them in their liberation. Thus they became clients of the powers who came to their aid, and the rivalries, already violent, were intensified by struggles for influence and conflicts of interest among the protecting powers.

What were some of the characteristics of the Balkan peoples? The numerous intermarriages practiced for centuries in the peninsula profoundly affected primitive physical types and ended up by creating, not a uniform type, but an appearance of similarity which, except for the Serbs, was related to eastern Mediteranean stock.

From north to south there is a climate appropriate to the mountainous terrain of the peninsula. Nevertheless, a common submission to the Turks and perpetuation of similar modes of existence affected the habits and customs of the inhabitants. Similar rural customs related to the great domains of the Turkish beys, who assembled Christian laborers on their estates, forcing the latter to vegetate under miserable conditions. The imprint did not vanish as soon as independence was achieved. Long after the fall of Turkish domination, the same rustic customs prevailed among peasants who enjoyed similar attire and adorned themselves with gaudy embrodiery, ornaments, and crude jewelry. They even decorated their livestock in a similar fashion. Almost everywhere patriarchal family life lent credence to a belief in the existence of a distinctive Balkan civilization.

For many years it was contended that the Balkan peoples had similar mental characteristics which were the result of long Turkish oppression. The yoke may have forced the people to acquire the habits of sneakiness and dissimulation which were found in all of them. Such were weapons of the weak to which conquered peoples are obliged to have recourse in order to attenuate the rigors of oppression. Finding it impossible to resist the master openly, they had to borrow devious methods to circumvent his authority. During the era subsequent to their liberation the Balkan nations may have continued to manifest these tendencies, which were too ingrained to disappear immediately, but they did rid themselves of these customs in proportion as the practice of independence became more natural to them. It would be unjust today to insist on this point and to see in it a common characteristic. On the contrary, each nation has presented unusual psychic differences. It may be difficult to distinguish a Greek from a Rumanian at first sight, but the manner in which the mind and reactions of either operates is clearly different.

Greece, a tiny kingdom squeezed into narrow limits, had in 1885 a population of only 2 million. The mountainous, arid terrain hardly offered any prospect of vigorous economic development. Cultivation of olive trees, grapes, figs, and tobacco constituted, along with fishing, very mediocre resources. Exploitation of lead and silver mines remained barely productive. Greece's true wealth lay in the aptitude of her people for commerce, once described as "not a mercenary task but a divine pleasure." This remarkable faculty was shared by poor and rich alike. The Greek was the businessman in Turkish villages having cosmopolitan populations. To go to the Greek was to go to the grocer. Many of these small retailers emigrated to seek their fortunes in America. They often succeeded and returned home to build houses which became the object of envy and to enjoy the wealth earned abroad. In the United States, the land of opportunity, and elsewhere, other Greeks became captains of finance, shipowners, businessmen of international fame such as Sir Basil Zaharoff (1850-1936), the famous armaments contractor born in Constantinople of a Russian father and a Greek mother, who made his fortune in London. In many foreign countries the presence of Greek enclaves, which had considerable fortunes at their disposal, contributed to the prosperity of the homeland, and had great renown as centers of Philhellenic sympathies.

The Greeks added a proverbial sobriety to these qualities. This facilitated their success. Having relatively few needs, the emigrant amassed savings in countries with high living standards. Once favored by fortune, many Greeks became philanthropic. The poverty of his soil made him accustomed to frugality. A handful of chick peas and a few olives sufficed to nourish him. And if he could add a bottle of grape wine or a glass of raki flavored with anise he was quite happy. At sidewalk cafés rows of chairs were grouped around tables at which indefatigable conversationalists discussed various topics before a miniscule cup of coffee and a large glass of water. The unchanging limpidity of the Greek sky added to the gentleness of life by spreading over everything the brilliance of its azure color like a ray of gaiety.

The remarkable development of commercial shipping added still another source of wealth. Greek ships of all sizes and shapes sailed the eastern basin of the Mediterranean and ventured even further. A coastline as irregular and gnawed away as that of Norway made Greece the home of peerless navigators. In tiny feluccas they moved from island to island, transporting the most diverse products. Where is the old soldier of the French Army of the Orient (which landed at Salonika in 1915) who would not remember the alignment of large sailing vessels laden with oranges, rising and falling on the lapping tide in the port of Salonika and whose cargo exuded aromas along the wharves? Steamships which plied the Straits, the Black Sea, the Mediterranean, and even the Atlantic were owned by Greeks. They conveyed tobacco, raisins, olives, figs of their native country, and returned laden with coal, oil, cloth, and other manufactured products.

Thus Greece constituted a "thalassocracy," possessing not only her own merchant marine, but also ports of call at Constantinople, Odessa, Alexandria, Trieste, Marseilles, London, Hamburg, New York. Greece was destined to gravitate into the orbit of the powerful English thalassocracy. French influence was also effective in Athens. It was perpetuated by an evident and obvious affinity of temperament which brought to Paris many Greek students and which made of French, as in all the Balkans, the second language of this country. Nevertheless, England had stronger attractions. A world of business inhabited by Greeks who had returned from America spoke English, a habit not entirely devoid of snobbery, and revealed to be rather deeply affected by Anglomania. More-over, England had always exercised on Greek politics an influence too obivous to be stressed here.

Greek strength resided more in the vivacity of the people than in these tangible advantages. From their ancestors the Greeks may have inherited brilliant intelligence, subtlety, suppleness, and and a taste for witty plays as well as a love of freedom. Like their forefathers, the Greeks appreciated eloquence. The word, envelope of the idea, carried them away even more than the idea itself. Like the Greeks of antiquity, they adored controversy, from which the ardor of their political passions arose, party quarrels, argumentation which grew so wild as to trouble and hinder the development of modern Greece. This is what made Greece so difficult to govern. A people enamored of independence, the Greeks too often proved to be rebels to discipline and fickle in their views. The same people who, pursuing personal fortunes with rigid willpower, allowed themselves to be seduced by the captious voices of politicians and were thus guilty of lacking strong convictions.

A too lively imagination frequently embroiled the Greeks in troubles. Inciting them to exaggerated ambitions, this imagination led them to neglect the realization of projects which were undoubtedly more modest but useful. Such was the dream of a greater Greece which dazzled so many of their politicians and obliged them to turn their attention to their co-nationalists in Constantinople, Asia Minor, and Egypt when so many other objectives should have diverted their attention to Greece proper. These were megalomaniac aims from which modern Greece suffered.

Greek patriotism was certainly exalted. The internecine squabbles lost their acrimony in the face of patriotism. Proud of the memories inherited from antiquity and capable of putting such thoughts to work, the Greeks proved worthy of their ancestors by their courage and attachment to the country. If they were not generally animated by an aggressive spirit, they gave proof of an unusual combativeness when the question of defending their homeland arose. Despite their deep attachment to the past, most Greeks were inclined to be westernized by putting into practice the most modern methods to which they were well adapted. This produced a double tendency whose contradiction was only explicable by Hellenic flexibility, a trait which probably underlay the unique continuity of their history.

Even when absent from their homeland for years, Greeks of cosmopolitan tendencies lived throughout the world, sometimes as English, French, or American citizens, but they continued to serve the motherland. Prolongation of their stay in foreign lands rarely diminished their loyalty. They proudly offered considerable donations to the homeland, which always remained their favorite country. The philanthropy of these wealthy benefactors, the *Evergets,* contributed to Greek prosperity and to adornment of Greek cities. For example, the marble stadium known as the Zappeion, a famous Athens landmark, was named for the Zappas brothers who donated a portion of their wealth acquired in Rumania to the construction of the edifice.

Many Greeks believed their culture was superior to that of all other Balkan peoples. During the Turkish occupation their zeal and energy singled them out and gave them an advantageous position, and an early release from bondage. The Greeks remained intensely nationalistic and produced very keen politicians. No foreign rule ever succeeded in killing the Greek spirit. Alien settlers were readly assimilated, except the Turks, and in that case the difficulty of religion was almost insurmountable. Thus, when symptoms of Turkish decadence became obvious, there was no need of a campaign to arouse Greek national consciousness—it was already alive.

Bulgaria, mutilated by the Congress of Berlin, had a population of about 3 million after Eastern Rumelia was annexed in 1885. Bulgaria's soil, unlike that of Greece, was quite fertile. An almost exclusively agricultural country, Bulgaria produced wheat, corn, tobacco, sunflower seed, and had made a specialty of cultivating roses whose essence appeared in excellent perfumes. When the Balkan Mountains were denuded of trees, the Bulgarians undertook steps to reforest the slopes partly to prevent the Turks, who feared the forests, from penetrating their country. Macedonian buffalo and sheep were raised in the country. The Bulgarians were essentially peasants who cultivated land partitioned into an infinity of small properties which sufficed to nourish their owners. The very few large domains were viewed with so much mistrust that the general rule was to have the land divided into modest parcels. The only appreciable industry was the rich Pernik coal mines, but their product was of inferior grade.

[According to the former generation of sociologists. *ED.*], the Bulgarian combined the characteristics of the Mongol (Tatar) with those of the mountaineer—generally slow, but thoughtful and tenacious. He had a swarthy complexion, very black hair and eyes, and his prominent cheekbones hinted of his Asiatic ancestry. Bulgarians were of average height, squat and robust, and many were considered sober, patient, obstinate, assiduous, industrious, and very attached to the soil they cultivated. The care with which a Bulgarian peasant plowed his little postage-stamp-size plot made him an excellent gardener. He was a market gardener of renown. In the Balkans the Bulgarian was the gardener while the Greek was the merchant. Besides these attractive qualities, his heredity, more Tatar than Slav, marked him with roughness, a violence bordering on brutality. Frequently cruel and excessively vindictive, Bulgarians lived in an atmosphere marked by assassinations and conspiracies which often poisoned their political life. The excesses in the Bulgarian character should not cause an underestimation of other distinctive traits. A great patriot, extremely courageous and long-suffering, not very demanding and easily disciplined, the Bulgarian made an excellent soldier. His brilliant conduct on the battlefield attested to this. He had a realistic mind, which could even be forthright and egotistical. Greek imaginativeness did not haunt him, and the Slav tendency to daydream was lacking in him. He was practical and taciturn. In the Bulgarian there was less inventive genius than an urge to learn and a rare aptitude to assimilate. When his Greek neighbor was willingly prodigal, the Bulgarian was as economical and frugal as he was avid for gain. While the Serb was often carried away by a penchant for risk and gambling, the more positive Bulgarian clung to reality and did not release the bird in hand in hopes of snaring two in the bush. Rather than borrow, he preferred to do forced labor. Never superficial, he often went to the bottom of things and liked to rationalize.

The Bulgarians possessed the qualities and defects of all peasant peoples to which should be added a primitive distrust of the foreigner, which may explain their suspicions of Russia's intentions. Their nationalism was intransigent. The Bulgarians, after achieving independence, became isolationist. Jealous of their freedom, they devoted considerable energy to forcing others to respect it. When no obstacles confronted them, the Bulgarians displayed an apparent calmness. But that appearance swiftly changed if they were challenged. More than the other Slavs, they perpetuated a certain solidarity but were obedient to orders. One outstanding trait of the Bulgarians should be noted. This was their very equalitarian temperament, a highly developed sense which made them rebel against social differences. The intense and rapid development of public education contributed to a leveling of the social classes. Although the vast majority of the Bulgarians came from the same peasant stock, the vagaries of life and a more or less admirable aptitude for study created among them a rudimentary social scale. For that reason Bulgaria inclined toward a kind of agrarian socialism.

Serbia's geographical location made her people the advanced sentinels inhabiting the junction of the great routes used by the Turks, Hungarians, Germans, Bulgarians, Albanians, and Rumanians. Serbia was the "guardian of Slav territories against German invasions," wrote Ernest Denis, the great French historian of the Slavs. In 1885 Serbia was still a very small country with a population of about 2½ million. Serbia was the only Balkan country lacking an outlet to the sea. The Danube and Save rivers formed her frontier with Austria in the north. Belgrade was separated from the powerful Hapsburg Monarchy by the Danube. Austria had encircled the country even more by occupying Bosnia and Herzegovina in 1878. Moreover, Austria had the right to maintain garrisons in the Sanjak of Novi-Bazar, a province wedged between Serbia and Montenegro. A common frontier with Bulgaria in the east was the subject of almost incessant dispute. The valley of the Vardar River passing through Macedonia to Salonika was the only route to the still distant sea. Serbia, so confined and delimited, was covered with mountains of medium height. The mountains nevertheless divided the country into almost impenetrable valleys, almost mutually inaccessible, and made Serbia a country of difficult accessibility.

Agriculture was the major source of wealth for this peasant people. The Serbs engaged principally in raising livestock, especially pigs, cultivating wheat, growing fruit trees whose plum varieties were renowned. Industry was almost non-existent except for rich copper and some gold mines in the region of Bor.

The Serb was essentially a warrior. From the age of 15 every male adolescent dreamed of bearing arms. The Bulgarian was an equally good soldier, but he had to leave his fields to fight when circumstances required it, whereas the Serb was generally animated by a more aggressive spirit which arose from his self-esteem and great confidence. Of fiercely independent temperament, the Serb, too, loved his country with pride. That inspired in him an almost excessive nationalism. Determined to secure all the territory inhabited by his co-nationalists, the Serb was ready to dedicate to this aim the courage and endurance which made him an excellent soldier. The Serbs delighted in hearing or intoning the endless romances celebrating the feats of their national heroes; for every true Serb lived as much in the past as in the present, and medieval wars still constantly furnished themes of new legends and ballads.

Less sober than the Bulgarians, the Serbs were, like the latter, attached to the soil, rude, and often violent. But their indisputable Slav origin inclined them toward that dreaminess of which their neighbors were insensible. Thus might be explained the certain instability which made the Serbs take hasty decisions, for they were more capable of heroism than of reflection. The poetic element was easily raised to the surface among the Serbs, and that is why their folklore was so rich regarding legends about Kossovo. Serbian religious sense was not very profound, and so they had a tendency to become enamored of an ideology to which the Bulgarians remained generally refractory, and more than the latter, the Serbs were sensitive to the effect of the spoken or written word. If their sentiment of Slav solidarity was developed and quite lively, their more profound individualism made them lean less toward unity and more toward rebellion against discipline. Less opinionated than the Bulgarians, the Serbs possessed an enthusiasm replete with resources. This enthusiasm, however, was frequently succeeded by depression. Like many Slavs, the Serbs had successive periods of exaltation and depression, with confidence temperament suddenly displacing discouragement. This disposition was apparently the result of a nervous and imaginative temperament. The Serb was more generous than his Bulgarian neighbor, who was more economical. While one held to the present and left nothing to chance, the other, less realistic, willingly banked on the future. The Serb easily borrowed and gambled.

Serbia was a land without aristocracy or middle classes in the 19th century. The inhabitants, less thrifty and industrious than the Bulgarians, less martial than the Montenegrins, less versatile and intellectual than the Rumanians, valued comfort more highly than progress. A moderate amount of labor enabled them to live well enough, and to pass their evenings at the village saloon; although being a relatively sober people, they met there rather to discuss politics than to drink. The Serbs never tired of politics, and still greater was their devotion to music, poetry, and dancing. Few countries in the Balkans were richer in myth and folklore. The peasants believed in charms and omens, in vampires, werewolves, ghosts, the evil eye, and white-robed spirits of the earth, air, stream, and mountains, with hoofs like a goat and henna-dyed nails and hair. Even at the beginning of the 20th century education had achieved little in dispelling such superstitions.

Specific physical characteristics could not be assigned to the Serb. Primitive Slav characteristics have been weakened as a consequence of centuries of intermarriage with non-Slavs. Nevertheless, most Serbs were often of considerable height, generally less brunette than their Balkan neighbors, and with lighter colored eyes. These characteristics were not typical of all inhabitants of that vast region which later became Yugoslavia, of which Serbia was only the nucleus. A prolonged existence under different regimes diversified the Serbs, Croats, Bosnians, and Montenegrins in whom it would be vain to claim to recognize the same temperament or type as that of the Serbs. History proves that, however blessed the Serbs may have been by events, they had a rare energy and admirable talent for growth to become a powerful and effective center of attraction for all south Slavs.

Rumania was considered about 1885 to be the leader among the Balkan nations. Despite amputations by Austria in the north, who seized the Bukovina, and by Russia in the east, who took Bessarabia, Rumania's territory extended over the lush plains between the Black Sea, the Carpathians, and the Transylvanian Alps, and the population of 5,200,000 was more than twice that of Serbia or Greece. Rumania was famed for her fertility. The plains of Wallachia and Moldavia were always considered one of Europe's granaries. The land system was one of great estates owned by nobles who had tremendous domains of more than 1,000 and sometimes 10,000 hectares (about 25,000 acres). At length, a social revolution occurred which carved up the land among a greater number of proprietors. The sub-soil competed in valuable resources. If in the 19th century petroleum was still far from offering the basic importance it acquired in the 20th, its use in modern equipment was beginning to appear. The Ploesti oilfields, exploited in crude fashion in the 1890's, revealed immense possibilities at the beginning of this century.

Social conditions in Rumania displayed extremely sharp differences from those prevailing in adjacent Serbia and Bulgaria. A relatively numerous nobility, from whose ranks the princes (*voevods*) who governed the Danubian Principalities had been selected, dominated the entire country by their possession of most of the land, wealth, and education. Far beneath their level was the peasant mass which struggled to maintain its miserable existence.

Rumania was probably the most multinational of the Balkan states at the beginning of the 20th century. Although Rumanians constituted about 90% of the total population in 1900, the population of foreign ancestry comprised many Jews, Armenians, Gypsies, Greeks, Germans, Turks, Tatars, Hungarians, Serbs, and Bulgarians. The Jews increased more rapidly than any of these peoples except the Armenians. They congregated in the larger towns. Bitter feeling against them was not so much due to religion as to a fear that if given political rights they would soon seize the entire country. Jews comprised majorities in many northern Moldavian towns, and their total number in Rumania (about 250,000 in 1900) constituted about 5 per cent of the total population, a larger ratio than existed in any other country in the world. In many places the Jews had a monopoly of the wine shops, and retail trade generally. Limited in their occupations to trade and money-lending, the Jews, who were probably more intelligent and better educated than the peasants, left little doubt that in a young country where the nobles were proverbially extravagant and the peasants in constant need, the soil would soon fall into Jewish hands were it not for stringent laws which prevented them from owning land outside the towns. When furthermore it was apparent that the Moldavian Jews, who were of Polish or Russian origin, spoke a foreign language, wore distinguishing attire, and remained aloof from their neighbors, the antipathy in which they were held may be generally understood.

The Gypsies, who were converts to the Orthodox faith, still clung to their vagabond existence, although their handicraft skills found them employment in the towns. The Greeks formed a mobile population of merchants and traders, anxious to amass fortunes and return home. German businessmen visited the country in large numbers, and colonies of German peasants flourished in Wallachia. In central Moldavia was a large Hungarian (Magyar) group, and the Serbian and Bulgarian minorities lived near the

Danube. The northern Dobrudja was inhabited by Turks and Bulgarians, with Tatars, Russians, and Armenians also in that province.

All the Rumanian peasants were not plowmen of the plains who cultivated wheatfields extending as far as the eye could see or the maize fields whose produce was constantly filling the grain elevators in Braila and Galatz. In the mountainous regions formed by the foothills of the Transylvanian Alps and the Carpathians, the Rumanians were sheepherders. They were nomadic shepherds on the move, ascending the high plateaus with their great flocks of sheep and pigs to find shelter in high chalets, then descending to the villages of the plains as the seasons changed. This occupation was so characteristic of the Rumanians that on the heights of the Pindus Mountains in Macedonia where groups of Kutzo-Vlachs exist, these shepherds were called Rumanians partly because of their calling. Thus a peasant who cultivated a wheatfield also knew how to be familiar with summits and forests.

Despite their vast numbers, the Rumanian peasants remained a negligible quantity, and the way they were treated left them very backward and usually illiterate. Gradually such misery was displaced by demands which the government had to consider when it initiated a series of agrarian reforms occasioned by general peasant refusal to be exploited any longer.

Few members of a middle class existed between the nobility and the peasantry. What should have constituted bourgeois activity was almost entirely monopolized by the Jewish minority, which was vital in the cities and towns. Finance, commerce, and the press were concentrated in the hands of this minority. Rumania did have a numerous intellectual élite. Quite talented, with supple and brilliant intelligence and a highly developed artistic sense, this intelligentsia was distinguished for its cosmopolitan spirit and particularly for its taste for things French, the heritage of a Latin spirit. Of refined culture and widely traveled, this élite had friends all over Europe, in Paris, London, Berlin, and St. Petersburg. Literature and music attracted fervent adherents. French studies were held in high esteem. Theatrical plays from Paris were performed, and the purest, wittiest French became the language of high society. The favor enjoyed by French literature was a forecast of the flourishing Rumanian writers who would someday enrich French *belles lettres*—the Countess de Noailles, Hélène Vacaresco, Princesse Bibesco, and Panait Istrati.

The long Ottoman domination, and especially the regime of

intrigue and corruption which flourished under the Phanariot *hospodars,* left a certain Byzantine imprint upon the Rumanians. Habits of softness, alleged immorality, and an apparent nonchalance were introduced into their way of life. Bucharest was renowned for its elegance and ease, and it was a pleasure capital of Europe. The very virile qualities of the descendants of Dacian warriors had softened over the centuries.

Two dissimilar types were recognizable among the Rumanians. One was fair-haired and blue-eyed; the other, more pronounced in the mountains, was dark, resembling southern Italians. Both were hardy, though rarely tall; and both, when of the peasantry, frugal and used to toil amid the rigors of the climate. All Rumanians were taught to regard themselves as true descendants of the Romans. The peasants retained their distinctive attire, long discarded, except on festivals, by the aristocrats. Men wore long linen tunics, leather belts, white woolen trousers and leather gaiters above slippers or sandals. Linen dresses of the women were fastened by long sashes or girdles, wound many times around the waist.

Many villages were built of thatch and timber, with floors raised on pilings several feet above the earth. The inner walls were often covered with hand-woven tapestries, which harmonized with the smoke-blackened rafters, the primitive loom, and the huge Dutch oven. Pagan beliefs lingered into the 20th century in Rumanian villages where vampires, witches, and the evil eye were dreaded. Peasants reassured themselves by using charms and spells, and by observance of the forms which their creed prescribed. A cross guarded every well or spring; every home had its ikons. Rumanian peasants subsisted on vegetables and *mamaliga,* a maize or corn porridge which formed the staple diet. Wine and plum brandy (*tsuica*) were drunk in quantity by peasants, but they were generally more sober than western Europeans. All classes delighted in music and dancing. Rumanian folk songs, often improvised by villagers, had exceptional beauty. National dances and music resembled those of the south Slavs.

The theories which Rumanian nationalists championed to elevate pride produced almost complete isolation for the people. Contempt for Russians, Ukrainians, Serbs, Hungarians, and Bulgarians sown among the ignorant Rumanian peasantry by the ideologists earned for Rumania only reciprocity of hatred and contempt, if not of derision and irony. Such was the price of perpetuating the Daco-Rumanian ideology.

Albania, wrote a Columbia University professor in 1914, "could almost be considered a sort of joke." A traveler returning from that country declared, the professor asserted, that the inhabitants, even the Moslems, considered themselves Greeks and the town of Koritza was actually an active center of Hellenism. Albania's existence did not really reveal itself as a political factor until 1913. Until then Albania was generally known as a very mountainous region, bristling with rocks, with a swampy, unhealthy coast, and of particularly difficult access. The country was bounded by imprecise frontiers with Montenegro in the north and Epirus in the south, and it faced the Adriatic Sea. It was a severely circumscribed country through which the celebrated Roman Via Egnatia passed on its way to Salonika.

The Albanians are apparently the most ancient people in the Balkans. History and legend offer no record of their arrival in the peninsula. They are probably descendants of the earliest Aryan immigrants, who were represented in historical times by the kindred Illyrians, who spoke a language unrelated to other tongues in the Balkans. Still known as clannish mountaineers, impatient of interference in their tribal customs, spurning civilizing influences, the Albanians submitted only with much sullenness to a superior power. The ancient Greeks imposed their authority over the region but never really Hellenized the stubborn inhabitants. Under the Romans obedience to the emperors depended precisely on military forces stationed in the region. The Albanians were superficially converted to Christianity, but probably nowhere did paganism survive longer or leave greater traces of superstition than in this inaccessible country. Despite a considerable mingling with Slavs, modern Albanians have physical characteristics which identify them with an earlier ethnic substratum. The Albanian language is not Slavic; it is a unique tongue of the Thraco-Illyrian family. The Albanians called themselves *Skipetare* (*Shqipetar,* etc.), "children of the eagle," and their country *Skiperia,* "land of the eagle." Two other names designating the Albanians are Gheg and Tosk, the former applied to northern Albanians, and the latter to the southerners. These two tribal groups were so divergent as to constitute almost separate nations. A curious diversity in religion developed after the Turkish invasions. Today about 70% are Moslem, 20% Greek Orthodox, and 10% Roman Catholic. All lived under a feudal system, grouped into tribes often at odds with each other, having nothing in common except a repugnance to all authority and distinguished by warlike attributes and an instinct for plunder.

The Albanians made the Turks pay dearly for the latters' conquest. In the 15th century Skanderbeg, their national hero whose real name was George Castriota, resisted Turkish rule and has become a semi-legendary figure. But resistance to the Turks was compensated by the ironic twist of Albanians performing a vital service to the sultans. Among the more remarkable grand viziers were the Kiuprillis, natives of Albania, who administered the Ottoman Empire at its height in the 17th century. Also from Albania came leaders who rebelled against the sultans such as Ali Pasha of Janina and Mehemet Ali, founder of modern Egypt. Services rendered to the sultans by the Albanians occasionally relieved the harshness of Turkish rule in such a way that, being the sultan's favored children, they could engage with impunity in raiding the neighboring Greeks and Serbs.

While other primitive peoples were either Hellenized or Latinized, or subsequently assimilated by the Slav migrations, the Albanians remained quite unaffected by foreign influences. Retaining their original tongue and preserving customs and institutions of remote antiquity, they still present an almost unique type, and differ dramatically from the other peoples of the Balkans. As one example, the blood feud and constant internecine warfare permitted few of them to die natural deaths. Their almost instinctive tribal system perpetuated obedience to chiefs and could have formed the basis of an Albanian empire. But they have no substantial national history, their literature consists chiefly of proverbs, and even today the Albanians remain isolated in the Balkans as Peking's only allies on the European continent. [A delightful and brief analysis of the Albanians is in Wolff, *The Balkans In Our Time,* pp. 25-31. The relative backwardness of Albania in the 20th century, probably Europe's most underdeveloped nation, is outlined in Leften S. Stavrianos, *The Balkans since 1453,* pp. 729-731. ED.]

These are then the five nations, different in origin, evolution, and character, who rubbed elbows in a relatively restricted area, the

Balkan peninsula, which has about as much territory as the Iberian peninsula at the other end of the Mediterranean basin. Five hostile nations whom a sixth came to dominate for a long time. The vast majority of these peoples practiced the Orthodox Christian faith, but it did not constitute a bond. The Orthodox Church did not have the same universal character as the Roman Catholic. It conceived its role to be national or autocephalous, not universal. Subjected early to political authority instead of rising above it, this church did not seek to unify nations as the Papacy succeeded in doing. Events clearly showed that in the Ottoman Empire the Greek Patriarchate had to submit to the control of the sultans, just as the patriarchs had to obey the Byzantine emperors. The same was true in Russia where ecclesiastical authority was subordinate to the tsars. The result was that each nationality strove to create its own national church, the symbol of its entity, so that Orthodoxy split into groups whose divergent political aspirations created rival groups.

One could impose a certain Slav community only on the Serbs and Bulgarians whose base would be an identity of culture rather than that of ethnic origin. But even this bond would be quite fragile and artificial. If it were fashionable to insist upon this tie from time to time to produce a rapport, most of the time the tie was broken by a resurgence of old antagonisms. Even these two nations, which had more in common with each other than with any other Balkan peoples, fought more fratricidal wars against each other than against other nations. Serbs and Bulgarians fought in 1885, 1913, 1915, and 1941. Perhaps this was due to the Congress of Berlin in 1878 which frustrated their national aspirations and fomented future wars. According to Stavrianos, the direct and logical outcome of the Berlin treaty was the Serbo-Bulgarian war of 1885, the Bosnian crisis of 1908, the two Balkan Wars of 1912-13, and the murder of Archduke Francis Ferdinand in 1914. The next section of this study treats this irrepressible nationalism which was also responsible in part for a penultimate resurgence of Turkish glory in the Young Turk Revolution of 1908.

Part IV

The Balkans
in Turmoil

.

CHAPTER I

The Young Turk Revolution and The First Balkan War

AFTER the Christian nations had been liberated, the Turks who, by a curious and rare anomaly, had been an ethnic minority in their empire now became the majority. Homogeneity and cohesion should have facilitated governmental administration, but general instability caused partly by attempts at reform merely perpetuated old problems. Although a constitution and parliament had been granted in 1876, both failed even before the outbreak of war with Russia a year later. Some Turks rejoiced at this failure to reform the old regime. Especially grateful was an old *effendi* (Turkish title of respect) who wittily remarked, "I thank Allah that my country has been spared the additional misfortune of a chamber of deputies."

Not all Turks concurred with this observation. A Young Turk movement had been created on liberal and national principles and inspired by ideas of the French Revolution. Its leaders wished to abolish the superannuated regime they considered responsible for Turkey's decline. This was a revival of Turkish nationalism in a new form. Not only very chauvinistic, but also very liberal in religious affairs, the Young Turks were imbued with a skepticism incompatible with Islam's rigid dogmas. Persecuted as dangerous agents of sedition and corruption, these partisans sought refuge abroad, notably in Paris where they formed an effective group. The movement had an intellectual orientation and hence few ties with the masses. Nevertheless, despite police surveillance, ideas circulated in large cities such as Constantinople and Salonika. Students and young army officers were attracted to the movement. Confronted with the inevitable end of his power in Europe, Sultan Abdul Hamid II appeared prepared to carry out a retreat into Asia which would later be executed by Mustapha Kemal Ataturk in 1919-21. The Young Turks, however, claimed they could preserve the empire by regenerating it. Their writings and newspapers prudently spread such ideas in such a manner as to circumvent the opposition of the authorities.

The clandestine character of the movement was so strictly maintained that it defied all suspicion for some time. The organization grew in membership and a network of branches. From the confines of his palace the sultan did not apparently suspect this threat when, in July 1908, he suddenly learned of an insurrection at Salonika which was inspired by the Young Turks. Why was that Macedonian city selected as the scene of the first strike? In Salonika the powers had already stationed their units to assist in governing Macedonia. The presence of foreign agents gave tangible evidence of European intrusion in the internal affairs of the Ottoman Empire. This was a painful humiliation for national pride and especially the sensitivies of the Young Turks. So it was quite natural that reaction should occur in the very place where their pride had been keenly wounded. Secondly, the arrival and subsequent operations of the international police force had disturbed the normal life of Salonika to the point where the Young Turk movement could be camouflaged.

The revolt assumed an essentially military character. It began in a barracks under the leadership of Enver Bey (1881-1922), a young, brilliant officer educated in German schools. Advancing upon Constantinople, the mutinous troops encountered no resistance in the capital and then restored the 1876 constitution. Sultan Abdul Hamid agreed to institute most of the reforms envisaged in the era of *Tanzimat*. For a few weeks a breeze of enthusiasm blew over a hopeful population. One probably incredible occurrence was reported: Moslems and Christians allegedly fraternized in the streets. Would they witness a regeneration of the decrepit, decadent empire and the establishment of an era of liberty and equality? Many apparently believed this without realizing such western ideas were incompatible with those practiced by the Ottoman regime and which contradicted the entire history of Turkey and the Moslem world. Nevertheless, the movement was welcomed with frank and open sympathy in many European nations. The powers decided to encourage it, and affirmed their confidence by withdrawing the international force from Macedonia. It was generally believed the Young Turks would reform conditions there as well as in the rest of the empire.

Leaders of the movement created a "Committee for Union and

Progress" to indicate the nature of their program. It soon became evident the Young Turks were motivated by unrestrained pride, unlimited self-confidence, and a very narrow nationalism. To their minds the word "Union," which had produced a magical effect upon the different peoples, signified "assimilation into the Turks." It would be union by willful absorption.

A first concern was the convening of a national assembly. To assure that the assembly would represent the entire empire, the Young Turks summoned delegates from Eastern Rumelia, which Bulgaria had annexed 20 years earlier, and from Bosnia and Herzegovina, occupied by Austria since the Congress of Berlin in 1878. This awkward display of exaggerated chauvinism was tantamount to an attempt to reassemble the Ottoman Empire as it had been before its most recent dismemberments. Reaction was swift. In October 1908 Austria proclaimed the outright annexation of Bosnia and Herzegovina. Inspired by Vienna's action, Prince Ferdinand of Bulgaria declared his nation's independence and proclaimed himself Tsar of the Bulgarians. Constantinople issued a strong protest and instituted a systematic boycott of Austrian products. What more could be done? Since her need for funds was desperate, Turkey had to recognize these acts in exchange for indemnity payments.

In the first decade of the 20th century intense anxiety gripped the ruling circles of Austria-Hungary. Agitation among the Slav inhabitants of the Hapsburg Monarchy, especially among the Croats, coincided with a general unease about possible dismemberment of lands from the Dual Monarchy as a result of moves by adjacent Slav states. Serbia's increasing attraction to the Monarchy's south Slavs inspired this anxiety. A south Slav conference was held in Fiume in 1905 at which Ante Trumbich (or Trumbic) (1864-1938), a Croat nationalist from Zagreb, and Frano Supilo (1870-1917), a Croat journalist from Dalmatia, launched the idea of a union of all south Slavs under Serbia's leadership. As a result of coercion and the maladroit policies of the Hapsburg authorities, the center of activity moved from Zagreb in Hungarian Croatia to Belgrade. This new orientation menaced the tottering Dual Monarchy. Thus Vienna decided to nip the movement in the bud by inflicting an irremediable humiliation upon Serbia who evinced an urge to become the point of crystallization of south Slav unity.

Baron Alois Aehrenthal was an aristocratic Austrian chancellor with narrow views. Encouraged by the military circles and under the influence of Emperor William of Germany, he was a partisan of strong action against the little neighboring country. Serbia was aware of these dangers as shown by King Peter's pursuit of a dignified, prudent, and conciliatory policy. To justify his tenacious hostility, Aehrenthal did not recoil from using any expedient. With a frivolousness which did no more to distinguish his honesty than his political sense, the Austrian chancellor formulated a series of accusations against Serbia. The first was the revelation of a plot against King Nicholas of Montenegro allegedly hatched by King Peter of Serbia, his son-in-law. Then in 1908 Aehrenthal concocted the infamous trial at Zagreb. The Austrian police manufactured the alleged existence of a vast conspiracy by Serbian propagandists to provoke agitations in the Slav-inhabited provinces of the Dual Monarchy. Influential Croat deputies to the Hungarian parliament were implicated. The courageous intervention of a professor at Charles University in Prague, Bohemia, Thomas Garrigue Masaryk (1850-1937), the future president of Czechoslovakia, revealed that the accusations were based on falsified documents. What history recorded by the term *faux d'Aehrenthal* confounded the Austro-Hungarian government by furnishing all Europe with evidence of its very pathetic police methods.

Vienna's rage intensified against little Serbia. Circumstances were still favorable to chastise Belgrade and terminate the allegedly malevolent agitation. Russia, recovering from her humiliating defeat by Japan, was in no position to engage in new struggles. What would Austria be risking? Would it not be wise to take advantage of an opportunity which might not be available again? This was the reasoning of the Austro-Hungarian General Staff whose officers urged a war. But Germany held the balance of power and, in 1909, considered a war too risky. Berlin thus restrained Vienna's bellicose ardor. This crisis, a dress rehearsal for 1914, certainly turned European public opinion in favor of the Serbs whose attitude during this period was reserved and replete with *sang-froid*.

In the southern Balkans the situation was becoming worse. Measures undertaken by the Young Turks, such as extension of military service and taxation imposed on all subjects, were arousing vigorous discontent in Albania and Macedonia. The Albanians, who had been attached to the old regime and to the sultan who heaped favors on them, protested innovations which violated their interests and customs. For the first time since the 15th century Albanian unrest became so intense that Europe's attention was drawn to this little known people. Austria and Italy, two littoral powers on the Adriatic Sea, followed with keen attention the course of Albanian discontent.

The program of forceful Turkification applied by the Committee of Union and Progress did not have the approval of all its members. The original group was soon splintered. A party with more moderate aims, the Liberal Union, attempted to restrain the Committee. Sultan Abdul Hamid, aware of dissension within the ranks of those dictating the law to him, believed the hour had arrived to reassert his authority. His attempt at a counter-revolution failed miserably. The old sultan was deposed April 27, 1909, and replaced by his brother Mohammed V, a sad puppet who was pleased to be released from a prison in which he had spent considerable time.

These shocks further weakened an already shaken empire. In Asia Minor the Young Turks, on the pretext of restoring order, allowed new massacres of the Armenians. Blood flowed as far as Cilicia in a cruel parody of the equality of races promised when the new regime assumed power. These excesses spread from Asia into Europe. The Greeks were molested, privileges of the Orthodox Church were curtailed, and new unrest occurred in Macedonia. Crete again demanded union with Greece. In Athens a military plot was organized to force King George into taking advantage of Turkey's crisis. At this time the name of a great Cretan destined to be the most capable statesman Greece would produce, Eleutherios Venizelos, was becoming familiar.

The Balkans were not the exclusive locale for international unrest. All Europe was watching developments in Morocco where Germany opposed French influence. The dispatch of a German warship to Agadir provoked a crisis which was terminated by an accord in November 1911. In exchange for granting concessions in the French Congo to Germany, the latter expressed disinterest in Morocco where France was about to establish a protectorate. The prospect of French expansion in North Africa and the turbulence Albania was provoking in the Ottoman Empire led Italy to realize her ambitions in Tripolitania. The Turkish colony of Tripolitania (modern Libya) lay directly south of Sicily. The Italians did not strive to justify their attack on this colony in 1911, declaring only that the Turks were obstructing Italy's economic activities in the region. Not content with merely shelling the ports, of which Derna and Tobruk became famous during the North African campaign in 1942, the Italians then shelled Beirut and seized the strategic island of Rhodes in the Dodecanese chain. In the interior of Tripolitania, however, the energetic Enver Bey led tribesmen in resisting the invaders. The brief war ended in July 1912 with Italy's possessions confirmed.

The Young Turk revolution was a sad disappointment for the Balkan Christians. The rebels had enticingly dangled before their eyes promises of liberty and equality, but it actually produced more chauvinism. When the Ottoman Empire appeared ready to collapse, partially as a consequence of the Italo-Turkish War, the Balkan states moved to take advantage of the occasion to realize their ambitions by expelling the Turks from Europe. But could they ignore their old hatreds and unite against the Turks? This was doubtful. Only a concerted effort could assure success since none was disposed to let his neighbor act alone or seize any Turkish territory without obtaining equal compensation. Although Turkey seemed weak, she was still strong enough to oppose them individually.

The idea of a union of the Balkan peoples was not new. One could cite the traditional friendship of Serbia and Montenegro. Suggestions about a union had already come from Athens during the government of Tricoupis and from Belgrade after Austria's annexation of Bosnia and Herzegovina. Since these were merely pious gestures, the states had never proceeded beyond the stage of establishing contacts. The Turks used every opportunity to incite the states against each other. They frequently favored the Bulgarians over the Serbs.

The Greek government was called upon to play a significant role in the formulation of plans. Crete named deputies to the Greek parliament after proclaiming her union with the mainland. The Ottoman government considered this sufficient cause for war. Nevertheless, the deputies were enthusiastically welcomed in Athens. Venizelos (1864-1936) was a member of the delegation. His appearance, which would someday become familiar in League of Nations circles, was tall, thin, a face elongated by a greying beard, and a steely look behind his spectacles. He inspired calm and confidence, and his was a clear and agile mind which surmounted contingencies of the present to envisage the future with magnanimity. A fervent nationalist but certainly no chauvinist, Venizelos knew how to accept necessary sacrifices when the need arose. More than once he would oppose public opinion to impose solutions he thought conformed to the realistic interests of Greece. Venizelos, said the Greeks, was the only man who could say no and be obeyed.

His adherence to liberal ideas was as keen as his nationalism. A true son of ancient Greece, he did not think a government could direct the destinies of a country against popular will. This sentiment would lead him to align Greece with the Allied Powers against the absolutism of their enemies. Arriving in Athens in 1909, a decisive moment for Greece, Venizelos succeeded in not only bringing about the unity of the nation by reconciling the royal family and the army officers, but also in inspiring full confidence in liberalism. His flexibility, argumentative abilities, eloquence, and even his personal charm rang out beyond the frontiers of his own country. Because of his authority, ability, and loyalty, Greece, despite the diminutive extent of her territory and the difficulty of her position, would play a vital role in international politics when World War I began.

King George, harassed by the Cretan crisis, appreciated in Venizelos the qualities of a real politician and, ignoring the fact that the latter had snatched the power of his own son in Crete, entrusted to him the direction of the Athens government in October 1910. The new premier knew how to impose himself on everyone, restore order rapidly in a country where it was lacking, and increase Greek military capabilities. He engaged a French mission to reorganize the army and an English team to train the navy. In foreign relations he sought a détente with Turkey by proposing a compromise to win time. He was ready to recognize Turkish sovereignty over Crete if Cretan deputies were permitted to sit in the Athenian parliament. The Young Turks, deaf to this argument, became more intransigent. They organized a strict boycott of Greek products. Kiamil Pasha (1832-1913), the new grand vizier, appeared conciliatory, but it was too late for an accommodation.

The Balkan states had already reached tentative agreements on common action against Turkey. Such steps were the result of Russia's encouragement and the skillful diplomacy of Venizelos, a convinced champion of a multilateral alliance system. Serge Sazonov, Russia's foreign minister, indicated early in 1912 his approval of a Balkan league. This prompted Serbia to sound out Bulgaria. Greece strove to dispel Bulgaria's reservations. The first public hint of a rapprochement came when the crown princes of Greece, Montenegro, Rumania, and Serbia participated in ceremonies marking the coming to age of Crown Prince Boris in Sofia. Exchanges of views among the five states increased thereafter.

Despite mutual antipathies, the kings of Montenegro and Serbia achieved a détente as a consequence of Austria's annexation of Bosnia and Herzegovina. In March 1912 Bulgaria and Serbia, ignoring former hostilities and rivalries in Macedonia, concluded a treaty of alliance providing for mutual assistance in the event of aggression. In May the two states modified the alliance by adding an anti-Turkish orientation to it. A dismemberment of Turkish territories seized in war was foreseen, as well as an indication of the size of the armies each state would furnish for combat. Both agreed to reveal the contents of the agreements to Tsar Nicholas II whose arbitration would be requested if dispute arose among them.

The Balkan League was being formed. To complete the chain a rapprochement was required between Bulgaria and Greece. This was an infinitely more delicate objective because of their rival aspirations and mutual hostility. Both claimed the region near Lake Okhrida in Macedonia and Thrace on the Aegean coast. Venizelos' skill modified old prejudices, and on May 29, 1912 a mutual assistance pact was signed. The treaty contained a few purely defensive stipulations, even providing for Bulgaria's neutrality in the event of a Greco-Turkish war over Crete. A military convention was added on October 5 which stipulated the precise obligations of each state in the event of a war with Turkey. No mention was made of territorial awards or communicating with Tsar Nicholas as had been provided in the Serbo-Bulgarian alliance. These interlocking treaties provided that Bulgaria contribute 300,000 troops, Greece 120,000, and Serbia 150,000.

The Turks had indirectly expedited the negotiating of these alliances. Violence committed by the Turks in Macedonia and subsequent brutal repression aroused a genuine revolt by the Albanians. Demanding the free use of their language and privileges for their schools, the Albanians massacred several Turkish officers at Ipek in Montenegro and occupied Skoplje (Uskub) in Macedonia. Already shaken, the Ottoman Empire had to confront a new insurrection while it was fighting the Italians in Tripolitania. This crisis was decisive for the Albanian rebels and also an opportune moment for the Balkan League.

Whatever may have been the degree of secrecy surrounding the negotiations leading to the Balkan League, the Turkish government, which had always relied on disunion among its adversaries, suspected a plot. The Turks mobilized troops near Adrianople on the pretext of conducting maneuvers. Despite counsels of prudence from Paris and London, the Balkan states decided to act. Intercessions failed to convince the Turkish government to offer concessions. The allied states began mobilizing their forces on October 1. Would Austria be tempted to intervene by undertaking a war against Serbia? This eventuality was feared in Belgrade even though Serbia anticipated Russia's assistance in the event of an Austrian invasion. The gravity of the situation forced Turkey to seek peace with Italy so that the former would regain freedom of action in the Balkans.

Montenegro, the smallest of the allied states, declared war on Turkey in a bold gesture on October 8, 1912. Constantinople broke all relations with the Balkan states on October 15, and on the 17th declared war on Bulgaria, Montenegro, and Serbia, but not on Greece whose intervention Turkey hoped to avert. The Greeks nevertheless entered the war. The Turks, overly confident of their strength and led by jealous generals, had to face in the Balkans four enemy nations and the Albanian insurrection while 120,000 of their troops were still stationed in Asia Minor.

The outbreak of hostilities found European opinion quite divided. A Turkish victory was anticipated by those for whom the invincibility of German strategy was dogma. Had not the sultan's troops been trained by German officers and furnished with German materials? Superb troops prior to German training, the Turks would now be invincible. Those who subscribed to this belief did not realize that the German experts did not have adequate time to teach the Turks. Greek troops had been trained by a French mission, and Serbia's army had been equipped with French materials. As in the Spanish Civil War a quarter-century later, the Balkan Wars of 1912-13 constituted a preliminary test of new strategy and materials used in the two European camps.

The armies of the Balkan allies achieved swift and spectacular victories. After a rapid mobilization, the Serbian army, highly disciplined and admirably led by General Radomir Putnik and Crown Prince Alexander, advanced toward the Sanjak of Novi-Bazar to effect a juncture with Montenegro's troops. The Serbs had to sustain at Kumanovo on October 23-24 a vigorous Turkish attack, but the excellence of Serbia's artillery routed a completely demoralized enemy. The hour awaited with tenacious and patient hope for four centuries had finally arrived for the Serbs. They made a triumphant entry into Skoplje (Uskub), the capital of Stephen Dushan, on October 26. They pursued the Turks, occupying Monastir on November 18, seizing 8,000 prisoners and 90 cannon, and reaching the Adriatic coast after overrunning northern Albania. The route to Lake Okhrida was now open. The Montenegrins led by King Nicholas made their juncture with the Serbs in Novi-Bazar.

The Greek forces under Crown Prince Constantine secured revenge for their reverses in Thessaly in 1897. The Turks were routed, and the Greeks entered the Vardar valley. Within three weeks they occupied Salonika on November 8 with its garrison of 26,000 Turks and 100 cannon. Then Crown Prince Constantine moved north to besige Janina in Epirus. The Greek fleet, the only navy the allied states had, prevented Turkish warships from leaving the Straits. This maneuver forced Turkish troops in Asia Minor to travel a long railway detour to reach the Balkan theater of operations. Because of an effective blockade, the Greeks paralyzed Turkish commerce and cut off provisions destined for Constantinople. The waters adjacent to the Balkan peninsula were freed of Turkish vessels. This facilitated the landing of 20,000 Greek-American volunteers who arrived to assist their compatriots.

Bulgaria's victories were more spectacular. Led by General Mikhail Savov, commander of a unit of the Bulgarian army in its victory over the Serbs at Slivnitza, the highly organized, well-trained army of this young nation which was resuscitated only thirty years before distinguished itself. The Bulgarians, who were located nearest to Constantinople, confronted the bulk of enemy forces in the vicinity of Adrianople and reaped a harvest of significant victories there. From October 22 to 24 the Bulgarians encountered at Kirk Kilissé in Thrace very strong resistance which they finally overcame. Exhausted by this effort, they could not pursue the Turks who retreated in disorder. A rapid advance would have brought the Bulgarians to the walls of Constantinople where, after a millennium, they might have seized the great city which had not been threatened by the Bulgarians since Simeon besieged it in 913. But the Bulgarians had to regroup their forces before marching again.

A new encounter occurred at Lulé Burgas where the Bulgarians, who relied on furious and tenacious use of their bayonets, forced the Turks to retreat further. But again the Bulgarians had to stop their advance. The Turks took advantage of this breathing spell to dig trenches in the area of the impregnable Chatalja lines immediately west of Constantinople and by reinforcing their artillery. When the Bulgarians reached Chatalja on November 16, the Turks stopped them about 20 miles from the coveted capital. Turkish troops, skilled in defensive warfare, inflicted severe losses on the Bulgarians which were rendered worse because Bulgaria's medical services were quite primitive. As for the fortified city of Adrianople, the Bulgarians could only besiege it while they continued advancing on the capital. The siege was continued because of determined Turkish resistance and the inadequacy of Bulgaria's artillery.

Turkey had thus experienced gravely irremediable defeats. Despite reverses the Turks still vigorously resisted the Bulgarians at Adrianople, the Greeks at Janina, and the Serbs and Montenegrins at Scutari in northern Albania. Europe was observing this collapse with anxiety and expectation. The Turkish soldier had lived up to his reputation until he emerged from a brief war with Italy only to face the opposition of four Balkan states. The Young Turks had committed the error of introducing politics into the army, which caused a serious weakening of discipline. And adequate time was lacking for the German instructors to complete their assignments.

The threat to Constantinople was grave especially since one could hear Chatalja cannons rumbling in the capital. Would the Bulgarians penetrate the city? Increasing fatigue among the Bulgarian troops and stubborn resistance by the solidly entrenched Turkish army complemented an outbreak of cholera among the

Bulgarians. The peril grew, and the neutral powers decided to act before Constantinople fell.

England and France decided to assume an active concern. Raymond Poincaré, the French premier, feared having his country dragged into a Balkan imbroglio by the consequences of his Russian ally's policy which, he believed, had not been fully communicated to Paris. Poincaré had not been fully advised of Russia's designs in the Balkans or of the material support extended to the Balkan League. The terms of the Franco-Russian Alliance of 1894 had indeed specified that the treaty did not extend to Balkan questions. But if the conflict were expanded into one which involved all Europe, what was the advantage of that restriction in the alliance? Poincaré preferred to circumscribe the fire and extinguish it before all Europe was ignited. He approached London and found support for French apprehensions. Anglo-French initiative produced a conference to terminate the war. Austria, obsessed with the idea of a preventive war to elevate the declining prestige of her empire, displayed a certain disinclination toward accepting an invitation, and her general staff still manifested bellicose tendencies. But Germany, still averse to launching a war over the Balkans, restrained her Austrian ally.

Austria announced her unalterable opposition to territorial access to the Adriatic for Serbia and came out for an independent Albania which would deprive the Serbs of an outlet. The Serbs remained steadfast and were supported by Russia. France assured Russia of aid in the event of war with Germany. Austria had the support of Italy who also opposed the granting of a maritime outlet to the Serbs. After hesitating, the Germans finally promised support to Austria if she were attacked while defending her interests. England sympathized with Austria's position and tried to cooperate with Germany without threatening her relations with France and Russia. The crisis became most acute in November when Austria and Russia began to mobilize their troops. Russia, still unprepared for war, then abandoned support of Serbia's territorial claims. The only alternative for the Balkan League was to seek an armistice.

A truce was signed on December 3. The allied states insisted on retaining their troops in the occupied regions. Greece refused to join in the armistice so that the siege of Janina could continue and the conquest of Aegean islands be completed. A peace conference began in London on December 17. The Balkan states, intoxicated by victory and despite obvious exhaustion, presented severe terms to Turkey. They demanded the cession of Adrianople, Janina, and Scutari, which had not yet been occupied because of Turkish resistance. When these demands reached Constantinople, they encountered categorical rejection. Indignation became so intense that a *coup d'état* was carried out on January 23, 1913 after reports arose of the government's readiness to cede Adrianople. Young Turk extremists, especially Enver Bey, who had become Enver Pasha, and his Germanophile supporters seized power after forcing the resignation of Kiamil Pasha, the grand vizier. After a month of vain discussions in London, the negotiations ended and hostilities resumed on February 3.

The Balkan states, because of their numerical superiority, finally triumphed over their adversary. The Greeks seized the islands of Chios, Samos, and Lesbos in the Aegean Sea. Janina surrendered to the Greeks on March 5 as a consequence of starvation. The Turkish commandant and 7,000 troops fled from the city and gained refuge in Albania. The Turks perpetuated a heroic resistance at Adrianople which had lasted six months. The city finally yielded after many Serbian reinforcements came to aid the Bulgarians. A general assault on March 26 overwhelmed the fortress city. Who was responsible for this victory? The Bulgarians, insisting upon exclusive credit, offended their Serbian allies by neglecting to invite them to participate in a victory march into the conquered city.

The siege of Scutari proved to be so difficult that the Montenegrins requested Serbia's assistance. The arrival of Serbian forces disturbed Austria who demanded their withdrawal. Scutari eventally capitulated to the Montenegrins on April 22 who permitted its defenders to surrender. Essad Pasha (1863-1920), the Albanian-born Turkish general who had commanded Scutari's defense, retreated to Tirana where he initiated intrigues to become king of Albania.

Alarmed by this advance toward the Adriatic, Austria and Italy, although perpetuating their rivalries, agreed to prevent the Slavs from securing access to the sea. Both pressed Montenegro to evacuate Scutari and Serbia to yield Durazzo in Albania on May 5. At the same time the Albanians demanded independence from Turkey. This demand made that country a seedbed of serious

international complications. To avert an incident with potentially grave consequences, an international flotilla was dispatched
to the eastern Adriatic to maintain the status quo until a decision
could be reached about Albania's claims. Another crisis arose
when, during an inspection of occupied Salonika, King George of
Greece was assassinated by a fanatic on March 18. This was a
sad loss for the cause of peace. His son and successor, Constantine
(1913-17 and 1920-22), the conqueror of Thessaly who was
married to the sister of the German emperor, was very concerned
with military prestige, had Germanophile tendencies, and was
stubbornly opposed to the policies of Venizelos.

A continuation of the struggle would have been veritable suicide
for Turkey. The Turkish government accordingly requested an
armistice which was granted on April 16. At least the Turks were
able to sign the truce with considerable pride because the honor of
their arms had been maintained by the courage of their armies at
Chatalja during the sieges of Adrianople, Janina, and Scutari.

Negotiations were resumed in London on May 20. The Treaty of
London was signed on May 30, 1913, after English foreign secretary Grey insisted on acceptance of terms agreed to by the great
powers. Turkey lost all of her European territories except Constantinople, the shores of the Straits, and a region east of a line
from Enos on the Aegean to Midia on the Black Sea. For all practical purposes this was a liquidation of Turkey in Europe. The
Ottoman Empire no longer existed on the European continent
except as guardian of the Straits. As for Crete, the Aegean islands,
and especially Albania, all were placed under the protection of the
great powers who decided their fate.

The question of distributing the spoils of war remained. Successes having exceeded hopes, the booty turned out to be more
considerable than had been foreseen when hostilities began. Rivalries among the allied states were not long in arising. Furthermore,
the creation of an independent Albania, demanded by Austria,
complicated the crisis even more by introducing a new factor.
Would the Balkan states, united during the hostilities, have the
wisdom to remain so in peacetime? Their histories inclined one
toward pessimism. New storms could be anticipated.

CHAPTER II

The Second Balkan War and the Outbreak of World War I

WITHIN 48 hours after signing the Treaty of London which terminated the First Balkan War on May 30, 1913, Greece and Serbia agreed to a treaty of alliance against Bulgaria. A victory more decisive than the allied states had anticipated was sharpening their appetites. Among these appetites that of the Bulgarians was the most demanding. Had Bulgaria not borne the heaviest brunt of the fighting, and were not the victories mostly due to Bulgaria's army and its sacrifices? Such was the clamor among the Bulgarians, especially after the distribution of territory produced a disquieting effect on them. Macedonia, to which each state had claims, constituted the major stumbling block.

Greece and Bulgaria bitterly disputed the disposition of Thrace and Salonika, the latter demanding a wide outlet on the Aegean Sea in Thrace and access to the Sea of Marmara in the Straits. Premier Venizelos of Greece, expressing a conciliatory spirit at the risk of arousing hostile opinion, favored a partition of the territories located north of the Aegean Sea. Greece would thus have abandoned a section of Thrace, principally the lower basin of the Maritsa River including the towns of Drama and Seres inhabited by Greek majorities. This gesture would have given the port of Dedeagatch on the Aegean to Bulgaria. But Venizelos refused to yield on the lower basin of the Vardar and Struma rivers including Salonika. The Greeks had conquered this region and now administered the port of Salonika which they absolutely refused to evacuate. Venizelos' firmness did not discourage Bulgaria's ambitions. Incidents soon occurred between the armed forces of the two states. Perhaps Venizelos' moderation, adjudged excessive by many Greeks, might have created domestic problems if he had been forced to proceed from intentions to deeds. Bulgaria's ill-tempered obstinacy enabled the Greek premier to withdraw from a potentially disconcerting crisis.

Tension was similarly critical between Bulgaria and Serbia.

Austria and Italy, who had insisted upon the establishment of an independent Albania which deprived Serbia of access to the Adriatic, wrecked the war aims of the Serbs. Rather spitefully cheated out of these shores, the Serbs, still squeezed in an untenable location, could not hope to find compensation toward the Aegean Sea. The Greeks were already occupying southern Macedonia, and its was impossible to claim Salonika at Greek expense. The Serbs could only indemnify themselves by increasing their award in Macedonia by seizing Monastir and Lake Okhrida, the central region originally destined to go to Bulgaria.

Bulgaria's pretensions assumed such hostile tones that Greece and Serbia agreed to arrange a common frontier in Macedonia to halt Bulgaria's aggrandizement and to prevent the creation of a common border between Albania and Bulgaria. Albania's independence was opposed by Serbia because the latter would be encircled by hostile states. A common Serbo-Greek frontier in Macedonia permitted the Serbs some hope for access to the sea in view of Greek friendship.

The Bulgarians clamored for the region promised them and which they considered due them by terms of the alliance of March 13, 1912. According to that agreement, Serbia would receive the Sanjak of Novi-Bazar and the territory north of the Shar Mountains (Sar Planina); the territory south and east of the Rhodope Mountains was to go to Bulgaria. The rest of Macedonia was to be autonomous, but if partition was decided on later, most of it was to go to Bulgaria, a disputed area being left to the arbitration of the Russian emperor. The Serbs, however, refused to evacuate territory promised to Bulgaria. Old hatreds were rekindled like an imperfectly extinguished fire. "Traitors, perfidious enemies," cried the Serbs. "Insatiable megalomaniacs," shrieked the Bulgarians. This exchange of invectives wrecked the fragile Balkan League. Once again Macedonia was transformed into an apple of discord to the satisfaction of Turkey who sought revenge as a result of disputes among her enemies. Austria, also jealous over Serbia's aggrandizement and the increase in Belgrade's prestige, rejoiced at the revival of territorial disputes which might diminish Serbian strength. Russia reminded the allied states of their adoption of arbitration as a solution to disputes and offered to assist in averting imminent war. Tsar Nicholas addressed personal messages to the kings of Serbia and Bulgaria in which he invoked the spirit of Slav solidarity.

Bulgaria did have a substantial grievance. The Sofia government justifiably asserted that in directing all its military efforts toward Thrace, the west or Macedonia had been neglected. Bulgaria had refused to divide her forces because of fierce Turkish resistance, and she had trusted her allies to occupy regions originally destined for her while contributing all her strength to the common goal. The mirage of a greater Bulgaria of the Treaty of San Stefano again haunted Bulgarian imaginations while the prospect of seizing Macedonia from Serbia and Greece seemed extremely remote.

Pashich, the Serbian premier, agreed to consult with Ivan Gueshov (Geshov, Guechoff), Bulgaria's premier, at Tsaribrod on their frontier. A compromise appeared imminent when the two statesmen agreed to a conference in St. Petersburg in response to the Tsar's invitation. The Bulgarians, however, were still intoxicated by their victories and immense pride, and their attitude stiffened. Gueshov was replaced by the more extreme Stoyan Danev. Victim of virtual blindness, Bulgaria scorned the Greek army and underestimated the Serbs whom she had once defeated at Slivnitza. Oblivious to a state of exhaustion, the Bulgarian general staff, encouraged by Austria, won over the government and launched the country into an adventure as doubtful as it was odious.

In Belgrade, meanwhile, Pashich was ready to heed Russia's advice. Rumania did not conceal intentions to intervene in renewed hostilities. In May 1913 Bulgaria had agreed to cede the fortress of Silistria in the Dobrudja to Rumania as compensation for the former's gains in the recent war. The Rumanians, however, now demanded more.

Suddenly and without warning, the Bulgarian troops of General Savov pounced on the Serbs near the Vardar River on June 29. A similar attack the next day surprised the Greeks near Salonika. This strategy was adopted to divide the Greek and Serbian forces. Who was responsible for this treacherous attack on her allies? Danev emphatically declared he knew nothing about orders to attack, and it appears he uttered this in good faith. The orders actually emanated from the general staff acting upon the instigation of Tsar Ferdinand who ignored his cabinet. Thus, blame for aggression must be assigned to the ruler. Ferdinand dreamed of entering Constantinople as a conqueror. His megalomania had infected his entourage which likewise envisaged Bulgaria's hegemony in the Balkan peninsula.

Fate reserved a demoralizing chastisement for Bulgaria. The Serbian forces led by General Putnik were on their guard and, after the surprise Bulgarian attack was repulsed, they reacted with an offensive and halted the Bulgarian advance at the battle of Bregalnitsa during the first week of July 1913. Developments regarding the Greco-Bulgarian fighting assumed a similar pattern. After an unanticipated shock, the Greeks repelled the Bulgarians from Seres. All along the front the Bulgarian forces, too confident of their superiority and the effect of their surprise attack, retreated in disorder.

Assured of support by Germany and Austria, her allies, Rumania announced her claims to southern Dobrudja. The Bulgarian government rejected these claims, and thus gave Bucharest an excuse to enter the fray. A new Balkan imbroglio offered Rumania an opportunity to establish a power equilibrium to her advantage. King Carol was swept up by the popular current, and he ordered mobilization on July 3. After crossing the Danube the Rumanian army pursued Bulgarian troops without any effective resistance. The widening of the war encouraged the Turks to renounce the Treaty of London on July 13 and resume the struggle by attacking the Bulgarians. Turkish forces recaptured Lulé Burgas, Kirk Kilissé, and Adrianople, thus erasing the memory of their recent losses.

Bulgaria's treacherous attacks had aroused a general outcry against them. The four allied states spontaneously united against their erstwhile ally. Soldiers of the allied forces shouted, "To Sofia!" Overwhelmed by the weight of so many enemies, Bulgaria fell to her knees after achieving the prodigious feat of mobilizing more than 600,000 men and assuming enormous sacrifies. In the paroxysm of defeat, Bulgaria's army retreated after massacring Greeks and burning their homes in Seres and Drama. These were new "Bulgarian Horrors," but this time committed by the Bulgarians.

Bulgarian premier Danev, humiliated by the terrible consequences of the act of which he was not an accomplice, resigned on July 15 and was replaced by Vasil Radoslavov (1854-1929), a Germanophile who would remain in office until the end of World War I. After merely one month of hostilities, hard-pressed Bulgaria requested an armistice on July 30. Peace negotiations opened in Bucharest. Since defeated Bulgaria was in no position to bargain, these deliberations were soon completed. A treaty of peace was signed in Bucharest on August 10. The Balkan states hastened to settle their differences before the great powers could again intervene in their affairs.

By the terms of the Treaty of Bucharest of August 10, 1913, Serbia's territory almost doubled in size and her population increased by more than one million as a result of the acquisition of the northern and central sections of Macedonia including Skoplje (Uskub), Monastir, Veles, and Okhrida (Ochrid) which gave Serbia the northern valley of the Vardar River. The obstacles which separated Serbia from Montenegro were thus removed, and the two nations became neighbors. Although Serbia's frontier was moved to within 40 miles of Salonika, direct access to the sea was still denied to the Serbs. Nevertheless, Greece agreed to furnish facilities to Serbia in the port of Salonika on the Aegean Sea.

Greece acquired the southern section of Macedonia, the shore of the Aegean Sea including Salonika, a part of Thrace as far as the Mesta River including Drama, Seres, and Kavalla, the southern part of Epirus, and the Aegean islands of Lemnos, Samothrace, and Thasos. Turkey retained the islands of Imbros and Tenedos at the entrance to the Straits. Rumania was compensated for her entry into the Second Balkan War with all of the southern Dobrudja including Silistria, a marshy region in which Rumanians were the minority inhabitants. This acquisition could not be justified on an ethnographic basis. Nevertheless, the Bucharest government believed that Rumania, as the strongest nation in the Balkans, must acquire territory since her neighbors were being aggrandized.

Rumania also raised the question of the Kutzo-Vlachs, whom she considered her compatriots. Too distant to be annexed by the so-called motherland, the Kutzo-Vlachs were abandoned in consideration of the compensating award of the southern Dobrudja. The Rumanians pointed out that they had observed a benevolent neutrality towards the allied states without assuming a really active role during the hostilities. Thus Rumania insisted she had turned the scales of the war. All these considerations led Rumania to claim a part of the spoils. This argument was accepted without serious objections because Bulgaria's attitude had not attracted much compassion.

Kirk Kilissé, Lulé Burgas, and Adrianople were restored to

Turkey despite Bulgaria's protests. The vanquished Bulgarians, denied fulfillment of their extravagant ambitions and hopes, did receive an appreciable advantage despite the severe defeat. Because of the moderating and conciliatory demands of Venizelos, Bulgaria was given a narrow coastline on the Aegean Sea and the mediocre port of Dedeagatch. Greece retained the better port of Kavalla which the Bulgarians craved. Dedeagatch and the coast were really insignificant concessions, but they constituted a moral victory. The right of access to the Aegean was granted to Bulgaria despite recent military reverses. Bulgaria thus had seacoasts on the Black and Aegean seas.

As for Montenegro, whose troops had fought valiantly in both wars, significant territorial extensions were granted in the direction of Albania and to the east near the Sanjak of Novi-Bazar. King Nicholas thus ruled over a much augmented state.

These frontier modifications did not produce much difficulty except for the situation regarding Albania. Doubtless the Albanians were a proud, ancient people with bellicose traditions. But they still failed to have a national state, being at most an ensemble of quite primitive tribes divided by religion and interminable feuds. But Austria and Italy had advanced Albania to the rank of a nation with the double intention of preventing a Serbian push to the Adriatic and a Greek hold on the two shores of the Corfu channel. These aims forced the Balkan League to stand by while Albania was granted northern Epirus and the city of Koritza (Koritsa) to the strong indignation of the Greeks who were scandalized to see numerous compatriots in that very Hellenized region pass under the domination of Albanians whom they considered barbarians. Venizelos' authority succeeded in calming the turbulence.

Albania's northern frontier with Serbia produced the most serious difficulties. The Serbs had to be evicted from certain localities granted to the new state. A sovereign was required for Albania, and the choice fell on a German prince, William of Wied, nephew of Rumania's queen, who would become a very ephemeral monarch.

Many problems created by the Balkan Wars required solutions. In terms of relative populations, the Balkan states had suffered considerable casualties: 11,000 Montenegrins, 68,000 Greeks, 71,000 Serbs, 165,000 Bulgarians, and 100,000 Turks. In territory and population Turkey was the only loser. Before the wars her European population was about 6 million, and her area 65,350 square miles. Of population she lost about 4½ million, and she was left with only 10,882 square miles of territory. Greece was the largest gainer, increasing her population from 2½ million to about 4½ million, and her area from 25,014 to 41,933 square miles. Serbia increased her population from just under 3 million to 4½ million, and nearly doubled her territory, increasing it from 18,650 to 33,891 square miles. Rumania added 286,000 to her population in securing the southern Dobrudja and now had a population of about 7½ million. Bulgaria's net gains were only 125,490 in population and 9,663 square miles. Montenegro increased from 250,000 to 480,000 people and her area from 3,474 to 5,603 square miles. The Treaty of Bucharest failed to settle questions of finance, economics, distribution among the allied states of part of the Ottoman debt, railway administration, or curbing the nationalistic appetites of the victorious states. The Balkan states had failed to incorporate all their nationals. Another war would be required to incorporate more, but still not all.

Europe welcomed the signing of the Treaty of Bucharest on August 10, 1913. After profuse bloodletting and considerable devastation, the exhausted Balkan peoples were obliged to recover their equanimity in a peaceful but brief interlude. Doubtless the peace was imperfect. Many counter-claims and much bitterness remained. But it was peace, and the people rejoiced to see it temporarily reestablished. The need for a rest would be imposed on the Balkan "nest of vipers."

Nevertheless, the tempest unleashed over the Balkans produced inevitable repercussions. The delimitation of Albania's frontiers continued to provoke resistance by Serbia and Montenegro. The award to Albania of the port of Dulcigno was made only after the Serbs were coerced into evacuating the city. Pacification of the conquered regions was not achieved until the restless minorities, particularly Turkish landowners, were appeased. Serbia realized that a prudent policy was vital to retain the fruits of her victory, and her government strove to avoid any pretexts which would arouse Austria's wrath.

Greek acquisition of islands in the Aegean Sea aroused Turkish discontent, even though the islands were inhabited by Greek majorities, which was manifested by reprisals on Greeks in Con-

stantinople and Asia Minor. The powers addressed protests to
Turkey. But the German government, true to its policy of friendship, abstained from joining in this move. The Greek government
considered sending an ultimatum to Turkey after intercessions
by the powers failed to terminate the repressions. Prior to taking
this step Athens consulted Belgrade on Serbia's interpretation of
their mutual alliance. Serbia hesitated in granting full support to
Greece for the intended ultimatum. A conference was scheduled
to be held in Brussels to settle the Greco-Turkish dispute. Venizelos departed for Belgium before events worsened and forced
him to return to Athens.

If there was any area on earth where the victories of the
Balkan League found an echo, it was among the Slav peoples in
Europe. That the Serbs and Montenegrins were proud of their
successes and joyful upon seeing their nations enlarged and having
common frontiers was a natural sentiment. Nevertheless, Serbia's
victories were equally applauded by the Croats, among whom a
lively enthusiasm was produced, and by the Czechs who were
quite distant. It could be said that a part of the glory of Serbia's
success was reflected by those who saw in it a source of national
pride.

What Austria feared was about to materialize. Basking in the
aura of victory, Serbia was becoming the focal point of the south
Slavs. Henceforth the south Slavs expected Serbia to assist them
in destroying the Austrian yoke. The Austro-Hungarian government, anxious for the stability of its fragile empire, had previously
lost opportunities to crush Serbia, its insolent neighbor. Vienna
was now firmly resolved to utilize the next pretext to secure
revenge. Albert Sorel, a specialist in Balkan history, had written
a decade earlier that "when the Eastern Question is settled, then
the question of Austria will be opened." Rarely had a statement
been more prophetic.

The advance of the Serbs and Montenegrins to the Adriatic had
provoked a series of counteractions by Austria, whose warnings
were supported by troop concentrations. The Serbs could only
yield to this by evacuating the ports denied them. Slav animosities
were no less aroused on the other side of the Danube. Viennese
authorities blamed several violent outbursts on the Serbian
government. To active Serbian propaganda were imputed the

fissures occurring among the mosaic of nationalities in the Hapsburg Monarchy. Increase of resistance by the Croats and Slovenes, Czech discontent, unrest among the Rumanians of Transylvania, and crises aroused by Albania, Austria's puppet, intensified restless repercussions. It appeared as if the Hapsburg Monarchy was coming apart, thanks to pressure from its subjugated peoples.

Only a war which could elevate Austria's prestige could save the empire from disaster. Germany, which until this time had restrained Austria's bellicosity, now lacked the same reasons to postpone a final showdown. Germany's military preparations had been completed in the autumn of 1913. An awareness of this readiness enabled the war party in the Dual Monarchy, principally Hungarian statesmen who were quite hostile toward the Slavs, to increase their influence. Emperor William and Archduke Francis Ferdinand, heir to the Hapsburg throne, met for the last time at Konopischt on June 13, 1914. Did they discuss common military action? What they actually discussed is still conjectural, but the Archduke apparently sympathized with the plight of the Slavs to whom he was willing to grant autonomy when he acceded to the throne.

In this tense and troubled atmosphere there rang out the shots which, by striking down the Archduke, signaled the beginning of the First World War. A peace had been signed in Bucharest on August 10, 1913; on June 28 of the following year, only ten months later, the inevitable storm clouds accumulated on the European horizon.

A brief recapitulation of the circumstances is useful at this point. Despite several warnings, the Archduke insisted on attending, with his morganatic wife, the Countess Sophie Chotek, military maneuvers near Sarajevo, capital of Bosnia annexed merely six years earlier. He was advised that the maneuvers, scheduled to begin on the anniversary of the battle of Kossovo, might arouse excessive agitation among the Serbs in the province. A few moments after the official procession had left the city hall, two bombs were hurled by an anarchist named Nedeljko Cabrinovich. Both exploded near the Archduke's automobile. The authorities assured Francis Ferdinand that this was an isolated act which would not be repeated. The Archduke continued his ride until he and his wife were killed by the shots of an 18-year-old Bosnian student, Gavrilo Princip, a timid-looking, nervous, and messianically inclined youth of Serbian ancestry. The Austrian police, who had been eager to fabricate false documents to rig the Zagreb trial, had been revealed as incredibly negligent in assuring the safety of their crown prince.

The Austro-Hungarian government immediately accused Serbia of having armed the assassins. Vienna insisted the murder was the obvious result of a plot whose machinations centered in Belgrade, the source of Slav agitation against the Hapsburg Monarchy. The assassins were indeed members of the Black Hand, a Serbian secret society. But between this fact and the accusation against the entire Serbian government there was a wide gap. Vienna was resolved to bridge that gap. No time was lost in realizing Vienna's will to punish Serbia as she had been tempted to do in 1908 and again in 1912. This time Austria would proceed to the very end by carrying out the threat since she was now assured of Germany's support.

The Austro-Hungarian government drafted an ultimatum containing draconic demands. Despite subsequent German denials, the contents of the ultimatum were certainly known in Berlin before it was dispatched to the Serbs. Submitted to Belgrade on July 23, the ultimatum gave Serbia two days in which to agree to suspend certain anti-Austrian newspapers, dissolve certain societies, remove some officials (a list of whom would be furnished), and, finally, to accept the participation of Austrian officials in an investigation designed to seek out the guilty persons on Serbian soil. All hostile propaganda directed against the Hapsburg Monarchy had to cease. Serbia accepted all the demands except one authorizing Austrian participation in the inquiry and trial. News of the unprecedented terms provoked indignant surprise in most countries. For a great power like Austria to seek deliberately to humiliate a small and weak country was an inglorious provocation unworthy of the honor of the plaintiff.

Inspired by Serbia's premier Pashich, a prudent statesman who was the real power in his nation, the reply was submitted before the deadline and was replete with dignity and a genuine spirit of conciliation. It satisfied all of Austria's demands except the one noted above, which was considered contrary to the sovereign rights of an independent nation. The Serbian reply, even on this reservation, was far from categorically rejecting the demand and left the door open for consultations and even compromise. Scarcely did the Austro-Hungarian envoy to Serbia have this moderate reply in his hands when diplomatic relations were broken, and he .departed from Belgrade with the personnel of his embassy. This reaction to Serbia's reply was absolutely inexcusable.

The consequences of Austria's ultimatum were very disquieting in Europe and especially distressing in Russia. Sentiments of Slav solidarity had aroused sympathy for Serbia in St. Petersburg. The Russian government announced on July 27 it would not abandon Serbia to the fate which appeared reserved for her. A long tradition of protection of the Orthodox and Slav peoples of the Balkans, which Russia considered her mission, could not be terminated without loss of prestige. On the contrary, it was more than ever vital in a crisis to show that Russia intended to remain faithful to this mission. At a time of crisis Russia could not abandon her Serbian protégé. Russia's Balkan policy was thus subjected to an unprecedented test. Russian public opinion supported the cause of the threatened Serbs. Amid great enthusiasm the Russian Duma (legislature) espoused the cause of the Slav brethren in the Balkans. It was now impossible for the Russian government to be indifferent or to retreat.

A retracing of events marking the outbreak of the First World War has been done in countless other sources and requires no retelling here. One can only note the interplay of alliances which widened the impending conflict. As Germany rallied to Austria's side, so France honored her obligations to her Russian ally which resulted in a German declaration of war on the French government. The German invasion of Belgium, in repudiation of guarantee treaties, provoked England's intervention. Europe divided into two armed camps during July 1914. The Central Powers of Germany and Austria-Hungary were ranged against Belgium and Serbia, respectively. On the opposing side was the Triple Entente—Russia, the protector of Serbia, France, the ally of Russia, England, the signatory of a treaty guaranteeing Belgium's neutrality, and the two little states which were victims of aggression, Belgium and Serbia. Thus the positions were clearly determined, and the reason for which the belligerents divided into two camps indicated what was at stake in the struggle, namely the safeguarding of weak countries against the ambitions of stronger ones.

The origins of, or perhaps the pretexts for, World War I were therefore clearly of a Balkan nature. Undoubtedly many motives contributed to provoking the war, and in the first place was the willpower of Germany who hoped to humiliate France whom she had subjected to a series of frequent alarms over the Moroccan question. It was nevertheless true that the war was unleashed by the resolve of Austria-Hungary to retard Serbia's progress and to prevent her from unifying the south Slavs. Serbia's victories in the recent Balkan Wars had gained for Belgrade a prestige which Austria had to destroy before the former could acquire more rewards. The war of 1914 was therefore the natural and logical outcome of the conflict which had just thrown the Balkans into turmoil. According to a famous formula, two culminating points had for years dominated European politics: the mountain peaks of the Balkans and the steeple of the Strasbourg cathedral in Alsace, symbols of the two dangers demoralizing the continent. In 1914 these two dangers reacted upon each other and became mingled in dragging the world into a catastrophe. In this study it is essential to realize that the war broke out at the point of intersection of the two great currents which were struggling for preponderance in the Balkans. German influence with its Austro-Hungarian vanguard would one day collide with Russian imperialism and its protection of the Slavs. Their confrontation in Serbia furnished the spark which set Europe afire.

European statesmen had been apprehensively observing the approach of spring. Their glances always turned anxiously toward the Balkan horizon which was always filled with storm clouds. Maurice Maeterlinck put into the mouth of a character in his drama, *Monna Vanna,* in 1911, "You make war when springtime comes, when the sky is as happy as a reawakening king, when the sea swells like a great basin of light . . . , when the land is so beautiful and loves men so much." He was mistaken by only a few months; men had chosen the summer to massacre each other.

The Balkan States after the Wars of 1912–1913

The Balkan States aft

of 1912-1913

Acquisitions		*At the expense of*
IIIII Bulgarians ————		
NNNN Greeks —————		Turkey
/// Serbs —————		
LLL Montenegrins ——		
::: Romanians ————————		Bulgaria

CHAPTER III

The Balkan States During World War I

THE Kingdom of Serbia was required to fight for the third time in three years when she was attacked by Austria-Hungary on July 29, 1914. Despite effective organization and high army morale, Serbia's forces reached the limit of their capacities without having had time to reconstitute the cadres or provisions. The situation appeared critical. An exhausted David confronting a Goliath, Serbia was surrounded by hostile or suspicious neighbors —Bulgarians thirsting for revenge, Albanians goaded by Austria, and Rumanians whose Germanophile king was feared. Serbia's frontiers had a vulnerability to which there were few similarities. The capital of Belgrade, located at the northeastern extremity of the kingdom, was exposed to the fire of cannons on the northern banks of the Danube in Hungary. In 1913 the Austro-Hungarian armed forces had perpetrated a series of provocations, sweeping the Serbian royal palace at night with searchlights and even photographing Serbian fortifications.

Austro-Hungarian forces crossed the Drina and Save rivers, two Danube tributaries, and penetrated Serbia on August 13, 1914. The slow mobilization of the Austro-Hungarian army permitted the Serbs to assemble heavy troop concentrations at the threatened points. Serbia faced an overly confident enemy with the heroism of a little nation completely aroused against the ancient foe and with the exemplary willpower of an aged king who was obstinate in conducting a war without yielding an inch. King Peter's officers, experienced in two recent and victorious wars, contributed their talents. To almost universal surprise, the little Serbian army, numbering only 300,000 seasoned men, successfully resisted the invader. General Putnik, the hero of Kumanovo, repulsed the Austro-Hungarian forces and then assumed the offensive. In merely twelve days Serbia was cleared of enemy forces who hurriedly abandoned many prisoners and much material.

The troops of King Peter, assisted by the Montenegrins, then invaded Bosnia.

The Austro-Hungarian general staff had underestimated the courage of the Serbs. Humiliated by defeat, a harsh affront to her pride, Austria resumed the attack with new reinforcements thrown into battle. Overwhelmed by sheer weight of numbers, the Serbs yielded and General Putnik ordered a general retreat. As a consequence, Austro-Hungarian troops advanced without encountering much resistance. They occupied Belgrade on December 2, and later took Kragujevatz and Nish. All of northern Serbia was occupied by enemy forces who then moved on the remaining Serbian outposts. Inspired by King Peter, age 71 and crippled by arthritis, the Serbs counterattacked on December 9 and routed the enemy at the foot of the Rudnik range. The enemy lost 60,000 men, 40,000 prisoners were captured, and more than 100 cannon abandoned. The heroic Serbian army had covered itself with glory. Brave King Peter returned to Belgrade a conqueror on December 15. The proud Hapsburg Monarchy, which had boasted it would inflict swift punishment on Serbia, was now cruelly humiliated.

While this epic, unilateral struggle prevailed near their frontiers, the other Balkan states prudently awaited the results of the war, each shading its policy to fit the changing scene. As already described, King Carol of Rumania had secretly bound his country to Austria and Germany without consulting his ministers. The question of the Rumanians in Transylvania had altered relations with the neighboring Hapsburg Monarchy because in that Hungarian province a national Rumanian party was demanding autonomy. As incidents occurred, the Rumanian monarch realized that his treaty of alliance had been signed in violation of the constitution and popular sentiment.

When the war began the Central Powers made vigorous efforts to remind Carol of his German ancestry and to drag him into the war. They attempted to excite Rumania's anti-Russian sentiments by dazzling her with the idea of recovering Bessarabia and even the seaport of Odessa. Rumania was divided in this difficult and dangerous position. But public opinion was generally favorable to the Allied Powers because Rumania's territorial ambitions were aimed toward Transylvania, an irredenta from which the people were impatient to expel the old enemy, the Hungarians.

At a Rumanian Crown Council session on August 3, King

Carol was obliged to reveal the treaty he made thirty years before and which had remained unknown to most of the succeeding governments. A glum silence greeted the disturbing revelation. When Petre Carp, a former premier, pleaded for the German cause, he was completely isolated. Aware of popular sentiment, the Crown Council refused to honor Rumania's commitment to the Central Powers. It was decided to maintain strict neutrality as Italy had done while proceeding with military preparations in case of any eventuality. For Carol this was a painful disavowal of his Germanophile foreign policy. The king, convinced his country had much to gain from a victory of the nation of his birth, which to him was not at all doubtful, again considered abdicating his throne as he had done in 1870. The French victory on the Marne River soon unleashed wild enthusiasm in Bucharest. Masses clamored for intervention on the Allied side. Some suggested an immediate attack on Austrian Galicia.

Cognizant of the profound gap which separated him from his subjects, King Carol's already declining health was undermined. After a reign of 48 years, during which he had rendered most eminent service to Rumania by his dignified life, his rectitude, and his qualities as administrator and soldier, King Carol died on October 10, discouraged and disillusioned for the future of a nation to which he had devoted his life. His nephew Ferdinand succeeded to the throne. More Rumanian than Carol, the new king was, by virtue of his marriage to Victoria's granddaughter, less influenced by German ties. Endowed with a cultured mind, he was somewhat slow in judgment and quite indecisive. From the moment of his accession Ferdinand imitated Italy's foreign policy. The Conservative Party, the Germanophile group led by Petre Carp and Alexandru Marghiloman (1854-1925), soon lost influence. Premier Ioan Bratianu, pressed by public opinion, announced that German forces could not cross Rumania to reach Turkey. Bulgaria took a similar step in prohibiting Russian troops to cross that country for the purpose of assisting Serbia.

Bulgaria equivocated at the instigation of enigmatic Tsar Ferdinand. Although many Bulgarians nourished warm sympathies for Russia, few could penetrate the ruler's sentiments or designs. Such a condition led the Allies to cherish the hope of dragging Bulgaria into the war. The Bulgarians could provide, by their strategic location and the proven valor of their troops, significant support to the Allied cause. The first approaches, however, met with

Bulgaria's inadmissible demands. Sofia claimed all of Thrace, a sizeable part of Macedonia, and the southern Dobrudja from Greece, Serbia, and Rumania, respectively.

As for Greece, that country was deeply divided. King Constantine, influenced by his wife, displayed a very obvious German orientation. Proud of his family kinship to the almighty German Kaiser, blinded by German invincibility, and sure of their victory, Constantine hoped to make Greece a beneficiary of that victory. Opposed to his policy was Venizelos who had been named premier in 1909. He wished to intervene on the side of the Allies in whom he saw defenders of justice and the mainstay of little nations menaced by German imperialism. Acrimony between king and premier would be marked by a duel for three years. This serious divergence would affect the Greeks who were again torn by two opposing parties confronting each other in very critical circumstances.

Serbia reminded Greece of their 1912 treaty of alliance when the war began. The Greek government replied that it would never join the Central Powers and would observe a benevolent neutrality during the hostilities. But Greece did promise to assist Serbia if the latter were attacked by Bulgaria. Athens then adopted a policy of neutrality which Venizelos, despite Constantine's pressure, succeeded in modifying by authorizing the beleaguered Serbs to utilize the port of Salonika.

As for Turkey, the simple reminder of friendship lavished by Emperor William on the sultan, German efforts to develop Turkish political, military, industrial, and commercial activities, and the pro-German orientation of the Young Turk leaders, were sufficient to attract Turkey into the German orbit. General Liman von Sanders had arrived in Constantinople in November 1913 at the head of a mission to reorganize the Turkish army. His arrival caused very strenuous protests by the Entente powers. The German ambassador, Baron von Wangenheim, as influential as his predecessors, exerted considerable authority over official circles. He had initiated negotiations of a Turco-German alliance which became a reality when the war began.

A unique naval incident precipitated Turkey's entry into the war. When hostilities began, two German cruisers, the *Goeben* and the *Breslau,* were in the Mediterranean. Both were caught as if in a trap. Not daring to pass under the English guns at Gibraltar and unable to pass through the English-controlled Suez Canal, the two ships sailed for the Turkish Straits. The cruisers shelled the French ports of Bone and Philippeville in Algeria, escaping the surveillance of the English and French squadrons and surpassing them in speed. The two cruisers entered the Straits and anchored off Constantinople on August 11, 1914. This was a forthright violation of Turkey's declaration of neutrality issued a week before. The Allied ambassadors protested Turkey's violation of the Straits agreements of 1856, 1871, and 1878 prohibiting passage of warships. To this joint statement the Turkish government replied that the two cruisers had just been officially purchased by Turkey. In fact, the Turkish flag was hoisted to the masts while the German crews exchanged their German for Turkish uniforms. The Allied diplomats were apparently convinced of Turkey's sincerity because discussions were resumed regarding Turkey's intervention on the Allied side.

What comprised a comic naiveté was explained by illusions Turkish friends contributed to lull the Allies into complacency. As far as France was concerned, there were those in Paris who were convinced that Turkey would never take up arms against a nation to which the Turks were indebted for their progress and security. Similar views were held in England. Thus the Allied envoys obstinately pursued attempts to bring Turkey to their side while Liman von Sanders accelerated Turkey's war preparations. Many German troops arrived in Turkey disguised as common laborers. Fortresses on the Dardanelles were manned, and the Straits were mined. A large loan floated by German banks furnished the necessary resources for Turkey to enter the war. Finally, the *Goeben,* renamed *Sultan Selim,* dashed into the Black Sea and sank a Russian ship. Both cruisers then bombarded Odessa and Sebastopol on the Russian Black Sea coast.

This defiant act ended the game. The Allied envoys, realizing that reassurances lavished by Turcophiles in the West had no solid basis, decided to leave Constantinople. War was declared on Turkey during the first week of November 1914. Russian troops then invaded Turkish Armenia, England proclaimed the outright annexation of Cyprus, and the Allies designed a project in March 1915 to partition the Ottoman Empire. Russia would receive Turkey in Europe except Constantinople which would be internationalized. France would acquire Syria, Cilicia, and Mosul. England was granted a free hand in Egypt and Mesopotamia. This was rather like selling the bear's skin before killing the animal. The Allies underestimated Turkish resistance.

The Russians, bottled up in the Black Sea as a result of Turkey's entry into the war, appealed for liaison with their English and French allies. The English were anxious to divert the Turkish threat to the Suez Canal. Military needs prevented the sending of troops from the Western Front. So an attempt to force open the Straits was planned. An Anglo-French expedition would seize the Dardanelles and thus open the waterway into the Black Sea and to Russia. This strategy was urged by Winston Churchill, the First Lord of the Admiralty, and it was hastily organized. The combined operation would suffer from lack of proper preparations.

To carry out this vast, dangerous, and risky operation, a combined Anglo-French fleet under English command began shelling the Turkish fortresses guarding the Straits early in February 1915. When the Allied commanders thought sufficient damage had been inflicted, the ships moved into the Dardanelles only to encounter stiff resistance which caused serious losses. The English dreadnoughts *Irresistible* and *Ocean* were sunk, the French battleship *Bouvet* went down, and severe damage was sustained by other ships. Apparently unconcerned about these losses, the French decided to continue the attack by risking new sacrifices. The English admiral, John de Robeck, considered it too rash an undertaking, and he ordered the combined fleet to withdraw. A more prolonged effort might have overcome the resistance of the Turks who were short of ammunition. In Constantinople the attack had been envisaged with pessimism, but news of the Allied withdrawal created a sense of relief. Nevertheless, the Allies had not abandoned the operation.

Allied troops were assembled in Egypt, on Lemnos, and other Aegean islands. An English ship, *The River Clyde,* went aground at the southern tip of the Gallipoli peninsula in the Straits, and was used as a landing pontoon for troop debarkation. The Allied troops secured a beachhead at a cost of heavy casualties. The Turks, strongly entrenched and capably advised by German officers, stopped the Allied advance after only two miles of penetration. The Allies were in a critical situation with the enemy in front, the sea to the rear, and bombarded on the flank by forts on the Asian shore of the Dardanelles. Disease and heat added more woes. The sick and wounded had to be evacuated under enemy fire to hospital ships because the front had no staging area in the rear. General Gouraud, commander of the French forces, lost an arm when struck by a shell. To alleviate the stalemate, the English attempted in August to surprise the Turks from the rear by landing at Suvla Bay to the north. After an appreciable advance by the Australians, the diversionary force was compelled to halt.

The Allies had insisted upon an undertaking which failed to make any progress. A complete evacuation of Gallipoli was carried out in December 1915, and this was the only successful feature of the entire expedition which cost more than 100,000 casualties. The Dardanelles Expedition (or the Gallipoli Campaign) was a staggering blow to Allied prestige in the Balkans, and for the conduct of the war in general a reverse laden with consequences. Russia, which would have been supplied as the result of a successful operation, remained bottled up in the Black Sea behind the lock of the Straits. The Allies had to supply Russia by a long and perilous ocean route to the White Sea in the Arctic. Field Marshal Paul von Hindenburg later wrote that the Allied defeat at the Straits was one of the most significant events of the war and one which contributed to lengthening that conflict.

Hostilities against Turkey were carried on by English troops in Mesopotamia and in the desert east of the Suez Canal. These theaters of operation are beyond the scope of this study. Nevertheless, the Allied forces evacuated from Gallipoli continued to struggle against the Turks in Europe. In October 1915 French troops landed at Salonika. They were joined by the Gallipoli evacuees in January 1916. This formed the nucleus of the Army of the Orient. Salonika, located near the mouth of the Vardar, the route of penetration into Macedonia, was a convenient base of operations for an army assigned to aid the Serbs. The Serbs continued to defend their country even after their misfortunes were compounded by the outbreak of a severe typhus epidemic which decimated their ranks and killed half their medical corps.

Did the Allied landings at Salonika violate Greek neutrality? The Allied cause certainly elated many Greek ministers. But from the viewpoint of international law, the legality of the operation, however justified, was debatable. King Constantine protested. The Allies ignored him, and their troops continued to land and establish several camps near Salonika.

While undertaking preparations at Salonika, the Allies strove to persuade the Balkan states to abandon their neutrality. In May 1915 Italy's intervention on the Allied side furnished a strong argument which apparently impressed Rumania. But the sudden reversal of Italy's offensive on the Isonzo and the Allied impasse at the Dardanelles only reaffirmed Bucharest in its reservations because the Central Powers were brandishing the specter of the Russian menace before the Rumanians, who were always sensitive to this danger. The cautious Bratianu continued to perform adroit maneuvers on the tightrope of neutrality.

The Allies intensified pressure on Sofia to bring about Bulgaria's entry into the war. Despite the disappointments of a Balkan mirage which had enticed and then deceived them at Constantinople, the Allies continued to interpret their desires to be reality. The Allied envoys in Bulgaria displayed a particularly impressive courtship when the Dardanelles expedition was being organized, but without any results. They renewed efforts at the time of the Salonika landings, still without succeeding in penetrating the Bulgarian sphinx. The Allies went even so far as to request Serbia to make concessions in return for Bulgaria's intervention. The Serbs were quite indisposed to concede because of their vexation in learning of the Allied promise to award Dalmatia to Italy for the latter's intervention. This promise was contained in the Treaty of London (April 26, 1915) whose secret contents became known to Austria who then divulged the information to the Serbs. Nevertheless, Allied pressure became so great that Serbia finally agreed to sacrifice a section of Macedonia to Bulgaria for the latter's intervention.

While the Allies were engaged in these tedious negotiations, Tsar Ferdinand was also negotiating with the Germans. Like their colleagues in Constantinople in 1914, the Allied envoys in Sofia, wrapped in a false atmosphere of confidence and deceived by fallacious assurances, experienced strange illusions about Bulgaria's designs. Finally, in September 1915, Bulgaria signed an alliance with the Central Powers. The Germans, outbidding the promises of the Allies, guaranteed to Bulgaria substantial annexations in Macedonia at the expense of Serbia and Greece, and assured Sofia of the support of crack troops under famed General von Mackensen. Despite these developments, the Allies persisted in negotiating with Bulgaria and even promised additional territory from Serbia. The only result of these talks was to convince Vasil Radoslavov, Bulgaria's premier, of the legitimacy of his claims to Macedonia.

Allied negotiations were prolonged by a peculiarly inveterate Bulgarophilia among the English ever since the denunciation of the Bulgarian atrocities by Gladstone. When Sofia issued mobilization orders on September 21, 1915, the Allies inquired as to the significance of this gesture. Sofia responded, "Nothing was more natural; our neutrality becomes an armed neutrality, but it does not necessarily lead to any consequences." If the Allies were displaying naive credulity, one of their number had adequate reason not to share this myopia. This was the Serbian government which did not cease to denounce the duplicity of Tsar Ferdinand. But the Allied Powers accused the Serbs of partiality and urged them to "be reasonable."

Russia demanded a clarification of Bulgaria's aims after exhausting her patience with the procrastinations of the Sofia government. When Bulgaria failed to produce a satisfactory response, Russia recalled her envoy. This was the break. The envoys of England and France also went home. Hostilities broke out on October 15 with all the vigor promised by the Central Powers. An immense offensive brought their troops into Belgrade on October 9. Bulgaria attacked the Serbs in Macedonia, and took Skoplje, Pirot, and Nish.

Tsar Ferdinand had doubtless acted according to his personal proclivities. An alliance with the German powers appeared the most promising to offer fulfillment of his grandiose designs which earlier defeat had failed to diminish. He proclaimed to his army at the end of the Balkan Wars, "Fold up your glorious flags while awaiting better days." The Bulgarian people viewed intervention more as a natural consequence of the Balkan Wars than as participation in the general European conflict. Was this not the time to gain for Bulgaria the frontiers traced at San Stefano? The war was an occasion for revenge after the reverses of 1913. This vindictive spirit impelled them to snatch from Serbia the share of booty which the latter had taken from them in Macedonia. A limited horizon made the Bulgarians more preoccupied with their own interests than the requirements of general strategy, and blinded them to the realization that they were engaged in a great war whose significance was more critical than any particular Balkan question. This observation explained why the Bulgarians, contrary to all expectations and despite tradition, were drawn into the camp of Russia's enemies.

Bulgaria's defection created in Allied circles a genuine consternation and a heartbreaking impression on public opinion. The Allied governments were accused of being duped by a sovereign whose attitude had earned for him in 1913 the epithet of "Ferdinand the Fox." Théophile Delcassé, the French foreign minister, had to resign because of popular discontent. Less severe repercussions were felt in the English government.

The position of Serbia's army became extremely critical as the result of Bulgaria's attack. Serbia had to face Austro-German forces in the north and Bulgarians advancing from the east. Almost totally encircled, only the western route to the Adriatic was open for Serbia's retreat. The army adopted this plan. The route across the precipitous mountains of Albania and along the edges of steep heights was worsened by the rigorous winter. The painful exodus, carried out with almost superhuman efforts, ranks among the most heroic episodes of the war. It was accomplished under the leadership of intrepid King Peter and Crown Prince Alexander. Poorly fed, ill-clothed, freezing in the snowdrifts, dragging along columns of civilians who were fleeing from the enemy, its convoys frequently capsizing into the ravines, the Serbian army proved its extraordinary endurance and rare willpower in those somber days.

At news of the first reverses, Allied units left Salonika to assist the Serbs. After advancing up the Vardar valley to the Struma and Cerna rivers, they encountered forces whose crushing numerical superiority rendered illusory all hopes of a breakthrough. The Allies had to retreat, abandoning their Serbian allies to the fate of yielding their entire homeland to the enemy. In January 1916 the French occupied Corfu as a refuge for Serbian troops. The Greek government protested, but the Serbs were nevertheless landed on January 15.

Bulgaria's entry into the war, succeeding that of Turkey, facilitated the Central Powers in establishing a solid, uninterrupted line of communications from Antwerp to Baghdad, passing through Belgrade, Sofia, and Constantinople. The Balkans, except for Rumania and Greece, were in enemy hands at the beginning of 1916.

After the Serbs had abandoned their homeland and the Central Powers occupied it, the question of maintaining Allied troops at Salonika was raised. An inspection by Field Marshal Herbert Kitchener, the English war secretary, led to England's decision to evacuate. But France insisted that, however tenuous the Allied positions were, the presence of a force on Greek soil was a constant notice to the Athens government of Allied determination to prevent Greek intervention on the enemy side. Aristide Briand (1862-1932), the French premier, considered deploying the forces as a threat to the flank of the Austro-German forces now concentrating on the Eastern Front. Retention of Allied troops, the majority of whom were French, at Salonika was ultimately agreed to by the English. Meanwhile, the Serbian army, encamped on Corfu where the Belgrade government also found refuge, was being reorganized by a French military mission so that it could someday resume the common struggle.

Continued stationing of the Army of the Orient at Salonika became precarious when Greek authorities produced an aura of insecurity by their equivocation. The duel between the Germanophile king and his pro-Allied premier reflected the alternating fortunes of the belligerents. Venizelos had submitted his resignation when the Allies landed at Salonika in October 1915. Constantine appointed a pro-German premier. Bulgaria's intervention then made the Greek position more delicate. Despite an earlier promise to assist Serbia in the event of a Bulgarian attack, the Athens government failed to display any token of honor. This disavowal of aid was explained by the pretext that engagements were valid only if Bulgaria alone attacked Serbia. Since Bulgaria's attack was part of a coalition strategy, Greece was not required to honor the pact. Greece was apparently pleased by her prudent policy after the Serbian debacle.

The Allied Powers had to avert an attack upon their Army of the Orient from the Greek side when troops advanced up the Vardar valley to assist the Serbs. The Allies again strove to entice Greece into the war by flattering her traditional ambitions in offering land on the shores of Asia Minor. England was even prepared to renounce her sovereignty over Cyprus. But King Constantine and his government resisted these seductive offers. In May 1916, after German and Bulgarian troops occupied a vital pass in mountainous Thrace and then seized Fort Rupel in Greek

Macedonia, Constantine ordered the Greek army to yield without any resistance. The Central Powers were then in a position to occupy the valley of the Struma River and the strategic city of Demi Hissar, a Greek fortress on the river.

The Greeks were playing a very risky game. The Allies risked a catastrophe if they tolerated an enemy advance toward Salonika and the Aegean. Certain control measures were necessary to avert a crisis which the Army of the Orient could not handle. This was the goal of a mission undertaken by the French naval flotilla in the Mediterranean. In August 1916 the mission landed in Piraeus to organize a group in opposition to the Germanophile government. German agents were expelled, and the police and postal systems came under Allied supervision. Greece was forced to yield most of her navy to the Allies. The imposition of a strict blockade served notice on the Greeks that the Allies would no longer be deceived. Venizelos, eluding Constantine's agents who had him under surveillance, surreptitiously abandoned Athens to take refuge in Salonika under the protection of the Army of the Orient.

The atmosphere in Athens intensified. Agitators aroused the populace against the Allies whose demands were considered injurious to national pride. Of course most Athenians refused to admit that Bulgarian and German forces had occupied Greek territory in Macedonia and that suspicions were growing that King Constantine was secretly bound to the Central Powers. On the other hand, Greek sympathies could have been alienated when Serbian forces, transported from Corfu, landed at Salonika on June 25, and contingents of Italian and Russian troops arrived in late August when the Allies advanced against the Bulgarians.

The English and French disagreed on steps to be taken against the Greek government. Furthermore, agreement could not be reached among the different French military units. The views of the French legation in Athens were not shared by the French military mission in Piraeus. The information services employed a different policy. This confusion was aggravated by the arrival of a French legislator who posted new demands. The Greeks were ordered to yield a number of cannon. Confronted by disunited negotiators, King Constantine took advantage of the confusion to employ aesopian language with the Allied Powers. He did not wish to appear submissive or to indicate to the Greeks that his hand was being forced. So it was agreed that sailors at Salamis would create a demonstration as a result of which the cannon would be delivered to the Allied Powers.

Meanwhile, the Bulgarians and Germans counterattacked and pushed the Army of the Orient back on Salonika. The Central Powers took Seres, Drama, and Kavalla. Venizelos established a pro-Allied government in Crete on September 29, 1916 which declared war on Bulgaria and Germany on November 23. The Allied Powers, angered by the surrender of Greek units to the Central Powers at Kavalla on September 18, demanded the surrender of the entire Greek navy. The Athens government yielded whereupon the Allies demanded the dismissal of the representatives of the Central Powers at Athens and the surrender of war materials. These demands were rejected by King Constantine.

French officers, ignoring the advice of espionage services which reported Greek troop concentrations and preparations for resistance, landed armed sailors on December 1. This contingent was attacked on the road from Piraeus to Athens; 51 men were killed and 134 wounded and strewn on the ground. Admiral Louis René Dartige du Fournet ordered the shelling of Athens. The barrage made quite an impact by landing near the royal palace. The admiral came ashore only to be seized by a crowd during a riot at the Zappeion stadium. Partisans of Venizelos were molested, arrested, imprisoned, and their houses robbed.

Allied prestige suffered a humiliating affront because of this incident on December 1, 1916. The English, French, but not Italian envoys left Athens to board ships in Salamis harbor. Would the Allies declare war on Greece? This was anticipated within a few days. After considerable reflection, the Allied governments were content to demand apologies, a ceremony of salute to their flags, indemnities for the families of the slain sailors, and reparations for the Venizelists who had been victims of the violence. The Allied forces then withdrew from Athens and Piraeus.

After Venizelos arrived in Salonika the National Defense Government was established there and granted Allied recognition. The region around Salonika, the island of Crete, and the Aegean islands rallied to the side of Venizelos. The remainder of Greece, guarding her neutrality, remained loyal to Constantine. Allied control measures were reinforced, the blockade tightened, and smoldering agitation aroused. The Allies demanded the complete withdrawal of Greek troops from Thessaly in December. The Athens government yielded on December 15. Meanwhile, the Army of the Orient under General Sarrail began an offensive in Macedonia, took Monastir, and pushed as far as Lake Okhrida. No Allied advances were made on the Bulgarian frontier.

After exhausting all patience and unable to effect any substantial changes in the Macedonian theater of operations in the spring of 1917, the Allied Powers entrusted a mission to Charles Jonnart, former governor of French Algeria, to secure the abdication of King Constantine. Jonnart's demand would be supported by several regiments of the Army of the Orient. Jonnart presented an ultimatum to Constantine on June 12, 1917, demanding his abdication and the renunciation of the claims of the Greek crown prince. At the same time Allied troops invaded Thessaly and a French force occupied the Isthmus of Corinth. The king was forced to yield, and he abdicated on June 12 in favor of his second son, Alexander, whom the Allies preferred to Crown Prince George. Venizelos returned to Athens on June 26 and was appointed premier again. The Germanophile faction terminated its vain agitation, while the Greek army of about 200,000 prepared to join the Allies in a victory to which it made a significant contribution. After many tragic vicissitudes, Greece, dissuaded for a time from her natural orientation by a king who was prone to German influence, was ranged on the side of the powers who had given her independence. There was no reason why Greece should not fight alongside her three godfathers of 1827, England, France, and Russia.

As for Rumania, whose attitude became more hesitant as the result of Bulgaria's intervention and the enemy occupation of Serbia, both of which events favored the Germanophile party, the Conservatives, in Bucharest, she was the object of particularly pressing overtures by the Allies in the spring of 1916. They strove to convince Bratianu that the time for a decision had arrived. Despite Allied and especially French pressures, the Bucharest government continued to vacillate. The political parties were divided. The Conservatives leaned towards Germany, but their Democrat wing, led by Take Ionescu, favored the Allies. Moreover, a pervasive fear of Russia served as a counterweight to sympathies for England and France. In June 1916 the situation improved as the result of an offensive led by Russian general Brusilov who, after forcing the Austro-Hungarian armies to evacuate eastern Galicia, approached the Rumanian frontier and the Hungarian plain. An argumentative Crown Council deliberated intervention. The partisans of Germany, Carp and Marghiloman, argued for non-intervention by citing a lack of preparedness, but they were ignored.

Bratianu had just concluded two years of tedious negotiations with both sides, always holding out for the biggest awards. The Allies won his favor and, on August 17, 1916, signed a treaty of alliance with Rumania and promised not to conclude a separate peace. The Allies promised a double offensive by the Russian army and the Army of the Orient, the latter still immobilized at Salonika, and the shipment of quantities of war material. In return for entry, Rumania was promised all of Transylvania and the Banat of Temesvar, most of the Bukovina, and an equal seat at the peace conference.

Rumania, emulating the action of Italy in May 1915 when Rome declared that Germany had not provoked the war, declared war on Austria-Hungary only, whom it accused of provoking the aggression against Serbia. Berlin was not deceived by this stratagem. The German press denounced the "degenerate Hohenzollern" ruling in Bucharest, and on September 5 a dirigible raid on the capital manifested Emperor William's anger. After appealing to their brethren in Transylvania, Rumanian troops imprudently crossed the Carpathian Mountains to liberate them while neglecting to take necessary precautions of defending their nation from an attack by Bulgaria. Scarcely had the Rumanians embarked on their Transylvanian campaign when Bulgaria declared war and crossed the Danube. The Russians, who had promised 500,000 men, sent only two divisions of rather mediocre quality whose units were already tainted with revolutionary spirit. In mid-September Brusilov's offensive was stopped by the powerful counterattack of German general Falkenhayn. General Sarrail's Army of the Orient seized Florina and Monastir after it finally did advance. But once these successes in Macedonia had been achieved, the army failed to proceed further.

The Rumanians were caught between Falkenhayn in the north and Mackensen in the south who was commanding a joint Bulgarian-German army. Wallachia was invaded after these two armies effected a juncture in November. The Rumanians hastily withdrew from Transylvania amid the encumbrance of thousands of refugees fleeing Hungarian reprisals. A Rumanian counter-attack on the Argesh River was routed. The government hastily moved to Jassy in northern Moldavia, and the capital, Bucharest, fell into enemy hands on December 6. Although the vital petroleum installations in Wallachia had been ignited by the Rumanians, Germany would soon have the oil flowing again into her great war machine.

For about a year the Rumanian government functioned at Jassy, and armed resistance continued despite protests of Germanophiles who insisted upon immediate peace. A French military mission headed by General Henri Berthelot reorganized the Rumanian army which halted the enemy advance into Moldavia. It even achieved at Marashti and Marasheshti (July-August, 1917) very considerable victories over Mackensen's forces and succeeded in maintaining a foothold on the banks of the Sereth River which bisects Moldavia. Nevertheless, the Austro-German armies had conquered and occupied the most valuable part of Rumania, namely the wheat-growing and petroleum-producing regions. As for the Russians, who were at first relatively indifferent to Rumania's intervention and then to her reverses, they finally sent reinforcements who were, however, corrupted by the decomposition gnawing away at their homeland. The Russian troops offered the dangerous example of fraternizing with enemy soldiers.

The Rumanians had been deeply disappointed by the failure of the Allied Powers to fulfill their treaty obligations. Bratianu justifiably complained of the scarcity of war materials and the failure of the Army of the Orient and the Russians to advance. In fact, the Rumanians witnessed a rout of the Russians in the fall of 1917 when the latter finally abandoned the struggle and requested an armistice. The Rumanian government refused to participate in armistice negotiations at Brest-Litovsk in December 1917. Bolshevik-inspired Russian troops in unoccupied Moldavia had to be disarmed and the unrest which they inspired had to be suppressed.

Confronted by a Bolshevik menace, Bessarabia, imitating the Ukraine's example, was proclaimed independent of Russia. Rumanian troops entered the province in April 1918 ostensibly to restore order. The pro-Rumanian nationalists in Bessarabia ultimately requested annexation to Rumania. Meanwhile, Bratianu, discouraged by the course of events, resigned in February 1918. He was replaced by General Alexandru Averescu (1859-1938), idol of the army he had led in the 1913 campaign against Bulgaria. After the Soviet government of Russia signed the Treaty of Brest-Litovsk on March 3, 1918, the Rumanians became resigned to the necessity of concluding hostilities. Left alone in the Balkans, the Rumanians signed preliminaries of peace at Buftea on March 5. The terms were reproduced in the Treaty of Bucharest of May 7, 1918 imposed on Marghiloman who had replaced Averescu as premier. Rumania had been lulled with the illusion that Marghiloman's pro-German orientation would attenuate the rigidity of the conquerors. This would not be the result of the maneuver. The treaty dictated to Rumania traced a harsh frontier rectification for strategic motives. About 150,000 more Rumanians were incorporated into Hungary as the consequence of the award to the latter of territory from Wallachia and Moldavia. The entire Dobrudja was not restored to Bulgaria but was instead to be administered by a condominium of the four Central Powers. Rumania retained an outlet to the Black Sea at Constantsa. No indemnity was contained in the treaty, but the methodically severe exploitation of Rumania took its place. Rumania was obliged to yield most of her wheat, undergo control of her petroleum production for 90 years, authorize use of her railways without compensation, assume payment of banknotes issued during the military occupation, permit this occupation until the signing of a general peace treaty, and generally agree to become an economic satellite of the Central Powers. The International Commission for the Danube, which had guaranteed freedom of navigation on that river, was replaced by a committee of riparian states. As consolation, Rumania was granted freedom of action in Bessarabia because the Central Powers were disinterested in that province which was contested by the Soviet Government of Russia.

While Rumania was suffering these harsh reverses, the Army of the Orient, inactive after the capture of Monastir, grew in size despite considerable difficulties. After the insecurity resulting from the Greek dilemma had subsided, the frequent sinkings of troop transports by German submarines, the outbreak of malaria among thousands of Allied troops who had to be hospitalized, and the success in securing their replacements, the entrenched army at Salonika finally achieved full strength. Not often in modern times had such a multi-national force been assembled at one point. The French, who formed the great majority, were joined by English, Serbian, and Greek forces. An Italian detachment, merely a symbolic assignment, rounded out the Army of the Orient. This large and diversified assemblage of 29 divisions with over 700,000 men had been the methodical accomplishment of General Sarrail, a talented organizer. After a brief tour of duty by his successor, General Louis Guillaumat (December 1917-June 1918), General Louis Franchet d'Esperey (1856-1942), a future marshal, was named commander. As harsh on himself as he was on subordinates, this vigorous officer, stocky, with more torso than legs, massive and endowed with indefatigable energy, immediately began preparations for a general offensive. It was unleashed on September 15, 1918, and directed against the mountainous positions of the Bulgarian forces. The Allied troops overcame these natural defenses and then pursued the retreating enemy forces. The offensive achieved its goal in twelve days. The Bulgarians requested an armistice which was signed on September 30 at Salonika. This was the first ceasefire destined to end World War I. This victory fully justified the concentration of troops at Salonika and also proved the valor of the Army of the Orient. This was the first Allied army to smash the enemy front and obtain an irrevocable decision.

Bulgaria decided on peace because of her enormous wartime sacrifices and disappointments experienced on the part of her associates. The harsh and demanding Germans had treated Bulgaria as a colony from which they exported the greater part of her produce, leaving to the inhabitants a barely adequate portion. The haughty, scornful German officers imposed their superiority on the Bulgarian army which, aware of its valor, was unjustly treated. In brief, Bulgaria was weary and discontented. As for Tsar Ferdinand, who had chosen the wrong side, he could do nothing but abdicate after this second defeat. He abandoned the throne to his son Boris on October 4, 1918. The armistice required the Bulgarian army to demobilize at once and its equipment placed in Allied hands. All Greek and Serbian territory had to be evacuated, all means of transportation placed at Allied disposal, and Bulgaria to be open to Allied military operations. The Army of the Orient proposed to split communications between the Austro-German and Turkish forces, attack the Turkish units in Thrace, and force an opening of the Straits. The Allied armies reached the Maritza River on October 30, crossed the Danube at Rushchuk on November 10, entered Rumania, and facilitated the latter's re-entry into the war on that date.

The victorious advance of the Army of the Orient permitted the Serbian army to re-enter Belgrade on November 1 after the capital had been occupied for three years. This was a triumph and a just compensation for the trials endured with as much tenacity as courage. General Franchet d'Esperey then crossed the Danube into Hungary, approached Budapest, and then threatened Vienna. The southern enemy front was broken from the rear. During October Emperor Charles of Austria-Hungary proclaimed a reorganization of the non-Hungarian sections of the Hapsburg Monarchy as a federal state, with full self-government for the nationalities. This was too late. The Czechs and Slovaks declared their independence on October 21, the Italian armies captured Trieste and Fiume during the first week of November, and the Yugoslav National Council proclaimed the independence of the south Slavs at Zagreb on October 29. That same day the Austrians offered to surrender to the Italians. Two days later an independent Hungarian government was established in Budapest. The Allied Powers then concluded an armistice with Austria-Hungary on November 3 which required a complete demobilization of enemy forces, surrender of half the equipment and of territory disputed by the Austrians, Italians, and Slavs, Allied occupation of strategic points, and surrender of the navy. A south Slav conference at Geneva on November 7 decided on the union of Croatia and Slovenia (formerly Carniola) with Serbia and Montenegro. Emperor Charles, the last Hapsburg ruler, abdicated on November 12, one day after Germany surrendered in France, and Austria was proclaimed a republic. Hungary was also declared a republic on November 16. King Peter of Serbia was proclaimed king of the Kingdom of the Serbs-Croats-Slovenes on November 24. One week later King Nicholas of Montenegro, who opposed this union, was declared deposed by his parliament which then voted for union with the new state. On the same day, December 1, a na-

tional assembly of Rumanians of Transylvania and the Banat at
Alba Iulia voted for union of these provinces with Rumania.

The Turkish front crumbled in similar fashion. The English
forces were victorious in that theater. After having suffered reverses in Mesopotamia, notably at Kut-el-Amara in April 1916,
and having seen the Suez Canal menaced, English troops recovered. Assembling a large army in Egypt, the English invaded
Palestine and Syria with the support of a French detachment.
Jerusalem was captured in December 1917, and a combined
Anglo-Arab force conquered Syria and Lebanon in October 1918.
The new Turkish sultan, Mohammed VI, who succeeded Mohammed V in July 1918, dismissed his Young Turk government
on October 13. The Turkish government appealed for an armis-
tice. It was signed by Admiral Sir Somerset Calthorpe aboard an
English dreadnought anchored at Mudros (October 30). The
Turks were obliged to open the Straits, release Allied prisoners,
demobilize their forces, and permit Allied occupation of strategic
points in the dwindling Turkish Empire. Two days after the
Germans surrendered, the war in the Balkans ended when an
Allied flotilla sailed through the Dardanelles and anchored at
Constantinople.

As for Albania whose elevation to the rank of an independent
nation and whose frontier delimitations had contributed to en-
dangering the tediously established Balkan equilibrium, her existence had also been threatened during the war. At the beginning of
hostilities her new ruler, William of Wied, after a reign of six
months, had to leave the country as a result of the hostility of his
subjects. The Austrians lost no time in occupying a greater part
of Albania after Serbia was crushed. The Italians landed troops
at Valona in September 1914, but they were driven out by the
Austrians only to return in the fall of 1918 when they proclaimed
a protectorate over the country. After Austria's surrender, Italy
attempted to extend the protectorate to cover the entire country.
The Italians did not leave until 1920 when Albania was admitted
to the League of Nations.

Most people have neglected the roles played by the Balkan
states in World War I so that attention can be concentrated on the
more critical operations on the Western and Eastern fronts. During
the holocaust which overturned and bathed Europe in blood for
four years, the role of the Balkan peoples was quite considerable.

It was in the Balkans that the spark of the war was ignited, and it was there that the fire began to die out. At the beginning of the war a third front existed in the Balkans, but it was secondary to the other two European sectors. After the collapse of the Eastern Front, the Balkan theater was substituted for the Russian sector to make up for its deficiency by becoming, because of the presence of the Army of the Orient, the second front. It would be from this southern front that would come the first decision, the one which by eliminating the Bulgarians was destined to produce other capitulations. This was essentially a French victory—French in its conception by virtue of the manuevers conceived by Briand, French in its execution by virtue of the command of Franchet d'Esperey and of the nationality of the majority of troops under his command.

Victory over Turkey, however, is recorded as an English success. England had been Turkey's principal adversary in the Dardanelles campaign and the only one in Mesopotamia and Palestine. The English finally forced the Turks to yield at Mudros. This lengthy struggle would provoke an antagonism whose consequences would be realized after the war.

The war was over. The Allied Powers had earlier declared that the peace settlement would have fateful consequences in the territories once contained within the defunct Ottoman Empire. "No peace," the European allies declared in 1916, "would be possible so long as . . . the principle of nationalities and of the free existence of small states" is violated. These principles were inconsistent with the continued presence of the Turks in Europe. Turkey had forfeited all claims to the protection of the powers. The Allies were pledged to liberate all Balkan peoples of non-Turkish nationality from rule by the Turkish government. This task had all but been achieved by the Balkan League in 1911-13. The unfinished task was completed by the Allied Powers. The peoples who had been submerged by the Ottoman tide had emerged. The Balkan lands had been divided among the Balkan peoples. The Turks ruled in Europe only a narrow stretch inhabited by a Turkish majority. The once vast empire of the sultans had come to an end.

Nevertheless, the geographical distribution of the Balkan peoples remained complex, the ethnographical demarcation was still disputed, and the frequent appeals to national self-determination would exacerbate the forthcoming peace settlement. Bulgarians, Albanians, Greeks, Yugoslavs, Rumanians, and many other smaller groups would have to learn to live together in the Balkans in an atmosphere of peace and goodwill. The Turks had imposed a fragile peace for almost five centuries. Would the final elimination of Turkish power entail a resurgence of medieval anarchy which characterized Balkan life before the Turkish conquest? Were the Balkans about to be Balkanized again?

CHAPTER IV

The Peace Settlement

A GREATER victim of World War I than Turkey in the Balkans was Austria-Hungary whose crumbled empire split asunder. The price of Germany's defeat was paid by the Hapsburg Monarchy, even as the reverberations were felt strongly by Bulgaria and Turkey. Despite Russia's defection from the war in March 1918, which was the consequence of the Bolshevik seizure of power the previous November, the final victory of the Allied Powers consecrated the triumph of the Serbs to whose aid they had originally come. The vast effort to unite the south Slavs around Belgrade would be realized according to the wishes of these peoples who until 1918 had been encircled by or incorporated within the Austro-Hungarian empire.

During the war Croat and Slovene spokesmen had succeeded in crossing Austria's frontier to confer with Serbian statesmen. The leading role in this movement was taken by the former mayor of Split (Spalato) in Dalmatia, Ante Trumbich, who in 1905 took the initiative for the Fiume resolution which was the beginning of manifestations favoring a union of Croats, Slovenes, and Serbs. As head of the Croat National Party, Trumbich, a voluntary exile, joined Serbian premier Pashich on Corfu after Serbia had been overrun by the Austro-German and Bulgarian armies. On that foreign island, animated by a unitary faith in the future, these two men, who lacked ties with their native soils overrun by enemy forces, boldly formed a program to establish a common homeland. In July 1917 they decided upon the union of the three south Slav peoples under the rule of the Karageorgevich dynasty of Serbia. This was the Pact of Corfu.

In August 1918 the south Slavs of the Hapsburg Monarchy held a congress in Ljubljana (Laibach), Carniola, under the leadership of Antun Korosec (Koroshetz), a Roman Catholic priest and head of the Catholic Slovene Populist Party, which demanded unification of all south Slavs. This action led to the adherence of the

Slovenes. In October 1918, when Austria-Hungary was in the process of decomposing, but prior to the armistice, a national congress of all south Slavs met at Zagreb (Agram) in Croatia. Delegates came from Croatia, Slovenia (formerly Carniola), Dalmatia, Bosnia, and Herzegovina. A resolution was adopted calling for the union of the empire's south Slavs with the Kingdom of Serbia, thus giving substance to the nightmare which had so often haunted the dreams of Emperor Francis Joseph (1848-1916). In November the parliament of Montenegro, disappointed by King Nicholas' attitude, repudiated its sovereign and voted for union with Serbia, thus formalizing the union of the two neighboring states, already united by blood, whose similar destinies had for centuries subjected them to the Turkish yoke. Crown Prince Alexander, who became regent for his ailing father, agreed to the wishes of these south Slav peoples on December 1. In March 1919 the Serbian Skuptshchina, to which delegates of the other south Slavs had come, formally proclaimed the establishment of the Kingdom of the Serb-Croats-Slovenes which ultimately became known as Yugoslavia.

The Treaty of Saint-Germain-en-Laye concluded with Austria (September 10, 1919) and that of Trianon with Hungary (June 4, 1920) determined the aggrandizement of the Kingdom of Serbia. Croatia, Slovenia, Dalmatia, Bosnia, Herzegovina, and the Sanjak of Novi-Bazar were awarded to Serbia without protest. The fate of the Banat of Temesvar, however, was contested by Serbia and Rumania, and ultimately terminated by partition. The region of Klagenfurt in Carinthia remained in Austria after a plebiscite. Infinitely complex questions arose regarding the Istrian peninsula and islands off the Dalmatian coast as a consequence of claims posted by Italy in the 1915 Treaty of London. At the Paris Peace Conference Italian premier Vittorio Orlando insisted upon fulfillment of that secret treaty which brought Italy into war. Since the Dalmatian coast and offshore islands were inhabited by Slav majorities, President Woodrow Wilson opposed their award to Italy and he was supported by England and France.

The Conference of Allied Ambassadors, charged with implementing the peace settlement after the treaties were signed, vacillated on this problem until the Adriatic port of Fiume was seized by Gabrielle d'Annunzio, the Italian poet-adventurer, in September 1919. Although the majority inhabitants of Fiume were Italian, the port constituted for the south Slav kingdom a vital outlet to the Adriatic. At the Conference of Rapallo in November 1920 the Allies attempted to resolve the impasse by making Fiume a free city. The Italians, however, persisted in their occupation without any indication of evacuating the port. Finally in 1924 the Conference of Allied Ambassadors decided to grant Fiume to Italy except for its suburb of Susak and the adjacent locality of Fort Baros which were awarded to Yugoslavia. The Dalmatian coast was ceded to the new kingdom with the exception of Zara and a few islands of strategic importance to Italy.

This settlement created in the fundamentally sensitive region a situation filled with dangerous complexities because of the general hostility between the Slavs and Italians. The Italo-Yugoslav border question foretold similar problems which the end of World War II would revive with so much acrimony and violence in the city of Trieste on the Adriatic. Nevertheless, in 1924 Yugoslavia had to yield to a decision which incorporated within Italy about a half-million south Slavs who inhabited Istria and part of Carniola.

Historic little Serbia was thus transformed into a significant state. Serbia's territory was more than doubled and the population almost tripled, from 5 to about 15 million inhabitants. The unwieldy new appellation, the Kingdom of the Serbs, Croats, and Slovenes, indicated a lack of homogeneity within the new country containing a juxtaposition of peoples of the same ethnic origins but who had preserved special characteristics. The new title appeared to presage the ultimate creation of a federal state. A constituent assembly met in Belgrade to draft a constitution. Since it was the first occasion for a reunion of all south Slavs, it was not long in furnishing considerable disappointment to those who had expected to see these brothers, so long separated, almost exclusively preoccupied with manifesting joy at being united in one family.

Rumania was also destined to harvest the fruits of her war effort. Doubtless her army had been swiftly crushed, but her sacrifices did contribute to the Allied cause despite Russia's defection. King Ferdinand renewed the struggle as soon as the opportunity arose. At the approach of the Army of the Orient, Rumanian troops were mobilized and by threatening the rear of Mackensen's forces, obliged the Germans to evacuate Wallachia during the second week of November 1918. The king then returned to liberated Bucharest at the head of the Allied forces. The Rumanians secured considerable gains at the Paris Peace Conference. Realization of Rumania's territorial ambitions was partly justified by decisions of the liberated peoples after the collapse of the Hapsburg Monarchy.

Internal conditions in the Hapsburg Monarchy were chaotic in 1918. After the death of aged Emperor Francis Joseph in November 1916, his successor, Emperor Charles, gave an impression of wishing to terminate the useless war. A mere handful of Hungarians remained obstinate. But events occurred so rapidly that Hungary's leaders precipitated the disintegration of the vast mosaic patiently assembled over five centuries by the Hapsburg dynasty.

A Rumanian national council assumed power in certain regions of Transylvania on November 10, 1918. At Alba Iulia on December 1 an assembly of many delegates voted in favor of the union of Transylvania with the Kingdom of Rumania. The assembly established its Directing Council headed by Iuliu (Julius) Maniu, uncontested chief of the Rumanian National Party whose long struggle for Rumanian rights under the Hungarian regime had won for him unequaled authority and popularity. The Saxon German minority in Transylvania supported these actions. The advance and occupation by Rumanian troops of most of Transylvania by December 1 helps explain these actions.

Before the armistice was signed, a national council was created in Austrian Bukovina on October 27 and proclaimed union with Rumania, whose army was invited to occupy the province. Bessarabia, after seceding from Russia as an independent republic and subsequently occupied by Rumanian forces in April 1918, also voted for union with Rumania. Thus Rumania's delegation to the Paris Peace Conference had substantial arguments to support their vast territorial claims. Infinitely more delicate was the question of the Banat of Temesvar, promised in its entirety to Rumania in the secret Treaty of Bucharest of August 17, 1916, which raised legitimate protests from Serbia because of the presence of a large Slav population in the Hungarian province.

From a legal viewpoint the stand of Rumania's delegation to the peace conference had certain weaknesses. By having concluded a separate peace in violation of the alliance of 1916, however inevitable it might have been, Rumania, according to some ex-

perts, had disavowed her commitments. The American delegation, on the other hand, was resolute in ignoring the territorial
promises of the Allied secret treaties to which the United States
had not been a signatory. The Rumanians had to find other jus-
tifications for their claims, and they succeeded in manipulating the
principle of national self-determination to which the influential
American delegation could not remain indifferent.

The head of the Rumanian National Council, established in
Paris in 1918 to promote Rumania's claims, was Take Ionescu, a
respected statesman, very cosmopolitan, and whose stature was
respected among the conference delegates. Ionescu, leader of the
pro-Allied Conservative Democrats, had been the most vocal
interventionist in his country. In the fall of 1918 he discussed a
possible compromise on the Banat of Temesvar with Serbian
premier Pashich. These discussions aroused apparent anxiety in
Bucharest. Bratianu, who became premier again in December
1918, repudiated these talks when he arrived in Paris at the head
of his delegation. Unlike Ionescu, Bratianu was monolithic and
intransigent, never ceasing to insist upon the absolute application
of the 1916 treaty, and he antagonized most of the delegates by
his rigid attitude maintained until he left Paris in June 1919.

The annexation of the Bukovina and Bessarabia, which had
clearly defined frontiers and Rumanian majorities, aroused energetic protests by the Soviet Russian government. Arbitration of
the Banat question resulted in a partition of the province between
Rumania and Serbia. The entire Dobrudja was restored to Rumania despite its large Bulgarian and Turkish populations. Rumania secured great territorial satisfaction even though not all
the promises in the 1916 treaty were fulfilled.

The Allied Powers had most difficulty in tracing the Rumanian-
Hungarian frontier. Territorial experts at the peace conference had
the complex task of tracing a boundary in a region where the
populations, principally at Szatmar (Satu Mare) and Arad, were,
as in Silesia, so intertwined that it was impossible to fix a frontier
without including on one side or the other groups belonging to the
opposite nationality. While these tedious negotiations were in
progress, grave developments were occurring in Budapest which
threatened the peace settlement.

While the Kingdom of Hungary was experiencing its death
throes, Bela Kun (1885-1938) established a communist regime in

Budapest. He governed by terror and paralyzed the economic life of that unfortunate country. The Hungarian communists crossed the frontier and attacked the Rumanians and Czechs in an attempt to establish a juncture with the Russian Bolsheviks. At first taken by surprise, the Rumanian army finally repulsed the Hungarians and, ignoring the injunctions of the Allied command, pursued them back to Budapest. The Rumanian army occupied Budapest in August 1919 and routed the communist regime. Advancing to the west, Rumanian troops, wishing to recoup from Hungary reparations for the damages inflicted in their country by the Germans, resorted to excessive requisitioning of goods which placed Hungary in the status of a dependency of Rumania. These regrettable activities combined with Bratianu's objections to the treaty on the protection of minorities in Rumania created serious tensions between Bucharest and the peace conference.

Jules Cambon, the esteemed French diplomat and chairman of the Conference of Ambassadors, later said in rendering homage to Rumania's role that "the victory of Bela Kun would have joined Hungary with Russia and menaced Central Europe and the Balkans. The Rumanians forced Hungary to respect the armistice. They accomplished this at much sacrifice and served as a rampart against Bolshevism up to the very gates of Vienna, and they were the instrument of European solidarity." This menace during the summer of 1919 was comparable to the Turkish threat to Vienna in 1683 which King John Sobieski of Poland ended. At length the Treaty of Saint-Germain-en-Laye with Austria and that of Trianon with Hungary settled the pending questions.

Rumania's territorial acquisitions completely modified her physical appearance. Formerly composed of two regions superimposed in the form of a crescent moon, Rumania now assumed the appearance of the full moon. The enlarged kingdom, more than 2½ times the original size, contained a population of about 16 million contrasted with the pre-war figure of 8 million. Rumania had finally realized her traditional aspirations by achieving the unification of all Rumanian lands. Nevertheless, the new delimitations excluded many co-nationalists in the following countries. These Rumanian statistics are juxtaposed to figures produced by the states in which Rumanian minorities lived. Thus a perpetuation of pre-war excessive nationalism was quite obvious. Rumanian statistics claimed there were 100,000 Rumanians in Hungary (Hungary claimed only 24,000); 330,000 in Yugoslavia (230,000); 50,000 in Albania (none claimed); 130,000 in Greece (none claimed); 100,000 in Bulgaria (16,500); 186,000 scattered in the Ukraine, Poland, and Czechoslovakia (Czechoslovakia was the only state to claim Rumanians—14,000). Thus about 900,000 Rumanians allegedly lived beyond the frontiers of the enlarged kingdom. These statistics must be viewed cautiously because census figures in the Balkans have been used repeatedly for chauvinistic purposes.

As in the era of Michael the Brave at the end of the 16th century, Rumania's population after the Paris Peace Conference included numerous and significant minorities. Rumania had become the Balkan state with the largest number of minority peoples. No census was held in Rumania until 1930. Therefore these figures are based on that census. 1½ million Hungarians, 725,000 Jews, 740,000 Germans, 577,000 Ukrainians, 360,000 Bulgarians, 288,000 Turks and Tatars, 415,00 Russians, 278,000 Gypsies, and about 150,000 Serbs, Poles, Slovaks and others. The minorities totalled about 5 million and constituted about 30% of the total population. As a result of this overlapping of nationalities, boundary disputes with neighboring states would keep public opinion at high pitch. These disputes were an obstacle to friendly relations, and within Rumania the numerous minorities became a constant source of inspiration to extremist nationalist groups which advocated violence and war as the only honorable solution. Furthermore, Greater Rumania was exposed to the avenging spirit of the Hungarians and Russian Communists, a double threat for a young state with still fragile foundations.

As for Greece, the Allied Powers concealed their rancor for Athens' tardy decision to enter the war. Had Greece not been restrained by the efforts of King Constantine? To plead her cause Greece had a statesman of great talent whose sympathies for the Allies began with the outbreak of the war and who now expected just compensation for the intervention he helped to bring about. Venizelos maneuvered with considerable dexterity to win the good graces of the nations. His supple, subtle mind knew how to flatter the inclinations of Allied statesmen. Nature, however, impeded the aggrandizement of the Kingdom of Greece. Surrounded on three sides by the sea, the only direction which could be offered for expansion was to the north. In the northwest Greece could not acquire territory from Serbia, while in the northeast the frontier in Thrace was adjacent to Bulgaria. The Allies compelled Bulgaria, an enemy state, to bear victory's expenses by ceding territory to Greece as the penalty for joining the Central Powers. The outlet to the Aegean Sea, awarded to Bulgaria by the treaties concluding the Balkan Wars, was awarded to Greece. The port of Dedeagatch was renamed Alexandropolis.

Greece thus acquired a common frontier with Turkey by securing a tentacle-shaped salient extending east along the Aegean coast toward Constantinople. Acquired proximity to that great city revived in imaginations always swift to overheat the ancient dream of recreating the Byzantine Empire to the advantage of Greece. Had God not imposed this mission upon the Greeks? The Allies, and principally England, aroused in the Greeks ambitions fraught with serious consequences by encouraging them to seek compensations in Asia Minor. Did not the region of Smyrna (Izmir in Turkish) contain a numerous Greek population? Was it not often called Homer's birthplace? To restore Greek sovereignty to that region would be an act of justice conforming to historical traditions, maintained the Greek nationalists. The English government envisaged an opportunity whereby it could dominate the eastern Mediterranean basin if an interposing state, too weak to inspire any misgivings and whose attachment to English policies was well known, could constitute a buffer. Such a solution would help check any possible resurgence of Turkish power.

But the English government soon realized the scheme to be too risky at the time. It was decided, instead, to award Greece several Aegean islands such as Mytilene and Chios, inhabited by Greek majorities and situated close to the shore of Asia Minor, which could become advance posts for the Greeks to leap onto the adjacent coast.

Bulgaria lay in the camp of the vanquished. The Bulgarians were shown no indulgence because their choice between the two belligerent camps had been determined by the personal sentiments of Tsar Ferdinand, an ambitious and devious character. Nevertheless, the nation was wholly responsible. The people had, after all, dutifully obeyed their sovereign. No actual protests were raised. So in October 1918, Tsar Ferdinand, to avert a potential storm, renounced his throne in favor of his son Boris who was known to

differ with his father. But this was a useless stratagem; Bulgaria
had to be punished. Although popular sentiment still favored
Russia, the latter could not plead Bulgaria's cause in 1919. Russia,
paralyzed by a revolution, was an outcast. Bulgaria was abandoned
to her fate. It was inscribed in the Treaty of Neuilly-sur-Seine,
signed November 27, 1919, which the nation considered harsh and
unjust. The Bulgarians had already suffered from the haughty German attitude which had spared neither deprivations nor humiliation. The alliance with the Central Powers had left bitter memories. Nevertheless, Bulgaria had to pay for the catastrophe into
which a harsh and arrogant ally had led her. The western frontier
was changed to Serbia's advantage. The towns of Tsaribrod and
Strumitsa were ceded. This was really an insignificant frontier
rectification, but it was painful to national pride.

The amputation in Thrace to the benefit of Greece was more
painful. The Bulgarians lost their access to the Aegean Sea, which
had been one of the constant goals of their foreign policy. From
the heights of the Rhodopes they could see the Aegean with its
warm waters sparkling in the distance. For five years this outlet,
formerly a forbidden area, was in Bulgarian hands. But after
Neuilly Bulgaria had only one seacoast which fronted on the
Black Sea, a closed body of water where her ports, of which
Burgas was the best, would be subject to the whims of the Turks
who retained the Straits. This deeply felt blow produced an urge
to eliminate the Greek barrier to the Mediterranean.

Bulgaria's humiliation was increased by the cession of the
southern Dobrudja which Rumania had seized in 1913. The existence in that province of a predominantly Bulgarian population
was destined to aggravate relations between the two neighboring
states to the point of discouraging communication at a time when
construction of a bridge across the Danube would have improved
traffic between Poland and the Mediterranean basin. Rarely had
a nation seen its frontiers so frequently modified in so brief a
period. For about a half-century the boundaries had been alternately extended and shortened like an accordion, traced expan-
sively by the Treaty of San Stefano in 1878, diminished the same
year by the Congress of Berlin, then expanded again in 1885 by the
acquisition of Eastern Rumelia. Expanded again after the First
Balkan War in 1913, the boundaries experienced the same year an
amputation due to the defeat inflicted by former allies. In 1915 a

small acquisition from Turkey near Adrianople encouraged Bulgaria's intervention. Then, profiting from Austro-German successes in the Balkans, Bulgaria recovered the lost territories in 1918, added more sections, and finally ended up by abandoning all the gains and more after defeat suffered as a member of the Central Powers. Before 1914 Bulgaria ranked second among the Balkan states. In 1919 Bulgaria became, except for Albania, the least significant country in the peninsula.

Turkey's situation was infinitely complex. The Ottoman Empire, primarily confined to Asia after 1913, had been the object of a premature partition by the Allied Powers. In March 1915 Russia proposed and England and France accepted a partition arrangement. When the question of attracting Italy into the war occupied the Allies, promises were finally made to Rome in the Treaty of London (April 1915) to the effect that Italy would secure the region of Adalia on the southern coast of Asia Minor. A year later (April 26, 1916), England, France, and Russia again determined the fate of Turkey's empire. This agreement had been maturing since March 1915 when England and France promised the Straits to Russia. This new understanding provided for the creation of an independent Arab state. England would secure influence in Mesopotamia and a part of Syria, France would have a sphere in the rest of Syria, Cilicia, southern Kurdistan, and Adana, and Palestine would be placed under international control. Russia would secure Turkish Armenia, a part of Kurdistan, and northern Anatolia. The English and French then specified their mutual claims to Turkey in Asia by the Sykes-Picot agreement of May 9, 1916. In April 1917 Italy was given further concessions in the regions of Adalia and Smyrna in return for recognition of the Sykes-Picot agreement. Russia's defection from the war upset these plans by reviving the question of the projected partitions. England and France then envisaged the creation of a new power equilibrium in the eastern Mediterranean as the consequence of Russia's apparent abandonment of interests in that area. Thus, during World War I, the Allied Powers had avidly planned to partition the heritage of the "Sick Man" who had been moribund for more than a half-century, but whose death now appeared certain. But unanticipated events, principally the outcome of certain military operations, confused the situation.

Turkey was defeated by English action. Constantinople and the Straits were first occupied by French detachments from the nearby Army of the Orient, but English forces soon arrived from Egypt, Malta, and Palestine to join the French. It soon became evident that England, victorious in the Middle East, intended to secure advantages from these successes to dominate the Levant by assuming the place vacated by Russia. The English apparently planned to extend to Constantinople the sphere in which India and the oil routes could be protected. To achieve this grandiose ambition, the English proposed to implant themselves in the region and encourage the appetite of the Greeks, their protégés. Emboldened by this patronage, numerous Greeks in Constantinople were ready to become England's agents. In the Levantine quarter of Pera they unfurled huge white and blue flags with dimensions as vast as their ambitions, whose satisfaction they joyously anticipated.

At this moment a great personage appeared in Asia Minor. Born in Salonika in 1881, Kemal Ataturk (formerly Mustafa or Mustapha Kemal, later Kemal Pasha), whom his mathematics instructor surnamed "Kemal" ("perfection" in Arabic), had earned early notice by the ardor of his military vocation and hostility to the regime of Sultan Abdul Hamid II. After being exiled, he returned to Salonika to participate in the Young Turk movement, although his views were more radical than party doctrine could tolerate. Wherever Turkey had to fight—in Tripolitania, the Balkans, the Dardanelles, the Caucasus—he proved a brilliant, intrepid officer who escaped bullets and shells miraculously. He daringly disapproved of the Germanophilia of the Turkish general staff, and later became pessimistic over the outcome of the war. He opposed the Mudros armistice which he considered humiliating. After Allied troops occupied Constantinople, Kemal, a noisy and rancorous officer, was appointed inspector of an army corps at Samsun in far-away Anatolia.

Exile to the vast interior of Asia Minor favored Kemal's plans. In that remote region, situated in the center of Turkey's indigenous, healthy population whose vigor had remained intact, Kemal undertook a nationalist campaign which would soon succeed, for this strategist had an orator's gifts which swayed crowds. With light chestnut hair, which he combed back tightly, heavy brows, an expansive chest, Kemal gave the impression of great physical vigor and rare willpower. This was the hero destined to resist Europe and regenerate his country.

Although the Allied Powers, and especially the English, noted this agitation which could threaten their plans, they could not undertake new military operations after four years of hostilities of which all were weary and exhausted. On the other hand, Greece had on combat alert an army which had intervened late in the war and which now requested authorization to fight the hereditary enemy in order to realize her dream of a greater Greece carved out of Asia Minor. The seductive Venizelos cleverly profited from this crisis, even to the point of convincing the rigid Woodrow Wilson. English prime minister David Lloyd George was pleased to see Venizelos so eager.

In May 1919, the Greeks were assisted by the English in landing troops at Smyrna. After seizing the city with English naval support, Greek forces began to penetrate the interior. The Italians also landed troops in southwestern Anatolia, a first step in their take-over of Adalia. Orlando, the Italian premier, opposed Greek military operations because of his country's claims to southern Anatolia. This crisis and Orlando's opposition to the proposed settlement in the Adriatic resulted in Italy's temporary abandonment of the peace conference. Italy's absence from the peace table led the English to push the Greeks forward. England thus schemed to eliminate rivals in order to install clients.

Reaction was swift and violent in Asia Minor. The debarkation of Greek troops at Smyrna unleashed a tempest of indignation. Protests reached the Allied high commissioners in Constantinople. Kemal was not a person to be content with Platonic gestures. The national resistance movement, of which he was the inspiration, actually coalesced as the consequence of the invasions of Asia Minor. He was now widely known as the chief organizer of resistance to the further dismemberment of Turkey, and for that reason the sultan, under English prodding, dismissed Kemal from the army and exiled him in July 1919. Kemal reacted by convening a nationalist congress at Erzerum in Turkish Armenia (July 23) which resolved to maintain the independence and territorial integrity of Turkey. This development was at first ignored in Turkey, but the spirit of revolt inspired by Kemal soon made rapid progress. Aided by officers as determined as he for a struggle, Kemal began to organize an army. The Allied Powers, ignorant of his success, underestimated the force they would soon encounter.

England reigned as mistress in Constantinople, and Sultan Mohammed VI and his government were puppets. Because of her army, England encountered no opposition in European Turkey, but this experience blinded London to the revolt smoldering in Asian Turkey and to the inevitable success of the Turkish nationalists. According to Count Carlo Sforza, the Italian foreign minister, Lloyd George's plans were the origin of Kemal's success. A secret agreement imposed upon the sultan placed the caliphate under English control.

In September 1919 a Turkish nationalist congress affirmed the inviolability of Turkish territory and declared its opposition to the Greek invasion and Allied occupation. The National Pact of September 13 announced the famous six principles, including self-determination, opening of the Straits, security of Constantinople, recognition of minority rights, and abolition of the capitulations. Elections to parliament in October resulted in victory of the Nationalists, and in January 1920 in adoption by the legislature in Constantinople of the National Pact. Confronted by such insubordination, the English authorities did not hestitate. English troops occupied Constantinople in full force and arrested members of the Nationalist opposition. Several escaped the English dragnet, and they became vehement agents of Turkish nationalism against the pretensions of the conqueror. The parliament was dissolved in April. In the same month a national assembly convened at Ankara which named Kemal as president of a provisional government. The Rubicon had been crossed as the result of the assembly's rejection of the sultan's authority. The sultan was accurately considered a mere English captive, but his religious authority as caliph was still respected.

In April the Nationalists signed an agreement with Soviet Russia from whom they secured needed military supplies. For the ensuing two years the national assembly governed Turkey in Asia. This secession produced a schism in the heart of the Ottoman Empire. On one side stood free Turkey in Asia, refusing to recognize defeat in the war and resisting the victors. On the other was Turkey in Europe, reduced in size and the only part of Turkey subject to the authority of the sultan who was supported by foreign and especially English guns.

Months had passed without the Allies having the time to prepare a peace treaty for Turkey because they were preoccupied in negotiating other treaties. At length the sultan's delegates arrived in Paris in August 1920, almost two years after the cessation of hos-

tilities, to affix their signatures, under protest, to the Treaty of
Sèvres, the fifth and last of the accords signed in the suburbs of
Paris, which theoretically put a formal end to the state of war with
Turkey. Greek military operations, encouraged by the English,
contributed to the Turkish decision to yield. The Greeks defeated
the Turks in Anatolia, occupied Bursa (Brusa), and captured
Adrianople on July 25. Signing of the peace treaty caused the final
break between the Nationalists and the sultan.

The Treaty of Sèvres required Turkey to yield another area of
her dwindling empire in Europe. Adrianople and a major part of
Thrace were ceded to Greece. The entire Straits region, including
the northern European shore and the southern Asian shore, were
neutralized under interallied administration and destined to be
demilitarized. The ancient capitulations, abolished during the war,
were reestablished, and a commission was created to manage
Turkish finances. Dismemberments of Turkey in Asia were very
considerable. Not only did the Bedouins of Arabia, whom England
had succeeded in arousing against the Turks, see their independence promised, but Syria, Mesopotamia, and Palestine were detached. The region of Smyrna, although still under Turkish sovereignty, was entrusted to Greek administration. These were the
losses consented to by Sultan Mohammed VI, who ruled without
actual authority and who had been virtually dethroned. The
Treaty of Sèvres would not be implemented.

The Ankara nationalists received news of the treaty with hearts
full of rage. This painful humiliation aroused the anger of Turks
in free Turkey. An urge to resist gained in intensity and scope.
The Ankara assembly proclaimed Kemal, the national hero, president of a government endowed with a constitution affirming the
principle of national sovereignty (January 20, 1921). The assembly was determined to pursue the struggle for liberation and independence. This was no longer a simple partisan movement opposed to the Allies. It now had a solid organization supported by
masses of Turks and the strength of an army of about 100,000.
The military valor that the Turks had already shown was augmented by the enthusiastic patriotism with which they were imbued
by their idolized chief. In February a conference in London failed
to produce agreement among the opposing sides. Kemal's first
diplomatic coup came in March when France agreed to evacuate
Cilicia in exchange for economic rights in that province. His sec-

ond success occurred on March 13 when Italy agreed to withdraw from Anatolia in return for similar economic concessions. Kemal negotiated a treaty with Soviet Russia on March 16 by which Turkey returned Batum to Russia and the latter recognized Turkey's possession of the fortresses of Kars and Ardahan.

After gaining this international recognition, Kemal did not hesitate to fight on all sides. The English were soon forced back. Armed and encouraged by their English allies, the Greeks began to establish themselves in Asia Minor in order to make a Greek lake of the Aegean Sea. This old ambition held so irresistible a temptation that a mind as well-balanced and perspicacious as that of Venizelos allowed itself to be duped by this mirage without realizing the gravity of the risks. But was Greece not profiting from England's support? Becoming more rash, the Greek premier launched his country into an adventure which led the Greeks, who could be ungrateful, to reject Venizelos in the elections of November 1920. A vigorous offensive was started in Anatolia. Greek troops seized Afiun-Karahissar and Eskishehr in the center of the Anatolian plateau, but they were soon repulsed by Ismet Pasha (1884-   ) in the battle of Inonu. Advancing again, the Greeks encountered Turkish resistance and decided to stabilize the front along the Sakharya River.

Appointed generalissimo, Kemal took advantage of a lull in the conflict to reorganize his army and to make it an élite corps. When he believed it ready, he struck a demolishing blow on the Greek lines on August 18, 1922. After a savage battle lasting 20 days, the Turks penetrated the Greek lines and advanced to Smyrna. The Greek army, almost hurled into the Aegean, hastily boarded ships by the light of burning Smyrna. Who was responsible for igniting the city on September 9? The two sides cast blame on each other. Smyrna, the pride of Asia Minor, was almost entirely destroyed. All of Asia Minor was evacuated by the Greek army. Their co-nationalists in the region were now terrified by possible reprisals. The Turkish army, enthusiastically grateful for his leadership, conferred upon Kemal the title of *Ghazi* ("the victorious"), which was the epithet conquering sultans had called themselves. General Ismet Pasha became known as Ismet Inonu, the surname taken from his victory over the Greeks.

England appealed to the Allied Powers to assist in defending the Straits against the Turks. The French and Italians refused to become involved. The castastrophe wrecked Greek dreams of grandeur which had been cherished over the centuries. It disturbed the Greeks all the more because they had believed they were about to realize their ideal. Since Venizelos, the inspirer of the ill-fated campaign, was out of office, and the Greek commander had been captured by the Turks, Greek wrath was turned on King Constantine, who had been restored to the throne in 1920 after Alexander, his son and successor, had suddenly died. A plebiscite in December 1920 had voted for Constantine's return. After a second reign of only two years Constantine abdicated for the last time. The Allies then intervened to put an end to the hostilities by arranging an armistice at Mudania on October 11, 1922.

Battlefield victories opened the road to Constantinople to Kemal's armies. When they reached the Straits, only English troops were guarding the seaway. As a result of an agreement with France, the latter had evacuated its troops from the Straits to the dismay of the English who reproached the French for abandoning the common cause. This was one of the grievances, added to divergent views regarding Germany, which aggravated the atmosphere of Anglo-French relations to the point of creating tensions. Resolved to use force in overthrowing any obstacle to their entry into the capital, Kemal's troops confronted English forces. A grave incident was narrowly averted by the *sang-froid* of the English commander. London finally realized, especially since Lloyd George's government had fallen in October 1922, that the new Turkish regime arising from the nationalist revolt had become a force with which it would be wise to treat, if not, indeed, to befriend. The Ankara assembly declared Mohammed VI deposed on November 1, and the English conveyed him to Malta. As Kemal's forces near Constantinople, revision of the Treaty of Sèvres appeared inevitable.

That revision was accomplished at the Lausanne conference (November 1922—July 1923). Rarely had negotiations been so extended, laborious, and difficult because of the rigidity of the Turkish delegation. Unlike the other peace treaties concluding World War I, which were dictated to the enemy states, this treaty was negotiated. Kemal's close associate, Ismet Inonu, was a most obstinate diplomatist. He was supported on many points by Georgi Chicherin, the Soviet foreign commissar, who had been invited to participate in the conference. Territorial losses were inevitable, but Turkish resistance was most pronounced regarding the sovereignty of the new Turkey for which Ismet demanded international respect. He tenaciously rejected internationalization of the Straits agreed to in the Mudania armistice, revival of the capitulations, and anything which resembled extraterritorial privileges for foreigners. The Allied Powers could not move him on these points. Negotiations were temporarily suspended, but that was no solution. The Turkish army still posed a threat to the Greeks in Thrace and England's troops were still deployed in certain Turkish areas. If these forces collided, a new conflict would have dangerous repercussions for an unstable and scarcely peaceful Europe.

After a recess for two months the conference resumed its deliberations which finally ended when Turkish demands were conceded. The Treaty of Sèvres was annulled. The peace substituted for it, signed at Lausanne July 24, 1923, was noted for its recognition of the full sovereignty of the new Turkey. Turkey recovered her European frontiers of 1913, and Adrianople and other sections were retroceded by Greece. The Aegean islands of Tenedos and Imbros were restored to Turkey, Greece secured the rest of the islands, Italy retained the Dodecanese, and England kept Cyprus. The capitulations, which originated during the reign of Francis I in the 16th century and which had exempted foreigners from Turkish jurisdiction, were abolished in return for Turkey's promise to introduce judicial reforms. This was very gratifying to Turkish pride. Henceforth every person residing in Turkey became subject to that state's jurisdiction, and all inhabitants without distinction as to religion became equal before the law. The Straits were demilitarized, open to ships of all nations in time of peace and in time of war if Turkey remained neutral; if Turkey was at war, enemy ships, but not neutrals, could be excluded. An international commission under the auspices of the League of Nations would assure freedom of navigation through the waterway. The Straits question was one of the few points on which Turkey failed to impose her demands, but the Turks would revive this debate within a decade.

Greece was required to renounce claims to Asia Minor. A unique principle was introduced into international politics to solve the problem of Greek minorities in Asia Minor and the small Turkish minority in Thrace. A separate Greco-Turkish agreement provided for the compulsory, bilateral exchange of populations.

THE BALKAN STATES AFTER THE FIRST WORLD WAR
G. Acquisitions of Greece:
   1) At the expense of Bulgaria; —2) at the expense of Turkey.
   The territories indicated by dots were acquired by Greece in
   the Treaty of Sèvres (1920) and retroceded to Turkey by the
   Treaty of Lausanne (1923).
R. Acquisitions of Rumania:
   1) At the expense of Russia; —2) At the expense of Austria-
   Hungary.
Y. Acquisitions of Yugoslavia:
   1) At the expense of Bulgaria; —2) At the expense of Austria-
   Hungary.

The Treaty of Lausanne, completed five years after the Mudros armistice, terminated a troubled period known as the era of World War I. Except for Constantinople, Adrianople, and the Straits, Turkey had been almost totally expelled from Europe. At the same time Turkey lost vast territories inhabited by the Arabs. Events would soon prove that Turkey had no reason to regret this dismemberment. Regenerated by a new leader who had originated from among the masses and who was endowed with spectacular energy, Turkey, now limited mostly to Asia Minor to which the capital was moved, rediscovered energy from the old, nourishing soil like the giant Antaeus in the ancient legend.

Albania, which had been occupied by the Italians when the war ended, lost her ephemeral monarchy established by the powers in 1913. Italy aimed to secure sections of the eastern Adriatic coast, and proposed to Greece and Yugoslavia projects of partition or exchange. But Albania found a friend in Woodrow Wilson who demanded a restoration of independence. During the summer of 1920 the Albanians rebelled against the puppet regime which Italy had installed. The Italians withdrew but managed to retain the island of Saseno which commanded the entrance to the bay of Valona. In 1925 a national assembly proclaimed Albania a republic with Ahmed Zogu as first president.

The Paris Peace Settlement established a precarious peace in Europe. In the perpetually troubled Balkans, the treaties divided the nations into two categories—satisfied and dissatisfied. Among the first, Rumania and Yugoslavia, enlarged by new territories and absorbed in the task of organizing and assimilating them, were preoccupied with safeguarding their acquisitions. Among the latter group, Turkey, because of her courage and tenacity, succeeded in obtaining justice for herself and turned to the vast effort of domestic reforms destined to revolutionize her institutions and traditions. Greece, having failed in her dream to extend Hellenic culture to Asia, had the wisdom to abandon that idea and come to terms with her former enemies. There remained Bulgaria, suspected by all, in litigation with all her neighbors, an easy victim for the revisionist powers whose minds were determined to change the treaties imposed by their conquerors.

CHAPTER V

The Balkan States Between the Wars

DURING the two decades separating the two great wars, Turkey was completely dominated by the vigorous personality of Kemal, to whom the Turks owed their regeneration. A remarkable leader—one is tempted to characterize him as a genius—Kemal, by the effect of a rare willpower, resuscitated his country by reuniting and modernizing it. Respected and obeyed as few chiefs of state have ever been, Kemal became the object of a veritable cult of worship after his death in 1938. At first called *Ghazi* because of his victories over the Greeks, then *Ataturk* ("father of the Turks"), he has remained the eternal leader in the view of his grateful people.

Kemal's greatest merit lay in his realization that the salvation of Turkey could be achieved in a return to Asia, her original cradle, while simultaneously adopting reforms inspired by Western European models. Not reforms in theory, such as during the era of the *Tanzimat,* but rigorously executed reforms. Kemal fulfilled his ambitions which, at first sight, appeared paradoxical when he attempted to Europeanize Turkey while leading her back to her Asiatic birthplace.

To effectuate this change in orientation, the Turkish capital was transferred from Constantinople to Ankara in the depths of the Anatolian plateau. Ankara, with a population of only 170,000, contrasted with the cosmopolitan Constantinople, with almost 1 million inhabitants and which would henceforth be known by its Turkish name of Istanbul, soon grew in size at the expense of the latter city. The old capital was destined to die slowly, retaining only the nostalgia of its faded splendor. Kemal's decision forced the government to take the road to the Anatolian steppes. The diplomatic corps followed, regretfully abandoning the graceful shores of the Bosporus and the embassies which had so often witnessed the keen rivalries of the powers besieging the Sublime Porte with their conflicting demands.

The Ankara national assembly had decreed the abolition of the sultanate in 1920, but the caliphate, the supreme authority in religious affairs, remained under the control of the displaced sultan's cousin. This was a temporary measure. The caliphate was abolished in 1924 and all members of the Osmanli house were banished from Turkey. Thus was eliminated the religious bond of all Moslems to the Turkish sovereign which had made the caliph commander of the faithful since 1517 and an object of veneration by the entire Islamic world. This radical step was inspired by a dual motive. Kemal undertook this move to terminate non-Turkish Moslem dependence on his nation and to acquire for his secular state the undivided attention of the Turks. He also wished to secularize institutions and customs which had been dominated by the requirements of a meticulous religion whose prescriptions interfered in all human activities.

Secularization was carried out with a rapidity and energy of which the transformation of Russia by Peter the Great offers the only comparison. In a state whose basis was formed by Islam, religion was veritably banished overnight. A legal code based on the Swiss model was substituted for Koranic justice. There would be no more Moslem courts; a single justice for all was decreed. Distinction between believers and infidels, which had prevailed for five centuries, was wiped out with the stroke of a pen by the proclamation of equality of all citizens before the law. Similarly the schools, formerly appendages of the mosques, were secularized. Those schools under the administration of foreign governments, particularly France, had to conform to the official curricula and bow to the control of the government.

The revolution in institutions was accompanied by a change in customs. Turkish females, formerly hidden behind their veils, had to appear in public with uncovered faces by order of the government. This was a frightful scandal in the eyes of old Turks who were attached to old traditions. Men were urged to abandon their traditional headdress, the fez, and the turban of religious origin to adopt European hats, preferably the democratic cap.

As in Russia under Peter the Great, this reformation of customs, symbolized by a Europeanization of dress, proceeded without much regard for personal feelings. Veils were occasionally removed from the faces of women who stubbornly insisted upon covering themselves, and a few fezzes were dashed to the ground without any prejudice to the refractory Turks who had exposed themselves. The new regime was forcibly imposed, but the respect inspired by Kemal was such that he alone, by his ascendancy and popularity, could insist on having the regime accepted.

Among other measures transforming old customs were the adoption of the Gregorian calendar of the West for the Koranic calendar, the purification of the Turkish language by the elimination of foreign words such as Arabic, Persian, and Greek terms, and the abolition of Arabic letters in 1928 and the substitution of the Latin alphabet which all Turks under age 40 were required to learn. All citizens were obliged to adopt last names; until that time they had been designated by their first names only.

A change of regime was instituted to crown this unparalleled work. The Turkish republic had been proclaimed in 1923. Its appellation of republic, national, popular, and secular in character, established its character. Kemal was, of course, named its president. He theoretically shared power with an assembly of 429 deputies. Nevertheless, he governed as an indisputable leader whose authority was law. So sudden and radical were the modifications introduced into all phases of life that it was necessary for Kemal to rule with an iron hand. Employing the police and strict censorship, Kemal's regime was not always devoid of repression. Opposition political parties, whose policies were incompatible with Kemal's plans, were suppressed. The rebellious Kurdish tribes were suppressed. The beginnings of Kemal's regime manifested all aspects of authoritarian systems arising out of a single political party. Turkey's new course could not have been otherwise if the nation was to be modernized in a hurry.

Turkey's modernization could not be placed in jeopardy. Not content with superficial reforms, Kemal strove to develop Turkey's prosperity by introducing western methods and machinery. Machines and fertilizers were introduced into agriculture. New techniques were applied to industrial production. Railways were extended, mines were exploited, and coal and chromium deposits were unearthed. Heavy taxation improved public finance. Taxes had weighed far too long on the peasants. Henceforth urban residents were the most heavily taxed. Energetic steps forced recalcitrant citizens to obey the tax laws. Special attention was accorded the army. Highly disciplined, expertly trained, and composed of sober, experienced, and courageous troops, the Turkish army was an essential element in the life of the country. Military expenditures absorbed more than half of all budgetary resources.

Turkey, like China in the 19th century, had been another land renowned for foreign exploitation. The investors disputed concessions and profits. But Kemal's reorganization was achieved without European assistance, and even to the detriment of foreign capitalists. A rigorous economic nationalism prevailed in the realm of business. Kemal's order of the day was to modernize without the Europeans by initiating new enterprises without their aid and by gradually eliminating them from the commerce which they had created. Turkey's businessmen, animated by Kemal's spirit, molded the country in such a way as to make it self-sufficient and completely free of all foreign economic domination.

Kemal Ataturk died in 1938 on the eve of World War II. His death was the occasion for national mourning in the strictest sense of the term. Turkey was overcome with grief at finding herself deprived of the man who, after having led the Turks to victory, had regenerated the nation. A multitude attended his funeral in November 1938, and statesmen were seen weeping. All were conscious of their indebtedness to this great warrior, a great reformer, and to the creation of a modern Turkey to which all were proud to belong. Kemal's successor was his close associate, Ismet Inonu, the conqueror of the Greeks and negotiator of the Treaty of Lausanne, who had been president of the council of ministers. Turkey persevered along the path traced by Kemal under the direction of Ismet and his foreign minister, Shukru Saracoglu.

The Kingdom of Bulgaria, with 6½ million inhabitants, offered the spectacle of a vanquished people, discontented, embittered, rancorous against those who had dragged the country into the war, and bristling with revenge against the Allies. Mutinies had occurred at the end of hostilities. The most serious occurred at Radomir where troops, having proclaimed a republic, prepared to march on Sofia while a German guard protected the flight of Tsar Ferdinand. Bulgaria had to bear an increase in financial burdens and the disbanding of most of her army according to the terms of the Treaty of Neuilly-sur-Seine.

The first step for Bulgaria was to create a peasant dictatorship. In a nation with 75% of the population tilling the soil in small plots according to quite primitive methods, the establishment of an agrarian-oriented government was only natural. Alexander Stambulisky (or Stamboliski) (1879-1923), a former schoolteacher and son of a peasant, animated this movement and became its leader. Widely esteemed because of his opposition to Bulgaria's entry into the war, an attitude considered subversive at the time, Stambulisky was imprisoned for his views. Released at the end of the war, he assisted in hastening the abdication of Tsar Ferdinand. This herculean, mustachioed peasant signed the Treaty of Neuilly-sur-Seine in 1919. He was then at the head of the so-called "Green Dictatorship" without experiencing any opposition from King Boris, the young and inexperienced monarch whose temperament expressed a waiting attitude, or from the growing bourgeoisie who were denied a role in politics. Although Stambulisky favored the peasants by initiating an agrarian reform and instituting obligatory work laws, he struggled against communist tendencies which began to arise in Bulgaria.

Bulgaria's strategic location in the Balkan peninsula, the discontent of her people, poverty, an inclination toward democratic ideas, and violent tendencies led Soviet Russia to choose this country as one offering the most favorable opportunity for the diffusion of Marxist theories in the Balkans. After the failure of Bela Kun in Hungary, the Communist International (Comintern), established in 1919, directed much effort toward Bulgaria in the hope of communizing the country. The Comintern sought to make of Bulgaria the center of a Union of Slav Peasant States controlled by Moscow. The chairman of a Balkan communist federation was Vasil Kolarov, a Bulgarian, who organized communist cells in the villages. His efforts spread into neighboring Yugoslavia. Kolarov tried to enlist the IMRO, but that organization resisted because its program was essentially nationalistic. Communist propaganda succeeded, despite industry's primitive development, in provoking a few strikes. Commuist activities were supported by demobilized army officers, the miniscule proletariat, and a few Macedonian agitators. Stambulisky resorted to drastic measures. He ordered army mobilization to forestall a general strike, and entrusted the obligation of maintaining order to peasant volunteers.

Stambulisky also reacted against the fomentors of trouble in Macedonia who opposed his friendship policy with Yugoslavia. Despite his friendship with the Yugoslav government, Stambulisky was alienated from the extreme agitators, who adhered to communist theories, and nationalists who supported agitation in Macedonia. Discontent increased until June 1923 when a conspiracy of officers, merchants, and intellectuals, all hostile to Stambulisky's peasant orientation, was formed to remove him from office.

Led by Alexander Tsankov (Zankov), a right-wing socialist, this coalition removed Stambulisky from office and occupied Sofia without striking a blow. Pursued by vengeful enemies, the unfortunate Stambulisky, who had proved his courage and enlightenment, was ignobly tortured and obliged to dig his own grave before being murdered. His barbaric demise confirmed a well-estalished truth that a politician's profession carried a maximum of risks in Bulgaria. Many Bulgarians were still alive who could recall the death of Stambulov in 1895. As a result of this coup, riots broke out in the fall of 1923. The agrarians, numerous and highly organized, refused to be dislodged from power without resistance. Their agitation merely aroused a reactionary movement which assumed the character of a counterrevolution.

The communist conspiracy was revealed during the tragic events which shed blood during Easter week of 1925. King Boris narrowly escaped from an assassination attempt when his car rode through a narrow pass on April 14. Two days later at the funeral of a murdered minister a bomb exploded in the Sofia cathedral. Strewn about the floor were 123 victims. The king and cabinet ministers owed their lives only to chance which had prevented them from taking their customary seats above which the bomb had been rigged to fall. The composure of the government and the patriotism of the populace forestalled all agitation at a time when success of the plot would have been the signal for the outbreak of anarchic terrorism. An investigation confirmed the communist origins of the plot, especially since a leader of the conspiracy had recently returned from Moscow. The communists were outlawed in Bulgaria in May 1925.

While these bloody troubles were tormenting Bulgaria, a repetition of border incidents on the Greek frontier provoked serious tensions between the two neighboring countries. Both complained of violence committed against their citizens. General Theodoros Pangalos, the Greek dictator (1925-26), sent his troops across the frontier into Bulgaria. Intervention by the League of Nations prevented unfortunate consequences. Negotiations under League auspices began and resulted in a treaty by which Greece indemnified Bulgaria in 1925. Then, following a principle adopted by Greece and Turkey in 1923, an exchange of populations was planned. Bulgaria would absorb more than 200,000 of her conationals emigrating from Greek Thrace and Macedonia. This was a heavy burden for Bulgaria's already overtaxed finances. The League Assembly granted a loan whose management was assigned to a League official. The situation remained critical for several years. A semi-revolutionary agitation hindered Bulgaria's development. Terrorist attacks, bombs, and murders succeeded each other in a dramatic atmosphere intensified by demands of the agrarians who had developed the very influential Peasant Party.

During this painful era King Boris, still self-effacing, had gradually matured to the point where he emerged without any serious rivals. As crown prince he had been befriended by the German general staff. General Ludendorff had been struck by his maturity and assiduity. After acceding to the throne amid frightful circumstances in 1918, and then hurled back and forth by the events which shook violent Bulgaria, young Boris remained an observer. His supple mind remained aloof from the tragic events, and he was content with sounding out popular sentiments and second-guessing the politicians. The king's voice, however, soon assumed more authority. Boris maneuvered slowly and cleverly, setting one politician against the other, until he became the real boss of Bulgaria in 1934. In 1930 he married Princess Giovanna, daughter of the King of Italy, an event which marked a rapprochement between the two kingdoms.

Short and thin, the king's stature gave the impression of agility. His face, an elongated oval and rather flattened at the temples, was crowned with a bulging cranium, prematurely bald. What was striking in addition to his Bourbon hooked nose were the beady, gray-green eyes which animated his glum face. Very shifty, the eyes darted about incessantly. Many said he had a fleeting glance because it never became fixed. At any rate, he had an intelligent appearance enhanced by a thin-lipped mouth emphasized by a slight mustache. Boris' character, a combination of flexibility and subtlety, corresponded to his appearance. An uncommon cultural background enlivened his thinking. He had stored up encyclopedic knowledge about everything from botany to mechanics, not to mention those topics which are the usual lot of statesmen or his astonishing talent for languages. Eager to be popular, Boris tried to please his guests and to impress them with his charm. He was a rather enigmatic and complex person. Was he treacherous like his father or simply a perceptive sovereign conscious of the weakness of his nation and the dangers to which it was exposed? Was he attempting to sail adroitly between two reefs?

Whatever his aim, King Boris, after patiently waiting for several years, suddenly intervened in politics by staging a *coup d'état* in 1934 which suspended the constitution and established a royal dictatorship to terminate disorders and restore calm. After four years of this regime, Boris considered Bulgaria sufficiently stabilized to permit a restoration of the parliament in 1938. But the king's apparent inclination for authoritarian methods rendered illusory this concession to liberalism. Elections were held under police surveillance, and despite the election of a respectable number of opposition deputies, the results represented only a very imperfect idea of the condition of public opinion and, above all, the significance of the opposition. Boris continued his personal government, with an obedient parliament, and was encouraged in this by the example of numerous authoritarian regimes established in Europe in the 1930's. While he avoided revealing his hand, Boris excelled at molding his conduct according to circumstances, appointing and dismissing ministers without any discernible motive to explain their favor or disgrace, so secret and subtle did his thinking remain. George Kiosseivanov, former envoy to Yugoslavia, was the only Bulgarian premier who could remain in office for several years. His massive girth contrasted sharply with that of the diminutive king. He had a solid, common sense and a seriousness of purpose which, combined with a sharp understanding of foreign affairs, provided Bulgaria with valuable service during a difficult period until he was dismissed by Boris in 1940. This was at the beginning of World War II when Kiosseivanov's services would have been most valuable.

The Kingdom of Rumania during the interwar period should have been quite gratified by the territorial awards of the peace treaties. A nation endowed with considerable wealth, because of the fertility of the soil and the enviable mineral and petroleum resources, Rumania was also doubled in size by the treaties. But this aggrandizement produced hitherto non-existing problems.

The inhabitants of Transylvania, who had lived so long under Hungary's rule and a considerable number of whom were Hungarian and German co-nationals, had to adapt themselves to new institutions and conditions. It would be abusive to assert, as it was frequently claimed, that the inhabitants of the newly-acquired provinces were more "European" than their compatriots of the old kingdom, whom the former termed "Byzantine" or "Balkan." This problem of fusion had less difficulty in neighboring Serbia. But in Transylvania, as in Moldavia and Wallachia, a great peasant mass was animated by the same spirit of attachment to the soil, the desire for tranquillity, and tenaciously hard work. This common sentiment contributed to the forging of the unity of the Rumanian nation. The strong National Party, representing peasant interests in Transylvania, was soon integrated into Rumania political life. The guiding light behind this integration, Iuliu Maniu, as popular and respected on one side of the Carpathians as on the other, rallied peasants of the new provinces and the old kingdom to his party. Elections in November 1919, the first time in Rumania's constitutional history when they were not rigged, produced a victory for Maniu's National Party. Alexandru Vaida Voevod, Maniu's close collaborator and a former member of the Hungarian parliament, was given the task of forming the first Rumanian government after Bratianu's resignation. This choice of a Transylvanian nationalist was a wise choice to point out the unity of the Rumanian peoples.

The agrarian problem, an internal topic of anxiety for the government, continued to produce peasant unrest. King Ferdinand had promised reforms in 1917 to appease the peasants. New laws were enacted between 1918 and 1921 to expropriate the great estates and to sell them by lot. The reforms were widely applied, especially in Bessarabia, and appreciably immunized the peasants against the attractions of Bolshevik propaganda.

The reforms resulted in about 14 million acres being redistributed among 1½ million peasants. This vast redistribution completely altered Rumania's appearance. As recently as 1907, the year of the great peasant revolt, holdings of 2½ to 25 acres and those having more than 1,000 acres occupied the same area. In 1921, with about 22 million acres divided into small properties, there were no more than 3 million acres comprising holdings of more than 618 acres each. Formerly a land of immense individual estates, Rumania was now transformed into a country whose soil was more fairly apportioned. No estate exceeded 1,500 acres. All arable crownlands and institutional lands, and especially the estates of absentee landlords and foreigners, were expropriated. The original owners were compensated in bonds bearing 5% interest and maturing in 50 years, except that institutions, primarily clerical, were compensated in eternal bonds. The peasants receiving these lands had to reimburse the government 65% of the expropriation cost on easy terms over a period of 20 years. Agrarian reforms were also legislated for the provinces acquired from the Hapsburg Monarchy and Russia. Private holdings in Bessarabia were limited to 250 acres instead of the 1,500 acres authorized in Rumania. In the Bukovina the maximum estate was 500 acres, while in Transylvania and the Banat the normal exemption was 200 jugars (1 jugar = 1.473 acres). The fulfillment of this agrarian reform placed about 90% of Rumania's cultivable land in the hands of peasants.

Tense conditions arose after 1919 regarding Rumania's application of the agrarian reforms to the regions acquired from Hungary. The Treaty of Trianon with Hungary in 1920 authorized inhabitants of the transferred provinces to choose citizenship within one year (to opt for Hungarian or Rumanian domiciles). These individuals could transfer their residences and could retain immovable property in the places of former residence. Hungary protested that her citizens could not come under Rumanian law. This crisis kept alive the question of Rumania's right to the new provinces as opposed to the rights of aliens created by international treaty. Rumania refused to refer the dispute to the League of Nations or to the World Court, and Bucharest denied the jurisdiction of the mixed Rumano-Hungarian arbitration commission created by the Treaty of Trianon. The League of Nations decided in 1928 to authorize a bilateral settlement, but neither government could agree. The matter was settled in 1930 when the World War I Allied Powers agreed to abandon their share of Hungary's reparations and also donate their receipts from Czechoslovakia's liberation debt to reimburse the dispossessed Hungarian citizens. Hungary was expected to reduce the optant claims against Rumania.

The numerous peasantry gained a powerful champion when the National Peasant Party was created by the merger of Maniu's

National Party and the old kingdom's Peasant Party headed by Ion Mihalache, a schoolteacher of peasant origin. An unusually remarkable feature was added to Rumanian politics by the 1923 constitution which established a truly national legislative assembly with a chamber of deputies elected by universal manhood suffrage and a senate composed of elected and appointed members. The old three-class system of voting was abolished. Rumanian Jews were admitted to citizenship. Cabinet ministers were appointed by the crown. The constitution nationalized all mineral wealth and petroleum, and denied ownership of rural lands to aliens.

For three years after the war it appeared that the power of the Liberal Party had been broken. Electoral reform had given suffrage to millions of peasants. These peasants supported the National Party led by Maniu, a man of great courage whose role as a fighter against Hungarian rule in Transylvania assured him considerable prestige. Thin, with bony face, always well-groomed, Maniu appeared to be a model bureaucrat. Descended from a family which had played a strong role in the 1848 revolution, he was a calm, reflective man who lacked a trace of the demagogue. His party was the rival to the Liberals, a fief of the Bratianu family, which expressed the interests of industry, finance, and commerce. Ioan Bratianu's long exercise of power produced a belief that he was indispensable. Other prominent politicians of the 1920's included the Conservative Democrat Take Ionescu and his young disciple, Nicolae Titulescu (1882-1941), who was destined for a spectacular career.

Returning to office in 1922, Bratianu soon offended public opinion by his dictatorial methods. This spade-bearded, black-eyed, mercurial statesman, with leonine head, had been the real creator of Greater Rumania. He had bamboozled the Allied Powers and the Central Powers alike, took Rumania into a disastrous war, and yet he emerged with more rewards than any other small allied state. Bratianu, son of the man who created the Kingdom of Rumania, could not help but think the nation was his personal possession. He was reproached for disguising authoritarian tendencies with a liberal program when an unanticipated crisis arose to aggravate the situation. Crown Prince Carol (1893-1953) was more preoccupied with pleasures than with preparation for his duties as the future monarch. Carol seemed to be more the inheritor of the traditions of imperturbability and unconcern of the

Phanariot *hospodars* than the firm discipline of the Hohenzollerns. He had contracted a morganatic marriage of short duration in 1918 which public opinion criticized. Subsequently married to Princess Helen of Greece, he nevertheless had an affair of long duration with Elena ("Magda") Lupescu, a stenographer. This Jewish woman affected bold contempt for the royal family and surrounded herself with a little court which profited from her ascendancy. As a result of Bratianu's stern remonstrance, King Ferdinand ordered his son to terminate his liaison with Madame Lupescu. Carol, however, preferred to renounce his right to the throne in favor of his son Michael (Mihai), and he departed for exile in Paris with his inamorata. By a regrettable twist of fate, Ferdinand died within a few months (1927), leaving the throne to a six-year-old boy.

The regency was entrusted to Prince Nicholas, Carol's brother, Maniu, and Bratianu. Ionel Bratianu soon died (1927), bequeathing control of the Liberal Party to his two younger brothers, Vintila and Constantin. The party, which then experienced a critical battle for its life, had to yield to its rival, the National Peasant Party. Supported by an impressive majority in the elections, the National Peasants then undertook a vast program of administrative reform and economic improvements by appealing to the technicians. Maniu, who was premier 1928-30 and 1932-33, was less hostile to Carol than Bratianu had been. So he invited Carol to return home. In June 1930 the exiled prince flew to Bucharest where he was proclaimed king by parliament.

Tall, imposing, strongly built, with a stern face, the man who had until 1930 been considered a carefree playboy soon proved to be brilliant, industrious, and very energetic. Ambitious for power, full of self-confidence, believing he was destined to undertake great tasks, King Carol (Charles) II was passionately devoted to politics, avid for struggle and risks, and resolved to place all power in his own hands. Was this a legacy of his German ancestry? His penchant for uniforms and decorations may well have derived from that background. Surrounded by intriguers and sycophants, Carol enthroned favoritism which was accompanied by the inevitable defect of administrative corruption. The presence of Madame Lupescu at his side contributed even more to discrediting the monarch. Dejected by the surly attitude of the sovereign whom he had restored to power, Maniu repeatedly lectured Carol on morality which he rather naively sought to make the king adopt at a time when his adversaries were whispering that his efforts might be better devoted to something more significant. In 1931 Carol appointed a coalition government headed by his tutor, Nicolae Iorga (1871-1940), the great historian, which became the prelude for the ultimate royal dictatorship.

A new political party appeared on the scene which, although not numerous at first, quickly attracted many malcontents who were seduced by its totalitarian doctrines. Its program called for a war against Jews and communists. This was the Iron Guard led by an adventurer of fanatic temperament, Corneliu Zelea Codreanu (1899-1938). He professed a devotion to military discipline which explained the ardor with which he shared Nazi ideology, even going so far as to confer on himself the title of *capitanul* which meant "one who leads" in the original Latin sense, and which was the Rumanian equivalent of *Der Führer* and *Il Duce,* He had distinguished himself by killing with his bare hands a police prefect who was allegedly too kind to Jews. Acquitted of this crime, Codreanu saw in this vindication an urge to persevere in violent methods to the point of introducing assassination into Rumanian political life. The Iron Guard's Council decided that murders would be perpetrated in ceremonies of purification. The names of Guardists who would commit the murders were chosen by lots. It was as a result of this process that Ion Duca, National Liberal premier, was murdered by these madmen in 1933. Although morally responsible, Codreanu was not bothered by the police who were more concerned with seeking the actual assassins.

Duca's death caused still another change of government in what had become a virtual game of musical chairs. Premiers fell like houses of cards: Iorga, a better historian than he was a politician, Vaida Voevod, Gheorghe Tatarescu, and others. Popular agitation was the natural consequence of this government instability. Railway workers went on strike in 1933. Iron Guardists and their opponents fought in the streets.

King Carol did not appear disturbed by these events. He used his personal policy to repress political parties which were at dagger points. Rumania counted the Liberals, National Peasants, Christians, Anti-Semites, the weak Social Democrats, Communists, and the Iron Guard fascists who were the most dangerous because they were the most daring. Carol declared that the 1923 constitution could no longer function. It was later modified and finally suspended in 1938 when Carol established his royal dictatorship. Already seething and divided, Rumania would become even more restless. Discontent grew as a result of character assassination, strict censorship, and police surveillance. Around Codreanu rallied increasing numbers of enthusiastic youth, army officers, and especially university students with fascist tendencies. All were animated by an ultra-patriotic ideal and even by a certain Neo-Christian mysticism which distinguished them from Hitler's Nazis. Using the name "Legionnaires" and with a battle-cry of "All for the Fatherland," the Iron Guardists were prepared to use any means to reestablish order in Rumania. Although many Guardists were sincere romantics, their organization was actually infiltrated and ultimately controlled by gangsters.

Iron Guard activities became so savage that in 1938 King Carol, at last alarmed by their growing power and influence, decided to act. On April 19 Codreanu and many of his lieutenants were condemned to prison for libel. A month later they were sentenced to ten years at hard labor for treason. This was followed by a government crackdown on the Guard after revelation of an alleged plot against the king. When Codreanu and thirteeen of his principal partisans were being moved to another prison, they fell under the bullets of the police "at a moment when they were attempting to escape," as the official statement read. This execution aroused considerable emotion in Nazi Germany because, by a strange coincidence, it had occurred (November 30, 1938) just when Carol returned from Germany where he had met Hitler. The Nazis were angered by this sudden twist of Rumania's policy toward the Iron Guard which, until 1938, had been the beneficiary of an obvious toleration. At a time when the Nazi menace was threatening Eastern Europe, Carol had incurred the wrath of the Nazi chancellor.

Greece with 7 million inhabitants had the appreciable advantage, denied to Rumania, of having few national minorities. The exchange of populations with Bulgaria and Turkey had cleared Greece of these minorities and added a sizeable group of Greeks to the nation. This immigration at first constituted, as it had for Bulgaria, a burden which required financial aid from the League of Nations. This burden was clearly obvious from the fact that

Greece had to absorb 1,200,000 from Asia Minor and 50,000 from Bulgaria. But this influx ultimately became a source of wealth because of the ingenious and commerce-oriented spirit of the immigrants. They established industries which were unknown in Greece and developed others which had had only minimal activity before the exchange. The new industries which flourished were rug manufacture, a specialty of Smyrna, and silk textiles. The efforts of the immigrants enhanced the Greek economy to the point where it soon achieved relative prosperity even in the agricultural sphere. Numerous landholdings had been reserved for those who settled in Greek Macedonia and Thrace where reclamation projects permitted them to secure fertile land favorable for tobacco cultivation. Athens' appearance was transformed by the growth of new suburbs.

Despite these social and economic changes, Greece nevertheless remained disunited and tense. The intrusion of the military into politics increased the instability. The influx of immigrants, who were generally hostile to the monarchy, added another problem. So numerous and complex were the quarrels, which produced several seizures of power, changes of cabinets, and even a change in the form of the government, that a sinuous tracing of politics is hopelessly confusing. Politicians appeared on stage, made their exists, reappeared, and exchanged places in an imbroglio saddened by tragedies.

King Alexander, who succeeded his father Constantine at the behest of the Allies in 1917, died in 1920 as a result of a monkey bite. In the ensuing elections Venizelos and his party were defeated even though Greek forces had achieved success in their campaign against the Turks which the premier had inspired. When the Greek army suffered reverses in Asia Minor, the Greeks demanded the restoration of Constantine to the throne so that he could generate military successes. Constantine returned to Athens from which he had been expelled by the Allies. The Greeks thus thrust on the Allies a disavowal as painful as it was unexpected, particularly for the English who had so strongly supported Greek ambitions. When the campaign in Asia Minor turned into a disaster, the Greeks experienced the grievous defeat at Sakharya. The humiliating reverses for national pride provoked another crisis which caused the second abdication of King Constantine in September 1922.

Constantine's oldest son, George, denied the throne by the Allies in 1917, acceded to the crown, but only for one year. A revolutionary government of military officers, led by Colonel Nicholas Plastiras, was opposed by an ultraconservative group led by General Joannes Metaxas. Accused of having supported Metaxas, King George II had to leave Greece. As he was departing from Athens, Venizelos, the grand old man of Greek politics, was returning from exile. An interregnum regency was entrusted to Admiral Pavlos Koundouriotes. The Greek republic was proclaimed on May 1, 1924 after a plebiscite. It lasted almost ten years. But the multiplicity of political parties, political passions, personal ambitions, and coteries perpetuated an atmosphere which was conducive to violence.

At first named president of the republic, Venizelos was soon discarded. Seizures of power were followed by repressions during which partisans of fallen regimes were vindictively pursued by the new masters until the time when the pursued became the pursuers. In June 1925 General Theodore Pangalos seized power. A partisan of strong-arm tactics, he provoked an incident with Bulgaria, and in domestic affairs he governed so harshly that he was overthrown in 1926 by General George Kondylis, a partisan of Venizelos.

A new constitution based on the French model was promulgated in 1926. In 1928 Venizelos returned to power since he was the only one who could suppress the quarrels. Greece finally experienced an era of relative tranquillity for four years during which a series of general improvements was undertaken. Agriculture, industry, commerce, public health, and education were improved by measures designed to restore the economy and develop the nation's welfare. An agricultural bank was established, commercial treaties were negotiated, and enlarged facilities for the settlement of immigrants were provided.

But ambitious aspirants to dictatorship were not long in reviving trouble. Venizelos had restored the senate, which had been abolished in 1862, for the purpose of stabilizing the republican regime. In the 1932 elections the Venizelists failed to secure a majority, possibly due to displeasure with Venizelos' conciliatory policy toward Turkey and the Balkan states. The Greek premier had convened the first Balkan conference in Athens in 1930. So in October 1932 Venizelos resigned, and he was succeeded by a moderate, pro-royalist government under Panyoti Tsaldaris. The Tsaldaris cabinet could not solve a financial crisis, and this impasse again required the aid of Venizelos who returned to office in January 1933. Elections in March ousted the Venizelos regime again. A coup organized by the pro-republican Plastiras, now a general, an attempt on Venizelos' life, a return of Tsaldaris to office, a navy mutiny, the coup of General Kondylis in 1935, and a myriad of other disquieting developments prolonged the ferment. Kondylis finally decided to induce the parliament to vote for the recall of exiled King George II. Such a step could most likely restore stability. The Greek people voted in a plebiscite (November 1935), which was rigged, to restore the monarchy. Ninety-eight per cent of the voters replied affirmatively to the question with an ardor far more impressive than that expressed ten years before in abolishing the monarchy.

Imitating his father's example, George returned a second time to remount a shaky throne. As a result of exile in London where he developed lasting friendships, the king returned quite Anglicized in manners and outlook. As a realist able to control his emotions and having no illusions about his difficult task, George at once indicated his good will and benevolence. Although at the mercy of Kondylis, the king nevertheless favored adoption of a very liberal constitution and decreed a general amnesty for the un-regenerate republicans.

But his moderation and clemency failed to secure wide response. The king's magnanimity produced no effect on the parliament whose members still pursued a turbulent policy aggravated by symptoms of growing communist activities. A strike of workers in a Kavalla cigarette factory revealed the effectiveness of communist propaganda. Elections in January 1936 confirmed communist strength when fifteen communists were elected to parliament and the incumbent government secured only a bare majority of seats. Because of this crisis, the king summoned General Metaxas (1871-1941), an authoritarian officer, to form a government in April 1936. In August Metaxas carried out his *coup d'état* by proclaiming martial law, dissolving parliament, and proclaiming himself dictator. He began prosecutions of communists, abolished all political parties, and instituted a rigid censorship. The new dictator had studied in a Berlin military academy, enjoyed a meteoric rise in the army, and was consecutively a conspirator, prisoner, and now premier, war minister, and foreign minister all in one.

Now that he was the indisputable master, this industrious and ultranationalistic dictator, who was certainly favored by the deaths of his rivals Kondylis, Venizelos, Tsaldaris, and Zaimis in 1936, resolved to set Greece on her feet and reorganize the country by the use of authoritarian methods at that time so widely applied in Europe. The regime was supported by the army. Metaxas repressed popular discontent by such conciliatory gestures as wage increases, social welfare, termination of agricultural debts, low food prices, etc. A grandiose public works program increased taxes and led to considerable domination of the government by commercial interests. Greece remained under the iron hand of Metaxas until the outbreak of World War II. Anti-monarchist republicans were gagged, but accusations were nevertheless raised against King George II for having violated the constitution by remaining an accomplice of a military dictator.

The new Kingdom of Yugoslavia faced acute problems incurred by the incorporation of peoples who had lived for centuries under Hapsburg rule. To force these peoples to erase overnight the memories of this past and its unique characteristics was to demand the impossible. After the initial acclaim over reunion with Serbia, the Croats and Slovenes realized the profound differences separating them from their south Slav brothers who had experienced centuries of Turkish domination. The latter practiced the Orthodox faith whose churches had practiced a traditional flexibility with regard to civil power. The Serbs used the Cyrillic alphabet. Isolated from the rest of Europe for five centuries, the Serbs retained a manner of thinking tainted by their subjection to the Turkish yoke. Hence the Serbs were reproached for perpetuating a "Balkan mentality."

The Croats and Slovenes, on the contrary, were predominantly Roman Catholic and thus members of a church which had been rebellious to temporal power. Writing in the Latin alphabet, they believed themselves to be more European than the Serbs and hence superior to their south Slav brothers. While the Serbs were almost completely of peasant origin and thus perpetuating a social level that was relatively equalized, an aristocracy dating from the feudal era survived among the Croats in addition to a cultivated bourgeoisie and the usual peasant class which formed very distinct social levels. Economic interests of Serbia and Croatia were difficult to harmonize. To the Croats and Slovenes Belgrade seemed a very modest capital in contrast to the sumptuous setting to which Vienna and Budapest had accustomed them. Even Zagreb (Agram) in Croatia, with its monuments and memories, was to them a city much more representative than the old Turkish fortress which had become the capital of the new kingdom.

The Serbs did not conceal their intention to transform this ensemble of provinces into a unified, centralized nation. The Croats, on the other hand, wished the formation of a federative state in which each province would enjoy considerable autonomy. These opposing views could not be reconciled. Disagreements could only end in conflict. During the formative years of the new kingdom the Croat and Slovene nationalists naturally avoided raising these issues. Partisans of centralized power controlled the first parliament, and in 1919, still enjoying the euphoria of victory, the first government consisted of representatives of the three principal elements of the population. The first Yugoslav government, created in January 1919, was headed by Premier Stojan Protich, a Serb, Vice Premier Koroshetz, a Slovene, and Foreign Minister Ante Trumbich, a Croat.

In the first elections the Serbian Radical Party, acclaimed in Belgrade as the creator of Greater Serbia and which had controlled the country for two decades, received a large number of votes. Despite its title, this party was oriented toward a prudent conservatism. Its success was attributable to the immense popularity of its founder and chief, the robust old Pashich, age 75, a patriarchal figure with a long, white beard which gave him a peasant's appearance. Some were tempted to reproach Pashich for his lack of comprehension of political compromise, his indifference to the opinions of nations other than Serbia, his obstinacy, and his taciturn attitude. But in Serbia his prestige remained intact. He was the creator of the Radical Party, the one who had resisted the risky fantasies of King Milan and had regenerated Serbia. He was above all the symbol of Serbian patriotism during the war, and the statesman who, despite reverses, perpetuated a faith in Serbia's future with the stubborn love of a peasant attached to his native soil.

The Democratic Party, composed of more liberal Serbs than the

Radicals, contended with the latter for power. The Communist Party registered impressive results in the elections by winning 54 seats in the parliament. This success was due to sufferings caused by a long, pitiless war and the misery accompanying it, to discontent aroused by a few individuals who had acquired fortunes, and to Russia's prestige which remained for many the inspiration whose example should be imitated. Communist pressures worried the government. No pretext was needed to repress the Communist Party because the communists themselves furnished the occasion when the interior minister was murdered by a communist assassin. The party was immediately declared illegal and its deputies barred from parliament or imprisoned. All communists and others suspected of sympathizing with them suffered the rigors of the police system. The result was to drive the communists underground and to give their movement a clandestine character which was even more dangerous because it was almost impossible to observe.

Meanwhile the deputies from Croatia insisted upon negotiating their demands with the Serbs on the basis of equality. Belgrade did not see it that way. As has been shown, the peoples formerly distributed among five different states—Serbia, Montenegro, Austria, Hungary, and Turkey—discovered glaring differences in cultural levels, aspirations, and general interests. The Croats complained of oppression by the excessive centralism and bureaucracy of Belgrade. "The Serbs get the jobs and we get the taxes," they wailed. The Croats, in fact, possessed greater resources than the Serbs and were thus taxed more. They insisted that revenues collected in the new provinces were being utilized to improve the relatively backward state of Serbia. Indeed, Serbia required considerable revenue to place her on an equal footing with regions whose economies had not been shattered and whose roads and railroads had not been devastated by the war. Anti-Serbian voices were raised with all the more authority because they were tightly grouped around Stefan Radich (1871-1928), leader of the Croat Peasant Party, who was twice imprisoned for his agitation. As popular in Croatia as Pashich was in Serbia, Radich opposed the Karageorgevich dynasty. In the end, however, the Croats were resigned to accept the 1921 constitution which established a centralized form of government. Radich and his party, however, joined opposition parties in combating the government.

Against the background of this conflict came quarrels generated by a multiplicity of parties whose divergences prevented the formation of stable majorities in the parliament. After the death of Pashich in 1926, a proliferation of petty politicians created frequent ministerial crises. The climax occurred in 1928. During a debate in the chamber a Montenegrin deputy killed two Croat delegates and mortally wounded their leader, Stefan Radich. The repercussions from this incident shamed Yugoslavia. After Radich died on August 8, the Croat deputies withdrew from the parliament. They demanded the creation of a federal state as the price of their cooperation. When Belgrade rejected this demand, the Croats established a separatist legislature in Zagreb and refused to deal with the Belgrade government. A critical impasse had been reached.

This apparently insoluble crisis, whose continuation was replete with risks, required an immediate disposition. King Alexander (1888-1934) suspended the constitution in January 1929, dissolved parliament, and assumed dictatorial powers. At this point in her history, the name of the country—the Kingdom of Serbs, Croats, and Slovenes—was changed to Yugoslavia which means "land of the south Slavs." In Serbia, where the king's prestige was great because he was still the national war hero, these measures were accepted as necessary to prevent a collapse into anarchy. But this was not the reaction elsewhere. The royal dictatorship was interpreted in Croatia as confirmation of the permanence of a centralized, unitary regime. The change of names also aggravated anxieties.

King Alexander, a slender man, always tightly laced into his uniform, with a long face and a rather prominent nose framed in thick spectacles, gave the impression of being a true soldier. As a result of his courageous record during the war, he had preserved the aura of a warrior in great epics. His education in Russia had developed in him a natural taste for authority toward which his devotion to military discipline also inclined him. Fiercely proud of Serbia and ambitious to promote her power, Alexander considered an intransigent patriotism to be his ideal. The interplay of politics bored him because he considered it a hindrance to his program of developing the young kingdom. Thus he had a horror of everything resembling disorder and communism, a fear which became an obsession.

The assassination of Radich served to excite Croat opposition.

The dead leader, considered a martyr to the cause, was succeeded by his disciple Vladko Machek (Macek), an equally strong patriot, who demanded a new constitution establishing a federal union. Nevertheless, Alexander treated Croatia as a Serbian province administered by bureaucrats from Belgrade and policed by Serbian gendarmes. Reaction against this repressive system was so strong that the bourgeois political parties in Croatia joined forces with Machek's Peasant Party to present a united front against the pretensions of the nationalists in Serbia. King Alexander became the object of fierce hatred throughout Croatia. Members of a Croat terrorist organization, the Ustash, whose tactics resembled those of the IMRO and whose leader was Ante Pavelich (Pavelic), swore to assassinate the monarch. The Ustash secured clandestine support in Fascist Italy and Hungary.

Obsessed by a fear of communism, Serbian functionaries carried out mass, hasty arrests which were less a repression than a warning. These indiscriminate measures merely irritated a considerable number of youths who were then attracted to liberal ideas. Ignoring this reaction and believing that Yugoslavia had just about regained her equilibrium, Alexander drew up a new constitution in 1931 which provided for a bicameral instead of the old unicameral legislature (the Skuptshchina). But the dictatorship continued under this camouflage without succeeding in securing actual collaboration between the government and the political parties, and without lessening the hostility which was mounting against the king.

King Alexander fell victim to this hatred when, landing at Marseilles on a state visit to France, he was assassinated on October 9, 1934 by a Macedonian revolutionary working with Croat revolutionists having headquarters in Hungary. The murder, which also claimed Foreign Minister Louis Barthou of France, almost led to war between Yugoslavia and Hungary. The horror of this tragedy relieved the resentment of his subjects who accorded their slain king an impressive funeral. Alexander's son succeeded to the throne as Peter II (1934-41). Prince Paul, the dead king's cousin, was regent for the 11-year-old monarch. Paul was a dilettante, a prince charming who was raised in England for which nation he remained nostalgic. Western in his orientation, Paul felt ill at ease in his homeland. Artistic things attracted him more than politics until he became interested in the latter, and then his taste for power intensified. He chose for premier Milan Stoyadinovich (Stojadinovic), a banker of massive girth, full of self-assurance, and having an authoritarian personality. Seduced by the prevailing fascist regimes in Europe, Stoyadinovich governed with excessive firmness and oriented Yugoslavia in a direction which was contrary to her interests and traditions.

Alexander's death by no means attenuated the conflict between the Serbs and Croats. At the very most the Slovenes were given a share in government due to the skill of Father Koroshetz. As for the Croats, they repeated their demands with increasing violence which went as far as to threaten secession or the seeking of a German protectorate to "free themselves from the Serbian yoke." Belgrade tried to appease the Croats by an attempted accord with the Papacy. This design was calculated to soothe the Roman Catholic sensitivities of the Croats. But this project unleashed a wild tempest in Serbia, provoked less by a religious reaction than by an almost instinctive distrust of Rome which for many still evoked memories of the menace of Catholic Austria.

The prolonged crisis assumed such gravity that in 1937 the Radicals joined with the Croat Peasant Party in an effort to solve the thorny question of the kingdom's continued unity. Machek, having become a champion of democracy, traveled to Belgrade in August 1938 to confer with the royal government. He received such a warm welcome in the capital that the authorities became disturbed. Furthermore, the customary methods of pressure used in elections in December 1938 did not succeed in giving the government more than a 4% majority of the total vote.

This reversal led Prince Paul to carry out a coup by removing Stoyadinovich, who appeared solidly entrenched but whose personality was too overbearing for the regent's tastes. Stoyadinovich was replaced by two men whose relative obscurity made them pliant instruments of Paul's policy. Dragisha Tsvetkovich (Cvetkovic) of the Radical Party was appointed premier, and Tsintsar-Markovich (Cincar-Markovic), the envoy to Nazi Germany, became foreign minister. Since Machek appeared interested in negotiating with this new regime, discussions were inaugurated which ended in a compromise on August 26, 1939. Democratic government was reestablished, and new elections by secret ballot promised. The state would be reorganized on a federal basis, the Croats receiving complete autonomy in all cultural and economic affairs. The autonomous *banovina* (province) of Croatia was created which included a section of Bosnia-Herzegovina and the Adriatic port of Dubrovnik (Ragusa). Matters of national concern (foreign policy, defense, etc.) were reserved for the central government. Machek was named vice premier and five other Croats joined the cabinet. Ivan Shubashich (Subasic) was appointed *ban* (governor) of Croatia. These last-minute concessions on the eve of World War II could not establish unity in the troubled kingdom which was destined to become a very active theater in the approaching conflict.

As for Albania, which became an independent republic after the Italian evacuation, the nation had such small dimensions, ill-defined frontiers, and its general weaknesses endangered the security of neighboring Greece and Yugoslavia. This threat was perpetuated by Fascist Italy whose aims contributed to making Albania a satellite and a bridgehead for interference in Balkan affairs.

In August 1923 four members of an Italian mission were murdered while engaged in delimiting the Greek-Albanian boundary. Rome sent a harsh ultimatum to Athens and on August 31 shelled and occupied the island of Corfu. Greece appealed to the League of Nations. A Greek tragedy was narrowly averted when English pressure forced Italy to withdraw from Corfu. This was Mussolini's first assertion of fascist power in foreign affairs. To establish Italian influence in Albania, Rome gratified some large Moslem landowners, including the famed Toptani family. In 1926 Italy and Albania signed a friendship treaty, and in 1927 the Treaty of Tirana providing for military cooperation. This marked the beginning of a virtual Italian protectorate by which Rome secured valuable petroleum concessions, supervision of Albania's army, certain educational privileges, and the privilege of constructing roads. In 1928 Ahmed Zogu, a member of the Toptani tribe and president since 1925, was proclaimed king as Zog I (1928-38). He undertook a modernization of Albania under the inspiring example of Kemal Ataturk. Could he succeed in establishing a stable and truly independent country? Italy waited and watched. Soon Mussolini's attitude became more insinuating and persuasive. In 1932 Zog opposed the creation of a customs union with Italy. This marked the beginning of opposition to Italy's overbearing policies. After an Italian squadron sailed into Durazzo in 1934 to terrify Zog, Albania again submitted. The sham independence of Albania would last only five more years.

The era between the wars produced, as has already been shown, serious domestic problems for the Balkan states. The vanquished states, dismembered by the peace treaties, shared with the victors, who increased in size, a similar fate. The latter even had to pay the price of victory in the form of problems arising out of the incorporation of new populations. An almost identical evolution could be noted for all the Balkan states. Victory of the Allied Powers, a triumph for the democracies, had strengthened the establishment of parliamentary regimes. But parliamentarianism, for which the people did not yet appear ready, functioned imperfectly and ended up in disarray. To restore tranquillity the governments were forced to adopt methods inspired by the processes of totalitarianism. Created by the power of Kemal, the new Turkey was Ataturk incarnate. In Rumania King Carol II assumed power without even disguising an authority which his neighbor, King Boris of Bulgaria, took pains to camouflage. Albania had the authoritarian regime of King Zog. Yugoslavia bowed before the wills of Alexander and Stoyadinovich. And Greece, torn between monarchy and republic, decided again on George II only to give a free hand to General Metaxas.

The masses did not always gracefully accept these authoritarian regimes, but they had to submit to a force rendered obvious by the ubiquitous secret police. Many were dissatisfied in Serbia, and a smoldering discontent pervaded Bulgaria. Rumania was anxious and divided. Turkey alone, where political consciousness was less developed, evinced little hostility to methods responsible for rejuvenating the country.

Confronted by indiscriminate repression, those who disapproved of the regimes had to conceal their sentiments. Thus it became difficult to appreciate the significance of an opposition which remained silent. Fearful of assassination, character and otherwise, a man did not reveal his true thinking except in safe surroundings among people he could trust. Thus in Bulgaria the Peasant Party had to avoid surveillance and indulge in various precautions to communicate with foreigners who sympathized with their cause. If and when elections were held, they provided only a distorted reflection of a nation's spirit. Campaigns took place under the pressure of the authorities, police harassment, and threats. It required considerable courage to be a non-governmental candidate. When voting was completed, the accuracy of the results was usually in doubt. Behind the facade of popular support for the Balkan regimes were hidden cells of discontent. Ideas were disseminated in clandestine manners. No matter how imperceptible, this activity undermined the government's basis. Even among bourgeois circles many were won over by ideas which were secretly circulated. Their attraction was especially effective on the youth because the secrecy accompanying such activities was an added attraction to young adults.

The Communist Party, among the opposition movements, was the most virulent and difficult to unearth. In every Balkan state, after having appeared in the open at the end of the war, communist parties were declared illegal as the result of violent incidents. Communist influence was strongest in Bulgaria where it provoked disturbances for about a decade. In Yugoslavia, the communists early won several seats in parliament. In Greece the communists were slow to reveal themselves, while in Rumania communist doctrines, considered by many to be mere philosophical speculations, hardly attracted much support because most of the population were peasants. Rumania's Russophobia also militated against the appeal of communism.

Despite repression, persecution, and police surveillance, communism remained a challenging force in most countries as much by reason of its underground organization as by the passions it aroused among its partisans who were as eager for sacrifices as they were for violence. They recruited among industrial workers made rebellious by widespread poverty and among intellectuals made revolutionary by social and political injustice. To simple minds as to the theoreticians of the absolute, communism offered a seductive ideology full of dynamism. It promised a revolution—a word replete with prestige—a revolution which would overthrow an abhorrent system and regenerate the world.

Among many Balkan peoples, generally accustomed to favoring Russia over the other powers, the Soviet Union became a vigorous pole of attraction and a model. Ignorant of actual conditions within Soviet Russia, the Balkan communists had a distorted image of life under Bolshevism. To them Russia was the country without masters at a time when the Balkan peoples were kneeling under the rods of the authorities. These Balkan communists were ready to serve Stalin with a devotion almost equal to that formerly shown the Romanov tsars. The severity of directives given to the secret police to stifle communist activities had no result other than to make the communists vanish from the visible political horizon. They disappeared, but they only went underground and their influence grew because of secret organizations whose methods had been perfected as the result of a long familiarity with clandestine behavior.

During troubles inspired by Bulgarian communists between 1925 and 1934 a project was conceived in Moscow to Bolshevize the Balkans. The authors of this plan had to modify their tactics after failing in their attempts to overthrow the Bulgarian government. They then proceeded to organize cells which soon comprised a federation of representatives of the Balkan communist parties. Guided by the Communist (Third) International in Moscow, this federation planned for the installation of soviet-style regimes in each country. Its chief was Georgi Dimitrov (1882-1949), leader of the Bulgarian Communist Party and a member of the Comintern. After being forced to abandon Bulgaria the federation moved to Vienna and then to Moscow where Dimitrov, granted Soviet citizenship, became general secretary of the Comintern in 1935.

Since this so-called Democratic Federation of communist parties engaged in underground activities, it usually escaped detection. The authorities were aware that at the University of Belgrade extremist ideas were shared by several professors and many students. More numerous partisans of communist ideas inhabited Bulgaria. In Greece the communists were more limited in their actions. All communists hesitated to arouse the authorities while awaiting opportunities to reveal their power in attempts to seize control. This was what would happen in Yugoslavia during World War II. At the end of that war communist organizations would suddenly emerge and, with the cooperation of the Red Army of Soviet Russia, become the basis on which would be erected regimes inspired by Moscow.

The Balkan states were very active in international affairs during the interwar era. General foreign policies evolved from a defense of individual interests to the safeguarding of general Balkan interests. The signing of regional agreements had as their goal the assurance of individual security by stabilizing the new territorial configurations. These accords culminated in a system of pacts which attempted to integrate the peninsula into a vast system destined to preserve the peace of Europe.

Turkey presented a special case in point. Kemal Ataturk took initiatives in foreign affairs as bold as his innovations at home. His moves constituted nothing less than an overthrow of traditional Ottoman policies. The new Turkey was completely isolated at birth. England's hostility encouraged the Allied Powers to adopt a cold reserve toward Turkey. The activities of the Italians in the Dodecanese Islands, aroused by the triumph of fascism, produced fears of a reawakening of Rome's ambitions in Asia Minor. In her isolation Turkey grew closer to another power which, virtually outlawed by Europe, also exhibited a vastly different face as the result of a revolution. This was Soviet Russia. Hereditary enemies for centuries, the two countries came to depend on each other in their common isolation. The governments of Ankara and Moscow were the first to establish diplomatic relations. Their mutual recognition was followed in 1921 by the signing of a friendship treaty. To the ancient tradition of mistrust inspired by the ambitions of a powerful neighbor, a real détente ensued for twenty years. This relationship evolved into combined efforts to avert crises so that both nations would complete internal reorganization efforts in peace.

Turkey achieved a similar about-face toward another old enemy—Greece. Kemal encountered a partner in Venizelos who was equally realistic. The Treaty of Lausanne of 1923 provided for exchanges of populations between the two countries. Greeks in Asia Minor were moved to Greece while Turks in Greece were transferred to Asia. This was a delicate operation carried out under the supervision of the League of Nations. After the Greek evacuation of the shores of Asia Minor, the long cherished dream of the Athens government to extend its power over that region would become pointless. Since a basis for discord no longer existed between the two countries, why should they not have buried a hostility which only old traditions could justify? This was realized on both shores of the Aegean, and a rapprochement was arranged.

It was quite difficult to substitute almost overnight a sincere and open friendship for an old animosity The accord did not fully correspond to Greek expectations, especially the anticipation of those who hoped for aid from their new allies in the tragic days the Greeks had to experience. The Greco-Turkish rapprochement nevertheless contributed to relaxing the troubled Balkan atmosphere. This was an unprecedented development in eastern Mediterranean affairs which upset former conceptions founded on an animosity responsible for so many bloody struggles.

In 1932 Turkey was admitted to the League of Nations, attesting to the confidence which the efficacy of Kemal's reforms had won for his country, to say nothing of the appreciable progress of his foreign policy. Turkey took advantage of good will shown to Ankara by demanding a revisions of clauses in the Treaty of Lausanne concerning the Straits, a question on which Kemal had not been able to have his way. After lengthy negotiations a convention signed at Montreux in 1936 gave the Turks considerable satisfaction. The international control commission was abolished and its authority transferred to the Turkish government. Turkey secured the right to fortify the Straits, and the waterway would be closed to warships during wars in which Turkey was not a belligerent. The Turkish republic had succeeded in persuading Europe to adopt the original demands made at Lausanne. Turkish success was due to political acumen and remarkable obstinacy.

Rumania and Yugoslavia, ranged among the victors, were in the front rank of the Balkan states because of the ample proportions of their territorial acquisitions, which had transformed them from small states into medium-sized powers. As neighbors of Italy and Hungary, both would be more directly involved in central European politics. This orientation led them to join with Czechoslovakia in creating the Little Entente in 1920-21. These three states, the successors to the defunct Hapsburg Monarchy, mutually agreed to prevent a restoration of the Hapsburgs and efforts at vengeance by Germany and Hungary. This pact coincided with the aims of French diplomats to create a counterweight on Germany's eastern frontiers. The Little Entente states were in a position to contribute toward containing new German aggression. France soon entered into treaties with Rumania and Yugoslavia which bound them to the security system created by the French Foreign Ministry.

A more European policy was pursued by Rumania than by any other Balkan state because of the breadth of view of her statesmen and the distinction they acquired in international affairs. Rumania's cultural level had been more advanced than that of her neighbors, and the kingdom had been an ally of great powers since 1883. Statesmen like the Bratianus, Take Ionescu, and Nicolae Titulescu, all educated in the West, displayed real evidence of a European spirit. After serving as finance minister, ambassador to England, and foreign minister, the clever and enterprising Titulescu played a very prominent role as Rumania's permanent delegate to the League of Nations, 1932-36. With a smooth, almost beardless face, prominent cheekbones which gave him a Mongolian look, and sparkling eyes, Titulescu was ranked among the most popular statesmen in Geneva where his imaginative resources and eloquence gained for him first-rank importance whenever international problems were discussed. He acted in such a way that Rumania's policy was for several years intimately intertwined with general European policy, and he made determined efforts to bring his Yugoslav ally into agreement.

Rumania's case was quite exceptional. In general, the Balkan states were preoccupied until the outbreak of World War II in settling questions of a regional character rather than involving themselves in the evolution of events in Europe.

In 1923 Greece unexpectedly incurred the wrath of a great power. Several Italian officers of a commission instructed to delimit Albania's frontiers were murdered in Epirus. Mussolini's new fascist government in Italy seized this occasion to elevate its international prestige. Italy accused the Greek government of having subsidized the murders. Mussolini addressed a very harsh ultimatum to Athens and, without awaiting the opening of consultations, landed troops on the island of Corfu after it was shelled with considerable loss of life. The League of Nations displayed lamentable timidity during this Corfu incident. Apparently unwilling to arbitrate a dispute between a great and small power, the League asked the Allied Conference of Ambassadors to settle the crisis. At length Corfu was evacuated, and Greece was required to pay a heavy indemnity to Italy. Coincidentally the Geneva diplomats were occupied in subtle juridical interpretations of the League Covenant and its applicability to this crisis. Italo-Greek relations ultimately improved to the point where a friendship treaty was signed in 1928. But the presence of Italian officials in Albania, which was adjacent to Greek Epirus, Italy's ambitious projects to increase her influence in the Adriatic, and the bombastic outbursts of Mussolini still caused very real concern in Athens.

Bulgaria's chagrin probably caused the greatest concern among the Balkan states. Reduced in size by the peace treaties, Bulgaria's fate was associated with that of the revisionist powers, Germany and Hungary, who had also been defeated in the war. Bulgaria had claims against Yugoslavia, Greece, and Rumania. Yugoslavia had annexed additional sections of Macedonia, Greece had denied Bulgaria access to the Aegean, and Rumania had regained the southern Dobrudja. Added to this acrimony was Bulgaria's smoldering ambition to secure Adrianople despite improvement in relations with the new Turkey. In 1925 a friendship treaty between the two former allies eliminated some of the friction.

Despite the prudence of King Boris, Bulgaria's neighbors kept their guard. Since all shared the same suspicions regarding Bulgaria, the idea of uniting to assure mutual defense against a resurgence of Sofia's aggressiveness inevitably arose. Lengthy negotiations preceded the signing of the Balkan Pact in Athens on February 9, 1934. Greece, Rumania, Turkey, and Yugoslavia mutually guaranteed the security of their frontiers and pledged to consult in the event of the signing of a convention by any one of them with a third power. This entente, clearly defensive in character and designed to maintain the status quo, was not specifically directed against any state. But since its application was limited to the Balkans, the signatories refusing to bind themselves to any non-Balkan matters, it was obvious that Bulgaria was the object of the pact. Bulgaria's absence from the entente also weakened it. The frontiers of each signatory state were contiguous to Bulgaria, and that fact was the probable *raison d'être* for the pact. Bulgaria was invited to join the Balkan Entente, but Sofia's contention that adherence to the pact would imply tacit abandonment of territorial claims led to rejection of the invitation. Unable to achieve Balkan unanimity, the pact members had really created a threatening vacuum in their midst. The Balkan Entente assumed the character of an anti-Bulgarian coalition just as the Little Entente was insurance against the restoration of the Hapsburg dynasty in Austria or Hungary.

Despite continued ferment in the peninsula, a certain rapport did develop between Bulgaria and Yugoslavia. Points of friction still revolved about the eternal Macedonian question because each state tenaciously insisted upon claiming the same regions. To create an atmosphere conducive to a détente, Bulgaria rigorously suppressed the IMRO and prohibited the activities of the *komitadjis* (local guerilla bands operating at the frontiers). Exchanges of royal visits also cleared the air to the point that in January 1937 a pact of "eternal friendship" was signed. Ties uniting the "two brotherly peoples" were celebrated in ceremonies on both sides of the frontier. But, in reality, this rapport was quite superficial. Its continuation depended upon the personal relations, mutual confidence, and cordiality established between Stoyadinovich and Kiosseivanov. Events would soon prove that the aspirations of the two Slav nations would collide over Macedonia despite apparent efforts to muzzle such manifestations.

In 1938 a discernible détente in Greco-Bulgarian relations was achieved with the signing of a few accords. Bulgaria had secured a certain respectability in the views of her neighbors. This change in policy was culminated in July 1938 with the signing of a treaty of non-aggression in Salonika by Bulgaria and the four members of the Balkan Entente. Bulgaria, however, refused to join the entente. Nevertheless, Sofia's friendly gesture convinced the entente to abrogate the clauses of the Treaty of Neuilly-sur-Seine which had limited Bulgaria's armaments. A general détente was discernible on the eve of World War II, and this generated a degree of optimism in the Balkans. Perhaps such enthusiasm was attributable to the fact that all the Balkan states had authoritarian governments at the oubreak of war in 1939.

The Balkan States on the Eve
of World War II

THE BALKAN states, having achieved a certain détente, soon manifested divergent tendencies when confronted by the ferment produced by the aggressiveness of Adolf Hitler, the grandiloquent ambitions of Mussolini, and the enigmatic silence of Joseph Stalin.

Yugoslavia was the first to be impressed by the strength of the Rome-Berlin Axis. Since Stoyadinovich's appointment as premier, due as much to the authoritarian regime flourishing in Belgrade as to the hesitant and conciliatory policies of England and France, Yugoslavia tended to drift toward the dictatorships. Stoyadinovich's deliberate policy to respond favorably to the blandishments of fascist regimes soon overrode the mistrust of Italy, which had been a basic feature of Yugoslavia's foreign policy. Skillfully flattered by Mussolini, Stoyadinovich parried alliance proposals of the French government as he did the appeals of Titulescu for an extension of Yugoslav-Rumanian engagements. Thus a destructive blow was dealt to the solidarity of the Little Entente.

In 1937 Yugoslavia and Italy negotiated a political and economic agreement. By reciprocally guaranteeing their mutual frontiers, the two nations renounced their pursuit of irredentist aims in Dalmatia, Istria, and Venezia Giulia. Yugoslavia thus granted de jure recognition to Italy's annexation of Fiume in 1919. Moreover, both agreed to improve economic and cultural relations. Count Galeazzo Ciano, the Italian foreign minister who came to Belgrade to sign this agreement on March 25, endorsed the views of Stoyadinovich whom he believed to be a genuine fascist, especially after the latter characterized the accord as a first step toward a "natural and inevitable alliance."

The Yugoslavs scarcely shared the sentiments of their government, judging by the coolness which greeted the Italo-Yugoslav agreement. When Ciano again visited Belgrade in November 1937, he was greeted in Belgrade with cheers of "Viva Ciano," uttered by Stoyadinovich's stooges.

When considering relations with Nazi Germany, Stoyadinovich, who frequently expressed admiration for Hitler, did display a certain hesitancy when he envisaged the possibility of a Nazi descent into the Balkans. Since to Stoyadinovich Germany "represented the greatest force on earth," he strove for friendly relations and relied upon Italy's intercessions to avert complications with Berlin.

The Yugoslavs, considered instinctively democratic by some, were baffled by a policy which violated their most cherished traditions. The masses and especially the army preserved an affection and gratitude toward Serbia's allies in World War I, and toward France particularly. But what did public opinion matter? Did not the police stifle manifestations frowned upon by the government and disperse with blackjacks students who had assembled to mourn the passing of prominent French statesmen?

When the Nazis occupied Prague in March 1939, the Croats became restless. Was the advance of Nazi Germany toward Eastern Europe a signal for Croatia to seek support from Berlin? Italy, who considered all Yugoslavia to be within her sphere of influence, expressed concern to her German ally about further German advances. Hitler reassured Mussolini, affirming that since Italy had had no interest in the fate of Czechoslovakia, Germany had no interest in that of Croatia or any ambitions in the Mediterranean. Thus the two Axis partners delimited their zones of influence in the Balkans.

Rumania, a pillar of France's security system in Eastern Europe, began to vacillate in the mid-1930's. The nation which had pursued a policy of preserving the status quo witnessed the crumbling of the Little Entente and her monarch acquiring Hitler's wrath as a result of his suppression of the Iron Guard. Furthermore, Soviet protests against the 1918 annexation of Bessarabia assumed a persistently alarming character. Divergences in domestic affairs produced repercussions in international politics. The Liberals and the National Peasants favored England and France while partisans of totalitarianism were naturally enthusiastic about Nazi Germany. Thus conflict between the democracies and the Axis powers would be certain to exacerbate domestic tensions within Rumania.

When King Carol dismissed Titulescu as foreign minister in 1936, the Little Entente became drained of its vitality. Its death certificate was validated at Bled in Yugoslavia on August 23, 1938 when the Little Entente powers signed a non-aggression treaty with Hungary and recognized the latter's right to rearm. Originally a security measure against Hungary's possible revenge, the Little Entente produced an accord which, with Hitler's support, became an instrument to create troubles in the Danubian basin.

When the threat of a new war became irreversible, the Balkan states were drawn into the whirlpool which engulfed all Europe. It was no longer a question of isolationism or regionalism. By 1939 Europe was a continent where each country sought to prepare its defenses in order to meet the inevitable torment. The negotiating of alliances and the award of guarantees followed in succession. The Balkan nations were merely second-rate powers which the great states used as pawns in preparing for the formidable conflict about to break out. Abetted by Mussolini, Hitler sought to intimidate them into becoming passive witnesses to his rise to preeminence while waiting to subjugate them. Meanwhile, the democratic states attempted to make of the Balkans a barrier to resist the insatiable ambitions of the Axis Powers.

Assuming solid positions in the face of an imminent war was not an easy task for little states which were primarily concerned with self-defense. The latent discord between authoritarian regimes and democratic ideas was no longer evident. The masses were deprived of the means of displaying their sentiments, and governments became extremely cautious. Whatever their preferences or however impressed they were by Nazi strength, the Balkan states were reluctant to compromise themselves at the beginning of the war crisis. Experience had taught them that such crises held surprises. The little states awaited the opportune moment to "bet on the winning horse."

Germany enjoyed an undeniable prestige in the Balkans on the eve of World War II. Berlin flattered the governments and encouraged pro-Nazi groups such as the Iron Guard. In other nations lacking parties with such flamboyant labels, Germany strove to support groups which manifested sympathy for totalitarian ideologies. The high regard most general staffs professed for German militarism and war materials constituted one of the pillars of Berlin's influence. Many army officers were convinced of the superiority of the military organization they had come to admire at reviews and parades in Berlin.

Germany had another very effective weapon in her arsenal. This was economic penetration. Since agriculture still constituted the major resource of the Balkan countries, Germany's highly industrialized economy complemented this farming. Under these conditions Germany profited remarkably well. The Germans purchased the wheat, maize, and tobacco raised in the Balkans, and sold agricultural machinery, electric products, and chemicals produced in their factories. That shrewd financial wizard, Hjalmar Schacht, the Nazi finance minister, fixed the imaginary value of the mark at a high rate in contrast to local exchange values. In this way the Balkan peasant was very happy to receive numerous lei, leva, dinars, or drachmas for his products. He did not realize that he was also paying very dearly for materials he was acquiring from Germany.

Because of this ingenious arrangement and the relative proximity of Germany, the latter became the most important client of the Balkan states. Germany purchased 65% of Bulgaria's produce in 1937, and this figure rose to 75% after the Nazi annexation of Austria and the Sudetenland in 1938. By 1939 Germany was buying from Bulgaria nine times more than England and France combined. Germany enjoyed a quasi-monopoly on Bulgarian products. As Austria had once waged the so-called "pig war" on little Serbia, Germany used economic pressure to bend governments to her views.

When England and France realized what was happening and attempted to react, their efforts were too late. France tried to attract Bulgaria from Germany's economic orbit by offering to extend credits in 1939. Germany warned Bulgaria that all trade would be terminated if the latter responded favorably to the French. Anxious about a potential ruin of her foreign trade, Bulgaria had to yield to avoid economic disaster. France then negotiated a trade treaty more favorable to Bulgarian goods. Walther Funk, Nazi minister of the national economy, went to Sofia and declared, "I am ready to buy everything you produce and sell you everything you need." How could such an offer be resisted? Bulgaria's example, which was typical, is cited as evidence of the methods Germany used in all the Balkan states. As

Nazi ideology stated, nature had provided a great economic *lebensraum* to Germany which extended from the North Sea to the Black Sea. One result of this policy was the accumulation of unlimited German currency by the Balkan states and the banking of very little other currencies. To utilize their resources in German currency, the states invited German lecturers, musicians, athletes, purchased German books, and had their youth enroll in German universities to spend the marks at their disposal. Such were the powerful methods used by Germany while England and France, who depended upon general sympathies among the masses and opponents of Nazism, scrupulously avoided arousing these potential friends lest difficulties arise concerning alleged Anglo-French interference in the internal affairs of the Balkan nations.

As for Soviet Russia, relations with the Balkan states were devoid of confidence because the little kingdoms naturally feared the communist menace. Republican Turkey was the only state which had early resumed relations with Russia. Rumanian foreign minister Titulescu did achieve a détente with Russia because he and Maxim Litvinov, the Soviet foreign commissar, both championed collective security at the League of Nations in the early 1930's. Although Greece recognized the Soviet regime in 1924, Rumania and Bulgaria waited ten more years to follow that example. Yugoslavia had become a sanctuary for many anti-Bolshevik White Russians. The Karageorgevich family preserved its attachment to tsarism. As a consequence, Yugoslavia did not establish diplomatic relations with Moscow until after the outbreak of World War II. This relative lack of contacts did not prevent Soviet agents from taking advantage of widespread Balkan poverty to prepare the ground for revolt. Turkey was more insulated against this propaganda because Kemal Ataturk prohibited all communist agitation despite amicable relations with the Soviet Union.

The Munich Pact of September 29, 1938 marked a decisive turning point in European politics. The ephemeral impression of relief which followed the frantic, anguishing days was followed by a feeling that new concessions greedily snatched by Hitler would not halt his aggression. The final liquidation of Czechoslovakia, carried out six months after the Munich Pact, constituted the most serious warning to the Balkan states. It sounded the death-knell to collective security. By selecting Poland as its next objective, German aggression moved east, and the peoples of the Balkan peninsula were threatened. The policy of appeasement pursued by England and France had obviously failed. Perhaps the policy of obedience to Nazi pressures would likewise fail to protect the Balkan states.

Among the Balkan peoples the Rumanians realized their country was next in line. The relative wealth of the country, the tremendous grain and petroleum resources, and its strategic location aroused the greed of the Germans who were already irate at the execution of Codreanu and his lieutenants. Bucharest's efforts to reconcile Warsaw and Prague after the Munich Pact, and Rumania's refusal to participate in the dismemberment of Czechoslovakia aggravated Hitler's displeasure. A week after the Nazi takeover of all Czechoslovakia, Rumania agreed on March 23, 1939 to a convention which authorized large-scale German economic control of her economy. The consequences were not only the virtual surrender of Rumania's resources to German exploitation, without appreciable compensation, but the country was drawn into the Nazi political orbit.

These developments further confirmed Anglo-French opinions of the insatiability of Nazi ambitions and the urgency to establish a limit beyond which Hitler must not go. This new policy, characterized by a sudden stiffening of English attitudes, was the signal for intense diplomatic activity in all eastern Europe. Adopting a reversal of its policy, the English government resolutely moved from appeasement to resistance. Prime Minister Neville Chamberlain declared in the House of Commons on March 31, 1939 that in case of German aggression against Poland, England would defend Polish independence. France issued the same guarantee, reaffirming the Franco-Polish treaty of 1921.

The Anglo-French foreign ministries inaugurated negotiations to accord similar guarantees to Greece. France insisted upon extending assurances to Rumania. The existence of the Nazi-Rumanian economic pact worried the English government. Even if London was not yet determined to defend Rumania, a new development would overcome English hesitancy. The initiative lay this time with Italy and not with Germany.

The question of Albania had played a significant role in delaying a more cordial rapport between Italy and Yugoslavia. Belgrade refused to sanction Italy's annexation of her neighbor. With considerable duplicity the Italians succeeded in allaying this anxiety. Ciano informed his friend Stoyadinovich in January 1939 that no action against Albania would be undertaken without prior notice to Belgrade. When Stoyadinovich hinted at a possible partition, Ciano responded with a suggestion that unofficial talks be held on this subject.

The world learned on April 7, Good Friday, that Mussolini had seized little Albania which was already an Italian satellite. What had taken place between January and April? Stoyadinovich, so overly confident, had been dismissed by Prince Paul ten days after his talks with Ciano. The Italian foreign minister considered the ouster a pretext to drop his promise to Stoyadinovich. Germany's occupation of Prague on March 15 encouraged Mussolini to execute an analogous act of aggression to acquire coveted territory. Italy dispatched to Albania on March 25 plans for the establishment of a protectorate which was changed to an ultimatum because of King Zog's delay in responding. At the expiration of the deadline, Italian troops disembarked in Albania after shelling the coastline. Zog escaped with his wife and four-day-old son to the mountains.

This event produced anguished concern in Belgrade. To demands for an explanation submitted to Italy, Mussolini replied that the occupation of Albania, designed to protect Italian interests, was merely a temporary arrangement. The Italian dictator refused to make any commitment regarding delimitation of Albania's frontiers. A few days later King Victor Emmanuel III, already Emperor of Ethiopia, added to his head a third crown, that of the king of Albania, "in response to the wishes" of a so-called constituent assembly in Tirana. This shameful seizure carried out by Mussolini came as the first thunderclap announcing the storm about to darken the European sky. Greece was now threatened by Italy in the same way that Rumania was menaced by Germany.

In separate but identical declarations England and France assured Greece and Rumania on April 13 that in case of threats to their independence, which they resisted with force, both Western powers would send all available military assistance. This essentially defensive guarantee was accepted gratefully. Germany considered the Anglo-French military guarantees an encircling maneuver which was quite ridiculous because the guarantors were prevented from fulfilling their promises by the great distances separating them from their protégés.

England and France strove to erect in Eastern Europe a system or bloc of nations who were resolved to maintain peace. Turkey obviously found a place in this bloc. England and Turkey signed a pact of mutual assistance on May 12 which included military cooperation if hostilities penetrated into the eastern Mediterranean. France and Turkey signed on June 23 a similar treaty. Formation of a Balkan bloc dedicated to the preservation of peace was well on its way. This development appeared to satisfy Soviet Russia. Grigorii Potemkin, the Deputy Commissar of Foreign Affairs, had just undertaken a visit to the Balkan capitals where he gave an impression that Moscow looked with favor upon the success of the Anglo-French policy. Bulgaria had to be persuaded to join the anti-fascist bloc. Hints were circulated in Bucharest that Rumanian concessions in the southern Dobrudja might induce Bulgaria to join. Although discreet overtures were made to Sofia, Bulgaria's tenacious ambitions were merely reawakened regarding the Dobrudja, Thrace, and Macedonia.

Turkey's participation in the establishment of this bloc extended it beyond the limits of the Balkans. Turkey's cordial relations with Soviet Russia permitted Ankara to perform the role of a liaison agent among the English, French, and Soviet governments. London and Paris, however, rejected this indirect approach. Anglo-French negotiations were initiated in Moscow to secure Soviet adherence to the guarantees already given to Poland and Rumania, two neighbors of Russia. A treatment of these protracted and laborious negotiations would be inappropriate. Nevertheless, Soviet demands should be cited. These included extension of military guarantees to the Baltic states of Estonia, Latvia, and Lithuania and the signing of a trilateral military assistance pact. An impasse ensued, partly aggravated by the refusal of Rumania and Poland to open their frontiers to the Red Army. The Polish government was overly confident and did not wish to antagonize Hitler by drawing closer to Stalin.

Discussions lasted four months in Moscow. One reason for their prolongation was the dismissal in May 1939 of Litvinov and his replacement by Vyacheslav Molotov. Litvinov, it was believed then, was removed because he favored Western ideas, but inadequate attention was given to the real significance of Molotov's emergence.

The Axis powers profited from the prolonged Moscow discussions. Fascist Italy became fully linked to Nazi Germany on May 22 when their Pact of Steel was signed marking the full development of the Rome-Berlin Axis. Both dictatorships dispatched messages to Bulgaria, Hungary, and Yugoslavia suggesting the creation of a counter-balance to the bloc being erected by England and France in the Balkans. At the same time top secret negotiations began between Berlin and Moscow. Nazi-Soviet discussions were revealed only when Nazi foreign minister Joachim von Ribbentrop suddenly arrived in Moscow and, within 48 hours, had signed with Molotov on August 23 a pact of non-aggression. This melodramatic occurrence ruined the hopes of the infinitely patient English and French negotiators in Moscow who were required, after four months of talks, to leave empty-handed even though they had gone to the utmost limits of concessions.

When Stalin guaranteed Germany's security in Eastern Europe, Hitler secured complete freedom of action in the West. A year before the Munich Pact had sown the seeds of conflict which were now fertilized by the Nazi-Soviet Pact, which was called a non-aggression treaty but was in reality a second and final step in the march to war. Soviet Russia opened to Germany the doors to the West, and Germany opened to Russia those of Eastern Europe where, after years of repression, were again born the ancient imperialistic aspirations which had lain dormant since the fall of tsarism. The signing of the Molotov-Ribbentrop pact, whose secret protocol provided for a Nazi-Soviet division of Eastern Europe and the Balkans, unleashed World War II. The Nazi armies invaded Poland a week after the pact was signed.

The Balkan States During World War II

THE Nazi-Soviet pact of non-aggression, signed August 23, 1939, produced panic in the Balkans and especially in Rumania. Emotions would have run even higher if a secret protocol to that pact had been revealed. In it Germany recognized Soviet Russia's interest in recovering Bessarabia and declared a general disinterest in Balkan affairs. Thus the Balkan peninsula was apparently assigned to the Soviet sphere of influence. As soon as this pact was signed, Moscow altered its policy toward the Balkan states. Russia's former support of a security system was dropped in favor of seizing a share of prospective booty similar to the acquisitions of Germany in Poland and Czechoslovakia. The Balkan Entente, which Russia had encouraged but now deemed too weak to resist the new developments, almost overnight lost its *raison d'être*. This was realized during a visit to Moscow of Turkish foreign minister Shukru Saracoglu in October 1939. Saracoglu had come intending to discuss the formation of a bloc of neutral states in the Balkans. But after a month of talks, Saracoglu, realizing that the object of his mission no longer corresponded to Soviet policy, departed without having secured anything. Henceforth the Balkan Entente was nothing more than an abstract idea deprived of reality. Its representatives met for the last time in Belgrade in February 1940 to exchange useless assurances.

When Poland collapsed after three weeks of resistance to Nazi and Soviet invasions, Rumania was shocked to realize that a strong state could not resist the German blitzkrieg. Of course Rumania had failed to fulfill treaty obligations to assist the Poles. Nevertheless, members of the Polish government and the diplomatic corps fled to Rumania and were granted temporary refuge. Was this not proof of the crushing superiority of the Nazi armies, asserted the Iron Guard? Armand Calinescu, the Rumanian premier from whom the nation might have anticipated great service, announced Rumania's neutrality. Consequently, the Iron Guard murdered him on September 21.

King Carol strove to perpetuate his country's neutrality during the first months of the war. Then France surrendered to Nazi Germany after a lightning campaign on June 22, 1940. News of France's fall produced intense emotion among Rumanians who were deeply attached to the French. That the nation which had always been a guide for Rumanian culture had been so rapidly overwhelmed appeared inconceivable. The collapse of France, the evacuation of English troops from the continent, and the withdrawal of French forces from Syria, which deprived the eastern Mediterranean of an allied army, rendered useless the guarantees once issued by London and Paris. Carol began to look to Hitler when a Nazi triumph in the war appeared to be a certainty.

By a unique irony of fate, Rumania became the object of two injunctions, at least one of which was quite unforeseen. Encouraged by Berlin's consent in the Molotov-Ribbentrop pact, Soviet Russia launched a raucous press campaign about Bessarabia which was "being subjugated by Rumanian boyars." Moscow submitted a 24-hour ultimatum to Rumania on June 26, 1940 requiring the retrocession of Bessarabia and the cession of the northern Bukovina which had never been part of Russia. Germany advised Carol to yield, and the Rumanian monarch could only acquiesce. This blow dealt by Russia pushed Rumania even closer to Germany in an effort to preserve the nation's territorial integrity. Carol summoned new politicians among whom were Iron Guardists exhibiting a servile docility toward Nazi Germany. These Guardists would be poorly repaid for these services.

In March 1940 Germany, planning to send troops across Hungary to move into Rumania, secured from Budapest a guarantee of free passage in return for a promise to uphold Hungary's claim to Transylvania. When Hungary presented demands to Rumania, Bucharest requested negotiations. When the discussions broke down, the Hungarians hinted at unilateral action. To avert a conflict in the Danubian basin when every German effort was about to be thrown against England, Hitler and Mussolini decided to intercede in this crisis. Rumanian foreign minister Mihail Manoilescu was invited to Vienna to meet with Ciano and Ribbentrop. He was accompanied by territorial experts equipped with documents, but this was a useless precaution. Ribbentrop handed

Manoilescu a map on which a new tracing of the frontier snatched from Rumania more than half of Transylvania and ceded it to Hungary, and gave him a few hours to reflect on the disastrous, consequences of rejection. Manoilescu fainted. This brutal compulsion was euphemistically called the "Vienna Arbitration," signed August 30, 1940. The loss of 16,642 square miles and a population of 2,390,000 in Transylvania, the cradle of their nation and an intellectual center cherished by the Rumanians, was cruelly felt. But the cup of bitterness was not yet drained.

Their appetite whetted by these two dismemberments of Rumanian territory, the Bulgarians raised their voices to demand the retrocession of the southern Dobrudja. These demands were upheld by Soviet Russia. Mistress of Bessarabia, Russia saw in retrocession the means to draw Bulgaria into the Soviet orbit and thus facilitate additional steps toward the supreme goal of seizing the Straits. These territorial changes caused a political overturn in Rumania. The new government of General Ion Antonescu (1882-1945) yielded on September 8 to Bulgaria's demands. By the Treaty of Craiova Rumania retroceded the southern Dobrudja containing about 3,000 square miles. All these territorial cessions cost Rumania in all about 40,000 square miles and a 4 million population.

Within a period of two months Rumania, subjected to three amputations, had to restore most of the territory acquired since 1913. Confronted by general indignation, King Carol, stripped of all prestige, was in a tenuous position. Although he had invited its cooperation, the Iron Guard had never pardoned the king for the death of Codreanu, its leader. Supported by Germany and with the backing of malcontent officers led by General Antonescu, the Iron Guard forced Carol to abdicate on September 6 and go into exile for the second and last time. He was succeeded by his son as Michael V, aged 19, also for the second time.

Reduced in size, a prey to internal crises, Rumania virtually lost her independence under a regime of terror instituted by the Iron Guard with German connivance. General Antonescu took advantage of the youth of King Michael to negate royal power and to assume all authority. He resolutely allied Rumania with Germany. To strengthen the fascist and militarist character of his dictatorship, he adorned himself with the title of *Conducator,* which was a Rumanian equivalent of *Führer* or *Duce.* Antonescu benevolently tolerated the excesses committed by the pro-Nazi Iron Guard. Sixty-four prominent men, all associates of King Carol, were executed on the spot where Codreanu had met his death. In November 1940 the Guard murdered two distinguished scholars who had been involved in politics, the historian Nicolae Iorga and the economist Virgil Madgearu. Iorga had written extremely anti-German articles. The murder of such a luminary tended to dishonor the new regime.

In less than one month Rumania had fallen prey to utter chaos. Thus, on the pretext of reestablishing order and protecting the oil-fields, the first German troops arrived on October 8. Units continued to arrive until they numbered about 500,000 troops. This occupation weighed heavily upon the country which was henceforth tied to the Axis. This alignment was sanctioned on November 23 when a Rumanian diplomat went to Berlin to sign the Rome-Berlin-Tokyo (Tripartite) Axis pact which Hitler would use to force Rumania's adherence to his policies.

Antonescu had the support of Germany not only because of his Germanophile tendencies, but because he was considered an experienced leader capable of maintaining discipline in an army whose assistance Berlin had already envisaged in the forthcoming campaign against Soviet Russia. Anarchy in Rumania favored German penetration, but when Nazi troops had been stationed in the country such chaos was prejudicial to their interests. The Germans were in no mood to permit it to flourish. Nazi troops interned the most active members of the Iron Guard in a thankless gesture for services rendered. For four ensuing years Antonescu would govern as an absolute dictator, and on two occasions plebiscites apparently gave him almost unanimous approval of his policies.

In September 1940 the question of navigation on the Danube, a waterway vital to Rumania, became an issue. The Germans invited the riparian states to a conference in Vienna. Soviet Russia was invited because her annexation of Bessarabia facilitated control of the northern arm of the Danube delta. Moscow showed lively interest in the question, but in a manner irritating to the Germans. Russia was apparently planning a project, to be fulfilled in 1948, whereby the international commission would be liquidated and replaced by a committee of riparian states only. The Vienna discussions reached an impasse because of the clash of German

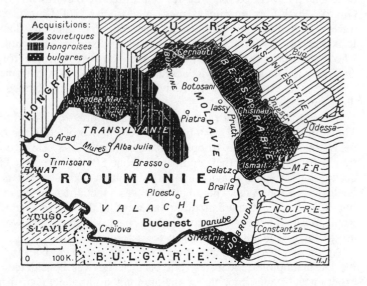

THE TERRITORIAL CHANGES OF RUMANIA SINCE 1940.

In 1940 Rumania was forced to cede a great part of her territory: in the last days of June, Bessarabia and the northern Bukovina were annexed by the USSR; at the end of August, Hungary, supported by Germany and Italy, occupied the major part of Transylvania, and a few days later Bulgaria secured the southern Dobrudja.

In September 1941, with German assistance, Rumania provisionally recovered the provinces ceded to the USSR and annexed the territory between the Dniester and Bug rivers.

But three years later, defeated by the Red Army, Rumania, by the armistice of September 12, 1944, had to renounce all these territories.

Rumania's eastern frontiers were fixed in the treaty of peace signed in Paris in February 1947. All of Transylvania was recovered, but Rumania was forced to recognize the loss of the southern Dobrudja to Bulgaria.

and Russian interests. Russia nevertheless proceeded to seize the Kilia arm, the most vital part of the delta, as well as several Danubian islands which were quite obviously the possession of Rumania. This was not the first cloud to darken the sky of Nazi-Soviet relations, but the spoliation at Rumania's expense, which highlighted the growing antagonism between Berlin and Moscow, also accentuated the bitterness Rumanians held for Russia. The Germans strove to perpetuate this hostility.

When Hitler unleashed a surprise attack on Soviet Russia on June 22, 1941, the assistance of his Rumanian ally had already been acquired for the "holy war against the godless Bolsheviks." For a long time Rumania was prepared to participate in a war from which she anticipated the defeat of her menacing neighbor and the recovery of the provinces snatched from her in 1940. The Rumanian army advanced at the side of the Nazi forces. After rapidly seizing Bessarabia and, after crossing the Dniester River, the Rumanians and Germans pushed the Russians as far as Odessa where a long and bloody siege was carried out. Odessa's defenders tenaciously resisted in the cellars of ruined buildings and homes. After the capture of Odessa, the Rumanians advanced as far as Sebastopol in the Crimea where resistance, as heroic as that of 1855, lasted eight months. Still further, the Rumanians marched into the very depths of the Russian steppes up to Stalingrad. Antonescu's troops had participated in the Nazi triumphs, but also at heavy sacrifices in human life and materials. Almost a half million soldiers were killed in a war that was not Rumania's. The price was very costly, but at least the Rumanians enjoyed the illusion of having conquered territories beyond the Dniester and also the seaport of Odessa. The region immediately east of the Dniester including Odessa was given to Rumania as a reward. Renamed Transdnistria by the Rumanian occupation forces, this region was despoiled and used as a virtual concentration camp for Rumanian Jews and other undesirables. Declarations of war by England and the United States did not disturb Rumania at first because they occurred during the flush of victory, but they would result in severe air raids on Bucharest and the oilfields.

The tide turned after the Nazi surrender at Stalingrad on February 2, 1943. The Nazi and Rumanian retreat from Russia began. By August 1944 the Red Army, hard on the heels of the fleeing Rumanians, crossed the Pruth River and entered Rumania which became a battlefield. The war was lost for Rumania.

King Michael, supported by a combination of Liberals, National Peasants, and even Communists, sent Prince Barbu Shtirbey, a venerable statesman, to Cairo in June 1944 to seek an armistice with the Allied Powers. Foreign Minister Mihail Antonescu, relative and confidante of the *Conducator,* negotiated with the Russians in neutral Sweden. Discussions in Cairo moved very slowly because of Moscow's suspicions and delays in responding to inquiries. As a result of this maneuver Rumania remained in the paradoxical and tragic position of being constantly bombarded by Anglo-American air raids while offering to break with the Germans.

King Michael finally resolved to act. Supported by a resistance group under Maniu's leadership, the young king executed a *coup d'état* against General Antonescu on August 23. The *Conducator* was imprisoned and a new government appointed. It was composed of Maniu, Constantin Bratianu, a few socialists, and even communists. This event is celebrated as Rumania's independence day. The first concern of the new regime was to terminate hostilities against the Russians and expel the last remnants of the German army, actions which led the Rumanians to hope for a modification of armistice terms.

Rumania, purged of Nazi forces after several hard battles, was easily occupied by the Red Army which entered Bucharest on August 31. The Cairo negotiations were transferred to Moscow where the Russians increased their demands. The armistice was signed on September 12 to which English and American representatives consented. The Russians had apparently delayed the signing until the Red Army was in complete control of Rumania. Despite their insistence, the Rumanian delegates failed to secure the inclusion of a clause requiring the evacuation of their country by the Red Army at the end of the war. The Russians considered such a clause simply superfluous, and they would profit from this omission to prolong their occupation of Rumania until 1956. The surrender of Rumania was one of the decisive events of World War II. The entire Balkan peninsula was thus opened to the Red Army.

Rumania, meanwhile, performed a complete turnabout in policy by joining the Allied effort. Like Italy in September 1943, Rumania was admitted as a co-belligerent and furnished about 15 divisions which, under the command of her recent enemy, Russia, marched off against her former ally, Germany. This new chapter in the struggle had for its objective the realization of an ideal dear to the heart of every Rumanian—the recovery of Transylvania. The Rumanians would suffer 150,000 more casualties in achieving this aim.

In Bulgaria symptoms of a pro-German orientation could be discerned at the beginning of the war. Kiosseivanov, a perceptive and moderate politician, was unexpectedly dismissed in February 1940 and replaced by Bogdan Filov, a professor of archaeology whose only qualifications were the esteem in which he was held by German scholars. It was rumored in Bulgaria that the king was pro-Allied, the army pro-German, and the population pro-Russian. This was a rather oversimplified view of a situation rendered more complex by the divergent tendencies of the Germanophile premier and an anti-German foreign minister, Popov. King Boris, a clever manipulator, managed to perpetuate Bulgaria's neutrality. For a while he succeeded in this endeavor by achieving a few triumphs which stabilized his nation's position in the Balkans. The retrocession of the southern Dobrudja in September 1940 was joyously greeted. A non-aggression pact with Turkey, prevailing friendly relations with Yugoslavia, and unusually cordial relations with Greece gave Bulgaria solid reasons to envisage continued security of her frontiers.

But Bulgaria's future did not lie in this area. German pressures became more imperious. Nazi infiltration became more accentuated in the economic realm. In November 1940 Hitler demanded Bulgaria's adherence to the Axis pact. Soviet Russia immediately dispatched an emissary to Sofia to offer a pact of non-aggression. Torn between two potential allies, Bulgaria became a battleground where Nazi-Soviet rivalries would be manifested. Rejection of Russia's proposition marked the beginning of tension with Moscow which would intensify. At the same time, however, Bulgaria rejected the Axis pact.

Premier Filov visited Berlin in January 1941. He pleaded the Axis cause when he returned to Sofia. Could Bulgaria really expect to prevent German troops, massed on the Rumanian banks of the Danube, from crossing that river? Instead of yielding to force, would it not be more advantageous to bow by accepting Ribbentrop's proposal to grant Sofia an outlet to the Aegean between the

Maritsa and Mesta rivers when Greece was defeated by the Italians who had invaded that country in October 1940? England, of course, denounced these German pressures. But even more severe was the undisguised warning issued by Soviet Russia. King Boris vacillated until March 1 when Nazi pressure forced him to yield.

Premier Filov flew to Vienna in Hitler's private plane on March 1, 1941. The ceremony of signing the Axis pact, to which Ciano was invited, proceeded with much fanfare. Invited to lunch by the Nazi chancellor, Filov believed himself treated as the representative of a great power. The next day German troops crossed the Danube to occupy camps in Bulgaria which had been determined before the signing. By this maneuver the Nazis advanced south in a leap of about 450 miles which brought them to the Turkish frontier. At the same time several thousand alleged German technicians, who had arrived previously in various disguises, shed their civilian clothing to don their uniforms again. By yielding to Germany, Bulgaria was transformed into a vital springboard for the Nazi army. When Mussolini's campaign against Greece turned into a rout for the Italian forces, German troops, lending a strong hand to their faltering ally, moved from Bucharest towards Athens across the Balkan Mountains in Bulgaria. When Yugoslavia incurred Hitler's wrath by overthrowing the Tsvetkovich government which signed the Axis pact on March 25, it was also from Bulgarian bases that German aircraft flew to punish Belgrade on Palm Sunday, April 6. Reactions were inevitable. The English embassy had left Sofia on February 24. Soviet Russia warned Bulgaria not to expect aid. Sofia soon suffered raids by the Royal Air Force operating from bases in Egypt.

Soviet Russia's warnings to Bulgaria about the latter's adherence to the Axis pact widened the abyss between the two accomplices of the Nazi-Soviet pact. These developments were perceived by a few deputies who had the courage to protest in the Sofia parliament against signing of the Axis pact. But their voices were drowned out by the frantic cheers of those who acclaimed Bulgaria's occupation of Thrace and part of Macedonia in April 1941 which marked a reconstitution of the medieval Bulgarian empire extending from Lake Okhrida to the Black Sea.

Then occurred the surprise Nazi attack on Soviet Russia, which forced Bulgaria to clarify her attitude toward this widening of the war. Moscow assured Sofia that a declaration of neutrality would be respected by Soviet Russia. King Boris, whose fingers had been earlier caught in the Nazi gears, was now jammed, despite his flexibility, in the implacable Nazi war machine which would grind him to pulp. He was compelled to institute anti-Semitic measures, adhere to the Anti-Comintern Pact, and declare war on England and the United States in December 1941 because of an ultimatum from Hitler. Bulgaria's entry into the war was a symbolic gesture without any actual plans to implement her decision. When the Anglo-American forces landed in North Africa in November 1942 and the Red Army defeated the Nazis at Stalingrad in February 1943, Bulgaria's fate was changed.

King Boris vainly strove to abstain from provocative gestures against Soviet Russia and persisted in his refusal to send troops to fight on the Russian front. Bulgaria's public opinion became disoriented by a policy whose aims were indecisive when evidence of an imminent German disaster became quite obvious. Bulgaria's foreign minister quit and communist underground activities assumed bold proportions. Threatened by these signs of disapprobation, Premier Filov undertook a cross-country campaign to win support for his pro-Nazi policies.

Bulgaria was thus being dragged to an uncertain fate. Germanophile declarations of the Filov government encountered bloody contradictions in the assassinations of several pro-Nazi officials. True to their heritage, the Bulgarians had recourse to the revolver and to sabotage to manifest opposition. Aware of German exhaustion and the alteration of the war situation, King Boris sought to extricate his nation from the imminent disaster by contacting American diplomats in Turkey. But Hitler was watching his unpredictable ally. He twice summoned Boris to Germany, the last time on August 14, 1943. One can readily imagine the violent scene which must have occurred between the furious tiger and the sly fox. The sudden death of Boris, two weeks after his return from Germany, confirmed beliefs that he had resisted Hitler's demands. His death remained mysterious for many years. In reality, Boris returned very disheartened and fatigued from a plane trip during which the German pilot took no precautions to pamper the condition of a royal cardiac patient. Suffering a relapse on his arrival, Boris succumbed on August 28 and was genuinely mourned by his subjects at a state funeral which terminated with his interment at the monastery of Rila.

The shaky barrier which Boris had erected to restrain Nazi pretensions collapsed with his death. While constituting the end of passive resistance to the Germans, it marked the birth of absolute domination by the Nazis. Since the king's heir, Simeon, was only six years old, a regency council was created and presided over by Boris' brother, Prince Cyril, a rather self-effacing person who had been distant from politics. Premier Filov and an army general were also members of the council. The Germans controlled Bulgaria behind this regency facade. Filov was soon replaced by the governor of the Bank of Bulgaria, Dobri Bozhilov, an unscrupulous former member of the Peasant Party and a notorious Germanophile. For one year this Bulgarian regime secured satisfaction in the form of revenge, dear to the masses. Without striking a blow and by merely being tolerant to German occupation, the Bulgarians exploited the Greek and Yugoslav territories which they had occupied and which had been the object of their eternal demands. Thus they briefly achieved the illusion of realizing the greater Bulgaria of San Stefano.

When the situation was reversed in the summer of 1944 and Rumania was occupied by the Red Army, a new Bulgarian government under Ivan Bagrianov tried to disengage Bulgaria from German occupation. The new premier demanded the evacuation of German troops on threat of internment, and, as Rumania had done, he dispatched a delegation to Cairo to negotiate an armistice with the Allied Powers. But Soviet Russia, with whom Bulgaria was not at war, refused to approve of Sofia's actions. When the Sofia regime decided to oppose Germany's demands, Ivan Muraviev, a Peasant leader and the next premier, procrastinated at Soviet urging. This delay permitted Moscow to recall to Bulgaria, in a brutal manner, the preponderant role Russia would play in the determination of Bulgaria's fate. Soviet Russia delivered to Bulgaria on September 5, 1944 a declaration of war based on allegations that the latter nation had rendered military assistance to Nazi Germany during the war against Russia. This was what Bulgaria least expected. Scarcely had stupefaction been diminished and without one shot being fired, Bulgaria asked for an armistice within six hours from the Red Army against whom Sofia made it a virtue never to bear arms.

What caused this tragicomedy? It was because the Soviet government did not wish to treat with a Bulgaria which, by

Bulgarie de 1939
Territoires enlevés :
à la Roumanie   à la Grèce   à la Yougoslavie
Territoire yougoslave occupé par l'Albanie

ACQUISITIONS OF BULGARIA, 1940-1941

The southern Dobrudja ceded by Rumania in September 1940 was the first Bulgarian acquisition.

Then in April 1941 Greece was forced to cede Western Thrace, Eastern Macedonia, and the islands of Thasos and Samothrace; Bulgaria thus regained access to the Mediterranean which she lost by the Treaty of Neuilly.

Finally, as a result of the dismemberment of Yugoslavia, Bulgaria received Western Macedonia. Bulgaria thus recovered the frontiers provided in the Treaty of San Stefano.

But all these acquisitions were shortlived. Only the southern Dobrudja was left to Bulgaria by the peace treaty of Paris in February 1947.

claiming the title of an ally, might have expected a less rigorous treatment or at the very least respect for her sovereignty and territorial integrity. Moscow demanded a defeated Bulgaria which would be obliged to submit to its demands. Bulgaria, forced to endure an occupation by the Red Army, contrived to establish a pro-Soviet government. This new regime was entrusted to Kimon Georgiev (Gueorguiev or Gheorghiev), an anti-fascist premier in 1934-35. The armistice was signed on October 28. Bulgaria thereby consented to an immediate retrocession of the Greek and Yugoslav territories which she had occupied during the war.

The beginning of hostilities had interrupted Yugoslavia in the midst of an internal reorganization which involved the award of autonomy to Croatia. The Serbian Radicals and Democrats were accusing Vladko Machek, the Croat Peasant leader, of treason, while the Croat nationalists considered the concessions to be inadequate. An expectation of reforms also aroused the Croat peasantry. Exchanges of protests and reproaches were added to the persistence of Croat discontent. Yugoslav army units even fired on the restless Croats. From the international viewpoint the Yugoslav government, torn between the democracies, with whom it had earlier contracted obligations, and the totalitarian states which were intimidating Belgrade, inclined toward the latter governments. Yugoslavia's location made that nation one of the most valuable pieces of real estate in the cruel contest which was about to begin.

When France surrendered in June 1940, the Serbs, who had remained faithful to the states to whom they were indebted for their territorial aggrandizement, experienced a genuine demoralization. The collapse of an ally, who had regularly contributed significant assistance to Yugoslavia, cast Serbian spirits into disarray. But the Yugoslav government was extremely sensitive to a show of Axis force. Yugoslavia had realized she was menaced since the Italian seizure of Albania and the signing of the Pact of Steel in September 1940. Prince Paul, the Yugoslav regent, was a sensitive person who dreaded violence, but he experienced the influence of brutal force. Terrified by Czechoslovakia's experience, Paul prudently sought security from Rome and Berlin since his foreign minister, Tsintsar-Markovich, was convinced of the invincible power of the Axis.

Yugoslavia's ultimate desire was to maintain neutrality at any cost. But threats increased on all sides. Rumania was occupied by German troops in October 1940 and Bulgaria was threatened. Greece was attacked by Italian forces in October 1940. Prince Paul realized his nation was encircled by the Axis powers. This fact hesitantly forced him to join the Axis as his neighbors had done. Germany had been wise not to place any conditions upon Yugoslavia's adherence. Although three members of the Yugoslav cabinet resigned in protest against joining the Axis, the Yugoslav government sent representatives to Vienna to affix their signatures to the Axis pact on March 25, 1941 in exchange for which Germany assured Belgrade of her respect for Yugoslavia's independence and territorial integrity.

Yugoslav reaction was spontaneous. The Serbs, in a paroxysm of national pride, rose in revolt against the cabinet's adherence to the Axis because their honor had been wounded and the signing was a prelude to shameful enslavement. Air force colonel Dushan Simovich was the leader of a plot which marched on the royal palace in Belgrade. Prince Paul quickly fled while the masses shouted, "Long live the king! Down with the Germans!" A mass was sung in the Belgrade cathedral in the presence of the 17-year-old King, Peter II, to celebrate the coup. The German diplomatic corps left Belgrade after having been exposed to rough treatment. This was a complete Serbian repudiation of Yugoslavia's foreign policy; the Croats remained hesitant and reserved. Nevertheless, Simovich formed a new government including Machek in the role of vice premier.

Nazi Germany's overwhelming and terrible reaction was quick to occur. In the early morning of Palm Sunday, April 6, a black cloud of Nazi aircraft appeared in the early spring sky over Belgrade to bombard with ferocity the ancient capital of Serbia amid scenes of abject spoliation. Most of the city was destroyed, and thousands were left lying under debris. Robert St. John, an American journalist in the Yugoslav capital on that Sunday, reported that the war was a "man lying on the sidewalk with his guts sticking out of his belly and a hole through his skull and both hands blown off, screaming because he can't reach into his pocket to get a drachma to buy aspirin tablets to stop the funny feeling in his head."

By a curious coincidence, Yugoslavia, after having renewed diplomatic relations with Soviet Russia for the first time since

1917, signed a non-aggression pact with Moscow on the night of April 5, 1941, a few hours before the Nazi blitzkrieg hit Belgrade. When Stalin learned of the resistance to Hitler raised by Simovich, he reportedly rejoiced at the courage of his Slav brethren. But Russia's obligations as Germany's formal ally forced Stalin to suppress his personal reactions which clearly indicated that Nazi and Soviet interests conflicted in Yugoslavia. Soviet policy remained contradictory about Yugoslavia, Rumania, and Bulgaria. The rift in the Nazi-Soviet alliance was growing wider.

Yugoslavia was quickly obliterated. King Peter and his government hastily fled to Palestine and eventually secured refuge in London. The Nazi forces, in a blitzkrieg more rapid than the campaign in the Lowlands, cut the Yugoslav army to pieces. The province of Serbia was quickly occupied by the Germans as an indication of the fact that the regions which, for two decades, had constituted the Kingdom of Yugoslavia, were dismembered. Serbia was reduced to her pre-1913 dimensions. Croatia was declared independent with Ante Pavelich, chief of the Ustash, leader of the state. The Duke of Spoleto, an Italian member of the House of Savoy, was proclaimed king of Croatia, but he refused to assume the obligations of his office, preferring instead the pleasures of Rome. Mussolini nevertheless took advantage of his chances to acquire Carniola, including Ljubljana (Laibach), and a substantial section of the Dalmatian coast if he could negotiate a favorable agreement with Pavelich to subject Croatia to Italy's mercy. Pavelich agreed to a treaty which placed Croatia under Italy's protection. Germany, however, annexed all of Slovenia including the city of Ljubljuana (Laibach). Hungary secured the Backa located between the Danube and Save rivers, and the city of Novi Sad (Neusatz) situated on the Danube. The major portion of Macedonia was awarded to Bulgaria, and Montenegro became an Italian protectorate.

The Yugoslavs preferred to resist rather than accept this fate. King Peter and his government appealed, from their sanctuary in London, to the courage of their subjects to fight the invaders. In mountainous Yugoslavia, inhabited by peasants animated by staunch patriotism and expert in guerilla warfare, fighting was soon organized on a wide scale. Dragoljub Mikhailovich (or Drazha Mihajlovic) (1893-1946), an army colonel, took the initiative to form a secret underground army in the region of Shumadia, the

Acquisitions:
allemandes
italiennes
hongroises
bulgares
albanaises

A·LL'GNE
SLOVÉNIE
CARNIOLE
Agram (Zagreb)
ITALIE
Drave
Save
CROATIE
Zara
DALMATIE
Split (Spalato)
Dubrovnik (Raguse)
ADRIATIQUE
ITALIE
H·O·N·G·R·I·E
Subotica
BAČKA
Novi'Sad
ROUMANIE
Danube
Belgrade
SERBIE
Sarajevo
Drina
Morava
Nich
Pirot
BULGARIE
MONTE NEGRO
Kotor (Cattaro)
Cettigne
Prizren
Skoplje
MACEDOINE
Vardar
Bitolj
ALBANIE
Tirana
Salonique
GRÈCE
0   100 K.
H.J.

THE DISMEMBERMENT OF YUGOSLAVIA IN 1941

In April 1941, attacked by Germany and Italy, Yugoslavia, after
two weeks of combat, was occupied and the Yugoslav state
ceased to exist.

At the beginning of hostilities Croatia proclaimed her independence. A month later, the Duke of Spoleto, the King of Italy's
cousin, became King of Croatia. Italy secured Carniola with
Ljubljana, and annexed most of the Dalmatian coast. Germany
annexed Slovenia and southern Styria with Marburg (Maribor).

The Axis allies were not forgotten: Hungary received the fertile
triangle of the Bačka and a small zone near the Mur and
Drava rivers; Bulgaria occupied Western Macedonia as far as
Albania (a satellite of Italy) who also received a part of the
booty. Montenegro followed the example of Croatia in proclaiming her independence.

cradle of Serbian independence. Another resistance movement was soon created and led by a mysterious person, a famed adventurer and consummate organizer who assumed the name of Tito. Actually named Josip Broz (1892-   ), a Croat who served in the Austrian army during World War I, was captured by the Russians, later converted to Bolshevism, and a prisoner in a Yugoslav jail for six years. Tito recruited volunteers for the Loyalists in the Spanish Civil War. He was general secretary of the illegal Yugoslav Communist Party. His guerilla force, called Partisans, hid in the mountains of Bosnia and Montenegro from which they fanned out to inflict blows and commit acts of sabotage against the Nazi occupation forces.

Mikhailovich and Tito at first pursued the common goal of expelling the invaders. Divergences soon appeared, and a permanent rift was soon apparent. The former and his Chetniks, resolved not to yield to the invaders, preferred to avoid operations which would produce enemy reprisals. The Chetniks sought to make use of the collaborationist regime installed in Serbia by the Nazis. They succeeded in infiltrating the regime and securing arms and useful information. Politically, Mihailovich was a Serbian nationalist who hated the Croats. Tito's Partisans, on the other hand, were absolutely intransigent in their hostility toward the puppet regime in Belgrade. Gradually the rivalry set the two groups against each other, and it degenerated into actual battles beween them. Added to the struggle against the Nazis on the soil of unfortunate Yugoslavia was a real civil war during which Tito's prestige increased.

Reports of these developments reached London where they produced a divergence of interpretation. Winston Churchill, the prime minister, finally won out in his insistence that aid be given exclusively to Tito because his Partisans were fighting the real enemy. After the Nazi defeat at Stalingrad in 1943 and with the westward march of the Red Army about to begin, the day no longer seemed remote when Yugoslavia would be liberated from the Nazi yoke. King Peter and his government in exile moved from London to Cairo in September 1943 to be closer to the homeland.

In November 1943 Tito's National Liberation Committee created a provisional government, of which he was defense minister, and demanded a federal and republican post-war Yugoslavia. A schism was thus established between the exile government and the Partisans. The Soviet government offered its full moral support to Tito whose very courageous military operation earned international acclaim for this communist. King Peter, initially adopting a hostile attitude toward Tito, now tried to achieve a rapprochement.

England dispatched liaison officers to Tito in March 1943. They succeeded in making contact with the Partisans who were harassing Nazi troops so effectively that the latter were required to maintain several divisions in the country. When he was about to be the victim of a vigorous Nazi offensive, Tito was rescued by the English who conveyed him by plane to an Adriatic island.

For more than a year various schemes were devised to effect a fusion between the National Liberation Committee and the royal government. Ivan Shubashich, the royal premier, appointed two Partisans to his exile government, and in June 1944 signed an agreement with Tito providing for post-war administration which would combine the Committee and the royal government. Events moved rapidly after this declaration. Soviet and Yugoslav forces liberated Belgrade on October 20. Rejected and abandoned, Mikhailovich went into hiding. England, who had always followed Yugoslav affairs very closely, was anxious to assert an influence over post-war Yugoslavia. Churchill and Foreign Secretary Anthony Eden discussed with Stalin in October the future of Yugoslavia and other Balkan states. At the end of their talks a communiqué indicated that they agreed on a policy to support a fusion of the Committee and the royal government. The Yugoslavs would be asked to decide on a future constitution. In March 1945 King Peter agreed to the formation of a coalition government in which Tito would be premier, four exiled politicians would have ministries, and Shubashich would become foreign minister. Nothing was mentioned about the return of the monarch; King Peter would never return home.

The Kingdom of Greece was on good terms with her neighbors, even with Bulgaria, at the beginning of the war because of a détente achieved in foreign affairs. The Metaxas dictatorship appeared eminently qualified for Axis membership, and so Germany exerted economic pressure and sent numerous "tourists," traveling salesmen, and propagandists to Greece. But the threat hanging over Greece came from Italy, and it became more menacing after Italy seized Albania in April 1939. In August 1939 the sinking of a Greek warship by an Italian submarine constituted a perilous warning. That Greece was destined to become Italy's share in the partition of the Balkans by the two Axis partners was written in the cards. The guarantees accorded Greece by England and France were rendered worthless when the Allies failed to help another of their allies—Poland.

The Greek government prudently observed strict neutrality until October 28, 1940 when Italy's ambassador awoke General Metaxas at 3:00 A. M. to deliver an ultimatum which was to expire within six hours. Asserting that Greece had granted bases to English warships, Italy demanded that Greece give her the same privileges. At that every moment, however, Italian troops were crossing the frontier into Greece. Mussolini was convinced that his numerical superiority and better weapons would crush the little Greek army with as much ease as he had overcome the troops of Ethiopia in 1936.

In an eloquent proclamation, Metaxas summoned the Greeks to war: "Greeks! Let us clench our fists and elevate our souls." These words produced an enthusiastic echo and an unanticipated miracle occurred. Just as in 1914 the heroic little Serbian army had repulsed the Austrians at the frontier, the Greeks soon defeated the Italians and within one month chased them back to the Adriatic after invading Albania. Worthy of their ancestors at Thermopylae, Greek troops astonished the world with their exploits and humiliated Mussolini's fascist soldiers.

In April 1941, however, Germany entered the conflict to rescue her associate. Nazi forces swooped down on Greece from Yugoslavia and Bulgaria. Despite English efforts to send assistance, the Greek army in Epirus had to capitulate before the overwhelming superiority of the Germans. In less than a month the entire Greek coast was in Nazi hands. The Germans entered Athens on April 27. King George and his government fled to Crete where English troops, supported by retreating Greek forces, prepared to defend the island. The Germans then descended upon Crete with a vast number of parachute troops, used for the first time in history on such a vast scale. Serious losses and damage were inflicted on the English naval ships in Cretan waters. The king and his ministers had to evacuate Crete, take up temporary residence in Cairo, and then transfer the exile government to

London. Surviving English forces in Crete were evacuated to Cyprus and Egypt. An appreciable Greek contingent also escaped from the island in a feat similar to that accomplished precisely a year before at Dunkirk. This Greek army would be augmented by volunteers who escaped from occupied Greece, and it would distinguish itself at the Battle of El Alamein in October 1942 and in the Allied invasion of Italy in July 1943.

The Nazi conquest of Greece and Crete marked the beginning of the enemy's occupation of the entire Balkan peninsula except for the small portion of Turkey in Europe. The Axis position in the eastern Mediterranean was greatly strengthened by this occupation. The Aegean Sea became dangerous for English ships. Turkey was terrified into preserving her neutrality. This situation prevented the English from delivering materials to Russia through the Aegean, the Straits, and the Black Sea.

If the Nazi occupation of Greece was harsh, then the regions seized by the Bulgarians were subjected to horrible conditions. Of a total Greek population of 7,350,000, about 23,000 Greek troops were killed; but over 400,000 civilians vanished. About 600,000 civilians were later executed by the occupation forces. Conditions became so unbearable during the three years of the occupation that about 200,000 died of hunger. Tuberculosis and malaria made dismal inroads among the civilian population, many of whom were huddled in prison camps while others remained without shelter in the devastated cities and towns. World War I had familiarized the Greeks with many horrors which now appeared inconsequential in contrast to what the Nazis and Bulgarians inflicted during World War II. Among the many occupied countries which suffered, doubtless none except Poland experienced more horror than Greece.

Despite this distress, the Greek people were far from being resigned to this oppression. They stubbornly resisted by initiating guerilla warfare and acts of sabotage. But even during those days which rank among the most tragic of her long history, Greece was unable to eliminate her customary dissensions. The National Liberation Front (EAM) recruited radical elements who opposed the Metaxas dictatorship and formed a resistance movement in the summer of 1941. The EAM organized a guerilla army, the ELAS, whose communist tendencies soon became apparent. As was inevitable in tortured Greece, opposition movements arose. One was the EDES (the Greek Democratic Army) which grouped monarchist elements with regular army officers under the command of General Napoleon Zervas. The turmoil in occupied Greece was similar to the divergences between Tito's Partisans and the Chetniks of Mikhailovich in Yugoslavia. Greeks were at each other's throats while struggling for the same cause, and the Nazis lost no time in stirring up rivalries which wrought death and destruction in the smallest villages.

The Greek exile government, like that of the Yugoslavs, also experienced vicissitudes. General Metaxas unexpectedly died before he could escape from his homeland. His successor committed suicide in the wake of Greek reverses. As soon as the government reached London, it experienced the first of many crises caused by frequent resignations which reflected differences among the leaders of the resistance movement at home. In April 1944 mutinies provoked by communist propaganda abroad Greek ships in Alexandria almost compromised the movement of Allied convoys in the Mediterranean. The courage of Greek naval officers and fear of English reprisals repressed a rebellion which revealed the deep unrest agitating public opinion at home and abroad. A royal proclamation was issued to produce calm at the conclusion of a conference of various resistance groups in Beirut, Lebanon. After indicating a desire to unify Greek democratic forces, King George II affirmed his decision not to return to Greece without popular approval. The radical elements, using as a pretext the severity of sentences meted out to the mutineers, of whom 35 were condemned to death, refused to participate in a royalist government.

The hour of Germany's collapse was soon approaching. In early September 1944 the Nazis began to evacuate the Peloponnesus and the Aegean Islands in a retreat which was soon accelerated. The English landed troops on the Greek mainland to support the partisans in October. Two days after the Nazi evacuation of Athens, the English entered the capital (October 13). The Greek communists failed to seize the city and were thus denied an opportunity to establish an interim government. After 3½ years in exile, the Greek government arrived home on October 18. Many hoped the country would now initiate the task of restoring the ruins and reorganizing the smashed administration, but this would not happen. On the contrary, serious difficulties and disputes erupted two days before the exile government was due to arrive in Athens. A communist uprising led to a virtual civil war in the blood-spattered capital where partisans of the left and right continued the struggle. Although officially dissolved by government decree, the resistance groups refused to disband. The monarchist and Anglophile EDES attacked the ELAS, which was communist and Russophile, and the two groups fought an internecine war aggravated by general strikes in Athens and Salonika and a prolonged ministerial crisis. The mournful December days marked a black period in Greek history. After having withstood so many trials, this unfortunate nation descended even further into misery, murder, and destruction. Only the resolute character of the English commander and his few troops housed in an Athens hotel finally restrained the disorderly factions.

Concerned by this state of affairs which, bordering on anarchy, threatened the security of the eastern Mediterranean. Churchill decided to go to Athens. He arrived on Christmas Day amid street fighting and resolved to use his prestige to restore order. After lengthy discussions the two major factions accepted Archbishop Damaskinos as regent of the kingdom until a plebiscite settled the question of the regime. In January 1945 a truce was signed by the English forces and the radical faction opposing English intervention. This crisis had left Greece with a legacy of misery superimposed upon the utter horror of the Nazi occupation.

Turkey, of all the Balkan states, was one which, at the outbreak of war, had most unequivocally sided with the Allied Powers. This was the result of a declaration of mutual assistance exchanged with England and France which entailed cooperation in the event of an extension of the war into eastern Mediterranean. The Turkish government had earlier participated in negotiations to form a bloc of peaceful Balkan states, but this had failed to materialize. Moscow's indifference toward this project, shown when Foreign Minister Saracoglu visited Russia in August 1939, was a disappointment which led Turkey into a policy of extreme caution. England and France continued to furnish effective assistance to Turkey in the form of abundant credits, arms, and munitions to facilitate potential fulfillment of commitments.

When the Axis invaded Greece, thus extending the war to the

eastern Mediterranean, conditions for effective cooperation arose. But Turkey decided to maintain a strictly neutral policy. This was stipulated in February 1941 by a declaration of non-aggression and friendship signed with Bulgaria when the latter state was being swept into the Nazi orbit. Turkey was quite obviously modifying her prior policy. Ankara apparently preferred defense of her own security to participation in a grouping whose members were at war. Hence Turkey's eagerness to renew the non-aggression act with Soviet Russia originally signed in 1925.

Nazi Germany lavished reassuring declarations on Turkey, repeating an avowal to respect Turkish neutrality. To support this policy, Germany dispatched to Turkey the ablest and most seductive of her diplomats, Franz von Papen, known as "The Sly Fox," who devoted his craft to perpetuating Turkish neutrality while attempting to inspire a revival of Germanophile sentiments which had been so widespread in 1914.

Nevertheless, the Ankara government perpetuated a strict and profitable neutrality without being influenced either by German intimidation or English reminders of Turkey's previous commitments. Allied victories aroused Turkish sensitivities about a possible renewal of the ancient Russian threat to the Straits. As the Red Army advanced into the Balkans in the late summer of 1944, ambitions were reborn in Moscow which Ankara had reason to fear. At the time of the Nazi counter-offensive on the western front in December 1944, which slowed down the Anglo-American advance, Turkey decided to break diplomatic relations with Germany and Japan. The Turks then opened the Straits to ships laden with supplies for Russia, and declared war on the Axis on February 23, 1945. The Soviet government pointed out, with some rancor, that this declaration was a tardy gesture, and Moscow's tone toward Turkey grew quite haughty.

Turkey's neutrality, often considered to have been inspired by excessive caution, was nevertheless profitable to the Allied cause. Turkish intervention early in the war would have unleashed a vigorous reprisal by Germany when the latter had almost the entire Balkan peninsula under her control. After smashing Turkish resistance, the Germans could probably have seized the oilfields of Iraq and fomented disturbances to threaten England's communications with India. But the neutrality which Turkey, alone among the Balkan states, succeeded in preserving with consider-

able difficulty rendered to the Allies appreciable services by preventing the extension of the war into the Middle East as had
occurred during World War I.

Among the myriad consequences of World War II was the birth
of disputes over the Balkan states which would provoke the Cold
War between Soviet Russia and the United States. The Nazi invasion and occupation had destroyed most of the old, pre-war
institutions in the Balkan states because the interwar regimes were
discredited as a result of their alliances with Hitler. The emergence
of resistance movements during the war years resulted in the creation of new elements ready to fill the vacuum created by the disappearance of the old order. An Anglo-American invasion of the
Nazi-occupied Balkan peninsula in 1944 might have averted its
incorporation into the Soviet orbit. But those who still argue this
conjectural assertion are ignorant of chronology. When the Anglo-
American forces crossed the English Channel to invade France on
June 6, 1944, in an amphibious operation considered to be a
military priority superseding any campaign elsewhere, the Red
Army of Soviet Russia had already crossed the Dniester River,
reached Jassy in Moldavia, and had obviously arrived in the
Balkans. When the Anglo-American armies crossed the Rhine into
Germany on March 7, 1945, the Red Army was already in control
of all Rumania and Bulgaria, about half of Yugoslavia had been
liberated with the aid of Tito's Partisans, and Russia's forces were
about 60 miles from Berlin. An Anglo-American attack upon the
Red Army was perhaps the only means by which Stalin could have
been denied the coming sovietization of Eastern Europe. And
no sane person advocated this madness in the days prior to the
collapse of National Socialism.

The Balkans in the Post-War Era

A SURVEY of the post-war period is essential before ending this study so that the evolution of the Balkan peoples to contemporary times may be understood. A glance at developments since 1945 is a precipitous undertaking because events occurred in a bewildering and still incoherent manner. Historical perspective required to appreciate the significance of these developments is still lacking. And conditions in the Balkans are still evolving in relatively unknown directions.

The Allied Powers did not wait until the cessation of hostilities before considering the fate of the Balkan peoples. After the Casablanca conference between Churchill and Roosevelt in January 1943, the former visited Adana to discuss with the Turks the probability of their entry into the war. But Roosevelt and his advisers, who were anxious about Stalin's reproaches over the delays in establishing a second front in France, disapproved of accessory operations in the Balkans and wished to concentrate all efforts on a western front. Churchill returned to the charge several times, insisting at the Teheran conference in November 1943 upon an offensive from occupied Italy into Yugoslavia and an advance toward Belgrade. He believed this operation would induce Turkey to enter the war and open the Straits to supplies for Russia. The memory of the success achieved by the Salonika offensive which repulsed the enemy in 1918 was apparently fresh in Churchill's mind. Moreover, he was anxious to liberate the peninsula before Russia could, or at the very least to deny the Red Army an entirely free scope in the Balkans. Naturally Stalin did not share these views, and he cleverly won Roosevelt to his point of view by denouncing an imprudent dispersal of forces to the Balkans since Germany was more vulnerable on French soil. The American general staff maintained that the few divisions which could be diverted to the Balkans would have weighed very feebly alongside the vast numbers of Soviet troops, and that the technical superiority of American materials could not be fully utilized in the mountainous terrain where communications were limited. Thus the hope of limiting Soviet influence by this diversion appeared very dim. The Americans insisted upon reserving these forces to hasten Germany's defeat in France, which was still considered the principal Anglo-American theater of operations. Churchill, the author of Allied intervention against the Bolsheviks in Russia in 1918, had difficulty understanding that the United States never established as one of its war aims the liberation of the Balkan peninsula or the containment of Soviet communism. Roosevelt had repeatedly insisted that the defeat of the Axis powers was his nation's chief war aim; all post-war political questions must await a post-war solution. The United States government fully realized that the final campaign against Japan would be undertaken almost exclusively by American forces. To expend more resources on European campaigns than were required to defeat Hitler would have jeopardized the campaigns in the Pacific. By the end of 1944 the Americans were hopeful of securing Soviet assistance in the liquidation of the Japanese Empire. Such aid would be considerably greater than England, exhausted after five years of war, could furnish to the war in the Far East. It must be recalled that no one could predict before July 16, 1945, the date of the detonation of the first atomic bomb in the New Mexico desert, what such energy would produce.

Despite these counter-arguments, Churchill could not be dissuaded from his views. He strove to make his opinion prevail until American forces landed in southern France on August 15, 1944. That diversionary operation forced him to abandon hopes of an Anglo-American operation in the Balkans. Within two weeks the Red Army had marched through Rumania and Bulgaria, reached the Greek frontier, and were poised near the boundaries with Turkey. This swift Soviet occupation may have justified Churchill's Cassandra-like warnings, but the alternative may well have been an alienation of Stalin and his signing of a separate peace with Nazi Germany once fascist troops had been evicted from Russian soil. Churchill should also have remembered Brest-Litovsk.

From the summer of 1944 the Balkan states were destined to become an arena for Soviet activities. Could a final attempt be made to limit Moscow's influence over the peninsula? England had pursued this policy since the time of Canning. And that is what Churchill and Eden attempted during a visit to Moscow in October 1944. They pointed out to Stalin that since Russia's contiguity certainly entitled her to reestablish order in Rumania and Bulgaria, a similar privilege should be assigned to England in Greece. As for Yugoslavia, that nation would become the object of joint Anglo-Russian concern. This partitioning of spheres of influence without American consent raised consternation in the U. S. Department of State. An Anglo-Soviet reassurance that this agreement was merely a provisional solution adapted to military operations consoled the Americans.

This Anglo-Soviet understanding, suggested by Churchill, was apparently designed to offer a practical basis for a division of spheres of influence in a region where English and Russian policies had clashed since the time of George Canning. Churchill recommended a 90% Soviet interest in Rumania, offset by a 90% English interest in Greece. Bulgaria was assigned to the Soviet sphere, but with a 75% to 25% division with England. Yugoslavia and Hungary were to be shared 50-50. Stalin agreed to this bargain. The Red Army was already occupying Rumania, Bulgaria, and half of Hungary so that there was no risk that English interests would become a serious obstacle.

Perhaps in deference to this partition, Stalin did not interfere when English troops landed in Greece in October 1944 to assist the royal government in its struggle against the pro-communist radicals. The tendency of Soviet occupation authorities to exercise exclusive preponderance in the other Balkan states soon became so obvious that one could wonder with U. S. Secretary of State Cordell Hull "whether their goal was to liberate or to conquer." At first confident in the spirit of collaboration which had so strongly contributed to imminent victory in Europe, the United States strove to minimize apprehensions. Roosevelt especially considered differences of opinion dangerous as long as Germany had not yet been defeated. He appealed for a diminution of prejudice and mistrust among members of the Grand Alliance.

Nevertheless, the conquering Red Army immediately and everywhere displayed methods which it would not abandon and which became more obvious. On the one hand Soviet authorities refused to establish liaison with their allies on matters of common policy.

On the other, they interferred in the administration of occupied territories to favor the establishment of pro-Soviet regimes.

Rumania, for example, signed an armistice with Soviet Russia on September 12, 1944. The Rumanians subsequently protested that Russia was violating its terms. Moscow's retort resulted in the collapse of the government of General Constantin Sanatescu which had replaced the Antonescu regime and consisted of ministers of the four anti-fascist parties—Liberals, National Peasants, Social Democrats, and Communists. A new government was formed by General Nicolae Radescu, the chief of staff who had been a prisoner in a Nazi camp, on December 2. The very few Rumanian Communists, with the support of the occupation forces, began a campaign of terror against the Radescu government. Andrei Vyshinsky, the Soviet vice commissar of foreign affairs, arrived for the first time in Bucharest on February 27, 1945 and demanded Radescu's resignation. King Michael had to comply with this ultimatum and appoint a new cabinet of ministers favorable to Soviet designs. At the same time Rumania had to agree to pay Russia $300 million in reparations.

Bulgaria, another example, was a country more receptive than Rumania to communist ideology. Nevertheless, Soviet chastisement measures were employed there, too. The execution of the three regents of the infant king, one of whom was Prince Cyril, signaled a bloody campaign against pro-Nazi suspects. And Yugoslavia became the scene of such anti-monarchical agitation that King Peter had to abandon plans to return to his homeland. A regency council was set up by Tito and Peter's premier, Ivan Shubashich.

These developments, occurring before the termination of hostilities in Europe, alarmed England and the United States. The recently concluded Allied conference at Yalta in the Crimea, February 4-12, 1945, had examined several interallied problems regarding the Balkan states. The final communiqué contained the famous "Declaration of Liberated Europe." One of its provisions provided for the establishment of interim governmental authorities in the occupied countries which would be broadly representative of all democratic elements in the population and pledged to the earliest possible establishment through free elections of governments responsive to the will of the people. These were the pious terms of a solemn declaration signed by Churchill, Roosevelt, and Stalin.

This charter of apparent liberties offered the Balkan peoples theoretical guarantees for the free exercise of their rights. But events which have occurred since the announcement of this declaration testify to the fact that the Soviet government had quite a different conception of the application of these principles from that of its English and American allies. The post-war era in the Balkans was, in fact, characterized by a constant increase of Soviet influence which even spilled over into central Europe, but it was contained in its southward march toward Greece and Turkey.

To retrace country by country the intricate details of the Sovietization or Stalinization of the Balkan states would be to attempt duplication of what has been achieved by many other available studies. Except for Yugoslavia, where the communist regime was not imposed but rather encouraged by Soviet Russia, the procedures used everywhere else were fundamentally identical. The only difference was that the timing was adapted to suit differing circumstances. This formula, carefully prepared and proven effective by experience, consisted essentially of an occupation by Red Army units deploying machine guns, tanks, and planes. This impressive military apparatus imposed upon the masses a respect which troop behavior converted into fear. The masses hoped it was merely a temporary state of affairs. But the presence of Soviet troops was prolonged, said Moscow, in proportion to the necessity of maintaining lines of communication between Russia and her armies of occupation in Austria and Germany.

Arriving in the caravans of the Red Army were native communists who had spent the war years in the relative security of Soviet Russia. The occupation forces provided them with vigorous support. Severe measures were simultaneously taken against those suspected of having collaborated with the Nazis. This vast purge, executed in its broadest sense, hit really guilty individuals, but it also gradually extended to moderates who were accused of being reactionaries or fascists. Renowned political personalities whose democratic sentiments were public knowledge and whose cooperation might have been useful to the Russians were accused of treason, espionage, and sabotage. Concentration camps, prisons, and even outright executions led to their disappearance. A time arrived when all leaderless political parties were reduced to inertia. Only the communist parties remained, their ranks swelled by opportunists and sycophants, some seeking to benefit from the authorities and others to avoid the worst. Some communists secured the most powerful ministries such as Interior and Defense which gave them control of the police and army, respectively. Many communist leaders, who had been in exile in Moscow for many years, were assisted by local communists who together gained absolute mastery over the administration of the Balkan states.

When this complex process was completed, it was merely a question of giving legal character to a *de facto* situation. Electoral lists were combed to expunge names of persons whose conduct had allegedly rendered them unworthy of exercising the right to vote. Those permitted to vote went to the polls under the watchful eyes of the secret police with full realization that a gesture of opposition would expose them to serious reprisals. Since only one political party existed, voters had no choice in the matter, and the election results indicated a massive majority in favor of the government, which then celebrated its victory over non-existent opponents. The victorious regimes affirmed, with figures at hand, that an almost unanimous popular mandate confirmed approval of the government so that it could now boast of standing upon a firm democratic base.

These regimes in Rumania, Bulgaria, Albania, and Yugoslavia (similar to regimes in the Soviet zone of Germany, Czechoslovakia, Poland, and Hungary) orbited as satellites in the Soviet galaxy. Each government dutifully aligned itself to the Soviet Union in all areas. The organization of each regime was naturally inspired by the Soviet example and principles, but in industrial and commercial fields the means of production and exchange were also incorporated into Moscow's orbit which oriented the economic policies of the Balkan states to the furthering of Russian interests. Delegates from the Balkan states at international meetings modelled their actions, speeches, and especially their decisions on the example handed down by Moscow. In the diplomatic realm the Balkan states became satellites to form a homogeneous bloc with Russia in the United Nations and in dealings with capitalist countries.

The Iron Curtain was slammed shut. The masses lived in a closed cell obedient to the Soviet formulas and maintaining only minimum contact with capitalist countries. Travel beyond the Iron Curtain countries was forbidden except for officials on missions, and it was extremely difficult for foreigners to gain access to the Balkan states. Refugees who succeeded in furtively crossing the frontiers joined former citizens who had earlier managed to escape before sovietization had been achieved. News from within the countries rarely reached the West, but it was generally known that freedom did not exist and that general misery prevailed.

All attempts by the western Allied Powers (England, France, and the United States) to prevent a stabilization of these conditions appeared to be vain efforts. At the Allied conference in Potsdam (July 17–August 2, 1945), the Allied Powers decided to review the activities of the Interallied Control Commission in the Balkans. But in London in September, Moscow in December, and Paris when the Axis satellite peace treaties were being drafted, discussions of Balkan problems invariably provoked discord and ended in frustration. The American and English diplomats questioned the incompatibility of regimes in Bulgaria, Rumania, and even Yugoslavia with the Declaration issued at Yalta. The Soviet diplomats tirelessly replied that the established governments in the Balkan states corresponded to the will of the peoples who had approved of them in elections and who were enjoying a happy existence under these regimes. When the western Allied Powers produced evidence of Soviet interference and pressure in local politics, Soviet diplomats replied by alleging that the situation was worse in Greece where harsh English policies prevented the people from displaying their true sentiments.

At most the four Allied Powers could only agree on the delimitation of new frontiers in the Balkans. The task was easy for Rumania. The Soviet government had announced unilaterally its intention to restore northern Transylvania when King Michael dismissed the Radescu government. This disavowal of the 1940 Vienna Award was really recognition of the predominantly Rumanian ethnical composition of the region. Soviet Russia, however, retained Bessarabia and the northern Bukovina which had been acquired in 1940. Bulgaria retroceded those regions of Macedonia seized from Greece and Yugoslavia in 1941. The southern Dobrudja was retained by Bulgaria, a decision obviously arranged by Russia's determination to befriend Sofia at Bucharest's expense, but the Bulgarians were still denied access to the Aegean

THE BALKAN STATES AFTER THE SECOND WORLD WAR

1. Acquisitions of Greece (at the expense of Italy).
2. Acquisitions of Bulgaria (at the expense of Rumania).
3. Acquisitions of the USSR (at the expense of Rumania).
4. Acquisitions of Yugoslavia (at the expense of Italy).

Sea. The Bulgarians, who had compromised themselves with the Nazis in a manner actually similar to that pursued by Moscow in 1939, were considerably favored by Soviet Russia, against whom Bulgaria did not fight during the war, in that the southern Dobrudja was retained. But Moscow's generosity was apparently based upon hopes of reviving the spirit of San Stefano. In truth, this policy may explain the loyalty Bulgaria has shown toward Soviet Russia since 1944; that nation remains today the most obedient of Moscow's allies in the Balkan states.

The Kingdom of Greece, who had fought heroically against the Axis, was ironically treated no better than Bulgaria, an Axis satellite. The Greek frontier with Albania in Epirus was not changed. The Allies merely awarded the Dodecanese Islands to Greece. Even this decision to award Greece these Italian-held islands incurred the grumbling opposition of Vyacheslav Molotov, the Soviet foreign minister, although the majority population of the archipelago was incontestably Greek. This justifiable award aroused the inhabitants of the island of Cyprus, also inhabited by a Greek majority, who demanded union with Greece. But England insisted upon retaining that vital naval base.

Yugoslavia's 1938 frontiers were restored, and Italy's possession of Zara and a few Adriatic islands was terminated. The retrocession to Yugoslavia of Macedonian territories produced incidents with Greece, but it was in northwestern Yugoslavia that the postwar delimitation provoked serious difficulties, particularly at Trieste. Yugoslav pretensions to the Slovene-inhabited regions of Carinthia retarded the signing of a peace treaty with Austria.

After almost two years of tedious negotiations among the four Allied Powers, the peace treaties with the Axis satellites of Bulgaria and Rumania were signed in Paris on February 10, 1947. These treaties were primarily frontier settlements. Agreement on recognition of the governments of Bulgaria and Rumania was not obtained because of Moscow's continuing disregard of the Yalta commitment.

In Bulgaria and Rumania, where allied control commissions were established after the war, Soviet authorities paralyzed the proper functioning of the constituted governments. Rumanian premier Radescu was tormented by the commander of the Russian occupation forces which were stationed in the country in a style quite unforeseen in the armistice. The Rumanian Communist Party, comprising only about 1,000 members in 1945, soon increased greatly in size at the instigation of agitators like Ana Pauker, a resident of Soviet Russia since 1940, Vasile Luca, also a Soviet resident since 1940, and Emil Bodnaras, another Moscow-trained communist. Foreign Minister Molotov affirmed on August 3, 1944 that the Soviet government envisaged in Rumania neither modifications of the social structure nor annexations of any territory. But Rumania's army was reduced to 10,000 troops thus permitting the negligible Communist Party to spread terror in the country.

Radescu, who was isolated and paralyzed, sought support from the western Allies to stem the growing anarchy. However discreet his requests may have been, they did not escape the vigilance of Soviet authorities. Denounced by the Moscow press and radio, the premier was finished. The communists deliberately incited street riots in Bucharest which had to be suppressed. At this point Andrei Vyshinsky appeared in Bucharest for the second time on March 2, 1945. While Soviet troops patrolled the streets as substitutes for the Rumanian police who had been disbanded by the Red Army, the royal palace was surrounded. Vyshinsky peremptorily advised King Michael that the inability of the Radescu government to maintain order constituted a danger to the security of the Red Army and it was therefore mandatory to grant power to another politician. When the king mentioned aged Prince Barbu Shtirbey, Vyshinsky brushed him aside and declared that only Petru Groza fulfilled the desired qualifications. Groza was a wealthy Transylvanian businessman and politician who had founded the so-called Plowmen's Front, a left-wing organization of Transylvanian peasants.

After giving Michael two hours in which to think this over, Vyshinsky withdrew, slamming the door vigorously. The king had to yield. Thus the Groza government was installed on March 6, 1945 with communists securing the strategic ministries. The appointment of Gheorghe Tatarescu, a dissident Liberal whose views aroused considerable criticism, appeared to constitute a certain balance. This new regime was entitled the National Democratic Front, and under its direction communism gained considerable strength because of the presence in Rumania of about 1 million Soviet troops. Purges were conducted despite the protests of Iuliu Maniu, leader of the democratic opposition. In a country devastated by war and whose communications were in a deplorable condition, sovietization measures were achieved without obstacles. Large landed estates were expropriated, factories were requisitioned, and Soviet-Rumanian economic organizations were established to export most of Rumania's production to Russia. Eighty per cent of Rumania's gross national product was being shipped to Soviet Russia. Added to these vicissitudes was a drought which caused a famine in the Danubian plains, a region that had once been a major European granary. To a ruinous inflation was added a radical currency reform which, on the basis of 20,000 old lei to 1 new leu, completed the ruin of the prosperous classes.

The American and English governments vainly attempted to enlarge the base of the Groza government. The West could not even protect its economic interests in Rumania which were compromised by the confiscations of the Soviet-Rumanian economic combinations. American and English citizens in Rumania were even expelled from that country. For a while a facade of respectability was maintained, and the Rumanians continued to display their attachment to King Michael. A few daring individuals raised their voices against this farcical democracy. They were arrested, and the leaders of the National Peasant Party, Maniu and Mihalache, were tried and sentenced to life imprisonment for allegedly plotting against the state (November 1947). News of the sentence imposed on aged Maniu produced in the world a revulsion against the partiality of the judges. Tatarescu resigned as foreign minister and was replaced by Ana Pauker who soon purged the foreign service of its personnel. Luca was named finance minister. Soon the Liberal, National Peasant, and Social Democrat parties vanished. Communism was proceeding at full speed to the liquidation of the bourgeoisie and the wealthier peasantry.

The implacable logic with which events were occurring in Rumania could only lead to the king's abdication. The Soviet government had ironically awarded Michael the Order of Victory in 1944 for his having shaken off the Nazi yoke. Michael, frustrated by his futile efforts to resist Moscow's domination and anxious to preserve his dignity, decided to abdicate on December 30, 1947 after attending the wedding of Princess Elizabeth in England. The Rumanian People's Republic was immediately and unanimously proclaimed in the national assembly. Elections

TERRITORIAL FORMATION OF RUMANIA

In 1861, the principalities of Wallachia and Moldavia (augmented by the award of southern Bessarabia in the Treaty of Paris of 1856) were united into the Principality of Rumania, a name which appeared for the first time.

At the Congress of Berlin the independence of the new state (which would become a kingdom in 1881) was recognized, but Russia obliged Rumania to cede southern Bessarabia (1) in exchange for the northern Dobrudja (2) taken from the Turks.

In 1913, after joining the Balkan coalition against Bulgaria, Rumania, by the Treaty of Bucharest, acquired the southern Dobrudja (3).

After World War I, in recognition of Rumania's participation, the Allies ceded Transylvania and a part of the Banat from Hungary (4), the Bukovina (5) from Austria, and Russia had to cede Bessarabia (6).

Greater Rumania maintained her frontiers until 1940 when she gradually began to lose most of her acquisitions: Bessarabia and the northern Bukovina annexed by the USSR; the southern Dobrudja to Bulgaria; and the greater part of Transylvania to Hungary.

The treaty of peace signed in Paris in 1947 restored Transylvania to Rumania.

which ensued assured 91% of the votes to the government. The only gesture permitted the intimated opposition was abstention from the elections. Rumania was brought to her knees, like her neighbors; and, because she was closest to Russia, found herself even more integrated into the Soviet system than the others. The land, forests, communications, and energy-producing enterprises became state property; banking was nationalized; and soil cultivation was gradually transformed into collective farms as a result of a campaign against the large landowners and the wealthier peasants. The lamentable consequence of these measures was a decline in agricultural production provoked by general peasant demoralization and a decrease in industrial production, chiefly in petroleum output, because of a shortage of tools and raw materials. Conditions deteriorated to the point where Soviet Russia was required to renounce a share of reparations so that Rumania's economy could recover.

In intellectual activities the efforts of the Rumanian People's Republic tended toward the suppression of the cultural élite, always prestigious in that country, and an irrevocable break with the West. Rumanian students abroad were summoned home. Whereas Rumania had been attached to French culture and was one of the brilliant centers of French culture in the Balkans and where the French language was rated second by the leading writers and French books were read more than anywhere else except in Belgium, the importation of French publications was prohibited, the teaching of French was dropped in favor of Russian, cultural agreements were terminated, French schools closed, and French teachers sent home. Titulescu had written in 1937, "Every Rumanian carries France within him. . . . The Rumanian soul vibrates for everything that is French. The glory of France is part of our national glory." What a denial had been forcibly imposed on the sentiments of these people!

The Kingdom of Bulgaria, after signing her armistice on October 28, 1944, was forced to join the Allied Powers and furnish a contingent to pursue the retreating Nazi forces. The mobilization of many Bulgarian soldiers, of whom more than 30,000 would be casualties, was an appreciable contribution to the struggle against the Axis powers.

The government of Kimon Georgiev was installed by the

bayonets of 20,000 Soviet soldiers on September 9, 1944. This new regime proclaimed the need to establish an "indissoluble alliance" with the Soviet Union and the new Yugoslavia. The Georgiev government undertook a series of internal reforms to transform the economy and reform the political system. The existence of numerous peasant cooperatives facilitated the task of collectivizing agriculture more than in Rumania and Yugoslavia. The new regime, called the Fatherland Front, contained Nicolas Petkov, leader of the Peasant Party, and other members of the pre-war liberal parties. But the radicals soon assumed an increasing ascendancy based on prestige secured by their active participation in the anti-Nazi resistance movement. The prisons were soon filled with those who had been reproached for Germanophile or reactionary sentiments. These victims, described as "repugnant persons," were denounced with as much vehemence as irresponsibility.

This massive purge, conducted by a growing police force, led its victims before so-called "popular tribunals" which meted out swift penalties. More than 3,000 persons were executed within one year after the end of the war, among whom there were 66 members of parliament, 2,000 sentenced to life imprisonment, and more than 6,000 given various other penalties. In a nation whose intellectual élite was relatively limited, Bulgaria's educated few were represssed and the moderate elements dispersed. Politicians known for their liberal views, such as Nikola Mushanov, former president of the Sobranie (Parliament), and Burov, a former League of Nations delegate, were threatened. The secretary of the Peasant Party, Dr. Georgi Dimitrov, was condemned to death, but he managed to escape and find refuge in the United States.

England and the United States were observing these excesses. Both signified their intention to recognize a government which represented every shade of Bulgarian public opinion. Elections, scheduled for August 1945, were postponed to November as a result of American insistence upon a free electoral campaign. Despite the presence of American observers, the opposition, maintaining that the conditions raised by the United States had not been fulfilled, abstained from the elections and thus permitted the Fatherland Front, now a coalition of radical parties, to win 85% of the vote. This result led Georgiev to orient the Front

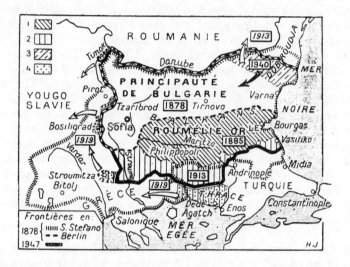

TERRITORIAL FORMATION OF BULGARIA

In March 1878 the Treaty of San Stefano created a great Bulgarian state which had been missing from the map of Europe
for five centuries. A few months later the Congress of Berlin
reduced Bulgaria to a small principality and the autonomous
province of Eastern Rumelia. (1) The two were united in 1885.
Proclaimed an independent kingdom in 1908, the Bulgarian state,
four years later, was a member of the Balkan League which
obliged the Turks to evacuate all territory west of the Enos-
Midia line. The disputes raised by Bulgaria's claims to Macedonia led her to attack her allies. Conquered, Bulgaria was only
permitted to retain a part of her conquests (2) and had to
cede the southern Dobrudja to Rumania (3).
At the end of World War I, Bulgaria, defeated in the camp of
the Central Powers, abandoned in 1919 by the Treaty of
Neuilly the entire shore of the Aegean Sea which was given
to Greece, and the districts of Timok, Tsaribrod, Bosiligrad, and
Strumitsa to Yugoslavia (4).
Her joining the Axis during World War II resulted in substantial
but temporary acquisitions (see the map of the acquisitions of
Bulgaria in 1940-41), but she was forced to yield everything
except the southern Dobrudja.

into the Soviet orbit. After his journey to Moscow and a return visit by Vyshinsky, Georgiev shuffled his cabinet in March 1946, announced his intention to revise the constitution, and thus placed his country in the hands of the communists. The Bulgarian people voted by a majority of 93% on September 8 to abolish the monarchy and create a people's republic. The widow of King Boris, Queen Giovanna, whose life had always been characterized by dignity and simplicity, departed from the country accompanied by her two children to join her relatives, the Italian royal family, in exile in Egypt. Young King Simeon II was probably too young to realize he had been a monarch. The plebiscite probably represented popular will in this country where there was little attachment to a foreign dynasty headed by an eight-year-old child.

After the question of regime was settled, the national assembly (Sobranie) had to be elected. Preparations for the elections were carried out in an atmosphere which was so agitated that it drew fresh criticism from the English and American representatives on the Interallied Control Commission. The Soviet delegate, a true despot, rejected the Anglo-American remonstrances, and the Fatherland Front secured more than 75% of the vote. Although the non-communist opposition won about 100 seats in the So-branie, the majority had very clearly gone over to the extreme left and communists. A month after the elections (November 1946) Georgi Dimitrov returned in triumph from Moscow. This veteran communist, renowned for his activities in the Comintern, formed a new Bulgarian government composed of a few members of the Peasant Party, the Social Democrats, and most from the Communist Party who held the strategic ministries.

The Communists used their government posts so effectively that, despite Anglo-American protests, Bulgaria rapidly became aligned with the Soviet Union. Nationalization and collectivization decrees followed in swift succession. Those who opposed this orientation refused to participate in a government which had passed into Communist hands. The Iron Curtain slammed down even more harshly than elsewhere, as was attested by the expulsion of French correspondents and the failure of an inquiry mission dispatched by the United Nations.

The most despicable event of this agitated period was the arrest of Nikola Petkov, leader of the Peasant Party, who had had the temerity to denounce the Dimitrov regime. Accused along with the deputies of the Peasant Party of participating in a treason plot, Petkov was condemned to death in September 1947. This news produced such emotions that the Anglo-American representatives were instructed to demand an explanation. Dimitrov merely replied that it was a matter of internal politics. Petkov was hanged despite the indignation of the civilized world sickened by the barbarism of these methods.

Freedom became a vain expression in Bulgaria where, after the conviction of their leader, Krustu Pastuhov (Pastukhov), the Social Democratic Party was soon dispersed. The large landowners were brutally dispossessed and locked out of their homes. Attendance at political meetings became compulsory. The black market flourished. As in Rumania, the teaching of foreign languages other than Russian was prohibited, and non-Bulgarian schools, among which were several renowned French secondary schools, were closed. The Soviet government rewarded Bulgaria's obedience by withdrawing Soviet troops from the country in December 1947.

Yugoslavia's post-war government, the Yalta conference recommended, should have been a coalition between Tito's Partisans and the royal regime. When the war ended Yugoslavia was still theoretically a monarchy, but real power was held by Tito and his National Liberation Movement. Ivan Shubashich was given the relatively unimportant ministry of foreign affairs in Tito's government. Hero of the resistance, Tito had promoted himself to the rank of Marshal and became the dictator of Yugoslavia. He produced the impression of reconciling the differences among the south Slavs and, at first sight, seemed to be succeeding where the Karageorgevich dynasty had failed. Were the efforts undertaken by Tito, a native Croat, designed to avenge the Croats for years of Serbian repression? Would the new Yugoslavia be dominated by the Croats? Marshal Tito, however, had risen to pre-eminence because of his heroic military qualities and intransigent patriotism. He was not a Croat nationalist, and he had fought against the fascist Ustash of Ante Pavelich. Among the poverty-stricken Yugoslavs whose homeland had been devastated by war and civil strife, Tito brought hope and the ideal of communism. Intense propaganda by Tito's regime soon produced a genuinely loyal Yugoslav mass, and the old internecine Serbo-Croat quarrels gradually subsided.

Tito's first concern was to claim all ethnically Yugoslav territory of which the country had been deprived in 1918-19—Istria, Venezia Giulia, Carinthia, Zara, and the Dalmatian islands. His troops expelled the Nazis from Trieste on May 1, 1945 and entered the city where they soon encountered Anglo-American forces. The question of that city's fate was posed with an acuteness which poisoned the critical post-war atmosphere and threatened a conflict in a region contested by Italy and Yugoslavia since 1918. Disputes between the Yugoslavs and the Anglo-American powers produced such tension that a provisional frontier was finally traced excluding the Yugoslavs from Venezia Giulia to avert incidents. The administration of Trieste was entrusted to the Anglo-Americans while the final disposition of the city was awaited. This decision aroused the indignation of Yugoslav nationalists whose sentiments were expressed by Tito when he declared that the sacred rights of his nation were being disregarded despite the sacrifices his people had made. Yugoslavia, he asserted, had lost about 1½ million people, 10% of her total population, as a result of invasion, civil war, and reprisals, and material damages amounted to several billion dollars. He refused to condone the retention by Italy, a member of the Axis, of the port of Trieste. England and the United States warned Tito that Trieste would remain under Allied control.

During this immediate post-war period propaganda against restoration of the monarchy was encouraged. Tito declared a monarchy to be incompatible with socialist doctrines. The National Liberation Movement echoed his sentiments and conducted a vast purge to eliminate moderate elements, even to the point of harassing needed technicians, antagonizing the peasants by methods of forced collectivization, and demoralizing the army by a purge of career officers. Seven officers of Mikhailovich's Chetniks were executed, several Skuptshchina deputies were arrested, and others condemned for allegedly revealing state secrets. Freedom of the press was theoretically tolerated provided nothing be printed which "might be of a nature prejudicial to the national interest." In Croatia, where the populace remained attached to the Roman Catholic Church and its clergy, vexatious measures were initiated and priests were imprisoned. Tito uttered the order of the day in denouncing the "corrosive tactics of the Catholic clergy" in a speech at Zagreb.

Elections were scheduled under these conditions. Foreign

Minister Shubashich resigned after protesting against actions taken by the government of which he was a member. Aloysiye Stepinac (Stepinats), Archbishop of Zagreb and Catholic Primate of Croatia, read a pastoral letter in which he denounced the persecution of the clergy. The forthcoming elections required a customary review of the electoral lists from which were expunged the names of persons adjudged unworthy of exercising the franchise. Several hundred thousand were thus disenfranchised. Elections to a constituent assembly were held on November 11, 1945. About 90% of the vote went to the National Front dominated by the Communists. The assembly unanimously proclaimed a federal people's republic of Yugoslavia on November 29. The new federation contained six states: Serbia, Croatia, Slovenia, Bosnia, Montenegro, and Macedonia. After expressing disapproval of the apparently fraudulent elections, England and the United States ultimately decided to recognize this *fait accompli*.

Supported by fanatic partisans, including most Yugoslav youth, Marshal Tito then began to transform the former Yugoslav kingdom into a new, people's republic by adopting Soviet methods of nationalization, intensifying secret police activities, remodeling the army, and reorganizing the government bureaucracy. He signed a pact of friendship and cooperation with Soviet Russia. The Iron Curtain slammed shut once again, this time on Yugoslavia from which disquieting news soon emanated.

Archbishop Stepinac was arrested, tried, and sentenced to sixteen years' hard labor for "subversive activities and an unpatriotic attitude," an act which unleashed even more violent religious persecution. In March 1946 General Mikhailovich was captured, and, after a humiliating trial, condemned to death and executed on July 17 after Allied protests only served to aggravate his case. A regime based on fear, which overturned the old social order, gained strength since the authorities had at their disposal innumerable means to force recalcitrants to yield. The government's program depended upon industrialization from which an improvement in living standards was anticipated. Despite exhausting labor imposed on everyone, prices remained high and poverty was rampant.

To this internal revolution was added the aggravation of a dispute over Trieste. Vigorously backed by Soviet Russia, Yugoslavia pushed her frontier to the west in a manner to increase

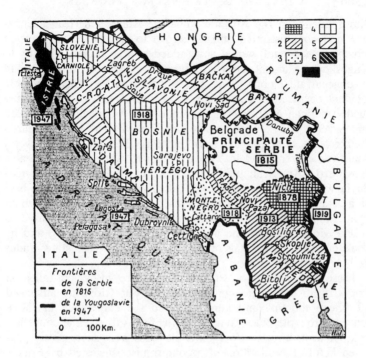

TERRITORIAL FORMATION OF YUGOSLAVIA.

It was not until 1815 that the Serbs secured from Turkey a certain autonomy. Their country became a principality under Turkish vassalage.

The Congress of Berlin granted to Serbia, in addition to recognition of her independence (Serbia became a kingdom in 1882) the region of Nish-Pirot (1).

At the end of the Balkan Wars Serbia received by the Treaty of Bucharest in 1913 the greater part of Macedonia (2), which gave her a common frontier with Greece.

After being completely occupied by the Central Powers during World War I, Serbia was transformed by the 1918 victory into a great state uniting the south Slavs in old Serbia, Montenegro (3), Bosnia-Herzegovina, Dalmatia, Slovenia detached from Austria (4), Croatia, Slavonia, and a part of the Banat detached from Hungary (5), and the districts of Timok, Tsaribrod, Bosiligrad, and Strumitsa annexed for strategic reasons.

The Second World War led to a temporary dismemberment of Yugoslavia (see map of this dismemberment in 1941). But Yugoslavia would recover her lost territories and secure Istria and some islands (Lagosta and Pelagosa) from Italy (7). Yugoslavia surrendered her claims to sections of Carinthia.

Slav influence in the Adriatic while the Anglo-American occupation and administrative officials strove to prevent this expansion which, if successful, would have added a large Italian minority to Yugoslavia. Marshal Tito, adopting a belligerent attitude, began to concentrate troops along the Italian frontier. The inevitable incident occurred in September 1946 when Yugoslav planes pursued American aircraft over Slovenia. Six Americans were killed and several others were imprisoned. The United States secured their release after lodging stern protests. The release of several American citizens held in Yugoslav concentration camps was also demanded. American public opinion was aroused against Yugoslavia which was, as President Truman declared, under the heel of a totalitarian regime which refused to recognize basic human rights. England also delivered a protest. During this crisis Tito visited Moscow, where he was encouraged in his actions, and he also stopped in the capitals of the other East European states under Red Army occupation.

These acts created a stormy atmosphere in which talks on Trieste were held. The same arguments were tirelessly advanced for fifteen months, and almost caused the conference in Paris, convened to write peace treaties for the five Axis satellite countries, to falter in its efforts. Four different plans were successively proposed before the adoption of a compromise suggested by France which gave to Yugoslavia a section of Istria and Venezia Giulia, the port of Zara, and a few islands in the Adriatic. Fiume was thus restored to Yugoslavia. As for Trieste, the intransigently divergent views were irreconcilable, and the negotiators decided to make Trieste a free city, thus duplicating the unwise precedent of Danzig. An Italian city encircled by Slovene-inhabited suburbs, which could have served as an access to the vast hinterland of central Europe, was placed under the protection of the Security Council of the United Nations. A governor with extensive authority was to be chosen after consultations between Italy and Yugoslavia, but the discussions collapsed. Yugoslavia displayed chagrin by boycotting the port of Trieste, and that once busy city gradually fell into an economic decline. In May 1948 England and the United States, accepting a French proposal, recommended that Trieste be restored to Italy so that the port could recover its status. The Soviet government at first rejected this proposal, but the subsequent Tito-Stalin rift occasioned changes in Moscow's attitude. In October 1953, the United States and England, abandoning the 1948 agreement to give all Trieste to Italy, announced plans to evacuate their occupation forces from the area. Italy and Yugoslavia would divide the disputed region. Marshal Tito threatened to seize the area promised to Italy. England, France, and the United States proposed a conference with Italy and Yugoslavia. After one year of discussion Italy and Yugoslavia reached an agreement on the nine-year-old Trieste dispute (October 1954). Italy regained the city of Trieste, and Yugoslavia secured the hinterland. Anglo-American occupation forces were then withdrawn. Soviet Russia did not oppose this settlement and hailed it as a step toward peace. Italy thus acquired 86 square miles including the city with its population of about 300,000; Yugoslavia secured 199 square miles with a population of about 70,000.

In the Kingdom of Greece the appointment of Archbishop Damaskinos as regent when Churchill visited Athens in December 1944 failed to produce prolonged stability. The radical elements, who surrendered only a negligible quantity of their weapons while concealing most of them, succeeded in eluding disarmament which had been decreed as the proper means to end a threatening civil war. The radicals also profited from the proclamation of a general amnesty. Nevertheless, unrest grew despite precautions, and a series of ministerial crises in 1946 added to the confusion created by strikes and riots inspired by the communists. The regent had to appoint six different cabinets during 1945, none of which could reconcile the moderate and radical resistance groups.

Elections were scheduled for March 1946 after Archbishop Damaskinos visited King George and the English government in London. The radical groups refused to participate in the elections because of the continued presence of English forces who strove to maintain order. The first post-war general election was won by an overwhelming majority for the royalist Popular Party. The radical EAM and other leftist parties had refused to participate in the voting. This election contributed to the outbreak of the Greek civil war in which thousands of communists, aided by Greece's communist neighbors, initiated widespread guerilla warfare.

As a result of the March 31 elections, Constantin Tsaldaris, the leader of the Popular Party, formed a cabinet on April 18. A plebiscite on September 1 decided 69% in favor of the monarchy. King George II returned for a third time on September 28, but his arrival failed to produce the needed pacification.

The radicals contended that the plebiscite failed to correspond to the popular will. They insisted the vote had been vitiated by reason of the support given to their adversaries by the English forces whose withdrawal they demanded. The Soviet government supported this argument. Whenever reproaches were addressed to Moscow on the subject of Soviet policy in the Balkans, Russia never failed to retort with complaints against the English occupation of Greece.

The Tsaldaris government ruled with an iron hand. Arrests and deportations were countered by frequent assassinations. Guerilla warfare flourished in which royalists struggled with the radicals. Both secured foreign support. It was feared that this civil war would degenerate as the Spanish Civil War had done into a general conflict in which foreign elements would confront each other to assure the victory of one of the opposing ideologies. The Security Council of the United Nations, concerned by the growing menace, decided to send an inquiry mission to Greece in December 1946.

An unanticipated development now occurred which was destined to have widespread repercussions. The English government declared on February 27, 1947 its inability to fulfill further commitments to Greece and Turkey. Weakened by an almost superhuman effort during World War II and with her wealth diminished, England was forced to recognize her exhaustion by yielding peacekeeping duties and recalling her troops from their remote posts.

The United States, apparently surprised by this decision, became determined to confront this new obligation with swift resolution. President Harry S. Truman announced on March 12, 1947 that his government would assume English obligations to furnish financial and military assistance to Greece and Turkey. As far as Greece was concerned, this was a guarantee to alleviate her misery and to assist in the struggle against a communist takeover. But the so-called Truman Doctrine had a more extensive scope. It signified the definitive renunciation by the United States of an isolationist policy and her will to assume a major role in an effort to defend common Allied interests. The United States henceforth became the leader in the struggle to encourage democracy in Europe and the eastern Mediterranean. While English troops were being evacuated from Greece, American warships cruised in Greek and Turkish waters. Was this action designed to protect the oil routes and the nations menaced by Soviet imperialism? The Soviet Union lost no time in condemning this American policy, and her ambassador to Greece was recalled home.

King George II died in April 1947 and was succeeded by his brother Paul (1947-63) while ministers continued to succeed each other in a disturbing rhythm. Internal unrest increased constantly. The radical partisans found an energetic leader in the militant communist, Markos Vafiades, whose ascendancy was rising. In December 1947 General Markos, leader of about 20,000 guerillas, proclaimed the creation of the first Provisional Democratic Government of Free Greece. The Athens government retaliated by dissolving the Communist Party and the EAM.

Evidence indicated that the radicals were being assisted by accomplices in the adjacent countries of Yugoslavia, Bulgaria, and especially Albania where attacks were mounted and the rebels secured refuge The Greek government denounced violations of international law committed by these infiltrations, but its ministers remained divided on the policy to be adopted regarding the insurgents, several being inclined to offer them an amnesty to restore calm and others urging nothing less than extermination. Appeasement measures were adopted at the urging of the United Nations inquiry mission which had arrived in Greece. Dissolution of the irregular rightist forces was decreed to avoid provocations, and an amnesty was promised to insurgents who surrendered.

These tolerant measures failed to appease the rebels. General Markos, whom the UN inquiry mission failed to locate, forwarded a report to the mission in which he accused the Athens government of fascist tendencies. His activities became intensified. At first localized along the northern frontiers, principally in the mountains of Epirus where he had his headquarters at Konitsa, the civil war attracted many adherents from distant Thessaly and the Peloponnesus. Markos claimed to control more than 25% of Greece, and in December 1947 he sought recognition from those Balkan states already within the Soviet orbit. Such recognition would have transformed secret aid furnished by the Balkan states into legal support of the Greek rebels. Realizing this, the Athens government led by Themostokles Sophoulis alerted the U. N. Balkan Mission, while London and Washington protested to Belgrade and Sofia for their aid to the rebels. American naval units sailed into Greek waters to support these protests. The

TERRITORIAL FORMATION OF GREECE

In 1830 the northern frontiers of the little kingdom of Greece did not go beyond a line from the Gulf of Arta to the Gulf of Volo.

In 1864 England ceded the Ionian Islands which she had occupied in 1815 after the collapse of Napoleon's empire.

The Congress of Berlin recognized Greece's right to Thessaly, but it was not until 1881 that the Turks evacuated that region.

As a result of the Balkan Wars, the Turks ceded the greater part of Epirus, southern Macedonia, and the Aegean islands (except Imbros and Tenedos, and the Dodecanese which Italy seized). Crete, autonomous since 1898, was also given to Greece.

In 1919-1920, by the Treaties of Neuilly and Sèvres, signed at the end of World War I, western Thrace was ceded by Bulgaria and eastern Thrace (up to the suburbs of Constantinople) by Turkey. Greece also secured a mandate over the region of Smyrna (shown in dots). But the Treaty of Lausanne in 1923 annulled these awards and made the Maritsa River the Greco-Turkish frontier.

Finally in 1947, by the Treaty of Paris, Italy abandoned the Dodecanese Islands to Greece.

United Nations called upon Greece, Yugoslavia, Albania, and Bulgaria to settle their disputes by peaceful means and established the aforementioned Balkan Mission to assure compliance with this appeal.

By 1948 the situation had not improved despite the outlawing of the Greek Communist Party, the dissolution of the EAM, and a vigorous Greek army offensive advised by American technical observers. Pitched battles near Konitsa were followed by the unexpected shelling of Salonika by Markos' artillery. The rebels then marched to within 40 miles of Athens. Confusion and terror increased as the result of the murder of a former Greek minister of justice, John Zevgos, in the streets of Salonika. The Athens government retaliated by executing over 100 communists, and the severity of this reprisal aroused European public opinion which became embarrassing to the Greek government which was compelled to justify its actions.

Hostilities in Epirus assumed the proportions of a virtual war. In the summer of 1948 the Greek government announced significant victories in the Grammos mountain massif and in the Pindus range, but the insurgents merely escaped across the Albanian frontier. Rumors of peace offers by General Markos were circulated, but it soon became apparent that the government's victories were not as decisive as had been anticipated. Furthermore, ministerial crises continued in Athens, and uprisings occurred across the entire breadth of the country.

In June 1949 aged premier Sophoulis died and was succeeded by Alexander Diomedes. By that date the Tito-Stalin rift had had its effect upon the Greek civil war. General Markos had opted for the Stalinists, and in February 1949 he was relieved of his command. Tito closed the Yugoslav frontier with Greece and thus prevented shipment of materials to the Greek rebels. The Greek government forces then initiated an offensive against the rebel strongholds. The rebel leaders ceased their resistance, and the Albanian and Bulgarian governments announced that insurgent refugees in their countries would be interned. After three years of fighting the civil war ended in October 1949. American aid to the Greek govenment and the termination of assistance to the guerillas contributed to the end of hostilities.

In March 1950 a general election in Greece gave the largest number of votes to the Popular Party (Populists), but the Center and moderate leftists secured a majority. This realignment, co-inciding with the termination of the civil war, contributed to a perpetuation of the government's instability as realized by the swift succession of five cabinets during the rest of 1950. Thus the end of the Greek civil war failed to produce stability, and the continuation of political crises lent credence to the frequently cited observation that Greece was fated to endure a tortuous existence regardless of the form of government ruling in Athens. Alas for tortured and martyred Greece, who contained millions of needy victims of two wars and who would continue to be the prey of political unrest.

As for Albania, the Allied Powers indirectly liberated this little country from Axis occupation. Actually the communist-dominated resistance movement forced the Axis to relinquish the occupation in 1944 as the result of the creation of the National Liberation Front led by Enver Hoxha (1908-   ), born into a bourgeois Moslem family, a student in France in 1930-36, member of communist discussion groups in Paris, then a teacher of French in Albanian high schools, founder of the Albanian Communist Party, and also leader of the resistance against Italian and German occupation forces. The Albanian resistance movement was origi-nally linked to Tito's Partisans in Yugoslavia. Hoxha's partisans refused to permit King Zog to return to Tirana, and they created a new government, imitating the Yugoslav example. After the fall of Mussolini in 1943 the Germans replaced the Italians in occupying Albania in September 1943. Some Albanian resistance groups cooperated with the Nazis, and this encouraged other under-ground forces to launch a civil war against these rivals. The anti-Nazi, communist guerillas emerged victorious after the Ger-mans evacuated Albania in November 1944 .

Albania was the only future Soviet satellite in the Balkans which was never occupied by the Red Army. Enver Hoxha could legitimately claim that his resistance movement was responsible for Albania's liberation. Nevertheless, weak Albania was destined to fall under Soviet domination because she was almost entirely surrounded by pro-Soviet Yugoslavia. In December 1945 general elections were held which returned a single list of official candi-dates. In January 1946 a constituent assembly proclaimed the People's Republic of Albania whose policies coincided with those of the other pro-Soviet states in the Balkans. Although the Western Allied Powers had recognized the Hoxha regime in November 1945, relations with them deteriorated rapidly after 1946. Naval incidents in the Corfu channel in 1946, which resulted in the loss of English lives, increased Anglo-Albanian tensions. Tensions arose between Albania and the United States in connection with a spy trial. The American legation quit Albania when the Hoxha regime refused to assume obligations of the pre-war government. Diplomatic relations between the two countries have ceased to exist for the past quarter-century. Albania's contiguity to the northwestern Greek frontier, bristling with mountains and difficult to penetrate, permitted that communist state to play a vital role in the Greek civil war. Little Albania, incidentally, was the first future Soviet satellite to be completely sovietized.

Turkey cannot be considered an authentic Balkan state after World War I because of her loss of territory in the peninsula and because experts consigned her to the geographical region of Asia. Thus Turkey's history is treated herein only in relation to her associations with the Balkan states. After the termination of hostilities in World War II, Turkey was subjected to Soviet intimidation because Moscow apparently desired a role in determining traffic through the Turkish Straits. In March 1945 Soviet Russia denounced her 1925 non-aggression pact with Turkey, but after a period of retrospection Moscow expressed regrets that "relations between the two countries had deteriorated." This rejoinder merely exacerbated relations. The Soviet government then demanded a revision of the 1936 Montreux Convention. Turkey replied that the convention involved all the signatory powers, not merely Turkey and Russia. Soviet Russia nevertheless insisted that Turkey relinquish exclusive control over the Straits. Moscow also demanded a rectification of the frontier in the Armenian region of Kars and Ardahan, as well as a democratization of the Turkish constitution—an unequivocal interference in Turkey's internal affairs. These demands clearly indicated that Soviet Russia considered the Straits to be within her sphere of influence.

Intense reactions resulted in Ankara. The Turkish government was determined to resist Soviet pressures. Since the Turks had been required to maintain a half million soldiers on active duty during the war so that neutrality could be assured, they were prepared to resist Soviet pressure. Although assured of American and English assistance, Turkey was resolved to strain her resources in resisting Russia. Public opinion was aroused to such a magnitude that Istanbul students demonstrated before pro-communist newspaper offices, which led Moscow to dispatch strong protests against the repression of these pro-Soviet journals.

The Soviet government, apparently preparing an argument which would later succeed in implementing changes of navigation on the Danube River, affirmed that control of the Straits concerned only those nations which were located on the Black Sea. Thus all other states had to be excluded. This was a reiteration of Nazi Germany's assertion about navigation on the Danube during the war years. The Soviet negation of the rights of the states which had signed so many conventions on navigation through the Straits angered the English government. Freedom of passage for Soviet warships through the Straits represented a grave threat to English hegemony in the eastern Mediterranean. Thus England strenuously opposed the Soviet project, and France and the United States supported England in this move. This raising of shields tempered Russia's aggressiveness, although Moscow did not renounce demands whose realization constituted an infringement on the sovereignty of Turkey from whom Russia subsequently demanded military and naval bases.

The issuance of the Truman Doctrine temporarily abated this crisis in the spring of 1947. The United States did not hesitate to throw its strength into the balance of power in order to contain Soviet imperialism. Since 1947 the United States has protected its exploitation of the Middle East oilfields and indirectly preserved the independence and territorial integrity of Turkey and Greece. And since that time Turkey has been a loyal member of the camp of those nations which have struggled to contain Soviet expansionism.

Albania, Bulgaria, Rumania, and Yugoslavia in the spring of 1948 constituted under Moscow's aegis a solid, coherent bloc adjacent to the central European states of Poland, Hungary, and Czechoslovakia, all of which formed a massive group of countries inhabited by about 100 million people, all of whom were subject to the same Soviet hegemony. An immense Slav front, augmented by the non-Slav Hungarians and Rumanians, had been created in

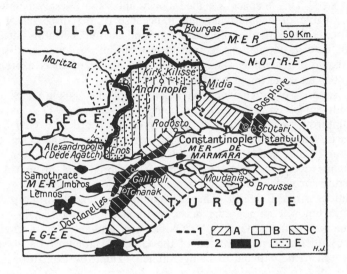

THE STRAITS

The broken line (1) indicates the frontiers of the Treaty of Sèvres (1920). This left to Turkey only Constantinople (Istanbul) and its environs (A). Greece received eastern Thrace (B). The Straits passed under interallied control and became a neutral zone destined to be demilitarized (C).

(This treaty was not put into effect. The defeat of her troops in the region of Smyrna obliged Greece to evacuate Thrace by the armistice of Mudania in October 1922).

The straight line (2) indicates the European frontiers resulting from a new treaty signed with Turkey in July 1923 at Lausanne. The Straits were demilitarized (D). Also demilitarized were the frontiers between the Aegean and Black seas (E).

Finally in 1936, at the Montreux Conference, Turkey recovered her former rights over the Straits.

which Soviet Russia played the role of an indisputable arbiter. The West anxiously observed the consolidation of this bloc whose amplitude recalled that of the greatest coalitions which have ever existed. This menace weighed down upon the West which was incapable of counterbalancing it because of the dispersal of its forces. The Kremlin suppressed, behind an impenetrable barrier, the diverse populations to transform them into a docile herd submissive to its orders. The West, lacking means to effect a breach in this mass, let things run their course.

A series of agreements concluded among the Balkan states and with Soviet Russia sealed the bonds. In August 1947 Tito and Dimitrov signed at Bled in Yugoslavia an accord by which Bulgaria, although offending popular sentiments, sacrificed on the altar of Slav solidarity her ambitions in Macedonia and even her claims over the frontier districts of Tsaribrod and Strumitsa in return for which Yugoslavia agreed to abandon her claims to reparations from Bulgaria. The two communist leaders discussed a tariff union, common currencies, and concerted action against the "monarcho-fascist Greeks." This idea of a Balkan federation, with the anticipated participation of the Greek Communist Party, appeared to be capable of being fulfilled. Dimitrov even broached the idea to Rumania during a visit in early 1948. A union of four Balkan states under Soviet control appeared imminent. But to universal surprise *Pravda*, the official organ of the Soviet Communist Party, expressed disapproval of such a federation. Moscow rejected any plans to threaten the complete independence of any interested state. Thus the hopes of generations of Balkan leaders, who recognized the pacification values of a federation, were laid to rest.

This strange rejection was still being discussed when another surprise occurred, and it was uniquely unanticipated. This new development would have far greater repercussions than the Bled conference. Until the summer of 1948 Yugoslavia had appeared as the Balkan state most favored by Moscow, and Marshal Tito was the most zealous of Stalin's disciples. The Soviet Union was indebted to Tito for his rapid communization of Yugoslavia and his challenge to the Anglo-American forces in Trieste. As a gesture of his good will, Stalin placed the headquarters of the Communist Information Bureau (the Cominform), successor to the Comintern, in Belgrade. This was an organization of the communist parties of nine countries whose activities would be coordinated by an executive committee in Yugoslavia. Stalin had abolished its predecessor, the Communist International, in 1943 to coddle the Western Allies, but he now realized such favors were of no strategic value. Yugoslavia constituted, because of her advance position from which communist doctrines could be exported to the West, a very special advantage of the communist bloc.

Despite all these virtues, Yugoslavia became the subject of an international crisis in 1948. At a congress of the Polish Communist Party in Warsaw on June 28, 1948, Yugoslavia was the subject of an excommunication from the communist bloc because Tito had allegedly deviated from Marxism-Leninism and he had been guilty of so-called nationalist deviations. This declaration had been preceded by Tito's repeated assertions of Yugoslavia's own interests. Differences between Tito and Stalin had grown to the point where the Soviet government recalled its technicians from Yugoslavia in March 1948. But the Cominform's expulsion of Yugoslavia from membership was certainly unexpected.

Marshal Tito denied the Cominform's accusations of deviation and received a note of confidence from his own party. He then initiated negotiations with the West, and notably the United States, for the purpose of securing economic assistance in view of deteriorating relations with members of the Soviet bloc. The headquarters of the Cominform were moved to Bucharest. Fears of a Soviet invasion became widespread.

Isolated and undeveloped Albania, economically dependent upon Yugoslavia, was the first to break trade relations with Belgrade and expel the Yugoslav specialists who had been invited to modernize the country. Ana Pauker, Rumania's foreign minister and the real boss of the Bucharest regime, engaged in a radio duel with Tito which ended with a suspension of deliveries of Rumanian oil to Yugoslavia.

In August 1948 a conference to discuss navigation on the Danube was scheduled for Belgrade. All were curious to see what stand the Yugoslav delegates would take. Those who hoped for Yugoslavia's break with Soviet Russia were disappointed to learn that Belgrade continued to remain a solid member of the communist bloc. By a vote of 7 to 3 (England, France, and the United States in the minority), the international commission on the Danube, one of the oldest and most productive institutions of

European public law, was liquidated and replaced by a committee of exclusively riparian states, all subservient to Soviet Russia. The Soviet government thereby achieved the ambition which Hitler had forced Moscow to renounce in August 1940. The entire lower course of the Danube, from Vienna to the delta, came under Soviet control. The "beautiful, blue Danube" became "The Red Danube," according to an oft-repeated quip.

Despite Yugoslavia's support of the bloc regarding navigation on the Danube, a fissure had indeed been created in the Soviet-controlled system. Would it be deep and lasting or, under the burden of his disgrace, would Tito be eliminated like so many other personages from whom Moscow had withdrawn its confidence after having heaped favors on them?

For a while Marshal Tito played a double game or at the very least maintained Yugoslavia in a state of equilibrium. He insisted upon loyalty to Soviet Russia while simultaneously seeking aid from the West. But soon the rigorous retaliations inflicted on Yugoslavia left Tito no freedom of choice. Belgrade was subjected to an economic blockade by the Cominform states. Yugoslav citizens in those states were molested. Yugoslavia became the target of vehement attacks in the press and on the radio. Belgrade had to ward off difficulties caused by economic strangulation which deprived the country of indispensable raw materials. Where once her exports were with the bloc states in proportions varying from 72% for copper to 100% for iron ore, with return imports of Soviet cotton and paper, Czech machinery and chemical products, Polish coal and rails, Rumanian oil, these exchanges suddenly decelerated and then almost terminated. Commercial agreements with Soviet Russia and the other bloc states were revised in an infinitely more modest form when they were not simply terminated. Yugoslavia failed to fulfill her first five-year plan and was obliged to intensify her domestic efforts.

After replying with analogous measures and denouncing the "incomprehensible and ignoble behavior" of her associate states in the bloc, Yugoslavia arranged commercial agreements with Sweden and Switzerland, and when conditions worsened Belgrade sought trade with England and the United States. Threatened with asphyxiation in the bloc, could Tito do anything other than turn to the West? He began by exchanging copper for American oil, then he requested American aid in equipping his modest industries, and finished by soliciting credits in private New York banks. The Americans were eager to encourage Yugoslavia to secede from the bloc. The American government freed Yugoslav gold deposited in New York and issued export licenses. American businessmen speculated on the profits to be derived from the crisis by investing in Yugoslavia's industrial development. In May 1949 the Yugoslav dinar was quoted on the international money market for the first time since the war. England negotiated commercial exchanges which amounted to about 9 million pounds sterling in five years. Thus Tito, out of necessity and not because of sympathy, oriented his nation toward the West which, in return for its economic assistance, anticipated political concessions over Trieste and the Greek civil war.

Soviet Russia did not expect to see Tito survive his disgrace. Striving to break him, the Kremlin intensified its propaganda to arouse internal opposition by denouncing alleged terrorism in Belgrade, accusing Tito of compromising with capitalism, and reminding Tito of his debt to the Soviet Union, the liberator and benefactor of the Yugoslavs. Moscow attempted to rekindle old antagonisms smoldering under the fragile mosaic of the Federal Republic of Yugoslavia. Many Yugoslavs were disturbed to hear their leader branded a traitor since they had been accustomed to glorifying him. Several communist officials doubted the wisdom of Tito's rift with Moscow, and a few fled to the bloc states. But on the whole the masses remained faithful to Marshal Tito.

The Yugoslav dictator defended himself with vigor. What was the use of insisting upon disguises when Stalin was bent on a rupture? After renouncing his customary gestures of devotion to Stalin, Tito decided to respond in kind. He did this by intensifying police activities, eliminating suspects, and strengthening the authority of his closest associates, Edvard Kardelj and Alexander Rankovich. Tito proclaimed the genuinely socialist character of his efforts and his fidelity to the principles of Marxism-Leninism. He vigorously protested against the campaign of vilification directed against him, and he repudiated compromise with Soviet Russia. Tito repeated incessantly that Yugoslavia was an integral unit of the socialist order and would never join the ranks of the capitalists. Yugoslavia, Tito declared, opposed the creation of the North Atlantic Treaty Organization (NATO) in 1949 and the Marshall Plan for the economic recovery of war-torn Europe.

Under Tito's leadership Yugoslavia had to rely upon her own capacity for hard work and her own resources exploited as only the Yugoslavs determined. Such was the program proudly announced by Tito in the spring of 1949.

Tito also asserted that Soviet Russia had no right to claim a monopoly on pure Marxist doctrine. He declared that any nation, including his own, was qualified to implement communist doctrines without blindly submitting to Stalin's will. These charges produced even greater tensions between Belgrade and Moscow. Within a year the rift changed from latent to official. After exchanging notes that were written in a harsh vocabulary which Soviet diplomacy had substituted for the delicately phrased formulas hitherto used, the rupture became complete in May 1949. The Yugoslav government, echoing Tito's address on his 57th birthday, a national holiday, addressed to Moscow a stern protest against its hostility and discrimination, notably against encouragement given to refugees and newspapers hostile to Belgrade. The Soviet government retaliated with accusations of "gross calumny."

The election of Yugoslavia on October 20, 1949 to a seat on the Security Council of the United Nations over strong Soviet opposition provided evidence that there was a limit to Soviet influence in East Europe despite all the methods of control it had at its disposal.

The Tito-Stalin break had repercussions beyond the Yugoslav frontiers. It created a new problem for communist consciences. Did obedience to Soviet discipline entail a renunciation of all nationalist spirit or was the implementation of Marxism-Leninism-Stalinism compatible with nationalism? The example of the Soviet-Yugoslav schism, born of a will to resist passive submission to orders from abroad, threatened to become contagious among the Balkan peoples. A sentiment of ethnic entity had remained very much alive since before the war. After having experienced centuries of foreign domination, the Balkan peoples had dearly paid for the independence so recently secured from their Turkish and fascist oppressors. Soviet Russia had to avert a crisis which threatened to wreck communist solidarity among the bloc states. Moscow had to halt, at any cost, an extension of this dangerous "nationalist deviation" of which Tito had given the example so that the so-called satellites would dance to the tune of Soviet orthodoxy.

Thus a general intensification of the Kremlin's control was carried out in the bloc countries. The communist parties extended their authority, and suspected politicians were eliminated so that Moscow-trained native communists could succeed to their posts. Accusations against Laszlo Rajk in Hungary, Rudolf Slansky and General Heliodor Pika in Czechoslovakia, Wladyslaw Gomulka in Poland, Traicho Kostov in Bulgaria, Lucretsiu Patrashcanu in Rumania, and others, all described as traitors and spies, illustrated the new purges.

The Balkan states were especially affected by the purge of native communists. In Rumania a quarter-million people were declared "unadaptable" and purged from the party. Owners of more than 20 acres of land were brutally evicted from their homes in the middle of the night. A left-wing Social Democrat and a member of the Plowmen's Front, ministers in the Groza coalition government, were forced to yield their posts to Vasile Luca, Ana Pauker, and Gheorghe Gheorghiu-Dej, the new vice premier. This shake-up in Rumania revealed the triumph achieved by Gheorghiu-Dej, (1901-65), first secretary of the Communist Party since 1945 and, unlike his colleagues, trained as a communist exclusively in Rumania where he had been imprisoned, at Dej, after leading the great 1933 railway strike until he escaped in 1944 to join the advancing Red Army. How he managed to escape liquidation because of his lack of a Moscow education is sufficient testimony to his skill. After a tightening of communist power in Rumania in 1949, Stalin rewarded this obedient satellite by undertaking a project to shorten the Danube's course to the Black Sea by eliminating the long curve made to the north by the river.

Similar steps occurred in Bulgaria. Tito's defection was stigmatized with horror, and demonstrations against alleged Anglo-American provocations were intensified. Accusations preceded harsh purges of government officials. In March 1949, a deputy premier, Traicho Kostov, hero of the anti-fascist resistance movement and one of the very few Balkan communists who had fought in his own country and not in Russia, was removed from his post and assigned work in the National Library on the pretext of his having encouraged nationalist deviations detrimental to Bulgaria's interests. Formerly minister of the national economy, Kostov had perhaps attempted, when negotiating trade treaties, to prevent a sacrifice of Bulgaria's interests to Soviet appetites. The dismissal of this genuine hero (during the war he was imprisoned by the Nazis and hurled himself from a jail window because he feared he could not resist further torture to make him reveal the names of his associates; both legs were fractured and he remained a cripple) occurred immediately prior to Dimitrov's last visit to Moscow for treatment of a fatal illness. Western concern over these developments led foreign experts to attempt a penetration of the mystery which always hovered over Moscow-inspired decisions.

Dimitrov had once declared, "The Soviet Union is as indispensable to the people's democracies as the sun is to human beings." Had Dimitrov become suspect? Or was Stalin planning to replace him with a more active person? These speculations were laid to rest on July 2, 1949 when Dimitrov's death was announced in Moscow. Soviet Russia mourned this veteran communist as a national hero. No eulogies or lamentations were adequate to deplore his passing. Stalin even took a turn guarding the body which was then conveyed to Sofia to be interred in a massive mausoleum during spectacular funeral ceremonies attended by world communist leaders. The old hero of the 1933 Reichstag fire trial in Berlin who later became a Soviet citizen and then dictator of Bulgaria was memorialized as Lenin had been in 1924. Dimitrov had carried intransigence to the extremes of inhumanity, and was always ready to sacrifice family and homeland to his blind devotion to the Comintern and Stalin. After his death, the causes of which still remain suspicious, Marshal Tito, the dissident contemporary of the late Dimitrov, increased his prestige in the Balkans.

Deprived of its leader, the Bulgarian Communist Party was doubly decapitated by Dimitrov's death and the liquidation of Traicho Kostov. Several party leaders, including Vulko Chervenkov, Dimitrov's brother-in-law, and Vasil Kolarov, the provisional premier, competed for the fallen mantle. The Sobranie, however, unanimously elected the 73-year-old Kolarov as new premier. Had Kolarov not spent 22 years in Russia? More and more Moscow bestowed confidence on those whose sentiments had been tested by long sojourns in the socialist motherland.

Tito and his unique brand of communism (called Titoism) was not the only threat to Soviet control of the bloc nations. The churches and other religious organizations formed another barrier to Soviet domination. In the Soviet Union the Russian Orthodox Church held a privileged position because the Communists had broken its spirit in the 1920's and then resurrected it as an agency subservient to party controls. The Patriarchate, revived in September 1943, but denied ties with the Greek Patriarchate in Istanbul, was the only church in Russia "capable of becoming democratic and popular." Thus it was ordered to exercise its influence over all the Orthodox peoples in Russia and nations under Soviet influence. The Russian Orthodox Church was given an old Pan-Slav mission to secure the loyalty of the non-Russian Orthodox peoples of the Balkan states. In this way Soviet domination would be enhanced by a holy aura.

As for the Roman Catholic Church in the bloc states, it was considered a citadel of resistance against socialism, an enemy with which compromise was deemed impossible and which had to be combated. The trial of Josef Cardinal Mindszenty, Primate of Hungary, in January 1949 furnished the model for discrediting the Catholic clergy by accusing them of treason, espionage, and black market activities. Originating in Yugoslavia with the trial of Archbishop Stepinac in 1946, it spread to Hungary and other Catholic countries behind the Iron Curtain. Archbishop Joseph Beran of Czechoslovakia fell victim to a purge. Archbishop Stefan Wyszinski of Poland was likewise mistreated. When the Papacy decided to excommunicate on July 15, 1949 those involved in persecuting clergy, the bloc regimes used this as a pretext to intensify the severe repression.

Roman Catholics, although not numerous south of Croatia in the Balkans, became the object of terror. In Rumania, whose majority population is Orthodox, a struggle against Catholicism constituted an aspect of the campaign against Western ideas. Intense persecution was aimed at the Uniate (Roman Catholic Church of the Byzantine Rite) clergy to force them into joining the Rumanian Orthodox Church. Bishops were dismissed, arrested, or deported. Their churches were expropriated, and 1½ million Uniates, principally in Transylvania, were terrorized. This culminated in an official decree of December 1948 which dissolved the Uniate Church in Rumania. As for the Roman Catholics, numbering about 1 million, their bishop at Alba Iulia was told to break with the Papacy. He refused to do so, and as a consequence all funds allocated to the Catholic clergy in the state budget were deleted and the higher clergy were arrested.

A similar situation prevailed in Albania. The Catholic minority, 10% of the population, was systematically terrorized. One of three bishops survived the ordeal, and he owed this feat to his advanced age. Protestants in Bulgaria, numbering about 15,000, were a special target. The Bulgarian people were treated to an unusual spectacle, but one which became classic during trials conducted according to the Soviet recipe, of accused persons confessing to crimes with tears in their eyes and voicing very touching repentance. Four Protestant clergymen were condemned to life imprisonment.

The peace treaties signed by Bulgaria, Hungary, and Rumania, the Axis satellites, in February 1947 had guaranteed freedom of worship in those countries. How could the Western Allies ignore such flagrant violations of the treaties? England ultimately joined the United States in protesting against these religious persecutions. A joint note, dispatched in April 1949, was rejected by these states on the pretext that it constituted interference in internal affairs and "tended to favor reactionary elements." The Soviet Union, a signatory to these treaties, was invited to join the Western Allies in this protest. But Moscow declined on the same grounds. The only recourse was an appeal to the United Nations.

The war of nerves waged inside Yugoslavia against Tito produced negligible results. So the Soviet Union decided to mount an external attack. Red Army units were concentrated on the Bulgarian and Rumanian frontiers with Yugoslavia. The Soviet government prohibited Albania from dealings with Yugoslavia. Cut off from other members of the Cominform by the interposition of Yugoslavia and Greece, little Albania was tied to Soviet Russia via air transport only. That was sufficient to transport a host of Soviet technicians who became masters of the Albanian economy which they organized for obvious strategic purposes. Moscow shipped war materials and established centers for the training of military personnel so that an Adriatic base could be used for the Greek communists in their struggle, or for anti-Yugoslav purposes as well.

The question of Macedonia, that eternal apple of discord among the Balkan states, seemed an effective jumping-off place for an assault on Yugoslavia's territorial integrity. By dangling the hope of a reunion of the sections divided among three countries, a revival of Macedonian nationalism might produce a triple success— a shaking of the foundations of the Yugoslav state, amputation of the entire Vardar valley to the detriment of monarchist Greece, and the creation under obedient Bulgaria's rule of an ostensibly autonomous Macedonia. Latent hostility between the Bulgarians and Yugoslavs could always be reanimated by the slightest pretexts. After Yugoslavia had been placed under the Cominform's ban, Bulgaria grabbed the opportunity to become Moscow's chief agent in the Balkans. Once again the dream of the greater Bulgaria of San Stefano was revived.

An independent or autonomous communist Macedonia would have linked isolated Albania to the rest of the Soviet bloc. The annexation of the Vardar valley by a new Macedonian state would advance Soviet influence to the shores of the Aegean and Salonika. Moscow would secure mastery of an outlet to the Mediterranean, the ambition of Russian imperialism for a millennium.

This grandiose scheme coincided with the desperation of General Markos in 1949. Why did Moscow decide to reproach him? Had he not resisted superior Greek forces near Mount Grammos? Nevertheless, Markos was discarded because he was a nationalist like Tito who had no intentions to sacrifice the interests of Greece to those of Soviet Russia by abandoning a section of Greek soil to create a greater Macedonia. This rigidity resulted in his disappearance, and the subsequent waning of the Greek civil war. After a harsh purge which did not spare resistance heroes, the Greek Communist Party was reorganized, and it now included several Macedonian representatives.

Yugoslavia's policy toward the Greek civil war had been affected by the Soviet scheme. Why should Tito continue to furnish assistance to an agency of Stalinist policy? When Yugoslav aid to the Greek communists was terminated, the Greek insurgents were destined to lose their vigor despite Moscow's efforts to force Albania, Bulgaria, and even distant Rumania to give assistance. When military operations diminished, the Athens government increased its chance of victory. Furthermore, recognition by the Greek communists of the legitimacy of a Slav claim to Greek Macedonia aroused considerable indignation. The insurgents soon suffered serious reverses near Florina, close to the Yugoslav frontier. Their operations soon became dispirited, and difficulties in recruiting obliged them to impress females into the combatant ranks.

Rumors of peace offers from the Greek communists coincided with a request that the United Nations mediate a truce on condition of an amnesty and a promise to hold elections under supervision of the four Allied Powers of World War II. Coming at the time of the Soviet-inspired Berlin Blockade, 1948-49, this move was suspected of being a Soviet scheme to relax tensions prior to the opening of negotiations on the question of Germany. England and the United States refused to react before sounding out the Athens government. Greece saw in this offer a confession of weakness on the part of the insurgents, and thus the Greek civil war was prolonged.

About 1 million famine-stricken people, 600,000 homeless refugees, 25,000 displaced children, partisan gangs who imitated the savagery of the ancient *komitadjis,* a severe budget deficit, astronomically high prices, unbridled speculation, merciless black market operations—such was the balance sheet of nine years of war and misery during which the strength of the unfortunate Greek people was thoroughly exhausted. While their homeland agonized in its unparalleled distress, the politicians tenaciously carried on their bazaar arguments in order to establish their subtle and ephemeral ministerial combinations.

The death of the indefatigable Sophoulis at age 87, who had been premier for the incredibly long period of 20 months, produced yet another crisis in June 1949. It was not easy to find a successor to this Nestor of Greek politics. For one week the Populists, Liberals, and Social Democrats struggled with incredible bitterness, their titles concealing disputes over clienteles rather than ideological differences. Alexander Diomedes, a liberal banker, formed a new coalition government with a program to crush the insurgent partisans. The new regime would have been wiser to recognize the discontent smoldering in the nation to the point where disconsolate politicians were contemplating a kind of fascist state to save the country. The United States had already furnished $170 million in technical assistance. To achieve its full effectiveness this generosity should have called forth from the Greeks a relinquishing of personal motives for the welfare of the nation. But Greco-American collaboration merely produced the inevitable crises with which England had been familiar for over a century.

American technical aid had also been given to the Republic of Turkey. Ankara received in September 1948 $118 million in credits which permitted the Turks to improve their defenses. Many American technicians assisted Turkish defenses and production. In May 1949 President Truman asked Congress for a supplementary appropriation of $50 million to continue aid to Greece and Turkey. On the alert for many years, Turkey did not anticipate any imminent alleviation of her anxieties. The Ankara government displayed interest in joining NATO, but the northern European member states refused to extend their obligations to the eastern Mediterranean in 1949. Weary of playing the role of a sacrificial sentinel in the Levant, Turkey began to display a certain ill-will toward the West. Generous American assistance produced certain misunderstandings. Some Turks did not always appreciate the quality of American materials or the advice of the technicians. Americans, in their turn, were frustrated by the backwardness of the country, its faulty finances, the primitive economy, and the army's disinterest in modern techniques. The American government, however, deemed it essential to draw Turkey into the free world's security system. The West had much interest in consolidating this arsenal of mutual assistance against the menace of communism. France took the lead to resurrect the military guarantees extended to Turkey in 1939. Subsequent Franco-American overtures to Turkey established a military security program in the eastern Mediterranean.

In the summer of 1949 an exchange of sharp notes between Moscow and Belgrade presaged a severe crisis. Attacks against Yugoslavia doubled in frequency and vehemence, orchestrated by the Soviet Union and taken up in a chorus by the bloc states. After rejecting Yugoslav attacks on the hostile Czech press, Prague accused Tito of having deserted the socialist camp. Bucharest affirmed that the regime of allegedly fascist terror in Yugoslavia demanded military intervention by the socialist states. Budapest terminated all trade relations.

These were the echoes of a polemical battle between Tito and Stalin which were sharpened at the time of the drafting of a peace treaty for Austria, 1949-55. Tito claimed the province of Carinthia which the four Allied Powers rejected as a result of their decision to retain Austria in her 1938 frontiers. To Tito's protests Soviet Russia replied that Yugoslavia had renounced her claims to Carinthia in 1947 and could not reopen the matter. One could recognize why the Soviet Government persisted so long in defending Yugoslavia's claims, and then abruptly switched its policy after the rupture. But Moscow's defense of Austria's retention of Carinthia was not based on an anti-Tito move; it was rather predicated upon delaying the conclusion of a peace treaty which, when ratified, woud have required a Red Army evacuation of its zone in Austria and the end of the pretext to maintain Soviet troops in Rumania and Hungary.

The next phase in the Tito-Stalin rupture was Moscow's protests against the alleged arrest and mistreatment of Russians residing in Yugoslavia. Tito retorted that they were anti-communist White Russians who were involved in spying activities. The Soviet Union considered this a ridiculous explanation by a renegade communist who was expected to take Yugoslavia into the capitalist camp. Then issuing an actual threat, Moscow declared that, "not being able to tolerate such a situation, the Soviet government would have recourse to more effective means of protecting its citizens."

The rupture was assuming alarming proportions. Would Soviet Russia undertake military operations or, at the very least, provoke incidents? For several days in August 1949 the question of war was raised after a flurry of sensational rumors about sabotage committed against a Yugoslav ship, oil refineries, railways, and factories. Reports circulated about overflights of mysterious aircraft, Soviet patrol boats moving up the Danube, infiltration of guerilla bands from Greece, and finally a price placed on Tito's head. If such news could be believed, Soviet Russia was apparently abandoning appeals to Slav solidarity and moves to establish an independent Macedonia. Moscow was apparently striving to overthrow Tito's regime with terrorist methods whose techniques it had perfected.

A Red Army force of 250,000 men in motorized divisions was concentrated in Hungary and Rumania. A conference of Red Army and bloc general staffs was held in Sofia. Rumors asserted that "American secret agents had set October as the date for the beginning of hostilities." Anxiety grew when there were reports of an artillery barrage across the Hungarian-Yugoslav frontier. Fortunately this shelling was not followed by an invasion. Nothing was being omitted from this harsh war of nerves. Stalin had unleashed a campaign whose vehemence recalled those associated with Hitler. A self-styled champion of world peace, Soviet Russia was playing with dynamite in the traditional powder-keg of Europe.

Tito displayed the qualities of a true hero during this crisis. He refused to reply to provocations and insults, and succeeded in maintaining his composure and Yugoslavia in a state of calm. At the same time he exhibited a firmness that could not be weakened by Stalin's intimidation. He declared in an address at Skoplje on August 2, 1949 that he was not afraid of anybody and was prepared to defend Yugoslavia against any attack. Tito then abolished the air and navigation combinations in which Soviet interests had predominated, and he drew closer to the West. He secured from the United States a project for the construction of a steel mill by an American company, a loan of $20 million from the Export-Import Bank, and a visit of representatives from the International Bank of Reconstruction to examine his request for a $250 million loan. The United States, ignoring its recent difficulties with Yugoslavia, was now encouraging Tito to join the free world.

A change of Tito's policy toward Italy was even more striking. In July 1949 the Italian government had protested the introduction of the Yugoslav dinar into the territory of Trieste. Rome interpreted this move as a prelude to annexation by Yugoslavia. Trade relations between the two neighbors were temporarily suspended. But as the Tito-Stalin crisis intensified, Tito minimized the Trieste dispute by agreeing to a new economic agreement with Italy. Italian electrical products were traded for Yugoslav mining resources. This unanticipated improvement in the formerly stormy climate indicated the beginning of the end of the Trieste dispute.

In September 1949 Yugoslavia boldly proposed her candidacy for membership on the Security Council of the United Nations against that of Czechoslovakia, who was the Soviet candidate. Coinciding with the trial of Laszlo Rajk in Hungary, Yugoslavia's election by a large majority so angered Stalin that he renounced the Soviet-Yugoslav treaty of friendship on September 27, expelled Yugoslav Embassy personnel from Moscow, and forced the bloc states to imitate his actions. Yugoslavia responded by using analogous procedures to hold at Sarajevo an espionage trial of 10 Soviet citizens who were sentenced to prison after confessing to spying charges. If Belgrade's spirit had become different from Moscow's, at least the methods remained the same.

Yugoslavia, the most critical Balkan chesspiece since the war, did not monopolize world attention. Developments in the Greek civil war did a favorable turn as a consequence of Tito's policies. In July 1949 Yugoslavia closed her frontiers as much to the insurgents as to the monarchists. Greek government troops took advantage of this move to launch a vigorous offensive which, supported by 50 American bombers, smashed the rebel resistance near Lake Presba. The almost impregnable Grammos range remained to be taken. A heavy concentration of forces in that mountainous region finally overcame rebel resistance. About 7,000 rebels secured refuge in Albania and Bulgaria. Athens was about ready to announce victory, but not the termination of the civil war because of the policies of Albania and Bulgaria.

It was feared in certain quarters that the Greek army, exasperated by Albania's complicity in the war and goaded by the Athens press which was demanding reprisals, might be tempted to cross Albania's border, which had so often been traced to the detriment of Greece, pursue the rebel forces, and, by the same stroke, occupy northern Epirus which Greece had never ceased to claim. Counsels of prudence from London and Washington convinced Athens of the risk of provoking Soviet reactions in that area. The Greek civil war ended on October 16, 1949 when the remaining insurgents agreed to a ceasefire. The free nations thus achieved a significant victory in containing the spread of Soviet influence to the Aegean Sea.

Albania, isolated and encircled by two hostile countries avid to neutralize this Soviet outpost on the Adriatic, now displayed considerable uneasiness. A genuine agitation arose in opposition to the dictatorship of Enver Hoxha. Hoxha had to react swiftly to preserve his power. Koci Xoxe, a former deputy premier, and a number of other high officials were convicted as Yugoslav agents, and Xoxe was executed. The Orthodox primate of Albania was replaced by a less critical cleric. A Committee for a Free Albania was established in Paris by exiles and even partisans of ex-king Zog. Arrests for sabotage and espionage forced large numbers of

Albanians to flee the country. In May 1950 Hoxha conducted elections which confirmed his policies. Albania was then under complete Soviet domination.

In Bulgaria the purge of Kostov was followed in December 1949 by his trial and death sentence on charges of being a spy for England, the United States, and Yugoslavia. Other officials who were also tried managed to survive because of their confessions, contrition, and the manner by which they overwhelmed Kostov with their accusations. The resounding condemnation of Kostov tragically illustrated the intense struggle against all who, however highly placed, were suspected to be infected with the Titoist virus which had to be mercilessly extirpated.

Such rigorous measures and the series of accusations could not fail to produce repercussions. To the malaise was added peasant discontent. Of all the classes in Balkan society, the peasants were traditionally and temperamentally the least fearful of Russia's influence. But post-war restraint measures, such as the requisitioning of crops and the expropriation of land, not only created poor harvests but also aroused mistrust of the incumbent governments. For that reason numerous Soviet technicians were sent to Bulgaria, for example, to assume control of agricultural production. Rumors circulated that Bulgaria was being groomed for incorporation into the Soviet Union. Resistance was either dispersed or terrorized into extinction. Opposition to complete sovietization came from Washington where a committee was established by members of the defunct Peasant Party.

As for Rumania, her contiguity to Soviet Russia, her Western-oriented culture, and her long anti-Russian tradition made that country, even more than the other bloc nations, the object of harsh Soviet controls. Rumania would be figuratively strangled for almost a quarter-century. Like the exile Bulgarians, Rumanians led by exiled General Radescu constituted a national liberation committee in Washington.

These developments indicated growing discontent among the Balkan peoples who, terrorized by the ubiquitous secret police, awaited the hour of their liberation. But too weak and oppressed to attempt it themselves, they saw in their destitution no means other than war to shake off the Soviet yoke. The existence in the Balkans, as well as in Hungary, Czechoslovakia, East Germany,

Poland, and the three Baltic States of millions who envisaged a new war as the only solution represented a possibly graver danger.

Marshal Tito's gestures which freed his country from the Soviet yoke mark a turning-point in the post-war history of the Balkan peoples. He actually created a new form of European Marxism called national communism. Known as Titoism, it would become a threat to Soviet communism. When Rumania was liberated by the Red Army in August 1944, Marshal Voroshilov, reviving an idea formulated by Stalin in 1928, declared, "The Soviet Union is the base of the world revolutionary movement. Anyone who thinks of defending this movement independently of or against the Soviet Union is against the revolution and ranges himself in the camp of our enemies." The message was quite clear: without Moscow there was no salvation. To which the Yugoslav radio later replied, "The policy of command and overlordship of the Soviet government is in flagrant violation of the principle of the freedom of peoples to decide their own destinies." The positions of both antagonists were clear. Between them there appeared no possibility of reconciliation, at least as long as Tito or Stalin lived. But one must not be misled. Tito is still alive, and he insists on being a communist. Any deviation from this stand would have alienated many of his own people from Tito as well as others whose support is indispensable for his security. One cannot lose sight of this fact in recapitulating the services the Yugoslav dictator has rendered to the free world in the past two decades.

Tito's voice indubitably resounded as an appeal to independence for the Balkan peoples. From the economic viewpoint Moscow's exploitation methods could best be seen in Yugoslavia. Subject to the most backward type of outright colonization, the bloc states were tyrannically controlled by a foreign power who directed them to the profit of Soviet Russia alone, and especially to the profit of reinforcing Russia's military potential. The depreciation of industrial equipment was accelerated by Russia's deliveries of inferior parts and products. Output declined. The consequences were a systematic jobbery which produced, not increased productivity, but penury and poverty in the 1950's. Yugoslavia, assisted by Western investments, escaped from this latest servitude and succeeded in achieving in the same period a rapid economic development. This achievement refuted traditional communist economic theories.

Events proved that Titoism spread gross fear in the Soviet camp until the death of Stalin in 1953. The contagion of this deviation had to be contained. The spectacular trial of Laszlo Rajk in Hungary was one proof of the rampant fear of this virus. The Rajk tragedy was a trial against Titoism. So that no doubts could be entertained about this, Moscow denounced its friendship treaty with Belgrade on the basis of a "revelation made at the trial of hostile actions carried on from Belgrade according to the directives of foreign imperialist circles."

Did this again denote an inevitable war? As is now known, hostilities did not break out. The Soviet Union, however, intensified the Cold War, in which Moscow was a past master, by provoking a revival of difficulties with Yugoslavia and by engineering draconian purges of those suspected of apathy. When Red Army forces were withdrawn from Rumania and Bulgaria by 1956, the governments of those bloc states had been so cleverly and strongly constituted that under the disguise of independence they were simply branches of Soviet Russia.

If these were trump cards of Soviet Russia and her Balkan allies, the West was not entirely lacking in them, either. Yugoslavia's go-it-alone policy tended to arouse in the Balkans an upsurge of nationalism. The monolithic bloc established with Soviet intervention was cracked in 1948, and it has not been intact for 20 years. Free world support of Marshal Tito enabled Yugoslavia to shake off Soviet influence. The victory of the Greek government in the civil war signified a resounding setback for Soviet communism, and it contributed to a consolidation of Turkish resistance. The ancient game of great-power rivalries over the Balkan peninsula has not ended. Soviet Russia has not relinquished efforts to break the lock which bars Moscow from the Mediterranean. The United States has assumed the initiative to prevent Moscow's acquisition of a foothold in the Mediterranean basin. It was not only on the banks of the Elbe River in Germany, but also on the shores of the Aegean Sea and the Straits that the Soviet push has been contained.

CHAPTER IX

The Balkan States Since 1950

By Sherman D. Spector

TO compress a history of the Balkan states during the past two
decades into a final chapter may appear to be a ridiculous
task, but this survey, which the author completed in 1949, would
not be complete without a brief outline of developments since
M. Ristelhueber put down his pen. Caution is essential in evalu-
ating recent developments which, unlike the events of prior centuries, must await digestion, analysis, and the assignment of significance by experts in Balkan affairs. Thus the major events of
primarily political importance will be outlined in this final chapter.
Those who wish extensive treatments of specific items are directed
to detailed accounts given in the Bibliography. Furthermore, the
appended chronology will assist in following historical continuity.

When M. Ristelhueber finished his book, a break-up of the
Soviet Empire in East Europe appeared quite remote even though
the Tito-Stalin rupture was producing a serious crisis in the
Balkans. Since that time, however, the threat of Balkanization,
that much maligned term, lurks in the peninsula. One may recall
the disruptions produced by the slow disintegration of the Turkish
Empire. Will the Balkan peninsula again become the scene of
great-power interference in the lives of the native peoples now that
Soviet Russia's controls have been relaxed? Must the Balkan
peoples regularly exchange long foreign domination for brief
periods of insecurity aggravated by an irresistible urge of the great
powers to resume their activities with a view to achieving their
exclusive domination over the peninsula?

If the Balkan peninsula again becomes the scene of a general
European war, then, inevitably, a genuine longing will arise to be
dominated by a great power if only to perpetuate relative peace.
Thus the nations will have struggled over the centuries for a vain
objective—national independence—of which fate has cruelly deprived them.

Tito's break with the Cominform in 1948 politically and psychologically shocked the communist regime in Albania. Stalin's death in March 1953 and the subsequent reconciliation between Moscow and Belgrade failed to produce a real rapprochement between Albania and Yugoslavia. On the contrary, Albania's hostility toward Titoism persists to the present day. Albania remains the only communist state in Europe which is identified with Stalinism and absolute intransigence toward Yugoslavia. Although Albania joined the Warsaw Pact (a 20-year mutual defense treaty signed by the eight European communist nations to counter the integration of West Germany into NATO), she has since refused to participate in its meetings or maneuvers. Efforts to produce a change in Albania's attitude were made by Soviet premier Nikita Khrushchev who visited Tirana in 1959 where he suggested the establishment of a nuclear-free zone in the Balkans. He also warned Italy and Greece to prohibit the installation of American missile bases on their territory. Khrushchev's failure to secure Albania's admission to the United Nations, not achieved until 1955, also contributed to a deterioration in bloc relations. In 1954 Enver Hoxha resigned as premier and assumed the office of first party secretary. His associate, Mehmet Shehu, became premier in a move reflecting adoption of the principle of collective leadership then in vogue in Moscow. Frequent purges have marked the period since these changes. The most recent occurred in 1960 when two prominent members of the Central Committee were dismissed.

Albania was the only European communist state to defend Communist China in its rift with Soviet Russia. By 1961 relations with Moscow had deteriorated to such a point that Khrushchev denounced Tirana and Peking in the same language. Soviet submarine bases were dismantled, and technicians were recalled in a prelude to the severance of diplomatic relations in December 1961. As a result of an end to Soviet economic and military assistance, Peking became Albania's major source of support. Diplomatic relations with other bloc states were also severed, but by 1967 Rumania had taken the lead in restoring relations. The Communist Chinese have rendered moral support to Albania's rift with Moscow by dispatching Premier Chou En-lai to Tirana on Albania with essential materials has led Tirana to negotiate trade agreements with several non-communist states. Diplomatic rela- several occasions since 1961. China's apparent failure to furnish

tions with England and the United States, broken in 1946, have not been resumed.

Albania, probably the most backward and undeveloped European nation, shares similar living standards with comparable states in Asia and Africa. This unfortunate country could not survive without aid from friendly states. The communist regime apparently disregards this inherent weakness when it boldly engages in verbal duels with other communist governments, and even with neighboring Greece with whom the question of northern Epirus still smolders. The failure of Albania's third five-year plan in 1966 indicated that isolation within Europe was retarding normal economic progress. The "Land of the Eagle" remains the most unknown country in Europe today.

In Bulgaria the death of Dimitrov in 1949 and the brief regime of Vasil Kolarov ushered in the rule of Vulko Chervenkov, Dimitrov's brother-in-law, in January 1950. Chervenkov was a typical Stalinist who dismissed thousands of suspected heretics from the Communist Party. Diplomatic relations with the United States were severed in 1950, and not resumed for a decade, because of espionage charges against American embassy personnel. The peasantry was subjected to hasty, enforced collectivization. The Bulgarian Orthodox Church was made a government bureau.

During the 1950's Bulgaria was completely isolated from Western contacts. Foreign schools were closed, foreign newspapers prohibited, purges of non-Orthodox clergy conducted, and other repressive steps were instituted to sovietize the country. Frontier disputes with Greece and bitter recriminations against Yugoslavia also marked the early 1950's.

When the bloc states followed Moscow's decision to terminate the cult of personality after Stalin's death, Bulgaria announced Chervenkov's abandonment of his post as first party secretary. In May 1953 Todor Zhivkov assumed that post. Growing antagonism against Chervenkov led to his yielding the premiership to Anton Yugov in April 1956. Khrushchev's reconciliation with Tito led to Bulgaria's resumption of relations with Yugoslavia. Chervenkov was denounced as a Stalinist in 1956. Traicho Kostov and others who had been executed for Titoism were posthumously rehabilitated (a practice later imitated in Hungary, Rumania, and Czechoslovakia), but repercussions from the Hungarian revolt in

1956 led to a tightening-up of controls. Chervenkov regained some of his lost power, and new purges of those accused of deviationism were conducted. When the domestic situation appeared normal, Bulgaria instituted new economic plans and introduced educational and administrative reforms.

Diplomatic relations with Greece were resumed in May 1954, but the question of wartime reparations has yet to be resolved. In March 1959 Bulgaria and the United States agreed to restore relations. Since 1955 Bulgaria has been a member of the United Nations and the Warsaw Pact.

In 1961 the regime was reorganized under the leadership of First Party Secretary Zhivkov, a native-trained communist, who enjoyed Khrushchev's confidence and is still in power today. Bulgaria, unlike the other bloc states, has remained the invariably faithful satellite of Soviet Russia. Bulgaria has consistently voted with Soviet Russia in the United Nations. Obedient to Moscow's lead, Bulgaria has sought improved relations with those states befriended by Russia. Trade with communist states still constitutes the vast bulk of Bulgaria's commerce, but recently Sofia has signed agreements with non-communist countries which promise expanded trade. Although relations with the United States remained proper for a while, a setback occurred in 1964 when a Bulgarian diplomat was tried and executed in Sofia on charges of espionage for the Central Intelligence Agency.

In March 1964 Zhivkov became the exclusive leader by removing Premier Anton Yugov from his post. This was in apparent imitation of Khrushchev's achievement in Soviet politics in 1957. Then in 1966 Zhivkov was unanimously elected premier while simultaneously holding the post of first party secretary. He embarked on foreign travels which marked the signing of various trade agreements with non-communist governments. Relations with the United States have improved since 1964 and their respective legations have been elevated to embassies.

Bulgaria's economic plans, executed in several consecutive five-year plans, have resulted in almost total collectivization of agriculture and nationalization of industry and commerce by 1966. Results were frequently disappointing, but this could be attributable to a lack of mineral resources and a determination to stress development of heavy industry at the expense of consumer goods. The discovery in 1963 of petroleum and natural gas deposits has promised new wealth. Nevertheless, Bulgaria, of all the bloc states, still has more than one-half of her trade with Soviet Russia. Perhaps this orientation can be attributed in part to Bulgaria's historical and traditional friendship for Russia.

Rapidly consecutive changes of regimes in the bloc states may perplex the reader, but the communists do not have a monopoly on this. Greece, labelled a democratic monarchy, had ten changes of government between 1947 and 1952. Many cabinets were formed from loose coalitions among the numerous factions that, according to the principle of proportional representation, elected the members of parliament. In 1951 the Greek Rally Party was created by disgruntled members of the Popular (Populist) and Unionist Parties, which had previously merged. The new grouping was led by aged Field Marshal Alexander Papagos; it won the elections in 1951 but refused to join a coalition. Not until November 1952 did the Rally Party win a majority of parliament seats when it then formed a government with Papagos as premier. A new constitution was promulgated during his ministry.

The Papagos regime undertook some economic reforms, but his death in 1955 left the Rally in a weak position. King Paul appointed Constantine Karamanlis, a member of the Papagos regime, to form a new cabinet. He established the National Radical Union in 1956 to replace the Rally, and the new party adopted a pro-Western, anti-communist program. Karamanlis won a questionable election victory, but he was threatened by the Union of the Democratic Left. In 1958 he won a decisive victory while the Union, dominated by radicals, lost seats. The longest premiership in modern Greek history ended in June 1963 when Karamanlis, in office since 1956, resigned over a rift with the monarch. In 1964 the Center Union Party won the national elections, and George Papandreou, its chief, became premier. Greek politics were thus perpetuating the 19th-century pattern of near-anarchy.

Anglo-American reluctance to favor Greek annexation of the island of Cyprus neutralized the anti-communist feelings of many Greeks. This attitude, in addition to Soviet diplomacy, favored the campaign of Papandreou's party which won the elections in February 1964. But the death of King Paul in March 1964 and the accession of his young son Constantine II marked a shift in politics. Latent hostility against Queen Dowager Frederika produced political unrest. This led to the collapse of the Papandreou cabinet in July 1965 after rivalries within his party had prevented any significant actions. Elected premier at age 76, Papandreou was frequently obliged to concentrate his attention on the ambitions of his subordinates, especially his son Andreas, a former economics professor at the University of California and a member of his father's cabinet, who fomented a serious rift within the cabinet. The elder Papandreou secured a parliamentary vote of confidence, but this was vitiated when General Grivas, chief of the Greek national guard on Cyprus, accused Andreas of trying to sap the strength of the Cypriote forces by creating a pro-communist secret society among their officers. The premier attempted to secure dictatorial powers during this crisis, but the young king's hostility led to Papandreou's resignation. At issue was a Papandreou plan to purge the army of reactionary officers. King Constantine opposed a purge because it would allegedly expose the army to communist influences. Papandreou's supporters staged riots in Athens as the king sought to form a new government which could win a parliamentary majority over Papandreou. Constantine won out with the appointment of Stephanos Stephanopoulos as premier in September 1965. Despite parliamentary approval, the new cabinet was confronted with serious pro-Papandreou opposition.

Outbreaks of violence encouraged by radicals continued to plague Greek politics in 1966, culminating in the collapse of the Stephanopoulos regime in December. In April 1967 a pre-election coup by reactionary army officers ousted the interim regime of Panayotis Kanellopoulos of the National Union. The new regime quickly imprisoned hundreds of radicals and anti-monarchists, including George and Andreas Papandreou. King Constantine believed the military junta would soon promulgate a constitution, but it has yet to be prepared. Serious difficulties between Constantine and the junta led to the former's attempt to reassert authority in the fall of 1967 and his subsequent flight to Rome where he was granted political asylum.

Greek political turmoils were also churned by the Cyprus dispute. In 1954 Greece renewed a demand that England transfer Cyprus to her. England rejected this demand. Riots ensued in Athens while the Greek Cypriotes led by Archbishop Makarios pressed for *enosis* (union). In October 1954 Greece succeeded in having the United Nations examine the dispute, and late in 1955 negotiations in London convinced the English to deport the Greek priest from Cyprus in 1956. Greek and Turkish diplomats met in Geneva in 1959 to draft a Cyprus agreement by which the island would not be annexed by either nation. The rights of the Turkish minority would be guaranteed.

In February 1959 England, Greece, Turkey, and Cyprus agreed to establish Cyprus as an independent republic. England would retain sovereignty over two military enclaves. The president would be elected from and by the ethnic Greek Cypriote majority and a vice-president from and by the Turkish Cypriotes. A 70-30% proportion of the Greek and Turkish communities would be represented in a national assembly. Separate Greek and Turkish communal chambers were established to treat religious, educational, and other communal matters. Archbishop Makarios, who was permitted to return, was elected president in December 1959, and Fazil Kutchuk became vice-president. The constitution was approved in April 1960, and England granted independence on August 16, 1960 when Makarios officially assumed the presidency.

But these developments failed to halt the violence between the Greek and Turkish communities. Makarios aroused Turkish hostility when he proposed constitutional changes in December 1963. The United Nations dispatched an international peace-keeping force to the island in March 1964, but the conflict raged after Turkey charged the murder of her people during an allegedly Greek-inspired battle. Turkish planes strafed Greek positions. Both sides agreed to a United Nations truce appeal in August.

In 1965 the Cypriote parliament extended the term of Makarios. He then declared the 1959 treaties of guarantee and alliance to be invalid. Turkey charged that Makarios was preparing for *enosis* with Greece. The Cypriote president countered by imposing an economic blockade on the import of Turkish goods. In 1967 the United States sent a special emissary to mediate the continuing dispute.

Despite constant turmoil since the end of World War II, the international position of Greece has improved. Resentment against Yugoslavia for assistance given to the Greek communists gradually disappeared after Tito broke with the Cominform. Diplomatic relations were restored in November 1950. Greek security was greatly improved when Athens was admitted to NATO in 1952.

In February 1953 a treaty of friendship, cooperation, and mutual defense was signed by Greece, Turkey, and Yugoslavia, but its fate has been jeopardized by the Cyprus dispute. The future of Greece depends upon the character of the harsh military dictatorship, not unusual for this country, imposed on the hapless country by politically inexperienced army officers who have strangled the democratic spirit in the land of its birth.

Rumania, the most populous of the Balkan states (19 million inhabitants), remains the most productive nation in the peninsula. Rumania has become heavily industrialized with all industry presently accounting for more than 55% of the gross national product. Farms and forests contribute 22% of the total product. State farms and cooperatives own 99% of the arable land. Rumania is the only bloc nation in the Balkans to have achieved full collectivization of agriculture.

In June 1952 ailing premier Petru Groza was replaced by deputy premier Gheorghe Gheorghiu-Dej, first party secretary. This change marked the beginning of a trend to identify the Party with the nation and to eliminate Moscow-trained puppets. Purges in May 1952 culminated in the downfall of two Soviet-trained stooges, Ana Pauker and Vasile Luca, and the emergence of Gheorghiu-Dej and his native communist associates. Stalin's death in 1953 encouraged Gheorghiu-Dej to go further. A new constitution established the customary "people's democracy." When Khrushchev decided upon de-Stalinization, Rumania could boast of having undertaken limited liberalization before the Soviet dictator's death. In 1954 Gheorghiu-Dej resigned as first party secretary, a post he had held since 1945, but he regained that post a year later after temporarily yielding the premiership to Chivu Stoica. The regime was reorganized again in 1961, and, as Khrushchev had done in Moscow, Gheorghiu-Dej became president while retaining the top party post. Prior to his death in March 1965 Gheorghiu-Dej had led Rumania into an obvious departure from Moscow-dictated policies. While observing international communist shiftings and the struggles for power in Soviet Russia, he steadily increased Rumania's independence. He built up economic strength by expanding heavy industry, placated Rumanian nationalists by replacing Rumanian for Russian street names, and he conciliated Marshal Tito with whom he planned a hydroelectric plant at their Danube frontier. At the time of his death Rumania was attempting to be the mediator in differences between Moscow and Peking.

Since 1962 Rumania has refused to comply with demands for a division of economic activities among the bloc states dictated by COMECON (Council for Mutual Economic Assistance), an organization created by Moscow in 1949. Bucharest has consistently refused to play a role subordinate to the more heavily industrialized Poland, Czechoslovakia, and East Germany. In May 1962 a top Soviet delegation in Bucharest tried to force Rumania back into line. But that summer Khrushchev yielded to Rumania's insistence, and during the past seven years Rumania has outstripped the other bloc states of the COMECON. To increase her foreign trade Rumania has regularly negotiated agreements with Soviet Russia, but trade with Moscow has consistently declined to the point where it is now hardly more than 35% of the total. West Germany has replaced Soviet Russia as Rumania's leading trade partner.

Khrushchev's removal from power in October 1964 was hardly mentioned in the Rumanian press. By that time Bucharest had already adopted a neutral position in the Sino-Soviet rift. Chinese premier Chou En-lai paid a visit to Rumania the previous summer, but Rumania has continued to urge Peking and Moscow to cease their public polemics. While walking the proverbial tightrope, Rumania has sought closer relations with the West. Numerous trade delegations have negotiated broad agreements with most of the world's developed nations. The achievement accounts for Rumania's phenomenal economic growth, which is currently rising at the fastest rate on earth.

In April 1965, at anniversary ceremonies of the party's 45th birthday, Nicolae Ceausescu, the youngest bloc communist leader who succeeded Gheorghiu-Dej as first secretary, announced Rumania's decision to pursue an independent road toward communism. The Communist Party issued a declaration bluntly insisting upon the complete equality and independence of all communist parties and states, and non-interference in Rumania's industrialization program. This was a risky proclamation of independence from Moscow, but Soviet leaders have not yet taken firm steps to dissuade Rumania from her Titoist path. Not even Ceausescu's assertion that Rumania should recover Bessarabia has aroused public fury in Moscow. Subsequent refusal of Rumania

to attend international communist conferences, convened to denounce Peking, and to participate in Warsaw Pact maneuvers have
indicated the new departure of a formerly obedient Soviet satellite.

Rumania's challenge to Soviet Russia within the bloc has been
primarily national in aim. The Rumanian party has not deviated
from its political and economic goals. Profiting from the prior
success of Titoist Yugoslavia and pro-Peking Albania, Rumania
still subscribes to general Marxist-Leninist dogma and to the need
of constructing an industrial base for her socialist society. Rumania cannot ignore the 800-mile frontier shared with Soviet
Russia. That fact was indelibly realized during the crisis over
Czechoslovakia in the summer of 1968. Rumania's fate is further
confused by traditionally cool relations with Hungary caused by
the smoldering question of Transylvania, and with Bulgaria over
the southern Dobrudja.

Rumania remains securely under the grip of a leadership
which has refused to exhibit any susceptibility to ideological
revisionism. The leaders have been strengthening their own power
while attempting to achieve domestic popularity in the process.
Rumania's habit of taking advantage of crises not of her own
making (such as Rumania's role in World War I) may explain the
cynical exploitation of the Sino-Soviet rift by which Bucharest has
enhanced its own freedom of maneuver in international affairs.
The election of Corneliu Manescu, the foreign minister, as the
first communist president of the United Nations General Assembly
in September 1967, the brief visits to Bucharest of such diverse
world statesmen as Chou En-lai and President Richard M. Nixon
(and a White House welcome for Ion Gheorghe Maurer, the
premier and first communist head of state to enjoy this honor)
attest to Rumania's incredibly successful policies.

Turkey since 1918 has been rightfully assigned to Asia and is,
therefore, no longer considered a Balkan state. Nevertheless, her
possession of Istanbul (Constantinople) and its immediate hinterland at the southeastern tip of the peninsula has enabled the Turks
to participate peripherally in Balkan politics.

When Soviet Russia denounced the 1925 pact of non-aggression
with Turkey in March 1945, the Turks realized that Moscow
would demand the right to participate in defending the Straits.
Turkey resisted Soviet pressure until after Stalin's death, when it

was relaxed. Despite the traditional Russian threat, Turkey has made considerable progress since the war and, for a while at least, enjoyed a multi-party system. The long tenure of President Ismet Inonu and his People's Party had produced corruption and extreme inflation. Celal Bayar, also a supporter of Ataturk, organized the Democratic Party in 1946. It came to power in an electoral landslide in 1950 in the first free elections ever held in Turkey, presaging the advent of democracy.

Turkish efforts to modernize were financed by an American aid program initiated by President Truman in 1947. The Democratic Party doubled agricultural production between 1950 and 1958 and increased industrial output by one-half. Turkey joined NATO in 1951, the Balkan alliance with Greece and Yugoslavia in 1954, and the Central Treaty Organization (CENTO) in the same year. As a staunch supporter of the United Nations, Turkey sent a battalion to fight in Korea.

Gains achieved by Bayar and Adnan Menderes, the premier, were mitigated by the high cost of debt repayment. Anticipating continued American assistance, the Turks acquired tremendous debt burdens which were aggravated by Washington's decision to restrict its aid. Inflation increased, consumer goods vanished, and popular unrest was aroused. The Bayar-Menderes regime resorted to oppressive measures to retain its power. In 1960 student unrest against the regime mushroomed into an army coup which over-threw the government on May 27. Led by General Jemal Gürsel, the army junta placed Bayar, Menderes, and other Democrats on trial. Menderes was executed, and Bayar imprisoned. Gürsel became president of the Second Republic. The military leaders appointed Ismet Inonu premier in November 1961, and a new constitution was promulgated. Although 77 years old, Inonu was still the national hero of the war against the Greeks. He could not, however, institute democratic procedures, and consequently he reverted to his old, rigid bureaucratic control of the economy. Disappointments over Cyprus increased discontent, and in 1965 Inonu was forced out.

The Justice Party took office on a program to stimulate industry and to seek a rapprochment with Soviet Russia. In 1966 President Gürsel, incapacitated by a cerebral hemorrhage, was succeeded by General Cevdet Sunay. Since its inception the Second Republic has been preoccupied with the Cyprus dispute. Turkey's opposition to *enosis* was bolstered by the visit of Soviet premier Alexei Kosygin to Ankara in December 1966. In recent years Turkey has concluded trade agreements with the bloc states. This swing from a pro-American orientation apparently hinged upon the Cyprus dispute. Turkey is working to establish an independent diplomatic position based on a vision of herself as the bridge between East and West and between Europe and the Middle East.

Yugoslavia's defection from the communist bloc was probably the most significant development in the Balkans since the end of the war. This event, carried out by the strongest Communist Party in the peninsula, marked the break-up of the Soviet empire in East Europe. With the exception of Albania, the Yugoslav communists had achieved the liberation of their country without any appreciable Soviet assistance. Tito and his Partisans were filled with exuberant self-confidence and pride in this accomplishment. The Tito-Stalin rift was based primarily upon the issue of a communist state pursuing its own road to socialism. This road was a marked departure from the Soviet experience. To indicate his resolutely independent route, Tito created workers' councils in 1950 to operate each factory. This measure provided an incentive for industrial workers and produced a competitive spirit between factories. Collectivization of agriculture was abandoned in 1953, and peasants were permitted to withdraw from the system. Decentralization of the government and other liberalization reforms increased Tito's popularity vis-à-vis Soviet Russia.

The deterioration of Yugoslavia's relations with the bloc states resulted in an almost immediate improvement of strained relations with the West. Tito concluded trade treaties with several West European governments, received grains from the United States when threatened with famine, and in 1951 signed a military assistance treaty with Washington. Relations improved with Greece and led to the signing of a defense pact in 1954. Relations with Italy were greatly improved by the solution to the Trieste question in 1954. Despite remaining a socialist country, Yugoslavia came to depend upon the West for economic assistance and military equipment.

Further changes in Yugoslavia's position came about as a result of Stalin's death in 1953. The break with the Cominform had been absolute, and the economic blockade by the bloc states had ended trade, credits, and vital industrial imports from Soviet Russia. The joint Soviet-Yugoslav companies had been dissolved. Tito's security was menaced for about four years. His defection had produced upheavals in the bloc states where accusations of Titoism were as serious as those of Trotskyism had been in Soviet Russia in the 1930's. Many communist leaders in the bloc states vanished as a consequence of charges of Titoism which were levelled against undesirable politicians by those who held absolute power.

Stalin's death was second only to Tito's defection in effectuating changes in the bloc. A rapprochement with Moscow was initiated by Khrushchev who visited Belgrade in 1955 to endorse a joint declaration condemning "all attempts to subject other countries to political and economic domination." Both communist leaders agreed to respect the sovereignty, independence, integrity, and equality of states and affirmed that questions of different forms of socialist development were the exclusive concern of individual countries. This incredible departure by Stalin's successor indicated that he had become a Titoist!

The 20th Party Congress in Moscow heard Khrushchev denounce Stalin in February 1956, and it adopted the Titoist principle of different roads to socialism. Not only was Tito vindicated by these developments, but Khrushchev's dissolution of the Cominform in April 1956 furnished more evidence of the impact of Tito's defection upon the bloc. The Yugoslavs acquired even greater self-confidence and prestige. The repudiation of Stalinism and Tito's successful resistance to pressures produced upheavals in the bloc states, and especially in Poland and Hungary. Led by Wladyslaw Gomulka, a Polish communist imprisoned at Stalin's orders years earlier, Poland broke away from tight Soviet controls despite the presence of Red Army troops on her soil. In Hungary, however, the removal of the Stalinist Rakosi was not enough. Moves toward independence from Soviet Russia led to disaster. The Hungarian revolution in October 1956 was severely suppressed by the Red Army, and the Titoist premier, Imre Nagy, was executed. This uprising ended the brief era of Tito's influence on Soviet policy. An escalation of the Hungarian revolution menaced the entire bloc, including Yugoslavia. Tito has been a rebel, but only when he controls the rebellion.

A long-range significance of Titoism lies in its example to other communist states of Yugoslavia's defiance of Soviet pressure and her development of a peculiarly nationalistic form of communism. Titoism has changed party controls from direct to indirect methods without yielding fundamental power to determine policies. In Yugoslavia two steps in this direction have been a revision of party rules in 1952 and 1964, and the adoption of a new state constitution in 1963. The latter document has successfully implemented Tito's federalism and has apparently ended the old internecine quarrels between Serbs and Croats. Decentralization of the economy also reveals the Titoist influence. The former centrally-planned economy has given way to market-influenced demands. The workers' councils have apparently succeeded in stimulating production. One should not assume that Tito, who has been in power longer than any other communist in Europe (with the possible exception of Enver Hoxha), has decided to loosen the reins of his authority. The 1963 constitution, which changed the country's name to the "Socialist Federal Republic of Yugoslavia," still limits political parties to the Communists and the communist-dominated Socialist Alliance of Working People, and provides that future presidents be elected by the parliament and restricted to two consecutive four-year terms. A new office of vice president has been created. Tito was reelected for four more years in May 1967 while simultaneously holding his powerful post of general party secretary. He ousted Vice President Alexander Rankovich, his heir apparent, in 1966 after a hidden microphone was found in Tito's home. Rankovich had been in charge of the secret police. Writer Mihajlo Mihajlov was imprisoned for publishing his books abroad. This denial of free speech was merely an additional indication of Tito's dictatorship, revealed earlier by his imprisonment of Milovan Djilas, author of *The New Class,* once a close Partisan associate, who had criticized the regime.

Despite continued rapport with Soviet Russia, Yugoslavia has never returned to the Soviet camp. Tito has, instead, been performing a delicate tightrope-walk between the two worlds. Although linked ideologically to the socialist camp, Yugoslavia does not wish to lose American military and technical assistance. To bolster his balancing act, Tito has joined with other neutral states to form "the third world." He has cooperated with Egypt, India, and Indonesia in appealing to the unattached Afro-Asian nations. No communist leader has traveled as widely and as often as

Marshal Tito in his efforts to mold the non-aligned nations into a cohesive force which can function independently of the great powers.

Yugoslavia, after a quarter-century of Titoist rule, has achieved much. Almost one-half of the economy is now devoted to industry. The majority of the peasants are independent holders tilling their own soil. Despite a large foreign debt, Yugoslavia in 1966 was in a better economic position than at any time in the pre-war years. But most significant has been Tito's triumph against efforts to unseat him. His strong government, regional autonomy, and his federalist policies have diminished the pre-war tensions between Serbs and Croats which once ravaged the country. A testing of Yugoslavia's national unity, which is probably Tito's greatest achievement, will come when Tito inevitably yields to a successor.

Conclusion

By René Ristelhueber

SITUATED at the juncture of the European and Asian continents, with the Dardanelles and the Bosporus as hinges, the
Balkan peninsula, by this exclusive fact, occupies a truly exceptional position: it forms a bridge extending towards Asia. This importance is still more enhanced by the location of the Black
Sea beyond the Straits which makes the latter a key to the passage
in whose depths Russia, Rumania, and Bulgaria are enclosed.
The mouths of the most international of rivers, the Danube, the
waterway of the products of Central and Eastern Europe, are
located on the same sea. Thus, freedom of the Straits and navigation on the Danube are related questions.

Geographically a meeting-place between Asians and Europeans,
the peninsula was destined to become the theater of their struggles.
Ambition to carry their authority to the neighboring continent
pushed the former to penetrate into the Balkans and the latter
to escape from them in quest of adventure. The incursions of both
alternated like a tidal movement. It was at Marathon and Thermopylae that the Greeks stopped Darius and Xerxes in their
attempt to impose Persia's yoke on Greece. Conversely, it was from
Macedonia that Alexander the Great leaped forward to the conquest of Asia. After bringing the Balkans into submission, Rome
seized Asia Minor and Syria, which later became the prizes of the
Byzantine Empire. Then came a new Asian push. The Arab incursions dislodged the armies of the *Basileus* and menaced the
walls of Constantinople. Hardly had the danger been averted
and the lost territories recovered when, from the plateaus of central
Asia, arose new conquerors, the Turks. Asia Minor and the
Balkans fell into their hands. There remained Byzantium, which
crumbled. An irresistible forward advance brought Suleiman's
soldiers to Vienna, the very heart of Christendom.

After having submerged part of Europe and placing the conquered nations in servitude, the Ottoman invasion began to recede.

For the Balkan peoples the moment came to seek liberation. But the strong hostility which divided them since ancient times prevented unity and a common effort. They preferred to invite foreign powers to aid them, powers which were happy to find in the region accommodations profitable to their interests.

Great-power rivalries created by the decline of the Ottoman Empire produced opposition between states having common frontiers. German Austria was the eastern march of Europe, and Slav Russia the prolongation of Asia. Their antagonism perpetuated the ancient struggle of the West against the East.

"When the Greek empire disappeared," the French historian Lavisse wrote, "the tsar found himself at the same time the inheritor of the Greek schism and the representative of Eastern Christendom opposed by the infidels; hence, by a double claim, he was the successor to the Byzantine emperor. A great future was opened before him." But the ambitious prospects offered to the Romanovs crossed the traditional ambitions of the Hapsburgs. For a long time the two dynasties confronted each other in this struggle until the direction of the German world passed from Vienna to Berlin. To a policy of resistance to Slav expansion were added the aims of an economic and military order which aggravated the conflict. From the inevitable clash between the two imperialisms came the spark which ignited Europe in 1914.

A quarter-century later, provoked by the eternal Polish question, the Second World War began as a resumption of the ancient conflict between Germans and Slavs. Their first victories permitted the Germans to dominate the entire Balkans for three long years. Russian influence there had been turned aside. But when the Nazi troops hastily evacuated the peninsula, the Red Army entrenched itself in the gaping vacuum which had been opened by Germany's collapse. Solidly reconstructed on a new base, the young Russian force encountered no resistance whatever. Once the German dike constructed so long ago to contain the Slav flood had been beaten down, this flood moved without any obstacles since the breaking of the equilibrium had permitted its passage.

The Russians had everything their own way. To secure from them a maximum effort in a war whose outcome still appeared uncertain, the Anglo-Americans not only furnished them with abundant materials, but, absorbed by other pressing concerns, voluntarily closed their eyes to the consequences of an exclusive

Soviet victory in the peninsula. Moscow did everything to re-assure them. The Communist International was dissolved. Molotov stigmatized Germany for having had no consideration for the will of little nations. Stalin went further by opposing to a program of vengeful hate one of equality of nations free to choose their own regimes. Not everyone was deceived by these assurances. Former foreign minister George Gafencu of Rumania noted in 1944 that the USSR was already "an implacable giant surrounded by silence" who would soon devour the region as far as Trieste, Prague, and Salonika. He correctly predicted that Soviet hegemony would prevail over the vast territory relinquished by the retreating Nazis.

Assuming for himself the historic role of the tsars, Stalin succeeded even more than his predecessors in realizing the most ambitious dreams of Peter the Great and Nicholas I. If Stalin had succeeded in gaining control of the Straits, the ancient ambitions of tsarist policy would have found their culmination. The Krem-lin's moves followed in a line of purest Russian traditions. Con-cerning the methods employed by the Romanovs in the Balkans during the 19th century, French historian Emile Bourgeois wrote in 1915 that in Romanov eyes "the only true Slavs were those who accepted Russian domination." "There as elsewhere," he added, "the supposed awakening of the peoples presaged a crusade whose object was conquest and whose means were force and intrigue." These statements were still valid in the post-war years when Moscow recognized as worthy of the quality of communist only those who were docile to its orders.

Furthermore, Stalin never missed an opportunity to use the methods of Tsarist Russia to attain the same results. As St. Peters-burg did earlier, Moscow insisted upon using the Orthodox Church to attain its ambitions. By the church's intercessions the Kremlin succeeded in reestablishing ancient bonds with the peoples of eastern Europe and the Asiatic Middle East. Of equal significance is the fact that Soviet Russia became the home of a new religion. That this new faith is materialistic exerted all the more attraction. Dangling immediate satisfaction before the eyes of the masses, the faith addressed itself to everyone without discrimination. And it must be recognized that strong communist convictions arouse people to the same enthusiasm and sacrifices as religious faith. As once the soldiers of Mohammed were made fanatical by Islam and followed the green standards of the Prophet across three continents, the Soviet armies, animated by a proselytism quite as vigorous, pushed the conquests of the red flag from the Pacific Ocean to the Elbe River. Possessing, as they insist, the monopoly on true democracy, these soldiers claimed the title of "liberators."

Analogies other than the exploitation of an ideology for political ends can be adduced. At the beginning of the 19th century, Capo d'Istria, the Greek adviser to Tsar Alexander I, presided over the destinies of a resurgent Greece while other Greeks, the Ypsilanti brothers, served in the Russian army and tried to incite an uprising in the Danubian Principalities. And just recently the Croat Tito, the Bulgarian Dimitrov, the Rumanian Pauker—all trained in the Moscow school—were the masters at Belgrade, Sofia, and Bucharest where, to the profit of Russian influence, they applied the communist doctrines which it was their mission to propagate.

Would it be unjustifiable to advance the idea that Soviet Russia occupied the place of the former Ottoman Empire in the Balkans? Between the two dominations, the peoples of the peninsula, except the Greeks, have hardly known anything but a respite of about sixty years in which they controlled their own destinies. Pushing its domination into Central Europe much further than the sultans, Soviet-controlled territory in the Balkans remained, it is true, somewhat less than that of the former Turkish Empire. But administratively the authority of the Kremlin was much more rigorous and exacting. Whereas the Ottoman Empire was characterized by a nonchalance bordering on carelessness and by extensive freedom left to local governors, that of Soviet Russia, on the contrary, was strongly centralized in the hands of a meticulous, tyrannical bureaucracy which implacably watched over its implementation. Tito's disgrace indicated the degree of obedience demanded by Moscow.

Furthermore, the Turks did not convert the conquered peoples by force; they were content to scorn them while frequently brutalizing them. It was quite different for Soviet Russia. She imposed the Soviet faith on countries occupied by the Red Army. To attain her ends, Russia did not always use force because she had at her disposal an infinity of resources to render life impossible for those who were tempted to adopt creeds other than communism.

Inspired by the United States, the free world has strived to consolidate the resistance of Greece, the cradle of democracy,

and that of Turkey, who still possesses the "key to the world."
These are the barriers which in the first years of the post-war
era contained Soviet expansionism to prevent it from spreading
into the Mediterranean on whose shores Western Civilization was
born. To say the least, it is curious to find Turkey among today's
defenders of that civilization of which she was for such a long
time the adversary.

Its geographic location, lack of cohesion among its states, and
old rivalries among the great powers mark the Balkan peninsula
as one of the principal theaters of the debate which divides hu-
manity. At the present time it is no longer a question of hostility
among peoples, or even between continents, but instead a conflict
between two parts of the world which confront each other from
Peking to Berlin, the West and the East, champions of opposing
ideologies of which the Balkans were once the stakes.

Conclusion

By Sherman D. Spector

THE major theme which predominates in this historical survey is that of the force of nationalism whose rampant manifestations have been aggravated by the interference of greater powers in Balkan affairs. When nationalism produced the greater powers of Europe, in a period spanning about four centuries, that force was acclaimed as the rightful expression of an innate right to independence. But when the force came to be applied to the Balkans, it was called "Balkanization." If granting freedom to little peoples struggling for it means their Balkanization, then the term should not be an opprobrium. In the pages of this book the small and medium-sized nations regained their freedom, which they had earlier possessed, but of which they had been deprived by the Ottoman Turks, the Nazi Germans, and Soviet-inspired Communists. As a consequence of nationalist efforts the Balkan peoples achieved by 1918 liberation from hostile and undemocratic domination in a process labelled "Balkanization"; why should these peoples be denied the force already employed by their neighbors in western, central, and eastern Europe? The small nations were regarded with suspicion as if by their insistence on their sacred sovereignty they made international affairs more complex. Indeed, the Balkan peoples have been indiscriminately accused of being international troublemakers. But this survey should smash that myth. Since 1800 there have been about eight wars in the peninsula. Of these only two were local—between the Serbs and Bulgarians. The other six were contests waged among the great powers over the Balkans ruled by the Turks in which the Balkan peoples were militarily involved. The term "Balkanization" should convey the sense of a lack of some form of international or even regional organization which could guarantee peace in the peninsula. If specific areas of the Balkans, especially those still inhabited by mixed populations, are still considered by the great powers as irredenta or routes of expansion, perpetual disorder will remain.

Our survey has shown that the little peoples rarely entered into conflict without great-power machinations. The establishment of great-power spheres of influence, which still prevails, has produced the major wars in history. The small nations are then placed in the unfortunate situation of becoming the arenas for warfare whose fateful consequences leave undying scars. As the communist-controlled nations emerge from under Moscow's yoke, will they again become the pawns of the great powers? If so, then perhaps the Balkan peoples would have been better off under a single, alien domination. The future should tell us whether the Balkan nations can live in peace and harmony in that troubled peninsula; one assurance which will promote peace will be the adoption of a policy of disinterestedness by the great powers.

CHRONOLOGICAL TABLE

THE GREEKS	THE BULGARIANS	THE SERBS	THE RUMANIANS	THE TURKS
486 B.C. Victory of Salamis.			150 B.C. The Romans seek an alliance with the Dacians.	
146 B. C. Roman conquest.			101 A.D. 1st expedition of Trajan against the Dacians. 271 Evacuation of Dacia by Roman legions.	
330 A.D. Founding of Constantinople. 395 Birth of the Eastern Empire. 529 Closing of the University of Athens.				
	679 Asparuk crosses the Danube. 813 Krum besieges Constantinople.	540 The Slavs are scattered to the north of the Balkans. 830 Voislav becomes great zhupan.		
863 Schism of Photius.	864 Boris is converted to Christianity.	879 Conversion to Christianity.		
	921 Simeon the Great proclaimed tsar. 963 Revolt of Shishman. 977-1014 Reign of Samuel.		1003 Arrival of the Hungarians in Transylvania.	
	1018 Byzantium conquers Bulgaria. End of the 1st Bulgarian Empire.	1040 Stephen Voislav fights the Greeks.		
1071 Defeat of the Byzantines by the Turks at Manzikert.				

THE GREEKS	THE BULGARIANS	THE SERBS	THE RUMANIANS		THE TURKS
			THE WALLACH-IANS	THE MOLDAVIANS	
		1171-1196 Reign of Stephen Nemanya, founder of the Serbian dynasty.			
	1186 Revolt of the Asen brothers at Tirnovo. John Asen tsar of the Bulgarians.				
		1196-1228 Reign of Stephen the Great.			
1204 Seizure of Constantinople by the Crusaders.	1205 Victory of Kaloyan over the Crusaders. 1218-1241 Reign of John Asen II.		1241 Invasion of the Tartars.		
	1257 End of the 2nd Bulgarian Empire.				
1261 Fall of the Latin Empire of the East.					1300 Osman I takes title of Sultan.
			1290 Radu Negru arrives from Transylvania according to legend. 1330 Basarab frees the Wallachian state from the Hungarian yoke.		
	1330 Defeat of the Bulgarians by the Serbs at Kustendil.	1334-1355 Dushan the Great. Height of the Serbian Empire.			1356 The Turks cross the Hellespont.
				1359 Bogdan declares himself independent.	1361 Adrianople becomes Turkish capital.
		1367 Death of Stephen Urosh V. End of the Nemanya dynasty. 1371 Election of Lazar.			
	1382 The Turks reach Sofia.		1386-1418 Mircea the Great	1387 Moldavia vassal of Poland.	
		1389 Defeat of the Serbs by the Turks at Kossovo.			1389 Victory of Kossovo over the Serbs.
	1392 The Turks at Tirnovo. 1396 End of Bulgarian independence.				1402 Defeat of Bayezid by Tamerlane.
			1417 Mircea vassal of the Sultan.		

| | | | THE RUMANIANS | | |
THE GREEKS	THE BULGARIANS	THE SERBS	THE WALLACHIANS	THE MOLDAVIANS	THE TURKS
1428 Byzantium reconquers the Peloponnesus. 1453 Capture of Constantinople by the Turks.					1444 Turkish victory at Varna over the Hungarians and Poles. 1453 Capture of Constantinople.
				1457-1504 Reign of Stephen the Great.	
		1459 Fall of Semendria, last Serbian fortress.			
1460 The Peloponnesus conquered by the Turks.				1492 Moldavia a vassal of the Sultan.	
					1517 Selim I becomes caliph. 1520-1566 Suleiman the Magnificent. 1529 1st siege of Vienna. 1535 Signing of Capitulations with Francis I. 1571 Defeat of Turkish navy at Lepanto.
			1593-1601 Reign of Michael the Brave. Height of Wallachia.		
1669 The Turks push the Venetians from Crete.					1683 Defeat of the 2nd siege of Vienna. 1699 Treaty of Karlowitz.
				1711 Signing of alliance with Peter the Great. 1st appearance of Russians in Moldavia. Government of the Phanariots.	
			1716 Government of the Phanariots.		

[419]

CHRONOLOGICAL TABLE: THE STRUGGLES FOR INDEPENDENCE

GREECE	SERBIA	RUMANIA	BULGARIA
			1762 Paissy writes in Bulgarian a history of the Bulgarian people.
		1770 Catherine II occupies Moldavia. 1774 Treaty of Kuchuk Kainarji. 1775 Austria is ceded the Bukovina.	
	1787 Some Serbs join the Russians to fight Turkey.		
		1792 Treaty of Jassy. Russia becomes the neighbor of Moldavia.	
	1804 Revolt of the Janissaries at Belgrade. 1806 Kara George and his partisans fight the Turks at Michar.		
		1812 Treaty of Bucharest. Russia is ceded Bessarabia.	
1814 Founding of the *Hetairia Philiké* at Odessa.	1815 Insurrection led by Milosh Obrenovich. Turkey recognizes Serbia as an autochtonous state.		
1820 Turkish expedition against Ali Pasha at Janina. 1821 Mgr. Germanos of Patras at the head of the insurgents. 1822 Assembly at Epidauros proclaims independence. 1825 Conferences at St. Petersburg. 1826 Ibrahim Pasha lands Egyptians in the Pelopon-		1821 Alexander Ypsilanti tries to liberate Moldavia and Wallachia. End of the Phanariot regime. 1826 Convention of Akkerman assures to Russia a privileged position in the	

[420]

1826 Ultimatum of Nicholas I to Turkey. Protocol issued by England and Russia at St. Petersburg. Convention of Akkerman.
1827 Missolonghi and Athens regained by the Turks. Treaty of London in favor of the Greeks. Naval battle at Navarino.
1828 Nicholas I declares war on Turkey.
1829 Treaty of Adrianople.

1830 Protocol recognizing Greek independence.
1832 Prince Otto of Bavaria becomes king of Greece.

1850 The Don Pacifico Affair.

1854 Blockade of Piraeus by England and France during the Crimean War.

1830 Firman recognizes hereditary succession in Obrenovich family.

1839 Abdication of Milosh Obrenovich; short reign of Milan.
1842 Return of Alexander Karageorgevich.
1848 Some Serbs join the struggle against the Hungarians.

1852 Secularization of power in Montenegro.

1856 Treaty of Paris. Serbian autonomy guaranteed by the Powers.

1828 New Russian occupation during war with Turkey.
1829 Treaty of Adrianople increasing Russian influence.

1832 1st teaching of French in a Bucharest college.

1856 Treaty of Paris substitutes the guarantee of the Powers for that of Russia.
1857 Voters pronounce in favor of the union of the Principalities.

1835 Aprilov opens at Gabrovo the 1st Bulgarian school.
1839 1st printing press using Bulgarian letters.

1851 Peasant unrest at Vidin encouraged by Russia.

GREECE	SERBIA	RUMANIA	BULGARIA
	1858 Victory of the Montenegrins over the Turks at Grahovo. 1858 Abdication of Alexander Karageorgevich. 1859 Return of Milosh Obrenovich, his death, succession of his son Michael.	1858 Conference of Paris decides to maintain separation. 1859 Alexander Cuza is elected by the two Principalities.	
1862 Abdication of King Othon (Otto). 1863 George of Denmark becomes king of Greece. 1864 England cedes the Ionian Islands. 1864 New Constitution. 1866 Revolt in Crete.	1862 Conflict in Belgrade. The Turkish fortress bombards the city. 1863 Army of Omer Pasha crushes the Montenegrin revolt. 1867 Turkish garrisons evacuate Serbia. 1868 Assassination of Michael. Succession of his nephew Milan. 1875 Insurrection in Bosnia-Herzegovina. Armed intervention of the Serbs on the side of the insurgents.	1864 Agrarian reform. 1866 *Coup d'état* forces Cuza to abdicate. Prince Charles arrives in Bucharest.	1870 Creation of the Bulgarian Exarchate. 1873 The patriotic agitator Levski is hanged. 1876 Violent repression by the Turks of the Bulgarian insurrection.

1877 Russia declares war on Turkey. Capitulation of Osman Pasha at Plevna.

1878 Treaty of San Stefano creates a big Bulgaria. Congress of Berlin dismembers Bulgaria.

1879 Constitution of Tirnovo.

1881 Alexander of Battenberg elected prince of Bulgaria.

1885 Eastern Rumelia proclaims union with Bulgaria. The Bulgarians are victorious over the Serbs at Slivnitza.

1886 Peace of Bucharest between Bulgarians and Serbs. Abdication of Prince Alexander.
1887 Election of Ferdinand of Saxe-Coburg.
1894 Ferdinand separates himself from Stambulov.
1895 Reconciliation with Russia.
1908 Ferdinand proclaims Bulgaria independent and assumes title of "Tsar of the Bulgarians."

1877 Treaty of alliance between Rumania and Russia. King Carol proclaims his independence and declares war on Turkey.

1878 The Treaty of Berlin recognizes Rumanian independence, but requires the cession of southern Bessarabia to Russia.

1881 Rumania becomes a kingdom.

1877 The Serbs, beaten by the Turks, seek an armistice.

1878 The Serbs re-enter the war and take Nish and Pirot.

1878 The Treaty of Berlin recognizes the independence of Serbia and Montenegro.

1882 Serbia becomes a kingdom.

1881 Rectification of the frontier in Thessaly to the benefit of Greece.

Chronology 1883-1967

I. Period from 1883 to 1908

1883   Secret treaty of alliance signed by King Carol I of Rumania with Austria.

1889   Voyage of Emperor William II to Constantinople.
Troubles in Crete.
Abdication of King Milan of Serbia.

1890   Grant of *firmans* to the Bulgarian bishops at Okhrida and Uskub.

1893   *Coup d'état* of King Alexander of Serbia.
Creation of the I.M.R.O. (Internal Macedonian Revolutionary Organization).

1895   July. Murder of Stambulov.

1896   22 August. The Sultan decides on reforms in Macedonia.

1897   January. Aggravation of troubles in Crete; massacres at Canea.
April. Austro-Russian agreement on the Balkans.
April. Greco-Turkish War.
December. Statute of autonomy accorded to Crete.

1898   Creation of the Greek Commission on Finances.

1903   April. Aggravation of agitation in Macedonia; bombs thrown in Salonika.
10 June. Murder of Alexander Obrenovich and Queen Draga at Belgrade.
Accession of King Peter I Karageorgevich.
29 September. Austro-Russian agreement at Mürzsteg regarding Macedonia.

1905   2 October. First Congress of South Slavs at Fiume.

1907   Peasant Revolt in Rumania.

1908   The Agram Trial.

II. The Young Turk Revolution and the Balkan Wars

1908   23 July. Beginning of Young Turk insurrection at Salonika.

5 October. Austria annexes Bosnia-Herzegovina.

5 October. Ferdinand proclaims himself tsar of independent Bulgaria.

12 October. Crete proclaims union with Greece.

1909   13 April. Sultan Abdul Hamid attempts a counter-revolution.

25 April. Deposition of Abdul Hamid. Accession of Mohammed V.

1910   April. Insurrection in Albania.

1911   28 September. Italy declares war on Turkey.

1912   13 March. Serbo-Bulgarian alliance.

29 May. Greco-Bulgarian mutual treaty of assistance.

1 October. Mobilization of the Balkan armies.

8 October. Montenegro declares war on Turkey.

17 October. Turkey declares war on Bulgaria and Serbia.

18 October. Treaty of Lausanne ending Italo-Turkish War.

22 October. Bulgarian victory at Kir-Kilissé.

24 October. Serbian victory at Kumanovo.

5 November. Bulgarians stopped before the lines at Chatalja.

8 November. Entry of Greeks into Salonika.

3 December. Armistice.

13 December. Conference at London.

1913   23 January. *Coup d'état* in Constantinople.

5 March. Capitulation of Janina.

26 March. Capitulation of Adrianople.

22 April. Capitulation of Scutari.

30 May. Preliminaries of peace at London.

28 June. Surprise attack by Bulgarian army against Serbs and Greeks.

13 July. Rumanian army crosses the Danube.

31 July. Bulgaria seeks an armistice.

10 August. Treaty of Bucharest.

III. The War of 1914-1918

1914   28 June. The Assassination at Sarajevo.

23 July. Austrian ultimatum to Serbia.

2 August. Secret Turco-German treaty of alliance.

10 August. Arrival of the *Goeben* and *Breslau* at Constantinople.

12 August. The Austrians invade Serbia.

10 October. Death of King Carol I of Rumania. Accession of Ferdinand.

31 October. The Allied ambassadors leave Constantinople.

9 December. Serbian victory over the Austrians at Rudnik.

1915   19 February. Naval attack on the Dardanelles.

18 March. Failure of the attack.

25 April. Debarkation of the Allies at Gallipoli.

26 April. Treaty of London with Italy.

October. First debarkation of Allied troops at Salonika.

12 October. Bulgaria joins the Central Powers.

1916   7 January. End of the retreat of Allied forces at Dardanelles.

17 August. Treaty of alliance with Rumania. Rumania declares war on Austria.

September. Offensive of Sarrail's army. Capture of Monastir.

1 December. Ambush at Athens.

6 December. Entry of German troops into Bucharest.

1917   12 June. Jonnart demands the departure of King Constantine from Greece.

20 July. Declaration at Corfu regarding the union of the South Slavs.

5 December. Rumania seeks an armistice.

1918   6 February. Bessarabia proclaims her independence from Russia.

7 May. Treaty of Bucharest imposed on Rumania.

17 August. Congress at Laibach.

15 September. Offensive of the Army of the Orient begins.

28 September.   Armistice with Bulgaria signed.

3 October.   Abdication of Ferdinand of Bulgaria.

17 October.   Congress at Agram.

30 October.   Armistice with Turkey signed at Mudros.

10 November.   Creation of a Rumanian national council in Transylvania.

12 November.   Montenegro votes for union with Serbia.

1 December.   The national assembly at Alba Iulia votes for the union of Transylvania with Rumania.

10 December.   Bessarabia decides on union with Rumania.

16 December.   The agrarian law in Rumania.

IV. The War Settlement and the Period between the Wars 1919-1939

1919   15 May.   Entry of the Greeks into Smyrna.

23 July.   A Turkish national congress at Erzerum decides to resist the Allies.

27 November.   Treaty of Neuilly signed with Bulgaria.

1920   28 January.   The Parliament of Constantinople votes the "National Pact."

16 March.   The British occupy Constantinople.

23 March.   Elections in Bulgaria. Dictatorship of Stambulisky.

23 April.   Meeting of the National Assembly at Ankara.

4 August.   Treaty of alliance between Yugoslavia and Czechoslovakia.

10 August.   Treaty of Sèvres signed with Turkey.

25 October.   Death of King Alexander of Greece.

14 November.   Elections in Greece. Departure of Venizelos.

5 December.   Plebiscite in favor of restoration of King Constantine of Greece.

1921   16 March.   Russo-Turkish treaty of friendship.

29 April.   Treaty between Rumania and Czechoslovakia.

7 June.   Treaty of alliance between Rumania and Yugoslavia.

27 August.   The Greek offensive in Asia Minor is halted on the Sakharya River.

20 October. Franco-Turkish agreement on the evacuation of Cilicia.

1922   26 August. The Turks defeat the Greeks on the Sakharya River.
24 September. Second abdication of King Constantine of Greece.
11 October. Armistice signed at Mudania.
1 November. Abolition of the sultanate.
November. Conference opens at Lausanne to revise the Treaty of Sèvres.

1923   9 June. Fall of Stambulisky.
Convention on exchange of populations between Greece and Turkey.
24 July. Treaty of Lausanne signed with Turkey.
31 August. Bombardment of Corfu by the Italians.
29 October. Proclamation of the Turkish Republic.
15 December. Departure of King George II of Greece.

1924   3 March. Abolition of the caliphate; secularization of the Turkish state.
25 March. Proclamation of the Republic of Greece.
29 September. Convention on the exchange of populations between Greece and Bulgaria.

1925   1 February. Ahmed Zogu becomes president of Albania.
14 April. Attempted assassination of King Boris of Bulgaria.
16 April. Plot in the Church of St. Nedelia in Sofia.

1926   4 January. Crown Prince Carol of Rumania renounces the throne.
October. Founding of the National Peasant Party of Rumania.
27 November. Italo-Albanian treaty.

1927   Revolutionary activity in Bulgaria.
11 November. Franco-Yugoslav treaty of friendship.
22 November. Italo-Albanian treaty of alliance.

1928   20 June. Acts of violence in the Belgrade Parliament.
1 September. Accession of King Zog I of Albania.

1929   6 January. King Alexander of Serbia suspends the constitution.
          May. Venizelos regains power.
1930   6 June. Return of King Carol II to Rumania.
1931   New Yugoslav constitution.
1932   Admission of Turkey to the League of Nations.
1933   December. Assassination of Rumanian premier Duca by members of the Iron Guard.
1934   9 February. Creation of the Balkan Entente. King Boris suspends the Bulgarian constitution.
          9 October. Assassination of King Alexander of Serbia at Marseilles.
1935   3 November. Restoration of the monarchy in Greece; return of King George II.
1936   24 July. Convention of Montreux regarding the Straits.
1937   24 January. Treaty of "eternal friendship" between Yugoslavia and Bulgaria.
          25 March. Italo-Yugoslav treaty.
1938   February. New Rumanian constitution; dictatorship of King Carol.
          King Boris restores the Bulgarian constitution.
          31 July. The Balkan Entente accords freedom of armaments to Bulgaria.
          30 September. The Munich Conference.
          25 October. German-Yugoslav commercial agreement.
          10 November. Death of Mustapha Kemal Ataturk.
          30 November. Death of the leader of the Iron Guard, Codreanu.
1939   4 January. The Regent of Yugoslavia breaks with Stoyadinovich.
          22 March. German-Rumanian economic agreement.
          8 April. Italy occupies Albania.
          13 April. France and Britain offer guarantees to Greece and Rumania.
          12 May. Pact of assistance between Britain and Turkey; France adheres to this pact.
          20 August. Granting of autonomy to Croatia.
          23 August. Signing of the Pact of Non-Aggression by Molotov and Ribbentrop.

V. The War of 1939-1945

1940   26 June. Russian ultimatum to Rumania demanding the cession of Bessarabia.

29 August. The Vienna Arbitration obliges Rumania to cede part of Transylvania.

6 September. Cession of the southern Dobrudja to Bulgaria. Departure of King Carol II; accession of King Michael V.

8 October. Entry of German troops into Rumania.

28 October. Italian ultimatum to Greece.

23 November. Rumania signs the Tripartite Pact.

1941   1 March. Bulgaria signs the Tripartite Pact.

25 March. Yugoslavia signs the Tripartite Pact.

6 April. Bombardment of Belgrade by the Germans.

27 April. Entry of Germans into Athens.

22 June. The Germans invade the Soviet Union.

1942   5 June. The United States declares war on Rumania and Bulgaria.

1943   May. Britain sends liaison officers to Tito.

28 August. Death of King Boris of Bulgaria.

November-December. The Teheran Conference.

1944   April. Mutiny of Greek sailors at Alexandria.

23 August. *Coup d'état* in Rumania. King Michael arrests General Antonescu. Cessation of hostilities against the Russians who enter Rumania.

5 September. The U.S.S.R. declares war on Bulgaria.

18 October. Return of Greek government to Athens.

20 October. Entry of Russian troops into Belgrade.

VI. The Postwar Era in the Balkans

1944   25 December. Churchill arrives in Athens.

1945   February. The Yalta Conference.

23 February. Turkey declares war on Germany and Japan.

6 March. Vyshinsky forces the Groza cabinet on King Michael of Rumania.

19 March. The U.S.S.R. denounces the pact of non-aggression with Turkey.

1 May. Entry of the Yugoslavs into Trieste.

11 November. Elections in Yugoslavia give 90% of the votes to the National Front. Proclamation of the Republic of Yugoslavia (29 November).

18 November. Elections in Bulgaria give 87% of the votes to the Patriotic Front.

2 December. Elections in Albania give 93% of the vote to the Democratic Front.

1946   July. Condemnation to death of General Mikhailovich at Belgrade.

July-October. Conference preparatory to the treaties of peace with Rumania and Bulgaria in Paris.

1 September. A plebiscite in Greece favors the return of King George II.

15 September. Proclamation of the Republic of Bulgaria.

28 September. Return of King George II to Athens.

September. Tension between Yugoslavia and the United States as a result of an attack upon American planes.

11 October. Condemnation to hard labor of Archbishop Stepinac of Zagreb.

18 October. The United Nations decides to send a commission of inquiry to the Balkans.

1947   10 February. Signing of treaties of peace between the Allies and Rumania and Bulgaria.

27 February. Britain decides to terminate assistance to Greece and Turkey.

12 March. Truman's declaration of aid to Greece and Turkey.

1 April. Death of King George II of Greece.

2 April. The Soviet ambassador leaves Athens.

2 May. Arrival of an American squadron at Istanbul.

4 July. Arrest of communists at Athens.

1 August. Complaint of Greece to the U. N. regarding aid to the partisans given by Yugoslavia, Bulgaria, and Albania.

2 August. Signing of a political and commercial agreement between Yugoslavia and Bulgaria.

23 September. Execution of Nicolas Petkov in Sofia.

11 November. Condemnation of Julius Maniu to life imprisonment in Rumania.

5 December. Dimitrov becomes chief of the Bulgarian government.

24 December. General Markos creates a dissident Greek government.

30 December. Abdication of King Michael of Rumania.

1948　28 March. Elections in Rumania give 90% of votes to the government bloc.

28 June. Excommunication of Tito by the Cominform.

18 August. Signing at Belgrade of a new convention relative to the Danube by the U.S.S.R. and her satellites.

End of August. The Greek civil war is intensified near Mount Grammos.

November. The U. N. in Paris condemns the aid given to the Greek rebels by Yugoslavia, Bulgaria, and Albania.

December. Dissolution of the Uniate Church in Rumania.

1949　31 January. General Markos, leader of the Greek revolt, is relieved of his functions.

April. Disgrace of Traicho Kostov in Bulgaria.

April. Protests of the United States and Britain against infractions of the treaties committed by Hungary, Rumania, and Bulgaria.

2 July. Death of Dimitrov.

25 July. The U.S.S.R. accuses Yugoslavia of mistreating Soviet citizens.

End of July. Italo-Yugoslav commercial agreement.

August. Arrival in Belgrade of delegates of the International Bank for Reconstruction to study conditions of a loan.

End of August. Victory of government troops over the Greek insurgents at Mount Grammos.

End of August. Serious tension between Moscow and Belgrade following an exchange of notes.

28 September. The U.S.S.R. denounces her treaty of friendship with Yugoslavia on the basis of revelations during the trial of Rajk in Budapest.

21 October. Election of Yugoslavia instead of Czechoslovakia to the U. N. Security Council.

October. The U.S.S.R. and her satellites denounce their treaties of friendship with Yugoslavia.

27 October—1 November. Hungarian troops fire on the Yugoslav frontier.

14 December. Condemnation to death of Kostov by the Bulgarian tribunal.

1950   (Chronology by S. D. Spector)

January 23—Bulgarian premier Kolarov dies and is succeeded by Vulko Chervenkov. U. S. envoy Donald Heath expelled from Bulgaria for alleged espionage.

February—Rumanian Communist Party reorganizes certain organs to tighten up on internal party discipline.

Bulgaria signs trade agreement with the USSR.

February 10—Albanian Orthodox Church withdraws from jurisdiction of the Patriarch in Istanbul and comes under the Russian Orthodox Patriarch.

February 15—Rumania prohibits private law practice.

March—Bulgaria purges one-fifth of the membership of the Communist Party.

Bulgaria breaks diplomatic relations with the U. S.

March 6—Albania withdraws from the World Health Organization.

March 12—Albanian finance minister Avedim Shehu purged.

May—First free elections in Turkey. Leader of Democrat Party Celal Bayar elected president.

May 15—Municipal elections in Bulgaria.

June—All Yugoslav personnel withdrawn from Albania.

June 24—Rumania purges 200,000 Communist Party members on charges of Titoism.

June 25—South Korea invaded by North Korean forces; U. N. intervention spearheaded by the U. S.

July—Greece sends a battalion to assist the U. N. forces in Korea.

August 5—Bulgaria demands Yugoslavia's cession of Tsaribrod and Bosiligrad in Macedonia.

September 23—Arrival in Albania of numerous Soviet officials who assume control over the government and economy.

September 26—Yugoslavia grants concessions to the Serbian Orthodox Church.

October 4—Greece and Turkey accept invitations to join NATO (to become effective in 1952).

October 15—Turkey sends combat troops to assist U. N. forces in Korea.

Turkey and Bulgaria engage in border clashes.

November 3—U. N. General Assembly condemns suppression of civil liberties in Rumania.

U. S. sends food to Yugoslavia to avert famine.

November 11—Albania terminates diplomatic relations with Yugoslavia.

November 25—Yugoslavia terminates diplomatic relations with Albania.

November 28—Yugoslavia restores diplomatic relations with Greece.

Greece restores diplomatic relations with Yugoslavia.

December—Yugoslavia institutes profit-sharing methods to stimulate production.

December 3—Elections in Rumania.

1951

January—Rumania embarks upon her first Five-Year Plan.

March—Rumanian military officials assume control of the oilfields.

Albania completes her fourth railroad.

Soviet-Albanian treaty concluded.

U.S. sends military assistance to Yugoslavia.

May—Yugoslavia sponsors the formation of a free Albanian federation.

Bulgaria conducts purge trials of alleged Titoists.

May 12—Rumania introduces new military manpower system.

June—The first West German diplomatic mission arrives in Yugoslavia.

Yugoslavia walks out of meeting of the Danube Commission in Bucharest.

June 1—Yugoslavia introduces a new criminal code.

Greece introduces currency reform.

Rumania initiates relocation of Yugoslav minorities within the country.

June 27—U. S. terminates trade agreements with Rumania.

July 12—Greek deputy premier Papandreou resigns.

July—Rumanian premier Groza shorn of much power.

July 21—Soviet deputy premier Molotov castigates Tito in Warsaw.

July 30—Greek field marshal Papagos announces intention to enter politics.

August 3—Albanian Roman Catholic Church forced to renounce ties to Papacy.

August 31—U. S. ends tariff concessions on Bulgarian imports. Yugoslavia announces introduction of decentralization of her economy.

September 9—Elections in Greece; victory of Papagos' forces.

September 15—U. N. charges Bulgaria was still assisting Greek communist rebels.

September 16—Salonika International Fair.

November 18—U. S. claims Rumania had violated the 1947 peace treaty.

December 7—U. N. abolishes the Special Commission on the Balkans.

December 22—Greece adopts a new constitution increasing emergency powers of the king.

1952

January—Rumania institutes a drastic monetary reform.

February 20—Greece admitted to NATO.

Turkey admitted to NATO.

March—Bulgarian premier Chervenkov departs for Moscow for a long stay.

March 31—Albania summons Albanian residents of Yugoslavia to revolt.

May 1—U. S. bans travel of her citizens to Bulgaria.

May 13—Bulgaria introduces a currency reform.

May 19—Albania introduces a Five-Year Plan.

May 22—Albania announces a new penal code.

May 31—Bulgarian premier Chervenkov elected president of National Committee of the Fatherland Front.

June—King Paul of Greece pays a state visit to Turkey.

Rumania suspends emigration of Jews to Israel.

Rumania introduces new system of state courts.

June 12—Albania decrees compulsory education of seven years for all citizens.

July 18—Rumania promulgates a new constitution. The new "Autonomous Hungarian Region" created in Transylvania.

July 30—Rumania signs trade agreement with Communist China.

August—Bulgaria signs trade agreement with West Germany. Bulgaria has border clashes with Greece.

September 29—Albania holds elections. The U.S.S.R. establishes a submarine base at Albanian port of Saseno.

October 3—The majority electoral system introduced in Greece.

October 5—19th congress of the Soviet Communist Party begins in Moscow.

November—Yugoslavia introduces decentralization of the government apparatus.

November 16—Elections in Greece; Papagos and the rightist Greek Rally win.

1953

January 14—Marshal Tito elected president of Yugoslavia.

January 23—Elections in Rumania.

February 28—Greece, Turkey, and Yugoslavia sign treaty of friendship and collaboration.

March—Tito visits England.

March 5—Joseph Stalin dies.

March 6—Georgi Malenkov becomes Soviet premier.

March 20—Malenkov yields his post as secretary of the Soviet Communist Party and is succeeded by a five-man secretariat which includes Nikita Khrushchev.

March 30—Yugoslavia announces decree on gradual liquidation of collective farms.

April 4—Former King Carol of Rumania dies in Lisbon.

April—Rumania announces a general amnesty.

May 10—Bulgaria names her first Orthodox patriarch in six centuries.

May 31—Rumania and Yugoslavia agree on joint administration of the Iron Gates.

July 11—Conference of Yugoslavia, Greece, and Turkey on common problems.

July 15—The U.S.S.R. requests resumption of diplomatic relations with Yugoslavia.

July 24—Government of Albania reorganized; Mehmet Shehu dismissed as secretary of the Communist Party.

August—Earthquakes shake the Ionian Islands.

August 2-16—4th World Festival of Youth in Bucharest.

September—Bulgaria reestablishes diplomatic relations with Yugoslavia.

September 8—New electoral reform in Yugoslavia.

September 9—New criminal code introduced in Yugoslavia.

October—NATO establishes a base at Izmir (Smyrna) in Turkey.

October 8—U. S. and England terminate joint administration of Zone A in the Trieste territory and relinquish it to Italy.

October 12—Greece permits the U. S. to establish military bases on her territory.

October 15—Albania requires compulsory study of Russian in the schools.

October 29—King Paul of Greece pays a state visit to the U. S.

November 24—Parliamentary elections in Yugoslavia.

December 31—Bulgaria completes her first Five-Year Plan.

1954

January 1—Bulgaria introduces a second Five-Year Plan.

February 1—Rumania introduces a monetary reform.

February 5—Congress of the Bulgarian Communist Party.

March 7—Turkey denationalizes her petroleum industry.

March 15—England announces her intention to grant independence to Cyprus.

April 20—Gheorghe Gheorghiu-Dej, First Secretary of Rumania's Communist Party, yields that post to Gheorghe Apostol and becomes premier.

April 30—Serious earthquake in Thessaly.

May—Bulgaria reaches agreement with Greece and reestablishes diplomatic relations.

May 1—Greece announces currency reform.

May 2—Elections in Turkey. Celal Bayar reelected president; Adnan Menderes named premier.

July 20—Mehmet Shehu replaces Enver Hoxha as party secretary in Albania.

August 6—Balkan military pact of Greece, Turkey, and Yugoslavia approved by NATO.

October—Yugoslavia signs trade agreement with Soviet Russia.

October 5—Italy and Yugoslavia accept compromise settlement of Trieste territory.

December—Milovan Djilas charges Tito with dereliction.

1955

January—Tito visits Burma and India.

February 8—Soviet premier Malenkov resigns and is succeeded by Nikolai Bulganin.

May 11-14—Warsaw Conference of eight East European states; Eastern Security Pact signed.

May 26—Khrushchev and Bulganin pay a state visit to Yugoslavia.

July—Outbreak of tension over the question of Cyprus.

September—London conference on future of Cyprus.

September 5—King Paul of Greece visits Yugoslavia.

October 3—Gheorghiu-Dej renamed first secretary of Rumanian Communist Party; Chivu Stoica becomes premier.

October 5—Greek premier Papagos dies; Constantine Karamanlis succeeds to post.

November 29—Government crisis in Turkey produced by harsh rule of Menderes.

December—Tito visits Ethiopia and Egypt.

December 14—Albania, Bulgaria, and Rumania admitted to the U. N.

1956

February 14—Khrushchev attacks Stalin and the "cult of the individual" at the 20th Congress of the Soviet Communist Party in Moscow.

February 19—National elections in Greece; Karamanlis reelected premier.

March 9—England deports Archbishop Makarios from Cyprus.

April 16—Dissolution of the Cominform.

April 17—Bulgaria posthumously rehabilitates Traicho Kostov; Chervenkov resigns as premier and is replaced by Anton Yugov.

June 2—Tito visits the U.S.S.R.

June 25—Rumania and Yugoslavia agree upon close cooperation.

June 28—Riots in Poznan, Poland.

September—Rumania joins UNESCO.

September 27—West Germany grants huge loan to Yugoslavia.
October 24—Beginning of the Hungarian revolution; suppressed by the U.S.S.R.
November 19—Milovan Djilas arrested in Yugoslavia.

1957

February 1—Government reorganization in Bulgaria; Chervenkov reemerges in post of minister of education.
April 17—The U.S.S.R. absolves Albania of paying for credits granted in period 1945-55.
Archbishop Makarios triumphantly visits Athens.
July 3—Molotov, Malenkov, Kaganovich, and Shepilov dropped from the Central Committee of the Soviet Communist Party and from their government posts.
July 5—Gheorghiu-Dej removes Stalinists Miron Constantinescu and Iosif Chisinevschi in Rumania.
October 4—The U.S.S.R. launches the first earth satellite, Sputnik I.
October 27—Turkey holds national elections; Bayar and Menderes win.
December 9—Tito asks the U.S. to terminate her military assistance.

1958

January 11—Ion Gheorghe Maurer succeeds the late Petru Groza as president of Rumania.
January 27—Strike of miners in Yugoslavia.
March 2—Greek premier Karamanlis resigns.
March 23—National elections in Yugoslavia; Tito reelected president.
March 27—Khrushchev becomes premier of the USSR and retains his post of first secretary of the Soviet Communist Party.
April 26—Yugoslav Communist Party Congress; Tito reelected first secretary.
May 11—National elections in Greece; Karamanlis wins.
June 1—National elections in Albania.
June 14—Greece severs NATO relations with Turkey over Cyprus dispute.
October—Rumania permits 50,000 Jews to emigrate to Israel.

November—Tito visits Egypt, Ethiopia, Burma, and Indonesia.
November 30—Dimiter Ganev elected president of Bulgaria; Todor Zhivkov becomes first party secretary.

1959

February 19—England, Greece, and Turkey sign agreement establishing Cyprus as an independent republic effective August 16, 1960.
March 1—Archbishop Makarios returns to Cyprus after a three-year exile.
March 15—Tito visits Greece.
March 27—Bulgaria resumes diplomatic relations with the U.S.
May—Greek premier Karamanlis visits Turkey.
May 13-16—Soviet-sponsored Council of Mutual Economic Assistance meets in Tirana.
May 25—Soviet premier Khrushchev visits Albania.
May 26—Khrushchev announces that the USSR would install missiles in Bulgaria and Albania if Greece permits American missiles in her country.
June—The Hungarian and Rumanian universities at Cluj are unified.
December 13—President Eisenhower visits Greece.
Archbishop Makarios elected president of Cyprus.
December 22—Bulgaria fails to achieve her 1959 production quotas.

1960

January 7—Turkey opens Europe's largest dam at Hirfanli.
February 10—Roman Catholic Archbishop Stepinac dies; Franjo Seper, his successor, voices acceptance of the Tito regime.
March—Soviet submarine base completed at Saseno in Albania.
Rumania signs long-range trade agreement with Greece.
April 9—Greece introduces new economic plan to increase national income.
Rumania signs COMECON charter.
May—Balkan alliance of Greece, Turkey, and Yugoslavia abandoned because of Cyprus dispute.
May 13—The U.S.S.R. protests use of Turkish airfields by American planes.

May 27—*Coup d'état* by Turkish army group. Government of Bayar and Menderes overthrown. General Jemal Gürsel becomes president.

June—3rd congress of the Rumanian Communist Party.

August 16—Cyprus proclaimed independent within the British Commonwealth.

September—U. N. General Assembly meets in New York. Tito, Gheorghiu-Dej, Khrushchev and other leading communists attend.

Albania proposes U.N. membership for Communist China.

Albania expels two prominent members of the Central Committee.

October 1—Albania and Communist China assume open friendship policy; first manifestations of approaching Sino-Soviet rift. Poland asks Albanian envoy to abandon his post.

October 14—Bayar and Menderes placed on trial in Turkey.

December—Rumania signs long-range trade accord with Yugoslavia.

1961

January 20—Milovan Djilas released from prison in Yugoslavia.

February 13-20—4th congress of Albanian Communist Party; criticism of the USSR voiced.

March 5—Reorganization of the Rumanian government; Gheorghiu-Dej becomes president of new State Council.

April 27—Turkey signs rail agreement with the U.S.S.R.

May—Albania tries pro-Soviet politicians; the U.S.S.R. abandons submarine base at Saseno.

July—Bulgaria introduces currency reform.

July 9—Turkey approves new constitution.

Greece becomes an associate member of the European Common Market.

August 13—the German Democratic Republic erects a wall between East and West Berlin.

September 1—Conference of non-aligned nations in Belgrade.

September 17—Turkish premier Menderes hanged for treason.

October 15—Turks elect General Gürsel president and Ismet Inonu premier.

October 16—22nd congress of the Soviet Communist Party opens in Moscow; attacks on Communist China and Albania.

October 29—Greek national elections; Karamanlis reelected.

November—Bulgaria breaks diplomatic relations with Albania.

November 29—Chervenkov expelled from the Central Committee of the Bulgarian Communist Party.

December 10—The U.S.S.R. and Albania sever diplomatic relations.

1962

February 22—Abortive coup by young army officers suppressed in Turkey.

May 14—New trial and imprisonment of Milovan Djilas in Yugoslavia.

May 31—Turkish premier Inonu resigns over amnesty dispute.

June—National elections in Albania.

June 18-25—Khrushchev visits Rumania to demand economic cooperation.

June 25-26—Khrushchev visits Bulgaria.

June 26—Turkish premier Inonu forms coalition regime.

June 30—Rumania announces achievement of 100% agricultural collectivization.

July 1—American assistance to Greece terminated.

August—U. S. vice president Lyndon Johnson visits Greece.

August 26-27—Lyndon Johnson visits Turkey.

October—Leonid Brezhnev, Chairman of the Presidium of the Supreme Soviet, visits Yugoslavia.

November—8th congress of Bulgarian Communist Party announces sweeping purges. Yugov removed from Central Committee, and Chervenkov expelled from the party.

December 3—Tito visits Moscow and addresses the Supreme Soviet.

1963

January 24—Crown Prince Constantine of Greece engaged to Princess Anna Maria of Denmark.

April—Turkey announces that NATO missile bases will be abandoned.

Albania refuses to sign limited test-ban treaty.

April 7—Yugoslavia adopts a new constitution electing Tito president for life.

June—Albania tries alleged American and Yugoslav espionage agents.

June 11—Premier Karamanlis of Greece resigns after eleven years in office. George Papandreou elected to succeed him.

July—Khrushchev informs Turkey of Russia's abandonment of designs on the Straits.

July 26—Massive earthquakes strike Skoplje, Yugoslavia, destroying 80% of all homes and killing 1,011 persons.

August 4—Rumania signs the limited test-ban treaty.

U.S.S.R. presses Rumania to cooperate with COMECON.

August 20—Khrushchev begins a lengthy visit to Yugoslavia.

October—President Tito begins an extended visit to the United States.

November 30—Rumania and Yugoslavia sign agreement to construct dam at Iron Gates gorge on the Danube River.

December—Violence between Greek and Turkish residents breaks out on Cyprus.

Chinese Premier Chou En-lai visits Albania.

1964

January—Albania orders all Soviet citizens to leave and confiscates Soviet property.

January 15—Bulgaria executes Kristov Georgiev as an American spy.

March 6—King Paul of Greece dies. Constantine II succeeds to throne.

March—A high Rumanian delegation visits Peking in effort to heal the Sino-Soviet rift.

Greek residents of Istanbul expelled during growing Greco-Turkish crisis over Cyprus.

April 21—Bulgarian president Ganev dies and is succeeded by Traikov.

April 26—Rumania rejects Moscow's economic guidance.

June—Turkish premier Inonu visits Washington to seek assistance in Cyprus dispute.

Rumania initiates her desatellitization process; Russian names are removed from the streets.

July—Bulgaria and Yugoslavia sign economic agreements.

July 9—Bulgaria and Greece agree to terminate post-war tensions.

August—Violence erupts on Cyprus.

September 18—King Constantine II of Greece is married.

Greek premier Papandreou frees most communists who had been imprisoned since the civil war.

October—Turkey and the U.S.S.R. agree to construct a dam in the Caucasus.

October 14—Khrushchev deposed; Leonid I. Brezhnev succeeds him as First Secretary of the Party, and Alexei N. Kosygin as Chairman of the Council of Ministers (Premier).

December 1—Turkey becomes an associate member of the European Common Market.

December 8—8th congress of the Yugoslav Communist Party; Tito calls for the independence of all communist parties.

1965

January—Albania refuses to attend Warsaw Pact meeting.

Bulgaria signs cultural agreement with the U.S.S.R.

Bulgarian president Traikov visits Moscow.

February 13—Turkish premier Inonu resigns after losing vote of confidence on budget proposals.

February 15—Afro-Asian students in Bulgaria demonstrate against U. S. policy in Viet-Nam.

March—Albania refuses to attend Moscow conference of communists from 19 countries. Communist China premier Chou En-lai visits Albania.

March 7—National elections in Rumania; Ion Gheorghe Maurer named premier, and Chivu Stoica president. Nicolae Ceausescu named first party secretary.

March 19—Gheorghiu-Dej, the Rumanian communist leader, dies.

April—Abortive coup suppressed in Bulgaria.

April 30—Yugoslav author Mihajlo Mihajlov sentenced to prison.

May—Completion of first direct railroad route between Athens and Sofia.

May 21—Archbishop Makarios calls for the union of Cyprus and Greece.

June—Soviet leader Mikhail Suslov visits Bulgaria.

Tito visits East Germany, Czechoslovakia, Soviet Russia, Bulgaria, and Hungary.

July 10—Daughter born to King Constantine of Greece.

July 15—Greek premier Papandreou resigns in rift with King Constantine over role of rightist elements in the army.

July 19-23—9th congress of the Rumanian Communist Party attended by Brezhnev; Rumania asserts her independence in the communist bloc.

July 24—Yugoslavia announces a general economic reform.

August—Albania announces currency reform.

August 21—Rumania adopts a new constitution.

September 25—Stephanopoulos forms coalition government in Greece.

October 10—National elections in Turkey. Demirel of Justice Party becomes premier.

November—Church-State crisis in Greece.

1966

January 31—Rumania and West Germany establish diplomatic relations.

February 27—National elections in Bulgaria; Todor Zhivkov elected premier.

March—Franco-Bulgarian trade agreement signed.

March 28—General Cevdet Sunay elected Turkish president replacing ailing Gürsel.

April—Albania refuses to attend 23rd congress of Soviet Communist Party.

April 28—Albanian premier Mehmet Shehu visits Peking.

May 7—Rumanian Communist chief Ceausescu announces outlines of his country's national policies.

June—Communist China's premier Chou En-lai visits Rumania. Chou En-lai visits Albania.

June 25—Yugoslavia and the Vatican restore relations.

July—Turkey issues amnesty for imprisoned Menderes supporters. Turkish battalion withdrawn from South Korea. Albanian national elections.

July 1—Alexander Rankovich ousted as Yugoslav vice-president and secretary of the Central Committee.

July 8—Former president Bayar of Turkey released from prison.

July 12—Bulgaria introduces 5th five-year plan.

July 14—Yugoslav foreign minister Koca Popovich elected vice president.

August 19-22—Severe earthquakes in Turkey.

August 28—Yugoslavia signs trade agreement with the U.S.S.R.

September—Greece and Rumania sign trade agreement.

September 14—Former Turkish president Gürsel dies.

September 22-25—Leonid Brezhnev visits Yugoslavia.

September 23—Yugoslav author Mihajlov imprisoned again.

October—Greek politician Andreas Papandreou accused of complicity in army plot.

October 4—Reorganization of Yugoslav Communist Party; Tito given title of president of the League of Communists.

November—Church crisis settled in Greece.

December—Soviet premier Kosygin visits Turkey.

December 21—Greek premier Stephanopoulos resigns.

December 31—Yugoslav author Milovan Djilas released from prison.

1967

April—Military junta seizes power in Greece.

July—Pope Paul VI visits Turkey.

August—Marshal Tito visits Arab capitals in attempt to mediate Arab-Israeli crisis.

September—Rumanian foreign minister Corneliu Manescu elected president of the U. N. General Assembly.

October 7—The Greek military junta releases George Papandreou from prison.

October 26—Greek Orthodox Patriarch Athenagoras visits the Vatican.

November 7—The U.S.S.R. celebrates the 50th anniversary of the Bolshevik revolution.

Selected Bibliography

[M. Ristelhueber listed the following books in his bibliography. His list is reproduced for the interest of those who wish to know the works apparently consulted by the author of the original edition of this book. *ED.*]

General Works

Ancel, Jacques. *Peuples et Nations des Balkans*. Paris, 1930.
————. *Manuel historique de la Question d'Orient*. Paris, 1931.
Choublier, M. *La Question d'Orient depuis le traité de Berlin*. Paris, 1899.
Driault, Edouard. *La Question d'Orient depuis ses origines jusqu'à la paix de Sèvres*. Paris, 1921.
Forbes, Neville, Arnold Toynbee, David Mitrany, & D. G. Hogarth, *The Balkans*. London, 1915.
Glotz, Gustave et Robert Cohen (eds.). *Histoire générale*, IX: *L'Europe orientale de 1081 à 1453*. Paris, 1945.
Iorga, Nicolae. *Histoire des Etats balcaniques*. Paris, 1925.
Seton-Watson, R. W. *The Rise of Nationality in the Balkans*. London, 1917.

Albania

Bourcart, Jacques. *L'Albanie et les Albanais*. Paris, 1921.
Jarray, G. L. *Les Albanais*. Paris, 1920.
Mousset, Albert. *L'Albanie devant l'Europe*. Paris, 1930.

Bulgaria

Bousquet, Georges H. *Histoire du peuple bulgare*. Paris, 1909.
Gentizon, P. *Le drame bulgare*. Paris, 1924.
Lamouche, L. *La Bulgarie dans le passé et le présent*. Paris, 1892.
————. *La Bulgarie*. Paris, 1923.
Léger, Louis. *La Bulgarie*. Paris, 1895.
Songeon, Guérin. *Histoire de la Bulgarie*. Paris, 1913.
Weiss-Bartenstein, Walther K. *Bulgarien—Land und Leute*. Leipzig, 1913.

Greece

About, E. *Le Gréce contemporaine.* Paris, 1854.

Deschamps, G. *Le Gréce d'aujourd'hui.* Paris, 1892.

Driault, Edouard. *L'Insurrection et l'Indépendance.* Paris, 1925.

Isambert, J. *L'Indépendance grecque et l'Europe.* Paris, 1900.

Rumania

Bratianu, Georges I. *Origines et formation de l'Unité roumaine.* Bucharest, 1943.

Iorga, Nicolae. *Geschichte des Rumänischen Volkes im Rahmen seiner Staatsbildungen.* 2 vols. Gotha, 1905.

————. *Histoire des Roumains et de leur Civilisation.* Bucharest, 1922 (An English translation by Joseph McCabe was published in 1925).

————. *La place des Roumains dans l'histoire universelle.* 2 vols. Bucharest, 1935.

Seton-Watson, R. W. *A History of the Roumanians from Roman Times to the Completion of Unity.* Cambridge, England, 1934 (re-issued 1963).

Turkey

Bérard, V. *La Macédoine.* Paris, 1898.

————. *La Révolution turque.* Paris, 1909.

Chéradame, André. *La question d'Orient.* Paris, 1903.

Gaulis, G. *La ruine d'un Empire.* Paris, 1913.

Iorga, Nicolae. *Geschichte des Osmanischen Reiches.* 5 vols. Gotha, 1908-13.

Pernot, M. *La question turque.* Paris, 1923.

Yugoslavia

Baerlein, Henri. *The Birth of Yugoslavia.* 2 vols. London, 1922.

Bain, R. Nisbet. *Précis d'histoire serbe.* Paris, 1917.

Denis, Ernest. *La grande Serbie.* Paris, 1915.

Haumant, Emile. *La formation de la Yougoslavie.* Paris, 1930.

Mousset, Albert. *Le royaume des Serbes, Croates, et Slovènes.* Paris, 1926.

Stanoyevitch, Stanoye. *Histoire de Yougoslavie.* Belgrade, 1936.

The Contemporary Period

Delage, F. *La tragédie des Dardanelles.* Paris, 1931.

Feyler, A. *La campagne de Macédoine.* Geneva, 1921.

Gafenco, Georges. *Préliminaires de la guerre à l'Est.* Fribourg, 1944 (English translation, *Prelude to the Russian Campaign,* London, 1945).

Gauvain, Auguste. *L'affaire grecque.* Paris, 1917.

Guéchoff, Ivan. *L'alliance balkanique.* Paris, 1915.

Mousset, Albert. *Le Monde slave.* Paris, 1946 (English translation, *The World of the Slavs,* New York, 1950).

Seton-Watson, Hugh. *Eastern Europe between the Wars, 1918-1941.* Cambridge, England, 1946 (re-issued 1967).

The preparation of an exhaustive bibliography to complement this text would require years of investigation and the printing of several volumes. This brief list of English-language items is designed, as is the entire book, to furnish the uninitiated reader with suggestions for further readings. Balkan specialists will fault the inclusion or exclusion of certain items. This list is not designed for the experts, but rather for those who are admittedly ignorant of the Balkans. An essential criterion for the selection of these items is the general availability of the books in average-size libraries. [*ED.*]

I. *General Histories.* The only English-language text of Balkan history since its beginnings in ancient times is still the classic work of Ferdinand Schevill, *History of the Balkan Peninsula,* revised by Wesley Gewehr (New York, 1933 and now available in reprint). The widely adopted text today is Leften S. Stavrianos, *The Balkans since 1453* (New York, 1958), which treats the modern period in a solid, expensive volume. Two recent studies furnish the novice with concise introductions to the Balkans: George W. Hoffman, *The Balkans in Transition* (Princeton, 1963), a thin paperback; and Charles and Barbara Jelavich, *The Balkans* (Englewood Cliffs, 1965), a succinct introduction for college students in 148 pages. Both slim books have selective bibliographies. Stavrianos has 73 pages of bibliography. He has also written a thin introduction to the Balkans during the 19th century: *The Balkans, 1815-1914* (New York, 1963), a paperbound in the Berkshire Studies designed for college students. A new sociocultural survey has been written by Traian Stoianovich, *A Study in Balkan Civilization* (New York, 1967), and its 215 pages are highly recommended. A new introductory text by Norman J. G. Pounds, *Eastern Europe* (Chicago, 1969), was published after this book was completed; it is apparently a geography survey by this noted specialist.

General surveys of East Europe have devoted considerable attention to the Balkans. The following do not concentrate upon the Balkans, but do treat the peninsula in a general coverage of the region between Russia and Germany. William H. McNeill's *Europe's Steppe Frontier* (Chicago, 1964) provides a stimulating analysis of the region where the Hapsburg, Ottoman, and Russian empires once confronted each other. An older study but still worthwhile is Harriet Wanklyn's *The Eastern Marchlands of Europe* (London, 1941). Although somewhat outdated, an anthology of the Peace Handbooks, *The Balkan States,* issued by the Historical Section of the English Foreign Office in 1920, still constitutes an excellent basic introduction to the region. A new study, which treats all East Europe, is by the English specialist F. B. Singleton, *Background to Eastern Europe* (New York, 1965), an inexpensive paperback. An advanced account of the medieval Balkans is by Francis Dvornik, *The Making of Central and Eastern Europe* (London, 1949), which is difficult to find; Dvornik's *The Slavs in European History and Civilization* (New Brunswick, 1962) is more accessible and quite complete to the 19th century. Renowned specialists have recently collaborated in a volume of essays, *The Balkans in Transition* (Berkeley, 1963), edited by Charles and Barbara Jelavich, which assumes a basic understanding of the peninsula's complexities. Robert Lee Wolff has interpreted developments between 1941 and 1955, and with some attention to the earlier eras, in his authoritative *The Balkans in Our Times* (Cambridge, Mass., 1956; now available in reprint). The great pioneer in East European studies, Robert W. Seton-Watson, wrote *The Rise of Nationality in the Balkans* in 1917; it is now available in reprint. His equally eminent son, Hugh, has produced two prodigious surveys: *Eastern Europe Between the Wars, 1918-1941* (London, 1946, and now in paperbound reprint) and *The East European Revolution* (New York, 1956) treating the period since 1941. Both are solidly packed with information hitherto scattered in many other studies. A pioneer but very brief survey was written by Wesley Gewehr, *The Rise of Nationalism in the Balkans, 1800-1930* (New York, 1931) for the Berkshire Studies; it is now available in reprint. A companion work is by Frank Nowak, *Medieval Slavdom and the Rise of*

Russia (New York, 1930), in the Berkshire series, which treats the southern Slavs and their medieval institutions. Two superseded works will furnish the reader with basic introductions to Balkan history: William Stearns Davis, *A Short History of the Near East* (New York, 1922), stressing the Turkish Empire; and J. A. R. Marriott, *The Eastern Question* (Oxford, 1925), a solid diplomatic history. Both items weaned many Americans in their first contacts with Balkan history. William Miller wrote very readable histories of the peninsula: *The Balkans* (London, 1923), and *The Ottoman Empire and its Successors, 1801-1922* (London, 1922). Both appear to be in most general libraries and are typical of historical popularization a half-century ago. George E. Mylonas, a Greek nationalist, wrote *The Balkan States* (Washington, 1947) to gratify his chauvinism; it is out of print and scarce. An English journalist and spy, Bernard Newman, wrote a popular account in *Balkan Background* (New York, 1945); factually questionable but delightful prose. A less controversial survey of little consequence, but widely available, is William M. Sloane, *The Balkans: A Laboratory of History* (New York, 1920). Joseph S. Roucek edited a text, *Central-Eastern Europe* (New York, 1946), containing chapters by experts which treat the individual Balkan nations; it is worthy of a reprint. The Royal Institute of International Affairs produced *South-Eastern Europe: A Brief Survey* (London, 1940). It is scarcely as commendable as *The Balkans* (Oxford, 1915) produced for the Royal Institute during another war by Nevill Forbes, Arnold J. Toynbee, David Mitrany, and D. G. Hogarth; it is still worthwhile reading. Leonid Strakhovsky edited a volume of essays by renowned experts, *A Handbook of Slavic Studies* (Cambridge, Mass., 1949), including chapters on the south Slavs. This anthology is especially valuable for chapters on south Slavic literature. The 11th edition of *The Encyclopaedia Britannica* (1914) contains valuable chapters on the Balkan peoples. A related account is by Sir Charles Eliot, *Turkey in Europe* (London, 1900), now in a reprint. The best treatment of 19th-century diplomacy affecting the Balkans is M. S. Anderson, *The Eastern Question, 1774-1923* (New York, 1966) which attempts to supersede Marriott. Carlile A. Macartney and Alan W. Palmer have written *Independent Eastern Europe* (New York, 1962), in paperback, a survey of the interwar era which competes with Hugh Seton-Watson's *Eastern Europe Between the*

Wars. Georg Stadtmüller wrote *Geschichte Sudosteuropas* (Munich, 1950), a survey from ancient times to 1918; it is valuable for the appendices of dynasties, grand viziers, princes, etc., which can be read without a prior knowledge of German. The late Walter Kolarz wrote *Myths and Realities in Eastern Europe* (London, 1946) to demolish long-cherished canards; it is worth finding and reading.

II. *Geography.* R. H. Osborne, an English geographer, has written *East-Central Europe* (New York, 1967), an inexpensive excellent introduction. Still valuable is the old *The New World: Problems in Political Geography* (New York, 1928), by the late Isaiah Bowman and available in most libraries. Other geographical introductions are by Wanklyn, Hoffmann, and Pounds (cited above).

III. *Economics.* Ristelhueber apparently decided to minimize economic development in his text. Those who wish specialized studies should consult Friedrich Hertz, *The Economic Problem of the Danubian States* (London, 1947); Antonin Basch, *The Danubian Basin and the German Economic Sphere* (London, 1944); Carlile A. Macartney, *Problems of the Danube Basin* (London, 1942); Wilbert E. Moore, *Economic Demography of Eastern and Southern Europe* (Geneva, 1945); and David Mitrany, *The Effect of the War in Southeastern Europe* (New Haven, 1936). These studies are difficult to find except in the largest university libraries. For studies of economies in the Balkans today, see *Balkan Communism* below.

IV. *Balkan Communism.* More studies about the Balkans since 1945 have been produced than all the works written in English prior to that date. Included here are only general studies accessible in most libraries and worthy of being consulted. Richard V. Burks, *The Dynamics of Communism in Eastern Europe* (Princeton, 1961, paper), and Zbigniew K. Brzezinski, *The Soviet Bloc: Unity and Conflict* (New York, 1968, paper) are essential. Joseph Rothschild's *Communist East Europe* (New York, 1964, paper) is very elementary. R. R. Betts (ed.), *Central and South East Europe* (London, 1950) is superseded by Stephen Fischer-Galati (ed.), *Eastern Europe in the Sixties* (New York, 1963, paper). John A. Lukacs attempts to explain how East Europe was sovietized in *The Great Powers and Eastern Europe* (New York, 1953). His massive study is superseded by Roger Pethybridge (ed.), *The*

Development of the Communist Bloc (Boston, 1965, paper); or J. F. Brown, *The New Eastern Europe* (New York, 1966, paper). A new journalistic account is by Paul Lendvai, *Eagles and Cobwebs: Nationalism and Communism in the Balkans* (Garden City, 1969). The defunct Mid-European Studies Center of the Free Europe Committee produced *East-Central Europe under the Communists,* a series of studies of the affected nations—*Romania* (Fischer-Galati), *Albania* (Stavro Skendi), *Bulgaria* (L. A. D. Dellin), and *Yugoslavia* (Robert F. Byrnes, editor of the entire series); all were printed in the 1950's and have been largely superseded by more recent studies. The U. S. Congress created special sub-committees in the 1950's to investigate conditions in East Europe; most libraries possess the published reports of these committees based upon hearings of defectors. Two studies of political institutions are Andrew Gyorgy, *The Governments of Danubian Europe* (New York, 1949) and H. Gordon Skilling, *Governments of Communist East Europe* (New York, 1966, paper). A more concise and lucid treatment of governmental institutions is by Cyril E. Black, "Communist Europe," in Taylor Cole (ed.), *European Political Systems* (New York, 1953).

V. *Bibliographies.* In 1943 the Division of Bibliography of the U. S. Library of Congress issued a general listing in 5 volumes—*The Balkans;* this will be superseded by the bibliography edited by Paul Horecky and published by the University of Chicago Press. Another outdated bibliography was completed by the late Robert J. Kerner, *Slavic Europe: A Selected Bibliography in Western European Languages* (Cambridge, Mass., 1918). A third, outdated but useful reference is Léon Savadjian's *Bibliographie Balkanique* in 8 volumes (Paris, 1920-38). Two general guides have sections on the Balkan states: George M. Dutcher (ed.), *A Guide to Historical Literature* (New York, 1936), and its sequel, George M. Howe (ed.), *The American Historical Association's Guide to Historical Literature* (New York, 1961). Paperbound books are given in Sherman D. Spector and Lyman Legters, *Checklist of Paperbound Books on Russia and East Europe* (Albany: The State Education Department, 1966). Numerous bibliographies of books on communism contain listings of works on the Balkan states. Virtually all the items listed in the above bibliography have extensive bibliographies. The American Association for the Advancement of Slavic Studies has issued its

American Bibliography of Russian and East European Studies annually since 1956. An excellent reference which should be reprinted is Jirina Sztachova (ed.), *Mid-Europe: A Selective Bibliography* (New York, 1953).

The most recent and probably most authoritative two-volume bibliography has been edited by Paul Horecky of the U. S. Library of Congress and published by the University of Chicago in 1970. Sponsored by the American Council of Learned Societies and the U. S. Department of Health, Education and Welfare, this massive bibliography has been annotated by noted experts. The first is *East Central Europe: A Guide to Basic Publications* which includes works on the region north of the Danube River; the second is *Southeastern Europe: A Guide to Basic Publications,* which is devoted exclusively to the Balkan peninsula and is therefore preeminently vital for students of that region. Both volumes are quite expensive, but university libraries should acquire them to assist interested students in locating additional readings about the Balkan peoples.

A penultimate opportunity prior to printing permits mention of items which have appeared while this book was in the publishing process. An English translation of Roger Portal's *Les Slaves* (*The Slavs*) has been published by Harper and Row (1969); in addition to treating the Poles, Czechs, Slovaks, and Russians, this survey devotes considerable attention to the south Slavs (Serbs, Croats, Slovenes, and Bulgarians) in a very attractive but expensive volume. Professor Stephen Fischer-Galati has edited a paperbound volume (Praeger, 1970) containing hitherto scattered items about the Balkans in his *Man, State, and Society in East European History*. A new and most appealing text has been written by Alan Palmer, the English historian, which treats East-Central Europe since 1815: *The Lands Between* (Macmillan, 1970); it is a model of concise and admirable English prose. Twayne Publishers has published a *Documentary History of Eastern Europe* (edited by Alfred Bannan and Achilles Edelenyi) which should serve as source readings for this study.

Index

(M. Ristelhueber did not incorporate an index in his study. The editor was required to Anglicize and/or Americanize many original French items— e.g., "Rumelians" for *"Roumeliotes,"* "Rumanians" for "Roumanians," etc.—and to render this index serviceable to those unfamiliar with the intricacies of Balkan history—e.g., "Danubian Principalities" as a synonym for "Moldavia" and "Wallachia" and the predecessor of "Rumania," also spelled "Roumania." Every effort has been employed to indicate such complexities in this Index, and to facilitate orthographical transliterations.

Among other difficulties encountered by Americans in studying the Balkan peoples is that of accurate pronunciation of proper nouns. One of the least difficult approaches to correct pronunciation is by Hugh Seton-Watson in his *The East European Revolution* [New York: Praeger, 1956, paperbound], pp. xvii-xix. *ED.*)

Index [463]

Index [463]

Hypselantes (see Ypsilanti)
Hypsilanti (see Ypsilanti)

Ibrahim Pasha, 71, 85, 86, 87
IMRO (Internal Macedonian Revo-
lutionary Organization), 172, 180,
285, 302, 312
Inonu, Ismet (Pasha), 276, 277,
284, 404
Interallied Control Commission, 352,
361
Ionescu, Take, 157, 253, 266, 291,
310
Ionian Islands, 81, 87, 89, 90, 91,
147, 149, 150, 168
Iorga, Nicolae, 44, 62, 293, 325
Ipek (see Pech)
Iron Curtain, 351, 352, 361, 364,
376, 383
Iron Guard, 293, 294, 314, 315, 322,
323, 324, 325
Isaac Comnenus, Emperor, 23
Isparik (see Asparuk)
Istrati, Panait, 203
Italy, 179, 180, 215; war with Turkey, 215, 216, 226, 230, 242, 246,
254, 259, 263, 264, 271, 273,
276, 287, 302, 304, 308, 310, 313,
314; occupies Albania, 318-19;
328, 336; invades Greece, 339,
340; 363, 366, 389, 405
Ivan III (Russia), 9, 68, 77
Ivan IV (Russia), 68

Jagiello, Grand Duke, 61
Janina (Epirus), 69, 79, 83, 153,
206, 220, 221, 222, 223, 224
Janissaries 63, 64, 66, 69, 79, 93,
94
Jassy, 118, 154, 255, 345; Treaty
of (1792), 58, 69
Jean de Brienne, 7
Jean de Majorque, 8
Jews, 174; in Rumania, 154, 155,
202, 203, 291, 292, 327
John Chrysostom, Saint 6
John Rilski, Saint, 25
John Tzimisces, Emperor, 20, 21
Jonescu, Take (see Ionescu)

Jonnart, Charles, 253
Jorga, Nicolae (see Iorga)
Joseph II, Emperor, 41, 58, 69
Jovanovich, Jovan, 163
Jugoslavia (see Yugoslavia)
Justinian, Emperor, 6, 48

Kaloyan, 23, 24, 33
Kanaris, Admiral Konstantinos, 83,
149
Kanellopoulos, Panayotis, 399
Karadzhich, Vuk (Karajich), 101
Kara George, 94, 95, 96, 97, 161,
190
Karageorgevich dynasty; Alexander,
Prince of Serbia, 98, 99
Karamanlis, Constantine, 398
Karatheodory Pasha, Alexander, 166
Karavelov, Luben, 126, 137
Kardelj, Edvard, 379
Karlowitz, Treaty of (1699), 40, 67
Kars, 276, 373
Kastriotis, George (see Skanderbeg)
Kaulbars, General Nicholas, 138
Kechko, Natalia, 160
Kemal, Mustapha Ataturk, 211, 272-
80, 281-84, 305, 308, 309, 317,
404
Khrushchev, Nikita, 395, 396, 397,
401, 402, 406
Kiamil Pasha, 217, 223
Kingdom of the Serbs, Croats,
Slovenes (see Yugoslavia)
Kiosseivanov, George, x, 288, 312,
329
Kiselev, Count Paul, 109, 110
Kitchener, Herbert, 250
Kiuprili family, 63, 65, 206
Klagenfurt, 263
Klein, Samuel (see Clain)
Klephts, 79, 80, 83
Kogalniceanu, Michael, 112, 118
Kolarov, Vasil, 285, 382, 396
Kolettes family, 83, 147, 149
Kolokotronis, Theodoros, 80, 83,
85
Komitadjis, 173, 312, 386
Kondylis, George, 296, 297, 298
Konopischt, 233